UNDERSTANDING BIOLOGY

UNDERSTANDING BIOLOGY

By

Ashok Kumar

Dept. of Zoology
Bundelkhand University
Campus Department
Jhansi

DPH

DISCOVERY PUBLISHING HOUSE PVT. LTD.
NEW DELHI-110 002

Published by:
Namit Wasan
DISCOVERY PUBLISHING HOUSE PVT. LTD.
4383/4B, Ansari Road, Darya Ganj
New Delhi-110 002 (India)
Phone : +91-11-23279245; 23253475; 43596065
E-mail : discoverybooksindia@gmail.com
discoverypublishinghouse@gmail.com
namitwasan9@gmail.com
web : www.discoverypublishinggroup.com

***First Edition:* 2010**

ISBN: 978-81-8356-508-0

Understanding Biology

Preface

The present title "Understanding Biology" has been written for those students interested in careers in diverse fields of biological sciences. It provides a structured approach to learning by covering all the important topics in a uniform, systematic format. The book has been comprehensively designed incorporating recent advances in this fast moving field. It also provides accessible information on molecular biology in compact form for undergraduate students in biology and related life sciences. It is intelligible to the educated layman, though it deals with some complex ideas. It is an adequate text for all the requirements of students in this area. In addition, busy lecturers who require a quick reference compendium will find it useful, particularly for tutional planning. Simple, yet hopefully clear figures and tables are provided throughout the book.

The over-riding goal of this book, and indeed of the whole *Understanding series,* is to present the essential information concering molecular biology in a compact, readily accessible form which leads itself to student learning and revision. The convergence of various approaches has generated a rich panorama of detail, the significance of which we are still attempting to unraval. The present text has been written as an introduction to this rapidly growing field.

To make the work more comprehensive and informative, the author has consulted many authoritative books, research journals, abstracts, monographs etc., so there can be no claim to originality except in the manner of treatment.

The author expresses his thanks to his friends and colleagues whose continue inspirations have initiated him to bring out this book.

The author expresses his gratitude to Mr. Wasan and staff of M/s Discovery Publishing House Pvt. Ltd. for their whole hearted cooperation in the publication of this book.

In the mean time, the author will remain sincerely responsible for any shortcomings of the book and be grateful to the readers for their suggestions and constructive criticism for the continuous betterment of the book. He takes this opportunity to appeal to the readers to send their suggestions straightaway to his Publisher.

Author

Contents

1

Biological Molecules

The universe began, astronomers tell us, with an explosion that filled all space, with every particle of matter hurled away from every other particle. The temperature at the time of the explosion—some 20 billion years ago-was about 100,000,000,000 degrees Celsius (10^{11} °C). At this temperature, not even atoms could hold together; all matter was in the form of subatomic, elementary particles.

Moving at *enormous* velocities, even these particles had fleeting lives. Colliding with great force, they annihilated one another, creating new particles and releasing more energy. As the universe cooled, two types of stable particles, previously present only in relatively small amounts, began to assemble themselves. (By this time, 100,000 years after the "*big bang*" is believed to have taken place, the temperature had dropped to a mere 2500°C, about the temperature of a white-hot wire in an *incandescent* light bulb.)

These particles-protons and neutrons-are very heavy as *subatomic* particles go. Held together by forces that are still little understood, they formed the *central core*, or *nuclei*, of atoms. These nuclei, with their positively charged protons, attracted small, light, negatively charged particles-electrons-which moved rapidly around them. Thus, atoms came into being. (Perhaps atoms existed before the explosion, but how will one ever know?)

According to current theory, it is from these atoms-blown apart, formed, and re-formed over 20 billion years-that all the stars and planets of the universe are formed, including our particular star and planet. And it is from the atoms present on this planet that living systems assembled themselves and evolved.

Each atom in our own bodies had its origins in this *explosion* of some 20 billion years ago. You and I are *flesh* and *blood*, but we are also stardust. This text begins where life begins, with the atom. At first, the *universe* aside, it might appear that lifeless atoms have little to do with biology. Bear with us, however.

A closer look reveals that the activities we associate with being alive depend on combinations and exchanges between atoms, and the force that binds the electron to the atomic nucleus stores the energy that drives living systems.

Table 1.1 : Atomic Numbers and Weights of Some Common Atoms.

Atom	*Atomic Number*	*Atomic Weight*
Hydrogen (H)	1	1
Helium (He)	2	4
Carbon (C)	6	12
Nitrogen (N)	7	14
Oxygen (0)	8	16
Sodium (Na)	11	23
Phosphorus (P)	15	30
Sulfur (S)	16	32
Chlorine (Cl)	17	35
Calcium (Ca)	20	40

ATOMS

There are 92 naturally occurring chemical elements, each differing from the others in the structure of its atoms. Each different type of atom has a different number of *protons* in its nucleus, ranging from the lightest, hydrogen, which has 1 proton, to the *heaviest*, *uranium*, which has 92. The number of protons in the nucleus of a particular atom is called the *atomic number*.

Outside the nucleus of the atom are electrons, attracted by the positive charge of the protons. The *electrons* determine the chemical properties of atoms, and chemical reactions involve changes in the numbers and relative positions of these electrons. Atoms also contain neutrons, which are uncharged particles about the same weight as

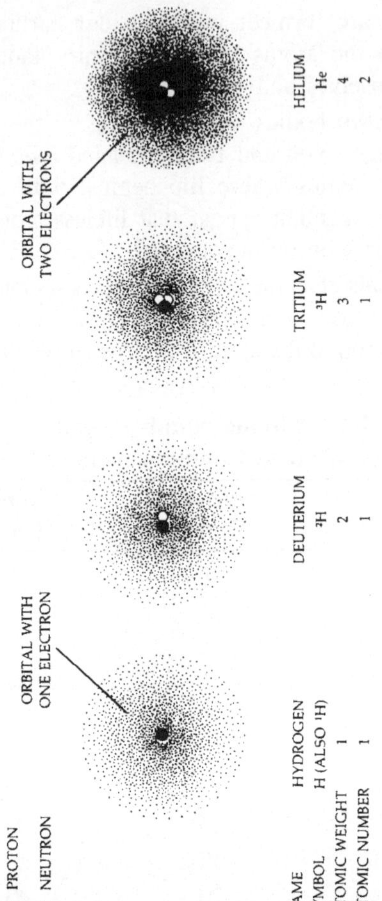

Figure 1.1 : Diagrams of atoms of hydrogen, deuterium, tritium, and helium. Note that hydrogen, deuterium, and tritium each have only a single proton and a single electron, and so they behave similarly chemically although they differ in the number of neutrons. Helium, which has one more proton and one more electron, is chemically very different from hydrogen and its isotopes.

protons. These, too, are found in the nucleus of the atom, where they seem to have a *stabilising* effect. The *atomic weight* of an element is essentially equal to the number of protons and neutrons in the nucleus. (Electrons are so light by *comparison* that their weight is usually disregarded. When you weigh yourself, only about 30 grams-approximately 1 ounce-of your total weight is made up of electrons.)

Isotopes

Atoms with the same number of protons but different numbers of neutrons are known as *isotopes*; they differ from one another in their atomic weights but not in their atomic numbers. For example, the common form of *hydrogen*, with its one proton, has an atomic weight

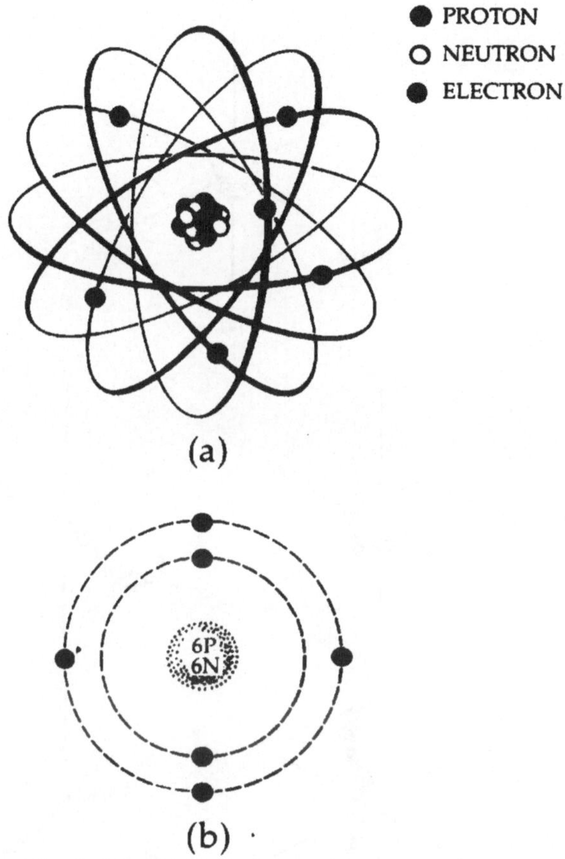

Figure 1.2 : Models of the carbon atom: (a) a planetary model and (b) a Bohr model.

of 1 and is symbolised as 1H, or simply H. Deuterium, ^{2}H, is an isotope of hydrogen that contains one proton and one neutron and so has an atomic weight of 2. Tritium, ^{3}H, the third isotope of *hydrogen*, has one proton and two neutrons and so has an atomic weight of 3.

Like many, but not all of the less common isotopes, *tritium* is radioactive, which means that its nucleus is unstable and emits energy when changing into a more stable form. The next heaviest atom is helium (He), which has an atomic number of 2 (two protons) and an atomic weight of 4 (two protons and two neutrons).

Hydrogen, *deuterium*, and *tritium* are all similar in their chemical properties because each can attract only a single electron, but helium with its two electrons (attracted by its two protons) is very different

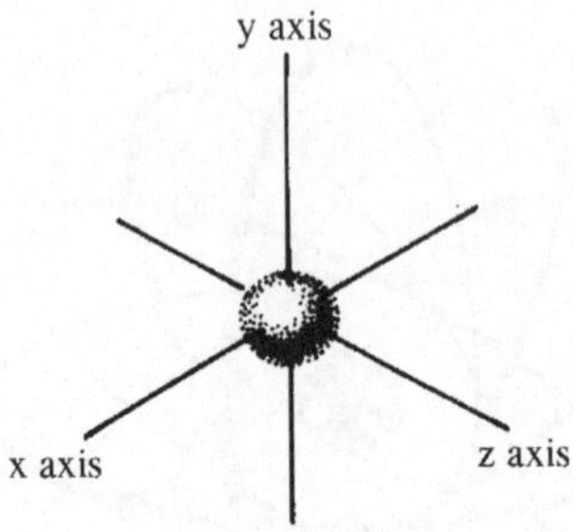

(a)

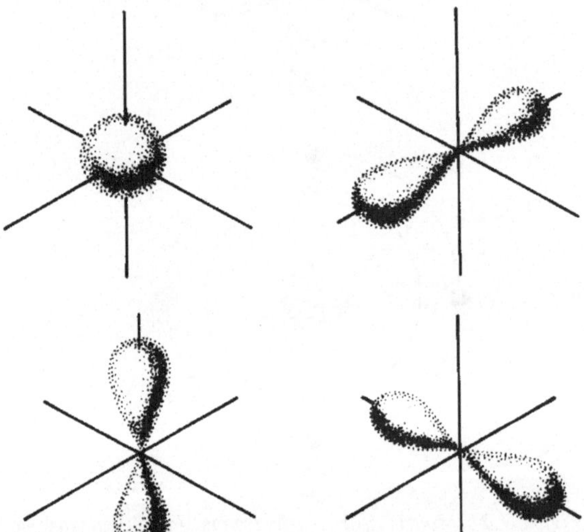

(b)

Figure 1.3 : Orbital models.

chemically from any of the isotopes of hydrogen. Thus, to repeat, the protons determine the number of electrons attracted to an atomic nucleus and those electrons determine the chemical properties of the atom.

Electrons and Orbitals

The concept of the atom as the indivisible unit of the chemical elements is almost 200 years old; however, our ideas about its structure have undergone many changes. These ideas, or hypotheses, are usually presented in the forms of models, as are many scientific hypotheses.

The earliest model, emphasizing the indivisibility of the atom, resembled a billiard ball. As it came to be realised that electrons could be removed from the atom, the billiard ball gave way to the plum-pudding model, in which the atom was represented as a solid, positively charged mass with negatively charged particles, the electrons, embedded in it. Subsequently, however, physicists found that an atom is, in fact, mostly open space.

The distance from electron to nucleus, experiments indicated, is about 1,000 times the diameter of the nucleus; the electrons are so exceedingly small that the space is almost entirely empty. Thus the more familiar planetary model of the atom came into being, in which the electrons were depicted as moving in orbits around the nucleus. More recently, the Bohr model (named after physicist Niels Bohr) became the most popular one.

It emphasizes the fact that electrons are found outside the nucleus at different energy levels; this concept of energy levels is, as you will see, of great importance in the chemistry of living systems. The current model of electron configurations is quite different from all previous ones and more accurate in terms of what we know about the behaviour of electrons.

According to this model, the electron moves unpredictably around the nucleus, and its position at any given moment cannot be known with certainty. For convenience, its pattern of motion is defined as the volume in which the electron will be found 90 percent of the time. This volume is known as the electron's *orbital.* Each orbital can hold a maximum of two electrons. Orbitals vary in shape.

The first two electrons occupy a single spherical orbital. (Thus, for instance, hydrogen's single electron moves about the nucleus-90 percent of the time-within a single spherical orbital, and so do the two electrons of helium.) This single spherical orbital, with its maximum of two electrons, makes up the first energy level. At the second energy level, there are four orbitals, each of which, as we noted, can hold two electrons. One of these orbitals is spherical, and the other three are dumbbell-shaped.

The axes of the dumbbell orbitals are perpendicular to one another. The spherical orbitals are filled first, and then the dumbbell-shaped ones. The second energy level can hold a total of eight electrons, and so can the third. Atoms tend to complete their energy levels, and the chemical behaviour of atoms is governed by this tendency.

For instance, helium (atomic number 2), neon (atomic number 10), and argon (atomic number 18) all have completely filled outer energy levels and so tend to be unreactive; they are thus called the "noble" gases because of their disdain for reacting with other elements. Hydrogen (atomic number 1), lithium (atomic number 3), sodium (atomic number 11), and potassium (atomic number 19) each has a single electron in its outermost energy level, and each tends to lose this electron.

As a consequence of such a loss, each has one more proton than electron and therefore acquires a positive charge: H^+, Li^+, Na^+, K^+. Fluorine and chlorine, by contrast, with atomic numbers of 9 and 17, tend to gain an electron in order to complete an outer energy level and so become negatively charged: F^- and Cl^- . Similarly, an atom with two electrons in its outer energy level may lose both of them, acquiring a double positive charge. Magnesium (atomic number 12) and calcium (atomic number 20) become Mg^{2+} and Ca^{2+}, and so on. Such charged atoms are known as *ions*.

Ions make up less than 1 percent of the weight of most living matter, but they play crucial roles, K^+ is the principal positively charged ion in most cells,and many essential biological reactions do not prceed in its absence. Both Na^+ and K^+ are involved in the production and propagation of the nerve impulse. Ca^{2+} is required for the contraction of muscles and Mg^{2+} forms a part of the chlorophyll molecule, the molecule that traps the energy from the sun. Some of the roles of ions in living systems will be discussed in future chapters.

Electrons and Energy

As we noted previously, electrons, which are negatively charged, are attracted to the atomic nucleus because of the positive charge of the protons. The orbital occupied by an electron is determined by the amount of energy of the electron. This energy is in the form of potential energy. An analogy may be useful.

A rock on flat ground may be said to have no energy. If you push it up a hill, you give it energy-potential energy. So long as it sits on the peak of the hill, it neither gains nor loses energy. If it rolls down the hill, however, it loses its potential energy as it rolls back toward its original level ground.

Similarly, water that has been pumped up to a water tank for storage has potential energy that will be released when the water runs back down.

The electron is like the boulder, or the water, in that an input of energy can raise it to a higher energy level-farther away from the nucleus. As long as it remains at this higher level, it possesses the added energy. Also, like the boulder or water, the electron tends to go to its lowest possible energy level, just as the rock rolls downhill, and not up.

Table 1.2 : Electronegativity of Some Common Atoms (On a Relative Scale of 0 to 4)

Atom	Electronegativity
Oxygen (O)	3.5
Nitrogen (N)	3.0
Chlorine (Cl)	3.0
Carbon (C)	2.5
Sulfur (S)	2.5
Hydrogen (H)	2.1
Phosphorus (P)	2.1
Sodium (Na)	0.9

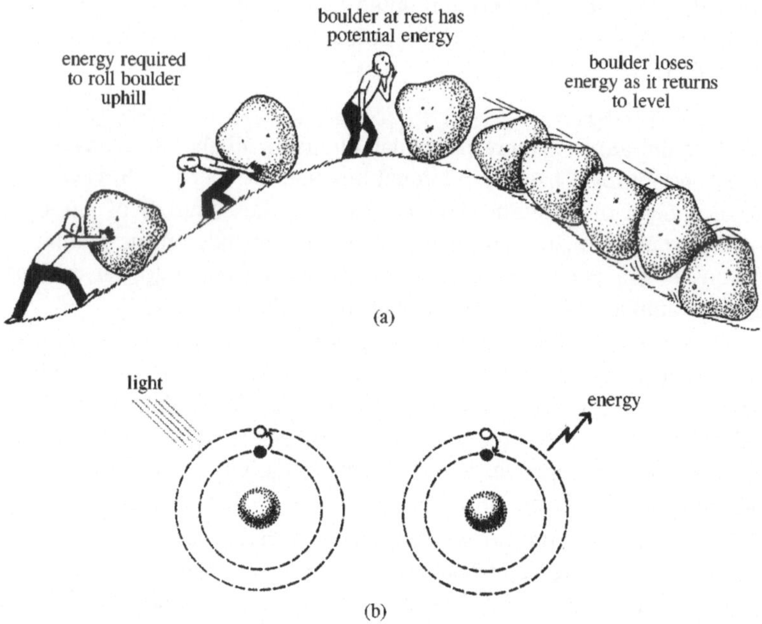

Figure 1.4 : (a) The energy used to push a boulder to the top of a hill (less the heat energy produced by friction between the boulder and hill) becomes potential energy, stored in the boulder as it rests at the top of the hill. This potential energy is converted to kinetic energy (energy of motion) as the boulder rolls downhill. (b) When an input of energy-such as light energy-boosts an electron to a high energy level, the electron, like the boulder, possesses potential energy that is released when the electron returns to its previous energy level.

In a given atom, the first spherical orbital is the lowest energy level-the ground state. The four orbitals of the second level are occupied by electrons with more energy, and so on. It takes energy to move a negatively charged electron farther away from the positively charged nucleus, just as it takes energy to position a boulder at the top of a hill.

However, unlike the boulder on the hill, the electron cannot be pushed part way up. With an input of energy, electrons may move from a lower energy level to any one of several higher ones, but they cannot move to somewhere in between. For an electron to move from one level to another, the atom must absorb a discrete packet of energy, known as a quantum, which contains just the precise energy needed for the transition and no more or no less.

Thus the study of electron movements is known as quantum mechanics, and the term quantum jump, which has invaded our everyday discourse, refers to an abrupt, discontinuous movement from one level to another.

Electronegativity

For the atoms of any particular element, all the electrons at any given energy level have about equal amounts of energy. However, the atomic nuclei of different elements have various degrees of attraction for electrons. The strength of the attraction depends on the number of protons in the nucleus, the closeness of the electrons to the nucleus, and the number of electrons outside the nucleus.

The affinity of an atom for electrons is called *electronegativity*. Electronegativity is expressed on a scale of 0 to 4. Helium and the other unreactive noble gases have electronegativities of 0. At the other end of the scale is fluorine with an electronegativity of 4. Oxygen, the next most electronegative, is 3.5. Electronegativity values for some of the elements are given in Table elsewhere in this chapter.

When an electron moves from an atom that is less electronegative to one that is more electronegative, it moves downhill, energetically speaking, and energy is released, as it is released when the boulder moves downhill.

In the green cells of plants and algae, the radiant energy of sunlight raises electrons to a higher energy level. In the course of a series of electron-transfer reactions, which will be described in other section of this chapter, the electrons are passed slowly downhill until they are finally accepted by oxygen. During this transition, the radiant energy of sunlight is changed to the chemical energy on which all life on earth depends.

BONDS AND MOLECULES

The ways in which atoms combine to form molecules are dictated by the number and arrangement of their electrons. The forces that hold molecules together are known as *bonds*. There are two principal types of bonds: ionic and covalent.

Ionic Bonds

Positive and negative ions attract one another. Thus the sodium ion (Na^+) with its single positive charge is attracted to the chloride ion (Cl^-) with its single negative charge. The calcium ion (Ca^{2+}) with its double positive charge can attract and hold two Cl^- ions, forming $CaCl_2$, with the subscript 2 indicating that two atoms of chlorine are present for every one atom of calcium. Such bonds, involving the mutual attraction of ions of opposite charge, are known as *ionic bonds*.

Covalent Bonds

Another way for an atom to complete its outer energy level is by sharing electrons with another atom. Bonds formed by shared pairs of electrons are known as *covalent bonds*. In a covalent bond, the shared pair of electrons forms a new orbital that encompasses both atoms. In such a bond, each electron spends part of its time around one nucleus and part of its time around the other.

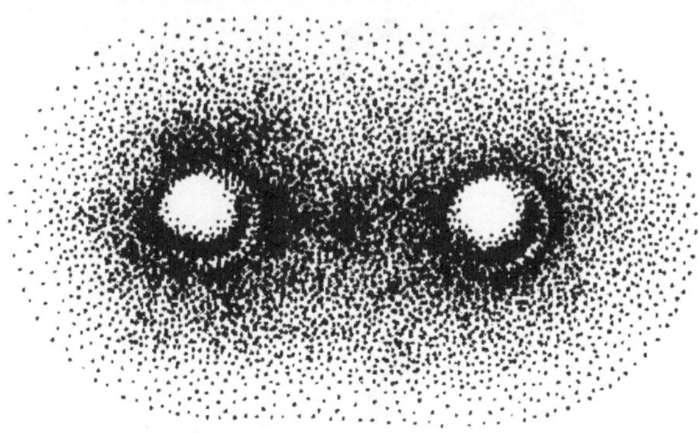

hydrogen molecule (H_2)

Figure 1.5 : In a molecule of hydrogen, each atoms shares its single first orbital electron with the other ato. As a result both atoms effectively have a filled first orbital, containing two electron—a hightly stable configuration.

Thus the electron sharing both completes the outer energy level and neutralises the nuclear charge. Covalent bonds are stronger and more stable than ionic bonds. Carbon, which has an atomic number of

6, needs either to gain or lose four electrons to achieve a filled and therefore stable outer energy level, and so is able to form covalent bonds with as many as four other atoms. When these bonds are formed, the electron pairs assume new orbitals.

These orbitals, as shown in Figure elsewhere in this chapter, are distributed symmetrically in space, forming a regular tetrahedron. Carbon's capacity to form four covalent bonds is crucial to its central role in the chemistry of living systems.

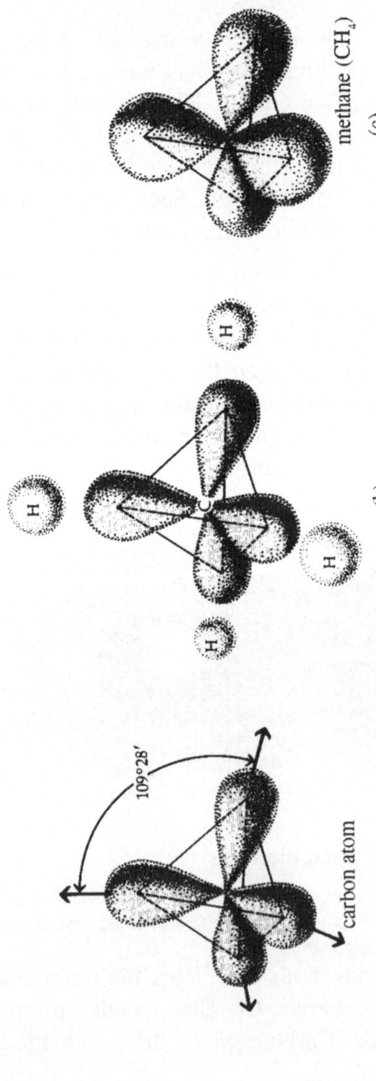

Figure 1.6 : (a) When carbon forms covalent bonds with four other atoms, new orbitals are formed. These new orbitals, which are all the same shape, are oriented toward the four corners of a tetrahedron. Thus the four orbitals are separated as far as possible. (b) When a carbon atom reacts with hydrogen to form methane, the four unpaired electrons of the carbon atom form pairs with each of the unpaired electrons in four hydrogen atoms, producing a methane molecule (c). Each pair of electrons moves in a new, molecular orbital. The molecule has the shape of a tetrahedron.

Double and Triple Bonds

There are various ways in which atoms can participate in covalent bonds and satisfy their valence requirements. Oxygen, with two unpaired electrons in its outer electron orbitals, has a valence of two and can thus form a simple compound with carbon, carbon dioxide (CO_2), in which each oxygen atom shares two pairs of electrons with a central carbon atom.

Such bonds in which two atoms are held together by two pairs of electrons (four electrons) are called double bonds. They are symbolised in a structural formula by two lines connecting the atomic symbols: C = C. Carbon atoms can form double or even triple bonds (in which three pairs of electrons are shared) with each other as well as with other atoms, and so the variety of kinds of molecules that carbon can form is very large.

Electrons shared in double and triple bonds form orbitals that differ in shape from the orbitals filled by single electron pairs. For instance, when four bonds satisfy the electron requirements of carbon, they will be directed toward the four corners of a tetrahedron that has the carbon atom at its center, as we saw in Figure elsewhere in this chapter.

Table 1.3 : Atomic Composition of Three Representative Organisms.

Element	*Man*	*Alfalfa*	*Bacterium*
Carbon	19.37	11.34	12.14
Hydrogen	9.31	8.72	9.94
Nitrogen	5.14	0.83	3.04
Oxygen	62.81	77.90	73.68
Phosphorus	0.63	0.71	0.60
Sulfur	0.64	0.10	0.32
CHNOPS total:	97.90	99.60	99.72

When two bonds are replaced by a double bond, the remaining single bonds form the arms of a Y with the double bond as its leg. When two double bonds are made by a single carbon atom, as in carbon dioxide, the three bonded atoms lie in a straight line.

Single bonds are flexible, leaving atoms free to rotate in relation to one another. Double and triple bonds hold the atoms relatively rigid in relation to one another. The presence of double bonds in a molecule can make a significant difference in its properties. For example, both fats and oils are composed of carbon and hydrogen atoms covalently bonded to one another, but in oils some of the bonds are double, and in fats the bonds are all single. As a consequence, fats are solid at room temperature and oils are liquid.

Polar Covalent Bonds

The electrons in covalent bonds are not always shared equally between the two atoms involved. Some atoms have a greater attractive force for the electrons than others-that is, they are more electronegative. As a consequence of this differential, the shared electrons tend to spend more time around the more electronegative atom.

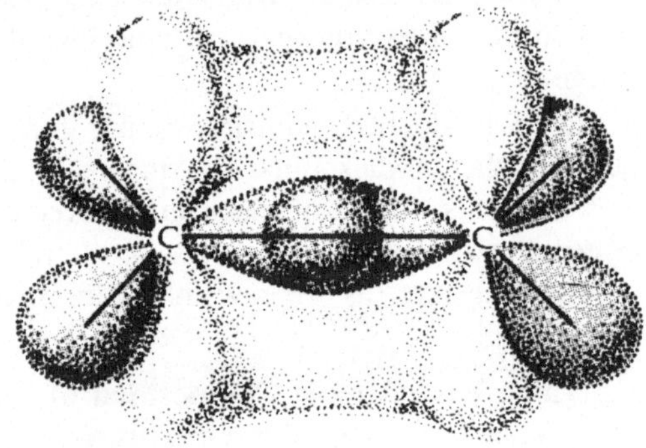

Figure 1.7 : An orbital model of a carbon-carbon double bond.

As a result, the more electronegative atom in the molecule will have a slightly negative charge, and the less electronegative atom will have a slightly positive one, since its nuclear charge is not entirely neutralised. The polar properties of some covalent bonds have very important consequences for living things.

For example, many of the special properties of water, upon which life depends, derive largely from its polar nature, as we shall see in the next chapter. Ionic, polar covalent, and covalent bonds actually may be considered different versions of the same type of bond. The differences depend on the differences in electronegativity among the combining atoms.

In a wholly nonpolar covalent bond, the electrons are shared equally; such bonds can exist only between identical atoms, H_2, $C1_2$, O_2, and N_2, for example. In polar covalent bonds, electrons are shared unequally, and in ionic bonds, there is an electrostatic attraction between the negatively and positively charged ions as a result of their having gained or lost electrons.

Chemical Equations

Chemical reactions-exchanges of electrons among atoms-can be compactly described by chemical equations. The equation for the formation of sodium chloride is

$$Na^+ + Cl^- \rightarrow NaCl$$

The arrow in the equation designates "forms" or "yields" and shows the direction of chemical change. Like algebraic equations, chemical equations "balance"; that is, there are the same number of atoms in the products of the reaction as in the original reactants. For instance, hydrogen gas can combine with oxygen gas to produce water. Hydrogen gas is H_2, and oxygen gas is O_2.

However, we know that each molecule of water contains two atoms of hydrogen and one of oxygen, and therefore the proportions must be two to one:

$$2H_2 + O_2 \rightarrow 2H_2O$$

Two molecules of H_2 plus one molecule of O_2 yield two molecules of water. The equation for a chemical reaction thus tells the kinds of atoms that are present, their proportions, and the direction of the reaction.

THE BIOLOGICALLY IMPORTANT ELEMENTS

Of the 92 naturally occurring elements, only six make up some 99 percent of all living tissue. These six are carbon, hydrogen, nitrogen, oxygen, phosphorus, and sulfur, conveniently remembered as CHNOPS. These are not the most abundant of the elements of the earth's surface. Why, as life assembled itself from stardust, were these chosen?

One clue is that they are all small, light atoms and such atoms, in which electrons are held more closely to the nucleus, form tighter, more stable bonds. Another is that they all form covalent bonds; and finally, with the exception of hydrogen, they can all form bonds with two or more atoms.

2

BIOLOGICAL SOLVENT

Life on this planet began in water, and today, wherever liquid water is found, life is also present. There are one-celled organisms that eke out their entire existence in no more water than can cling to a grain of sand. Some kinds of algae are found only on the melting undersurfaces of polar ice floes.

Certain bacteria can tolerate the near-boiling water of hot springs. In the desert, plants race through an entire life cycle-seed to flower to seed—following a single rainfall. In the jungle, the water cupped in the leaves of a tropical plant forms a microcosm in which a myriad of small organisms are born, spawn, and die.

Observations of the polar ice caps on Mars and of its "canals," first seen more than 100 years ago, kindled hope that life might be present there also. However, no liquid water was detected in the soil or atmosphere at the site of the first spacecraft landings.

Indeed, it was discovered that the air surrounding Mars is so dry and cold that liquid water could not exist on the planet. Nor was life discovered. On earth, by contrast, water is a common liquid. Three-quarters of the earth's surface is covered by water. In fact, if the earth's surface were absolutely smooth, all of it would be 2.5 kilometers under water.

Water makes up 50 to 95 percent of the weight of any functioning living system. If you weigh 60 kilograms, about 50 kilograms of that is water. But "common' is not the same as "ordinary." Water is not in the least an ordinary liquid. Compared with other liquids it is, in fact, quite extraordinary. If it were not, it is highly probable that life could never have evolved.

WATER AND THE HYDROGEN BOND

In order to understand why water is so extraordinary and how, as a consequence, it can play its unique and crucial role in relation to living systems, we have to look again at its molecular structure. As we noted in the previous chapter, each water molecule is made up of two atoms of hydrogen and one of oxygen held together by two covalent bonds.

The water molecule as a whole is neutral in charge, having an equal number of electrons and protons. However, the molecule is electrically asymmetric-that is, polar. This polarity occurs because oxygen is more electronegative than hydrogen. The paired electrons in the outer orbitals spend more time around the oxygen nucleus than they do around the hydrogen nuclei.

As a consequence, the region near the oxygen nucleus has two weakly negative zones, and each of the regions near the hydrogen nuclei has a weakly positive zone. Thus, the water molecule, in terms of its polarity, is four-cornered, with two positively charged "corners" and two negatively charged ones.

When any of these charged regions comes close to the oppositely charged region of another water molecule, the force of the attraction forms a bond between them, which is known as a *hydrogen bond.* Hydrogen bonds are not found only in water. A hydrogen bond can form between any hydrogen atom that is covalently bonded to an electronegative atom-usually oxygen or nitrogen-and the oxygen or nitrogen atom of another molecule.

In water, hydrogen bonds form between the negative "corners" of one water molecule and the positive "corners" of another. As a consequence, every water molecule can establish hydrogen bonds with four other water molecules. Liquid water is made up of water molecules bound together in this way.

Any single hydrogen bond is relatively weak and has an exceedingly short lifetime; on an average, each such bond lasts about 1/100,000,000,000th of a second. But, as one is broken, another is made. All together, the hydrogen bonds have considerable strength, making water both liquid and stable under ordinary conditions of pressure and temperature.

Now let us look at some of the consequences of these attractions among water molecules, especially as they affect living systems.

Surface Tension

Look at water dripping from a faucet. Each drop clings to the rim and dangles for a moment by a thread of water; then just as the tug of gravity breaks it loose, its outer surface is drawn taut, to form a sphere as the drop falls free. Gently place a needle or a razor blade flat on the surface of the water in a glass. Although the metal is denser than water, it floats.

Look at a pond in spring or summer; you will see water striders and other insects walking on its surface almost as if it were solid. These phenomena are all the result of *surface tension.* Surface tension is the result of the cohesion or clinging together, of the water molecules. *(Cohesion* is, by definition, the holding together of like substances. *Adhesion* is the holding together of unlike substances.)

The only liquid with a surface tension greater than that of water is mercury. Atoms of mercury are so greatly attracted to one another that they tend not to adhere to anything else.

Water, because of its negative and positive charges, also adheres strongly to any other charged molecules and to charged surfaces. The "wetting" capacity of water-that is, its ability to coat a surface-reflects its polar structure, as does its cohesiveness.

Table 2.1 : Comparative Specific Heats (The Quantity of Heat, in calories, Required to Raise the Temperature of 1 Gram through 1°C)

Substance	*Specific Heat*
Water	1.00
Lead	0.03
Iron	0.10
Salt (NaCI)	0.21
Glass	0.20
Sugar (sucrose)	0.30
Liquid ammonia	1.23
Chloroform	0.24
Ethyl alcohol (ethanol)	0.60

Capillary Action and Imbibition

If you hold two dry glass slides together and dip one corner in water, the combination of cohesion and adhesion will cause water to spread upward between the two slides. This is *capillary action.* Capillary action similarly causes water to rise in very fine glass tubes, to creep up a piece of blotting paper, or to move slowly through the micropores of the soil and so become available to the roots of plants.

Imbibition ("drinking up") is the capillary movement of water molecules due to adhesion into substances such as wood or gelatin, which swell as a result. The pressures developed by imbibition can be astonishingly great. It is said that stone for the ancient Egyptian pyramids was quarried by driving wooden pegs into holes drilled in the rock face and then soaking the pegs with water.

The swelling of the wood created a force great enough to break the stone slab free. Seeds imbibe water as they begin to germinate, swelling and bursting their seed coats.

WATER AND TEMPERATUERE

Specific Heat of Water

The amount of heat a given amount of a substance requires for a given increase in temperature is its *specific heat* (also called heat capacity). One calorie* is defined as the amount of heat that will raise the temperature of 1 gram (1 milliliter or 1 cubic centimeter) of water 1°C. The specific heat of water is about twice the specific heat of oil or alcohol; that is, approximately 0.5 calorie will raise the temperature of 1 gram of oil or alcohol 1°C.

It is four times the specific heat of air or aluminum and 10 times that of iron. Only liquid ammonia has a higher specific heat. In other words, it requires a high input of energy to raise the temperature of water. The high specific heat of water is also a consequence of hydrogen bonding.

Heat is a form of energy-the kinetic energy, or energy of movement, of molecules. In order for the kinetic energy of water molecules to increase sufficiently for the temperature to rise 1°C, it is necessary first to rupture a number of the hydrogen bonds holding the molecules together.

The reason that it takes more heat to warm a gram of water to a given temperature than to warm a gram of almost any other liquid is that so much of the heat energy added to the water is used in breaking the hydrogen bonds between the water molecules. Only a relatively small amount of heat energy is therefore available to increase molecular movement.

Note that heat and temperature are not the same. A lake may have a lower temperature than does a bird flying over it, but the lake contains more heat because it comprises many more molecules than the bird; therefore it has more molecular motion. Temperature is measured in degrees and reflects the average kinetic energy of the molecules. Heat is measured in calories and reflects both molecular movement and the mass and number of the molecules present.

What does the high specific heat of water mean in biological terms? It means that for a given rate of heat input, the temperature of water will rise more slowly than the temperature of almost any other material.

Conversely, the temperature will drop more slowly as heat is removed. Because so much heat input or heat loss is required to raise or lower the temperature of water, organisms that live in the oceans or large bodies of fresh water live in an environment where the temperature is relatively constant.

Also, the high water content of terrestrial plants and animals helps them to maintain a relatively constant internal temperature. This constancy of temperature is important because, as we shall see, biologically important chemical reactions take place only within a narrow temperature range.

Table 2.2 : Comparative Heats of Vaporisation (The Quantity of Heat, in calories, Required to Convert 1 Gram of Liquid to 1 Gram of Gas)

Liquid	*Heat Required*
Water (at 0°C)	596
Water (at 100°C)	540
Ammonia	295
Chlorine	67.4
Hydrofluoric acid	360
Nitric acid	115
Carbon dioxide	72.2
Ethyl alcohol (ethanol)	236.5
Ether	9.4

Heat of Vaporization

Vaporization-or evaporation, as it is more commonly called-is the change from a liquid to a gas. Water has a high *heat of vaporization.* It takes more than 500 calories to change a gram of liquid water into vapor, fifty times as much as for ether and almost twice as much as for ammonia.

Hydrogen bonding is also responsible for water's high heat of vaporization. Vaporization comes about because some of the more rapidly moving molecules of a liquid break loose from the surface and enter the air. The hotter the liquid, the more rapid the movement of its molecules and, hence, the more rapid the rate of evaporation.

But, whatever the temperature, so long as a liquid is exposed to air that is less than 100 percent saturated with the vapor of that liquid, evaporation will take place, right down to the last drop. In order for a water molecule to break loose from its fellow molecules-that is, to vaporise-the hydrogen bonds have to be broken.

This requires heat energy. At water's boiling point (100°C at a pressure of 1 atmosphere), 540 calories are needed to change 1 gram of liquid water into vapor. As a consequence, when water evaporates, as from the surface of your skin or a leaf, the escaping molecules carry a great deal of heat away with them.

Thus evaporation has a cooling effect. Evaporation from the surface of a land-dwelling plant or animal is one of the principal ways in which these organisms "unload" excess heat and so stabilise their temperatures.

Freezing: The Heat of Fusion

The freezing point of water is 0°C. So is the melting point. To make the transition from a solid to a liquid, water requires 79.7 calories per gram. As water melts in an icebox or other closed, insulated container, it draws this much heat from the contents of the container. Conversely, as water freezes, it releases the same amount of heat into its surroundings. This 79.7 cal/gram is known as the *heat of fusion*.

In this way, ice and snow also serve as temperature stabilisers, particularly during the temperate zone transition periods of fall and spring. Moderation of sudden changes in temperature gives organisms time to make seasonal adjustments essential to survival. Water exhibits another peculiarity as it undergoes the transition from a liquid to a solid.

As the temperature of a liquid drops, its density tends to increase. This increase occurs because the individual molecules are moving more slowly and so the spaces between them decrease. The density of water also increases, until the temperature nears 4°C.

Then the water molecules come so close together that every one of them becomes hydrogen-bonded to four others, forming an open latticework. In the course of this bonding process, water expands again, so that water as a solid takes up more volume than water as a liquid.

This increase in volume has occasional disastrous effects on water pipes, but, on the whole, turns out to be so beneficial for life forms that it would seem to be almost miraculously devised. If water contracted as it froze, not only would ice cubes fail to tinkle in our glasses, but also lakes and ponds and other bodies of water would freeze from the bottom up.

Once ice began to accumulate on the bottom, it would tend not to melt, season after season, and eventually the pond would freeze solid and life in the pond would be destroyed. By' contrast, a layer of ice tends to protect the life of the pond, keeping the liquid water beneath it at 0°C or above.

The presence of dissolved substances in water reduces the temperature at which water freezes, which is why salt is thrown on icy sidewalks and used in ice-cream freezers. The "hardening" process in several species of winter-hardy plants, by which they prepare themselves for cold weather, includes the breakdown of starch (which is insoluble) into simple sugars (which are soluble).

Freshwater fish, whose body fluids are salty compared to the pond or lake in which they live, do not freeze when the temperature of the water is at or near 0°C. However, logically speaking, saltwater fish, whose body fluids are less salty than the ocean water surrounding them, should freeze at the below-zero temperatures of Arctic water.

They do not, however, and animal physiologists investigating this phenomenon have discovered that at least one species, ghost fish, produces a complex protein named, appropriately, antifreeze protein. This protein, which is secreted into the bloodstream, appears, like the antifreeze in your car radiator, to prevent water molecules from crystallizing.

WATER AS A SOLVENT

Many substances within living systems are found in solution. (A solution is a uniform mixture of the molecules of two or more substances; the substance present in the greatest amount-usually a liquid-is called the solvent, and the substances present in lesser amounts are called solutes.)

The polarity of the water molecules is responsible for water's capacity as a solvent. The polar water molecules tend to separate substances such as NaCl into their constituent ions. Then, as shown in Figure elsewhere in this chapter, the water molecules cluster around and segregate the charged ions. Many of the molecules important in living systems-such as glucose (sugar)—also have areas of positive and negative charge.

(Such polar regions of partial charge arise, as you might expect, in the neighborhood of covalently bonded atoms of unequal electronegativity.) These molecules therefore attract water molecules and so dissolve in water.

Molecules that readily dissolve in water are often called *hydrophilic* ("water-loving"). Such molecules slip into aqueous solution easily because their partially charged regions attract water molecules and so compete with the attraction between the water molecules themselves.

Molecules such as fats that lack polar, or charged, regions, tend to be very insoluble in water. The hydrogen bonding between the water molecules acts as a force to exclude the nonpolar molecules. As a result of this exclusion, nonpolar molecules tend to cluster together in water, just as droplets of fats tend to coalesce, as for example, on the surface of chicken soup.

Such molecules are said to be *hydrophobic* ("water-fearing"), and the clusterings are known as hydrophobic interactions. We will encounter these properties of hydrophobic and hydrophilic molecules again in later chapters. These weak forces-hydrogen bonds and hydrophobic forces-play very important roles in shaping the architecture of large biomolecules and, as a consequence, in determining their properties.

IONIZATION OF WATER

In liquid water, there is a slight tendency for a hydrogen atom to jump from the oxygen atom to which it is covalently bonded to the oxygen atom to which it is

hydrogen-bonded. In this reaction, two ions are produced: the hydronium ion (H_3O^+) and the hydroxide ion (OH^-). In any given volume of pure water, a small but constant number of water molecules will be ionised in this way. The number is constant because the tendency of water to ionize is exactly offset by the tendency of the ions to reunite; thus even as some molecules are ionizing, an equal number of others are forming, a state known as equilibrium.

Although the hydrogen ion does not exist in a separate form, by convention the ionization of water is expressed by the equation:

$$HOH \rightleftharpoons H^+ + OH^-$$

The arrows indicate that the reaction can go in either direction. The fact that the arrow pointing toward HOH is longer indicates that, at equilibrium, most of the H_2O is not ionised. As a consequence, in any sample of pure water, only a small fraction exists in ionised form.

In pure water, the number of H^+ ions exactly equals the number of OH^- ions. This is necessarily the case since neither ion can be formed without the other when only H_2O molecules are present. A solution acquires the properties we recognise as acidic when the number of H^+ ions exceeds the number of OH^- ions; conversely, a solution is alkaline (basic) when the number of OH^- ions exceeds the number of H^+ ions.

The pH Scale

Chemists define degrees of acidity by means of the *pH scale.* In the expression "pH," the p stands for a negative power of 10, and the H stands for the concentration of hydrogen ions in moles per liter.

A mole is the amount of an element equivalent to its atomic weight expressed in grams, or the amount of a substance equivalent to its molecular weight expressed in grams.

Table 2.3 : The pH Scale.

	Concentration of H^+ Ions (moles per liter)		*pH*	*Concentration of OH^- Ions (moles per liter)*
	1.0	$= 10^{0}$	0	10^{-14}
	0.1	$= 10^{-1}$	1	10^{-13}
	0.01	$= 10^{-2}$	2	10^{-12}
Acidic	0.001	$= 10^{-3}$	3	10^{-11}
	0.0001	$= 10^{-4}$	4	10^{-10}
	0.00001	$= 10^{-5}$	5	10^{-9}
	0.000001	$= 10^{-6}$	6	10^{-8}
Neutral	0.0000001	$= 10^{-1}$	7	$10^{-7} = 0.0000001$
	10^{-8}		8	$10^{-6} = 0.000001$
	10^{-9}		9	$10^{-5} = 0.00001$
	10^{-10}		10	$10^{-4} = 0.0001$
Basic	10^{-11}		11	$10^{-3} = 0.001$
	10^{-12}		12	$10^{-2} = 0.01$
	10^{-13}		13	$10^{-1} = 0.1$
	10^{-14}		14	$10^{0} = 1.0$

Thus, a mole of atomic hydrogen (atomic weight 1) is 1 gram of hydrogen atoms, a mole of atomic oxygen (atomic weight 16) is 16 grams of oxygen atoms, and a mole of water is 18 grams of water molecules. The most interesting thing about the mole is that a mole- of any substance-contains the same number of particles as any other mole.

This number, known as Avogadro's number, is 6.02×10^{23}. Thus, a mole of water molecules (18 grams) contains exactly the same number of molecules as a mole of hydrochloric acid molecules (36.5 grams). Use of the mole in specifying quantities of substances involved in chemical reactions makes it possible for us to consider comparable numbers of reacting particles.

A liter of pure water contains 1/10,000,000 mole of hydrogen ions. For convenience, this is written exponentially as 10^{-7} mole per liter. In terms of the pH scale, it is referred to simply as pH 7. At pH 7, the concentrations of free

H^+ and OH^- are exactly the same, and thus pure water is said to be neutral. Any pH below 7 is acidic, and any pH above 7 is basic. The lower the pH number, the higher the concentration of hydrogen ions. Thus pH 2 means 10^{-2} mole of hydrogen ions per liter of water, or 1/100 mole per liter-which is, of course, a much larger figure than 1/10,000,000. The difference of one pH unit represents a tenfold difference in the concentration of hydrogen ions.

We can now define "acid" and "base" more exactly:

1. An *acid* is a substance that donates H^+ ions to a solution, that is, a hydrogenion donor. A solution with a pH below 7 (with more than 10^{-7} mole of H^+ ions per liter) is acidic.

2. A *base* is a substance that decreases the number of H^+ ions, that is, a hydrogen-ion acceptor. A solution with a pH above 7 (with less than 10^{-7} mole of H^+ ions per liter) is basic.

In short, a solution that contains more H^+ ions than OH^- ions is acidic, and one that contains more OH^- ions than H^+ ions is basic.

Strong and Weak Acids and Bases

Hydrochloric acid (HCI) is an example of a common acid. It is a strong acid, meaning that it tends to be almost completely ionised in aqueous solution into H^+ and Cl^- ions. Sodium hydroxide (NaOH) is a common strong base; in aqueous solution, it exists almost entirely as Na^+ and OH^- ions. Weak acids and weak bases are those that ionize only slightly.

Most organic acids owe their acidic properties to a group of atoms called the carboxyl group, which includes one carbon, two oxygens, and a hydrogen atom (symbolised as -COOH). When an organic acid is dissolved in water, the carboxyl group dissociates to yield hydrogen ions:

$$-COOH \rightleftharpoons -COO^- + H^+$$

Thus any compound containing carboxyl is a hydrogen donor, or an acid. It is a weak acid, however, because, as indicated by the arrows, the —COOH ionizes only slightly.

Compounds that contain the amino group (—NH_2) act as weak bases since the —NH_2 has a weak tendency to accept hydrogen ions (protons), thereby forming —NH_3+:

$$—NH_2 + H^+ \rightleftharpoons NH_3^+$$

Because of the strong tendency of H^- and OH^- to combine and the weak tendency of water to ionize, the concentration of H^+ ions will always decrease as the concentration of OH^- increases, and vice versa. If HCl is added to a solution containing NaOH, the following reaction will take place:

$$Na^+ + OH^- + H^+ + Cl^- \rightarrow H_2O + Na^+ + Cl^-$$

In other words, if an acid and a base of comparable strengths are added in equivalent amounts, the solution will once more be neutral.

Buffers

Solutions more acidic than pH 1 or more basic than pH 14 are possible, but these are not included in the scale because they are almost never encountered in biological systems. In fact, almost all the chemistry of living things takes place at pH's between 6 and 8.

Notable exceptions are the chemical processes in the stomach of humans and other animals, which take place at a pH of about 2. Human blood, for instance, maintains an almost constant pH of 7.4 despite the fact that it is the vehicle for a large number and variety of nutrients and other chemicals being delivered to the cells, as well as for the removal of wastes, many of which are acids or bases.

The maintenance of a constant pH-an example of homeostasis is important because the pH greatly influences the rate of chemical reactions. Organisms resist strong, sudden changes in the pH of blood and other fluids by means of *buffers.*

Buffers help maintain constant pH by their tendency to combine with H+ ions and thus remove them from solution as the H^+ ion concentration begins to rise and to release them as it falls. Buffers are often combinations of H^+ donor and H^+ acceptor forms of weak acids or bases.

The capacity of a buffer system to resist changes in pH is greatest when the concentrations of H^+ donor and H^+ acceptor are equal. As the ratio changes in either direction, the buffer becomes less effective.

The major buffer system in the human bloodstream is the acid-base pair H_2CO_3 HCO_3^-. The weak acid H_2CO_3 (carbonic acid) dissociates into H^+ and bicarbonate ions as shown in the equation below.

$$\underset{H^+\text{donor}}{H_2CO_3} \rightleftharpoons H^+ + \underset{H^+\text{acceptor}}{HCO^-}$$

The H_2CO_3 HCO_3^- buffer system resists the changes in pH that might result from the addition of small amounts of acid or base by "soaking up" the acid or base. For example, if a small amount of H^+ in the form of an organic acid is added to the system, it combines with the H^+ acceptor HCO_3^- to form H_2CO_3.

This reaction removes the added H^+ and maintains the pH near its original value. If a small amount of OH^- is added, it combines with the H^+ to form H_2O; more H_2CO_3 tends to ionize to replace the H^+ as it is used.

Control of the pH of the blood is rendered even "tighter" by the fact that the H2CO3 is in equilibrium with dissolved carbon dioxide (CO_2) in the blood:

$$H_2O + CO_2 \rightleftharpoons H_2CO_3$$

As the arrows indicate, the two reactions are in equilibrium and the equilibrium favours the formation of CO_2; in fact, the ratio is about 100 to 1 in favour of CO_2 formation.

Dissolved CO_2 in the blood is, in turn, in equilibrium with the CO_2 in the lungs. By changing your rate of breathing, you can change the HCO_3 concentration in the blood and thus adjust the pH of your internal fluids.

Obviously, if the blood should be flooded with a very large excess of acid or base, the buffer would fail, but normally it is able to adjust continuously and very rapidly to the constant small additions of acid or base that normally occur in body fluids.

3

Bio-organic Molecules

In this chapter, we present some of the types of molecules that are found in living things. Consider this, if you will, an introduction to the principal characters; the plot begins to unfold in other chapter. As you will see, the molecular drama is a grand spectacular with, literally, a cast of thousands; a single bacterial cell contains some 5,000 different kinds of molecules, and a eukaryotic cell-the sort of cell that makes up the tissues of animals and plants-has about twice that many.

These thousands of molecules, however, are composed of relatively few elements. Similarly, relatively few kinds of molecules play the major roles in living systems. If you bear with us, you will find that you readily learn to recognise the players and their roles and to distinguish the stars from the members of the chorus.

THE CENTRAL ROLE OF CARBON

As we noted previously, water makes up about 60 to 70 percent, on the average, of a living system, and ions such as K^+, Na^+, and Ca^{2+} account for no more than 1 percent. Almost all the rest, chemically speaking, is composed of organic molecules-molecules containing carbon.

In general, an organic molecule derives its overall shape from the arrangement of the carbon atoms that form the backbone, or skeleton, of the molecule. A carbon atom has six protons and six electrons, two electrons in its innermost orbital and four in its outer orbitals. Thus carbon can form four covalent bonds with as many as four different

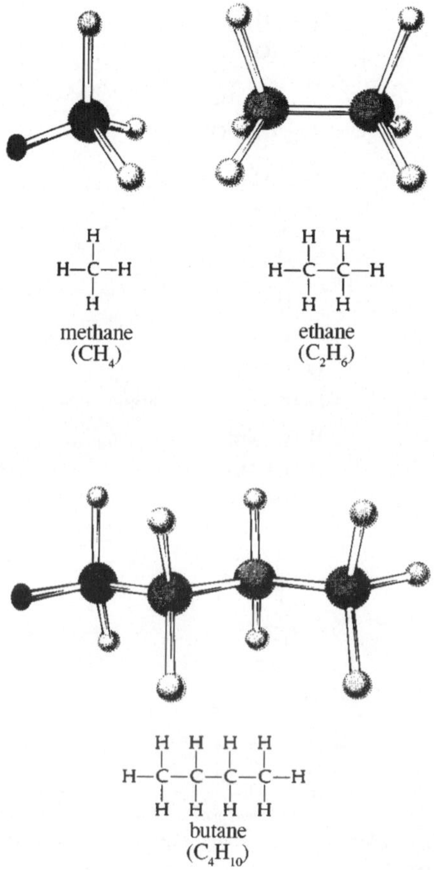

Figure 3.1 : Structural formulas and ball-and-stick models of methane, ethane, and butane. In these models, the large black spheres represent carbon atoms and the small coloured spheres represent hydrogen atoms.

atoms. Methane (CH_4), which is natural gas, is an example.

Even more important, in terms of carbon's biological role, carbon atoms can form bonds with each other. Ethane contains two carbons; propane, three; butane, four; and so on, forming long chains. In these compounds, every carbon bond that is not occupied by another carbon atom is taken up by a hydrogen atom. Compounds consisting of only carbon and hydrogen are known as *hydrocarbons*.

Chains containing oxygen atoms in addition to carbon and hydrogen are common in living systems. When these atoms occur in the ratio of one carbon to two hydrogens to one oxygen (CH_2O) the compounds they

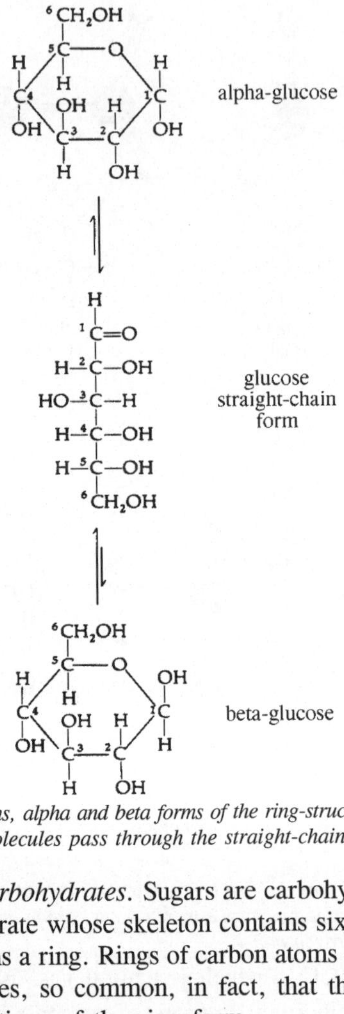

Figure 3.2 : In living systems, alpha and beta forms of the ring-structured glucose molecule are in equilibrium. The molecules pass through the straight-chain form to get from one ring structure to the other.

form are known as *carbohydrates*. Sugars are carbohydrates. The sugar glucose is a carbohydrate whose skeleton contains six carbon atoms. In solution, glucose forms a ring. Rings of carbon atoms are common types of biological molecules, so common, in fact, that the C's are usually omitted in representations of the ring form.

Functional Groups

The specific chemical properties of a molecule derive principally from groups of atoms, known as *functional groups,* that are attached to the carbon skeleton. An OH (hydroxyl) group is an example.* When one hydrogen and one oxygen are bonded covalently, one electron is left over for sharing.

A compound with a hydroxyl group in place of one or more of the hydrogens in a hydrocarbon is known as an alcohol. Thus methane

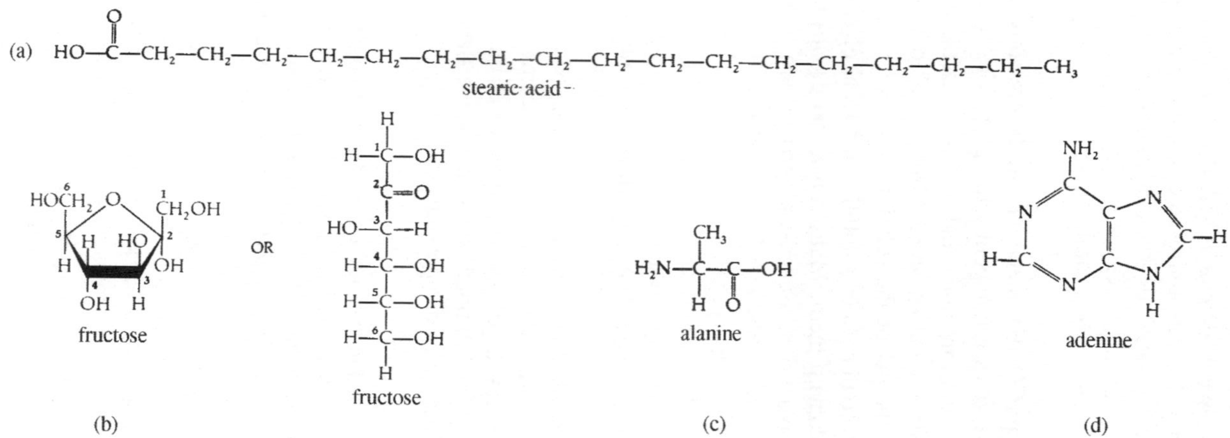

Figure 3.3 : (a) A fatty acid is a long hydrocarbon chain terminating in a carboxyl group (indicated in colour). (b) The sugar fructose. In the chain form, the ketone group is indicated by colour. (c) Every amino acid contains an amino group (NH_2) and a carboxyl group (COOH) bonded to a central carbon atom.

(CH_4), with the replacement of one hydrogen atom by a hydroxyl group, becomes methanol, or wood alcohol (CH_3OH), a pleasant-smelling, poisonous compound noted for its ability to cause blindness and death. Ethane similarly becomes ethanol, or grain alcohol (C_2H_5OH), which is present in all alcoholic beverages. Glycerol, $C_3H_5(OH)_3$, contains, as its formula indicates, three carbon atoms, five hydrogen atoms, and three hydroxyl groups.

The carboxyl group (COOH), mentioned in the previous chapter, is a functional group that gives a compound the properties of an acid.

Many functional groups are polar and so have a partial positive or negative charge in aqueous solution. Some of these tend to become fully ionised, depending on the pH of the solution.

Thus these groups confer water-solubility and local electric charge to the molecules that contain them. Many functional groups participate directly in chemical reactions. Functional groups are essential for recognising a particular molecule and helping predict its properties.

Alcohols, with polar hydroxyl groups, tend to be soluble in water, for instance, whereas hydrocarbons such as butane, with only nonpolar functional groups (such as methyl groups), are highly insoluble in water. Sugars contain hydroxyl groups plus an aldehyde group or a ketone group.

Aldehyde groups are often associated with pungent odours and tastes. Smaller molecules with aldehyde groups, such as formaldehyde, have unpleasant odours, whereas larger ones, such as the chemicals that give vanilla, apples, cherries, and almonds their distinctive flavors, tend to be pleasing to the human sensory apparatus.

Four Representative Molecules

Figure 3-3 shows four kinds of molecules found frequently in living systems. The first (a), as you will recognise, has a long hydrocarbon chain; this chain, being nonpolar, is hydrophobic. Because of the COOH, you know that it is an acid. It is a *fatty acid,* a major component of fats, lipids, and waxes.

The second molecule (b) is *a sugar.* It is recognisable as a sugar because it consists of a carbon skeleton with hydrogen and oxygen atoms in the ratio of CH_2O, and it has a ketone group characteristic of a sugar. In aqueous solution, it forms a ring, as shown here.

You can also tell that it is soluble because of the OH (alcohol) groups that confer solubility. This particular sugar is fructose. The third molecule (c) is an *amino acid.* An amino acid consists of a carbon atom bonded to one hydrogen atom and to three functional groups. One of these groups is always a carboxyl group, which gives the molecule its acidic properties. Because of the amino group, an amino acid is also a weak base. The third functional group varies from amino acid to amino acid; in this case it is a methyl (CH_3) group, and the amino acid is alanine.

The fourth molecule (d) is a *nitrogenous base*. It is called nitrogenous because the rings of the molecule contain not only carbon but also nitrogen. It is a base because of the amino group. This nitrogenous base is called adenine and it is definitely one of the stars in the biological drama.

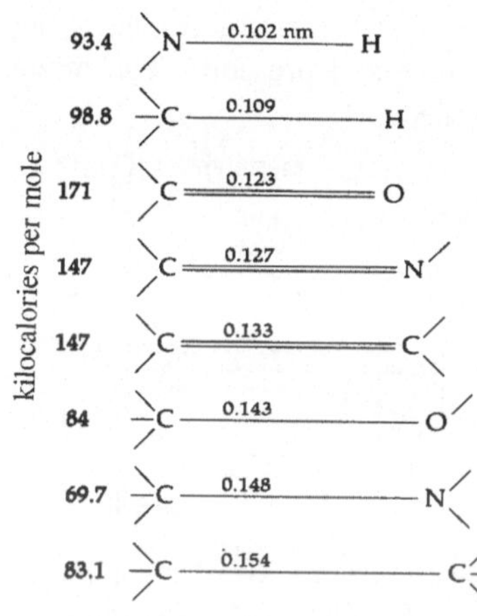

Figure 3.4 : A chemical bond is a force holding atoms together. The strength of the bond is measured in terms of the energy required to break it.

It has been said that it is necessary only to be able to recognize about 30 molecules for a working knowledge of the biochemistry of cells. One of these is a fatty acid; two others are the sugars glucose and ribose; five are nitrogenous bases such as adenine; and 20 are the biologically important amino acids. So, as you can see, the cast of characters is nearly complete.

The Energy Factor

Covalent bonds-the bonds commonly found in organic molecules-are strong, stable bonds consisting of electrons moving in orbitals about two or more different atomic nuclei. These bonds have different characteristic strengths, depending on the configuration of these orbitals. Bond strengths are conventionally measured in terms of kilocalories per mole. Chemical reactions always involve a change in electron configurations and therefore in bond strengths.

Consider, for example, the burning of methane, represented by the following equation:

$$CH_4 + 2O_2 \rightarrow CO_2 + 2H_2O$$

This reaction can be set in motion by a spark, which is what causes explosions in coal mines, and it releases energy in the form of heat. The amount of energy released can be measured quite precisely. It turns out to be 213 kilocalories per mole of methane. This can be expressed by a simple equation:

$$\Delta H° = -213 \text{ kcal}$$

The Greek letter delta (0) stands for change, H for heat, and the superscript ° indicates that the reaction occurs under certain standard conditions of temperature and pressure. The minus sign indicates that energy has been released.

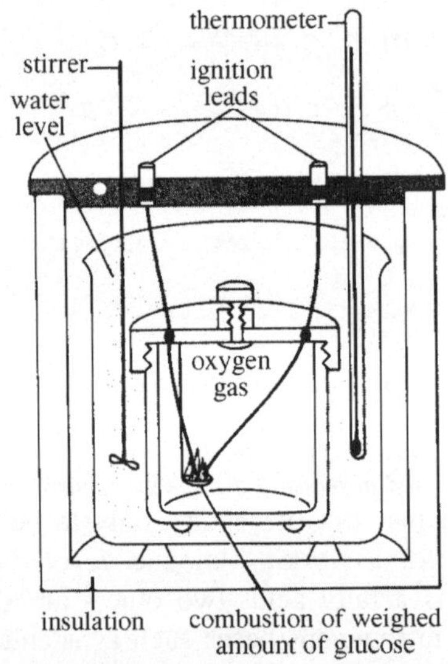

Figure 3.5 : A calorimeter. A known quantity of glucose or some other material is ignited electrically. As it burns, the rise in the temperature of the water is measured. Based on the specific heat of water, one can then calculate the number of calories released by the burning of the sample.

Similarly, changes in energy occur in the chemical reactions that take place in living systems. However, living systems have evolved strategies for minimising the energy required to set a reaction in motion and also the proportion of energy released as heat. (The word "strategy" in its ordinary meaning is a deliberate plan to achieve a specified goal. Biologists use it to mean a group of related traits evolved by natural selection to solve particular problems encountered by living systems.)

CARBOHYDRATES: SUGARS AND POLYMERS OF SUGARS

Carbohydrates are the principal chemical energy sources of most living things. In addition, they form a variety of structural components of living cells; plant cell walls, for example, are mostly made of cellulose, which is the most common organic compound in the biosphere.

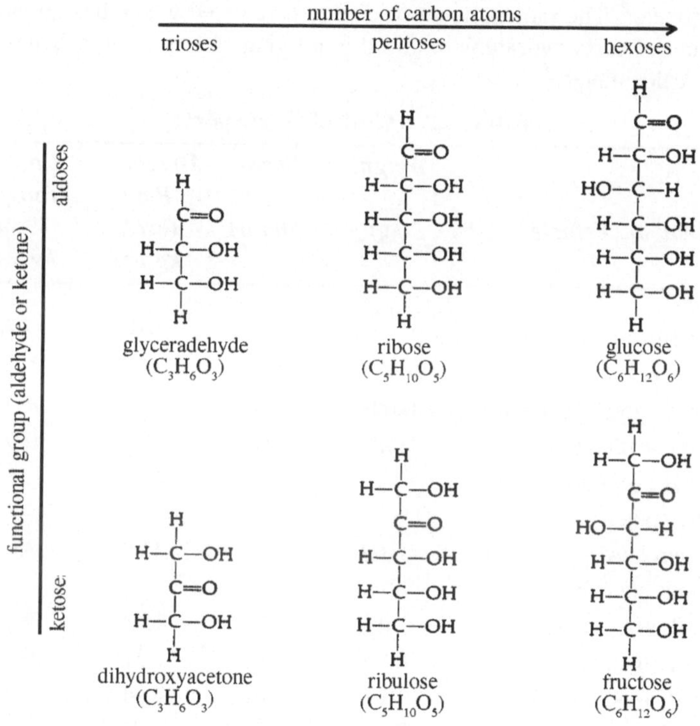

Figure 3.6 : Two different ways of classifying monosaccharides: according to the number of carbon atoms and according to the functional groups (indicated in colour). Glyceraldehyde, ribose, and glucose contain, in addition to hydroxyl groups, an aldehyde group. Dihydroxyacetone, ribulose, and fructose each contain a ketone group.

Large molecules that are made up of similar or identical subunits are known as *polymers* ("many parts") and the subunits are called *monomers* ("single parts"). In the case of carbohydrates, the monomers are monosaccharides, single sugars, and the polymers are polysaccharides.

Monosaccharides: Ready Energy for Living Systems

As we noted previously, *monosaccharides (sugars)* can be described as $(CH_2O)_n$; *n* may be as small as 3, as in $C_3H_6O_3$, or as large as 8, $C_8H_{16}O_8$. As shown in Figure elsewhere in this chapter, they are characterised by hydroxyl groups and an aldehyde or a ketone group.

Like hydrocarbons, carbohydrates can be oxidised to yield carbon dioxide and water:

$$(CH_2O)_n + nO_2 \rightarrow (CO_2)n + (H_2O)n$$

This reaction is also energy-yielding, and the amount of energy released as heat can be calculated by burning sugar molecules in a calorimeter. The same amount of energy is released when the equivalent amount of carbohydrate is oxidised in a living cell as when it is burned in a calorimeter.

Table 3.2 : Cost of Transport.

Animal or Vehicle	*Weight (kg)*	*Speed (km/hr)*	*Metabolic Rate (kcal/ kg hr)*	*Cost of Transport (kcal/ kg km)*
Flyers				
Fruit fly *(Drosophila)*	2.0×10^{-6}	7.4	104	14.05
Honey bee *(Apis)*	1.0×10^{-4}	30.0	450	15.0
Hummingbird *(Calypte)*	0.003	49.0	197	4.02
Pigeon *(Columba)*	0.384	58.0	55.1	0.95
Walkers and Runners				
White-footed mouse *(Peromyscus)*	0.023	1.08	37.8	35.0
Ground squirrel (Citellus)	0.198	2.80	15.2	5.43
Lizard *(Iguana)*	0.90	0.370	2.31	6.24
Dog (Canis)	10.7	5.84	7.94	1.36
Man *(Homo)*	70.0	5.58	4.06	0.73
Horse *(Equus)*	707.0	5.00	2.61	0.52
Swimmer				
Salmon (Oncorhynchus)	0.19	2.8	1.1	0.39
Vehicles				
Cherokee airplane	978	200	240	1.2
F105F jet fighter	17,200	1,150	1,750	1.52
DC-8 jet	107,000	965	550	0.57
Volkswagen	1,010	81	59.6	0.74
Cadillac	2,210	119	98.3	0.83

This statement comparing the oxidation of food molecules with that of fuel molecules is not a metaphor; it is a fact. Look for instance at Table elsewhere in this chpater in which energy costs for running different kinds of machinery-biological and manmadeare compared, and note the remarkable similarities. (There are at least two other interesting generalisations that can be formulated from these data. Can you find them?)

A principal energy source for vertebrates is the monosaccharide glucose. It is in this form that sugar is generally transported in the animal body. A patient receiving an intravenous feeding in a hospital is getting glucose dissolved in water. This glucose is carried through the bloodstream to the cells of the body where the energy-yielding reactions are carried out. As measured in a calorimeter, the oxidation of a mole of glucose yields 673 kilocalories:

$$C_6H_{12}O_6 + 6O_2 \rightarrow 6CO_2 + 6H_2O$$
$$\Delta H^\circ = -673 \text{ kcal}$$

Disaccharides: Transport Forms

Disaccharides consist of two single sugars (monosaccharides) covalently bonded together. Although glucose is the common transport sugar for vertebrates, sugars are often transported in other organisms as disaccharides.

Sucrose, commonly called cane sugar, is the form in which sugar is transported in plants from the photosynthetic cells (mostly in the leaf), where it is produced, to other parts of the plant body. Sucrose is composed of the monosaccharides glucose and fructose.

As is the case with all disaccharides and, indeed with most organic polymers, a molecule of water is removed in the course of bond formation, a reaction known as *condensation*. Thus, only the monomers of carbohydrates actually have a CH_2O ratio because of the removal of two atoms of hydrogen and one of oxygen every time such a bond is formed.

When the sucrose molecule is split into glucose and fructose, as it is when it is used as an energy source, the molecule of water is added again. This splitting requires the addition of a water molecule and so is known as *hydrolysis,* from *hydra,* meaning "water," and *lysis,* meaning "breaking apart."

Another common disaccharide is lactose, a sugar that occurs only in milk. Lactose is made up of glucose combined with another monosaccharide, galactose. Sugar is transported through the blood of

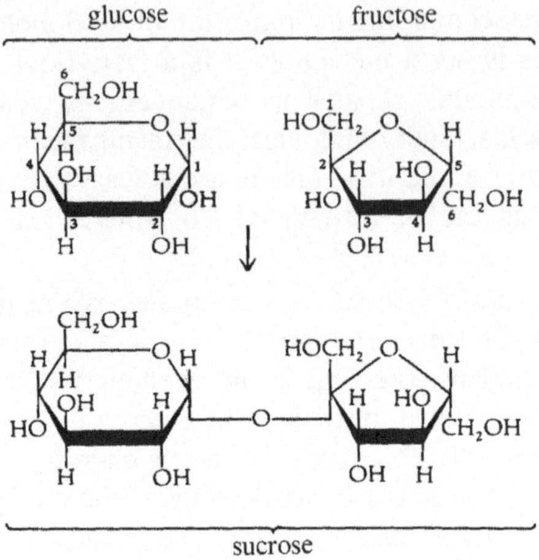

Figure 3.7 : Sucrose is a disaccharide made up of two monosaccharides, glucose and fructose. Note that the sucrose formed here is the beta form; the fructose has been rotated 180° and so can join to glucose in a 1→ 2 linkage. The formation of sucrose involves the removal of a molecule of water (condensation). Splitting sucrose requires, conversely, the addition of a water molecule (hydrolysis).

many insects in the form of another disaccharide, trehalose, which consists of two glucose units linked together.

Polysaccharides: Sugars in Storage

Polysaccharides are made up of monosaccharides linked together in long chains. Some of them are storage forms of sugar. *Starch,* for instance, is the principal food storage form in most plants. A potato, for example, contains starch produced from the sugar formed in the green leaves of the plant; the sugar is transported underground and accumulated there in a form suitable for winter storage, after which it will provide for new growth in the spring.

Starch occurs in two forms, amylose and amylopectin. Both consist of glucose units linked together. *Glycogen* is the principal storage form for sugar in higher animals. Glycogen has a structure much like that of amylopectin except that it is more highly branched, with branches occurring every eight to ten glucose units. In vertebrates, glycogen is stored principally in the liver and in muscle tissue.

When there is an excess of glucose in the bloodstream, the liver forms glycogen. When the concentration of glucose in the blood drops, the hormone glucagon, produced by the pancreas, is released into the bloodstream; glucagon stimulates the liver to hydrolyse glycogen to glucose, which then enters the bloodstream.

Formation of polysaccharides from monosaccharides requires energy. However, when the cell needs energy and these polysaccharides are hydrolysed, the energy released is available for cellular work.

Structural Polysaccharides

A major function of molecules in living systems is to form the structural components of cells and tissues. The principal structural molecule in plants is *cellulose.* In fact, half of all of the organic carbon in the biosphere is incorporated into cellulose. Wood is about 50 percent cellulose, and cotton is nearly pure cellulose.

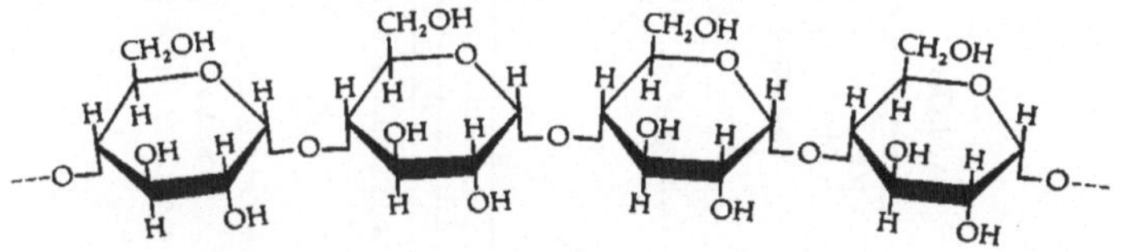

amylose
(a)

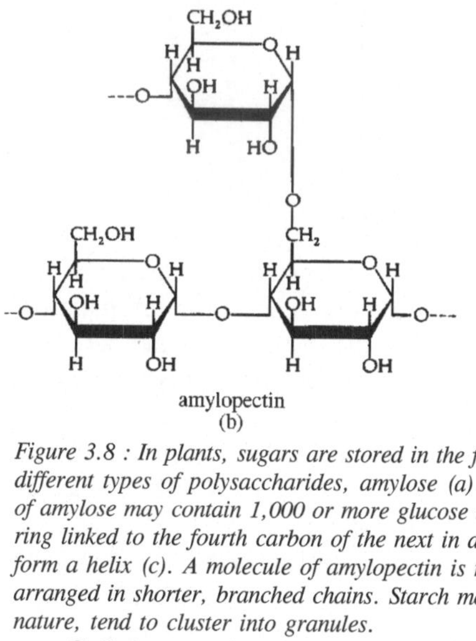

amylopectin
(b)

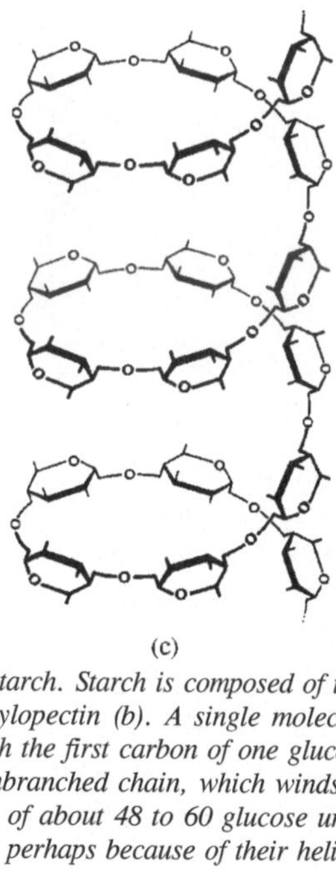

(c)

Figure 3.8 : In plants, sugars are stored in the form of starch. Starch is composed of two different types of polysaccharides, amylose (a) and amylopectin (b). A single molecule of amylose may contain 1,000 or more glucose units with the first carbon of one glucose ring linked to the fourth carbon of the next in a long unbranched chain, which winds to form a helix (c). A molecule of amylopectin is made up of about 48 to 60 glucose units arranged in shorter, branched chains. Starch molecules, perhaps because of their helical nature, tend to cluster into granules.

Cellulose molecules form the fibrous part of the plant cell wall. The cellulose fibers, cemented together by other kinds of polysaccharides, surround the plant cells, which, in effect, live in little cellulose boxes.

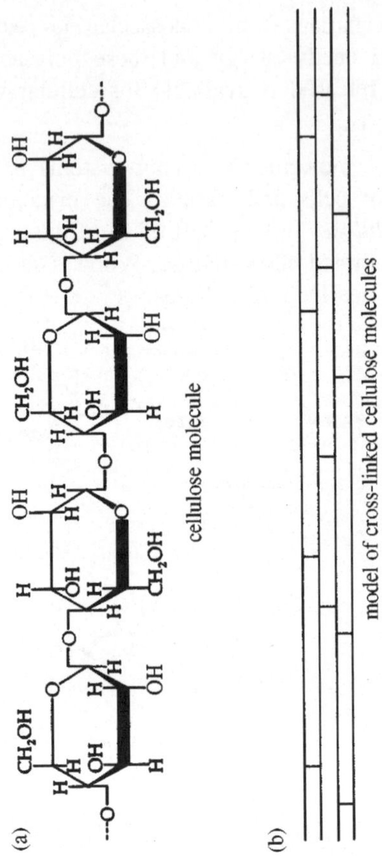

Figure 3.9 : Starch consists of alpha-glu-cose monomers. Cellulose (a) consists of beta-glucose monomers. The OH groups, which project from both sides of the chain, form hydrogen bonds with neighboring OH groups, resulting in the formation of bundles of cross linked parallel chains.

When the cells are young, these boxes are flexible and stretch as the cell grows, but they become thicker and more rigid as the cell matures. In some plant tissues, such as the tissues that form wood and bark, the cells eventually die, leaving only their tough outer cellulose-containing walls.

Cellulose is a polymer composed of monomers of glucose, just as starch and glycogen are. Starch and glycogen can be readily utilised as fuel by almost all kinds of living systems, but only a few microorganisms-certain bacteria, protozoa, and fungi-can hydrolyse cellulose. Cows and other ruminants, termites, and cockroaches can use cellulose for energy only because of microorganisms that inhabit their digestive tracts.

To understand the differences between structural polysaccharides, such as cellulose, and energy-storage polysaccharides, such as starch or glycogen, we have to look briefly once again at the glucose molecule.

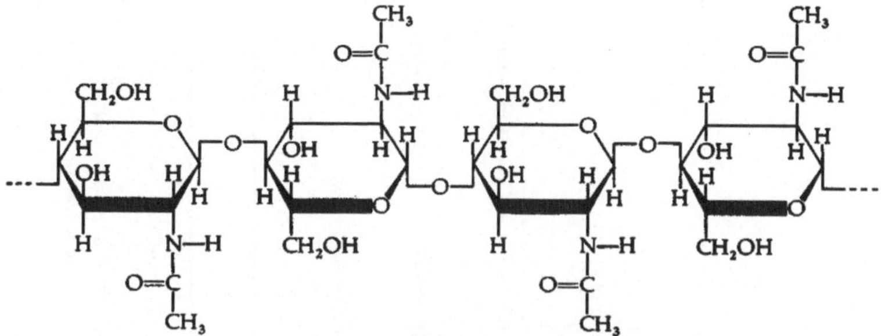

chitin

Figure 3.10 : Chitin is a polymer consisting of repeated modified monasaccharides.

You will remember that the molecule is basically a chain of carbon atoms and that when it is in solution, as it is in the cell, it assumes a ring form. The ring may close in either of two ways.

One ring form is known as alpha, and the other as beta. The alpha and beta forms are in equilibrium, with a certain number of the molecules changing from one to the other all of the time, going through the open-chain structure to reach the other form. Starch and glycogen are both made up entirely of alpha units. Cellulose consists entirely of beta units. Because of this slight difference in structure, cellulose is impervious to the enzymes that so successfully break down the storage polysaccharides.

Chitin, which is a major component of the exoskeletons of insects and also of the cell walls of many fungi, is a tough, resistant, modified polysaccharide.

LIPIDS

Lipids are a general group of substances, of which fats and waxes are particular examples. Unlike carbohydrates, lipids are hydrophobic. Many, although not all, contain fatty acids as major structural components. Lipids serve both as energystorage forms-usually in the form of fats or oils-and for structural purposes, as in the case of phospholipids and waxes.

Fats: Energy in Storage

Unlike many plants, such as the potato, animals have only a limited capacity to store carbohydrates. In vertebrates, sugars in excess of what can be stored as glycogen are converted into fats. Some plants also store food energy as fats (oils), especially in seeds and fruits. Fats contain a higher proportion of energy-rich carbon-hydrogen bonds (see Figure 3-4) than carbohydrates do and, as a consequence, contain more

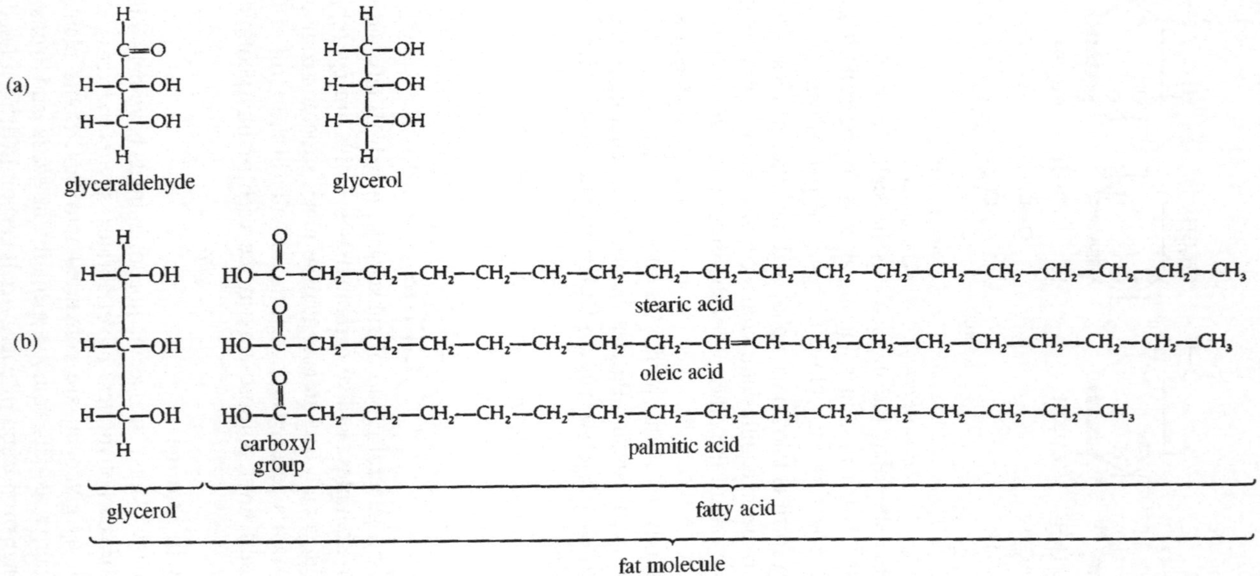

Figure 3.11 (a) Glycerol and glyceraldehyde differ by only two hydrogen atoms. The hydroxyl (OH) groups of glycerol are characteristic of an alcohol. Glycerol is one of the building blocks of fats. (b) A fat molecule consists of three fatty acids joined to a glycerol molecule.

chemical energy. On the average, fats yield about 9.3 kilocalories per gram as compared to 3.79 kcal per gram of carbohydrate, or 3.12 kcal per gram of protein. Also, because they are hydrophobic, they do not attract water molecules, as glycogen does.

Taking into account the water factor, fats store six times as much energy, gram for gram, as glycogen, which is undoubtedly why in the course of evolution they came to play a major role in energy storage.

For instance, a male ruby-throated hummingbird has a fat-free weight of 2.5 grams (about 1/10 ounce). It migrates every fall from Florida to Yucatan, some 2,000 kilometers.

Before doing so, it accumulates 2.0 grams of body fat, an amount almost equal to its original weight. However, if it were to carry the same energy reserves in the form of glycogen, it would have to carry 5 grams, twice its own fat-free weight. (Incidentally, as you will note in Table elsewhere in this chapter, flying is a more efficient method of travel for animals of comparable weight than walking.)

A neutral fat molecule consists of three molecules of fatty acid joined to one glycerol molecule. (Note the similarities of glycerol and glyceraldehyde.) Fatty acids, which are seldom found in cells in a free state (that is, not as part of another molecule), typically consist of chains between 14 and 22 carbon atoms long.

About 70 different fatty acids are known, which differ in their chain lengths and in whether the chain contains any double bonds (as in oleic acid) or not (as in stearic acid), and in the position in the chain of any double bonds. A fatty acid, such as stearic acid, in which there are no double bonds is known as a saturated fatty acid.

A fatty acid, such as oleic acid, that contains carbon atoms joined by double bonds is said to be unsaturated. Unsaturated fats, which tend to be oily liquids, are more common in plants than in animals; examples are olive oil, peanut oil, and corn oil.

Sugars, Fats, and Calories

As we noted earlier, when carbohydrates are taken into the body in excess of the body's energy requirements, they are stored temporarily as glycogen or, more permanently, as fats. Conversely, when the energy requirements of the body are not met by its immediate intake of food, glycogen and, subsequently, fat are broken down to fill these requirements.

Whether or not the body uses up its own storage molecules has nothing to do with the molecular form in which the energy comes into the body. It is simply a matter of whether these molecules, as they are broken down, release sufficient numbers of calories.

Structural Lipids

Insulators and Cushions

In general, fat stored in fat cells can be mobilised for energy when caloric intake is less than caloric expenditures. Some types of fat, however, seem to be protected from metabolic activity. Large masses of fatty tissue, for example, surround mammalian kidneys and serve to protect these precious organs from physical shock.

For reasons that are not understood, these fat deposits remain intact even at times of starvation. Another mammalian characteristic is a layer of fat under the skin, which serves as thermal insulation. This layer is particularly well developed in sea-going mammals.

Among humans, females characteristically have a thicker layer of subdermal ("under-the-skin") fat than males. This capacity to store fat,

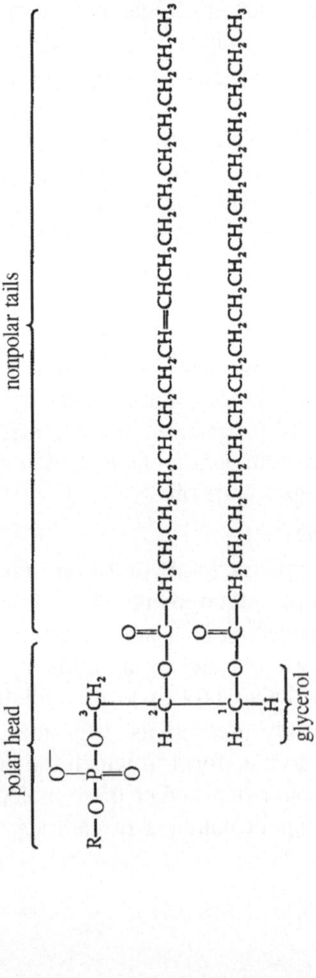

Figure 3.12 : A phospholipid molecule consists of two fatty acids linked to a glycerol molecule, as in a fat, and a phosphate group (indicated by colour) linked to the glycerol's third carbon.

although not much admired in our present culture, was undoubtedly very valuable 10,000 or more years ago.

At that time, as far as we know, there was no other reserve food supply, and this extra fat not only nourished the woman but more important, the unborn child and the nursing infant, whose ability to fast without damage is much less than that of the adult. Thus many of us are strenuously dieting off what millennia of evolution have given us the capacity to accumulate.

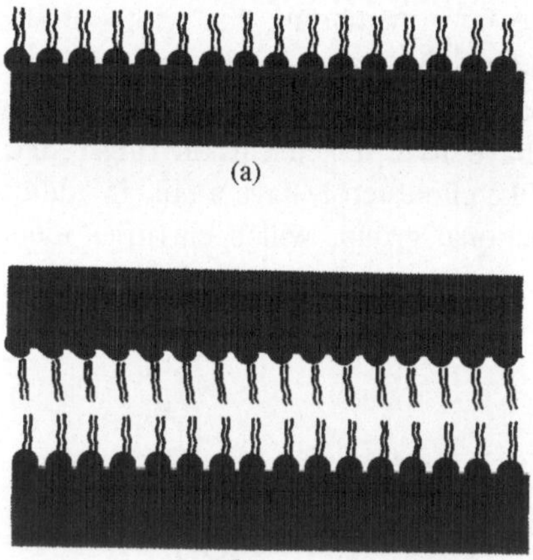

(a)

(b)

Figure 3.13 : (a) Because phospholipids have water-soluble heads and water-insoluble tails, they tend to form a thin film on a water surface with their tails extending above the water. (b) Surrounded by water, they spontaneously arrange themselves in two layers with their heads extending outward and their hydrophobic (water-fearing) tails inward.

Lipids and Membranes

Lipids also play extremely important structural roles. The lipids most important for structural purposes are phospholipids. Like fats, the phospholipids are composed of fatty acid chains attached to a glycerol backbone. In the phospholipids, however, the third carbon of the glycerol molecule is occupied not by a fatty acid but by a phosphate group to which another polar group is usually attached.

Phosphate groups are negatively charged. As a result, the phosphate end of the molecule is hydrophilic and the fatty acid portions are not. The consequences are shown in Figure elsewhere in this chpater. As we shall see, according to the present model, this arrangement of phospholipid molecules, with their hydrophilic heads extended and their hydrophobic tails clustered together, forms the structural basis of the cell membrane.

Waxes

Waxes are also a form of structural lipid. They form protective coatings on skin, fur, feathers, on the leaves and fruits of higher plants, and on the exoskeletons of many insects.

Cholesterol

Cholesterol is found in cell membranes (with the exception of bacterial cells). About 25 percent (by dry weight) of the membranes of red blood cells is cholesterol; it is also a major component of the myelin sheath, the fatty membrane that wraps around fast-conducting nerve fibers, speeding the nerve impulse.

Cholesterol belongs to a group of compounds known as the *steroids*. All the steroids have four linked carbon rings, like cholesterol, and several of them, like cholesterol, have a tail. In addition, many of them have the OH functional group, which classifies them as alcohols.

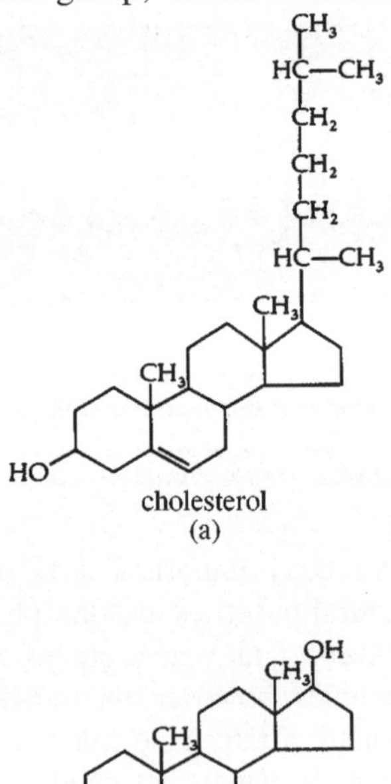

cholesterol
(a)

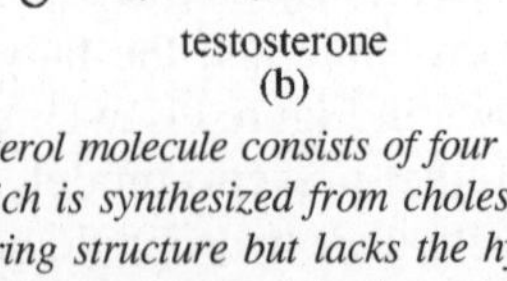

testosterone
(b)

Figure 3.14 : (a) The cholesterol molecule consists of four carbon rings and a hydrocarbon chain. (b) Testosterone, which is synthesized from cholesterol by cells in the testes, also has the characteristic four-ring structure but lacks the hydrocarbon tail.

Although steroids do not resemble the other lipids structurally, they are grouped with the lipids because they are insoluble in water. In some older people, cholesterol forms fatty deposits on the inner lining of the blood vessels. This blocks the vessels and decreases their elasticity, making such people more susceptible to high blood pressure, heart attacks, and strokes.

Attempts have been made to reduce the incidence and extent of such deposits by reducing the dietary intake of high-cholesterol foods, such as eggs and cheese. But since many cells of the human body are able to synthesize cholesterol, it is not clear that a reduction of dietary cholesterol will solve the problem.

Regulatory Lipids

Sex hormones and the hormones of the adrenal cortex are also steroids; they are formed from cholesterol in the ovaries, testes, and other glands that produce them. Prostaglandins are a recently discovered group of chemicals with hormonelike actions, which are derived from fatty acids. Both the steroid hormones and the fatty acids will be discussed more fully in other section of this chapter.

PROTEINS

Proteins are among the most abundant organic molecules; in most living systems they make up 50 percent or more of the dry weight. Only plants, with their high cellulose content, are less than half protein.

There are many different protein molecules: enzymes; hormones; storage proteins, such as those in the eggs of birds and reptiles and in seeds; transport proteins, such as hemoglobin; contractile proteins of the sort found in muscle; immunoglobulins (antibodies); and many different types of structural proteins.

In their functions, their diversity is overwhelming. In their structure, however, they all follow the same simple blueprint: They are all polymers of amino acids, arranged in a linear sequence. As we saw earlier, every amino acid has the same fundamental structure, which consists of a central carbon atom bonded to an amino group (NH,), to a carboxyl group (COOH), and to a hydrogen atom.

In every amino acid there is also another atom or group of atoms bonded to the central carbon. As shown in Figure elsewhere in this chapter, this side (R) group can be a hydrogen atom, in which case the amino acid is glycine; a CH_3 group, in which case the amino acid is alanine; and so on. The side group, depending on the atom or atoms that compose it, may have a positive charge, have a negative charge, be polar (with negative and positive zones), or have no charge at all (in which case it is hydrophobic).

Table 3.3 : Biological Functions of Proteins.

Types of Proteins	*Examples*
Structural proteins	Collagen, silk, virus coats, microtubules
Regulatory proteins	Insulin, ACTH, growth hormones
Contractile proteins	Contractile filaments in muscle cells
Transport proteins	Hemoglobin, myoglobin
Storage proteins	Egg white, seed protein
Protective proteins in vertebrate blood	Antibodies, complement
Membrane proteins	Membrane-transport proteins, antigens, permeases
Toxins	Botulism toxin, diphtheria toxin
Enzymes	Sucrase, pepsin

Amino Acids: The Building Blocks of Proteins

A large variety of different amino acids is theoretically possible, but only about 20 are used to build proteins. And it is always the same 20, whether in a bacterial cell, a plant cell, or a cell in your own body.

In proteins, amino acids are joined together by peptide linkages. The sequence of amino acids in the chains determines the biological character of the protein molecule; even one small variation in the sequence may alter or destroy the way in which the protein functions. Protein molecules are large, often containing several hundred amino acids.

Thus the number of different amino acid sequences, and therefore the possible variety of protein molecules, is enormousabout as enormous as the number of different sentences that can be written with our own 26-letter alphabet.

Organisms have only a very small fraction of the possible proteins. The singlecelled bacterium *Escherichia coli,* for example, contains 600 to 800 different kinds of proteins at any one time, and the cell of a plant or animal has several times that number. In a complex organism, there are at least several thousand different proteins, each with a special function and each, by its unique chemical nature, specifically fitted for that function.

The Levels of Protein Organisation

Proteins are assembled in living systems with the amino group of one amino acid linked to the carbonyl of another, like a line of boxcars. Such chains of covalently bonded amino acids may be called *polypeptides.*

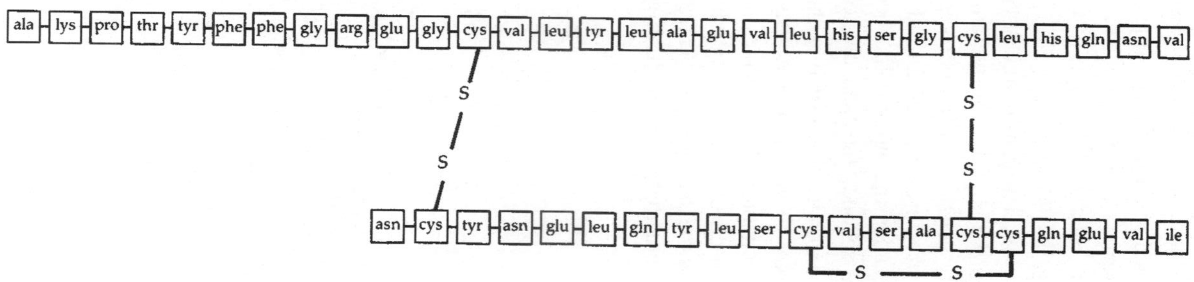

Figure 3.15 : Primary structure of a relatively small protein, the hormone insulin. This was one of the first proteins for which the primary structure was determined. As you can see, it consists of two polypeptide chains held together by disulfide bridges.

This linear sequence is known as the *primary structure* of the protein. Each different protein has a different primary structure. The primary structure of one protein is shown in Figure elsewhere in this chapter.

The protein is assembled in a long chain, one amino acid at a time. (This process will be described in some detail in other chapter of this book.) As it is assembled, interactions begin to take place among the various amino acids along the chain.

Linus Pauling and co-worker Robert Corey discovered that hydrogen bonds could form between the slightly positive amino hydrogen of one amino acid and the slightly negative carbonyl oxygen of another amino acid. They elucidated two structures that could result from these hydrogen bonds. One of these they called the alpha helix, because it was the first to be discovered, and the second, the beta pleated sheet.

Proteins that have an extended form such as the helix or the pleated sheet are known as *fibrous proteins*. These structures are shown in Figure elsewhere in this chapter. Biochemists refer to the regular, repeated configurations caused by hydrogen bonding between atoms of the polypeptide backbone as the *secondary structure* of a protein. Pauling won a Nobel Prize for his elucidation of the hydrogen bond and its role in protein structure.

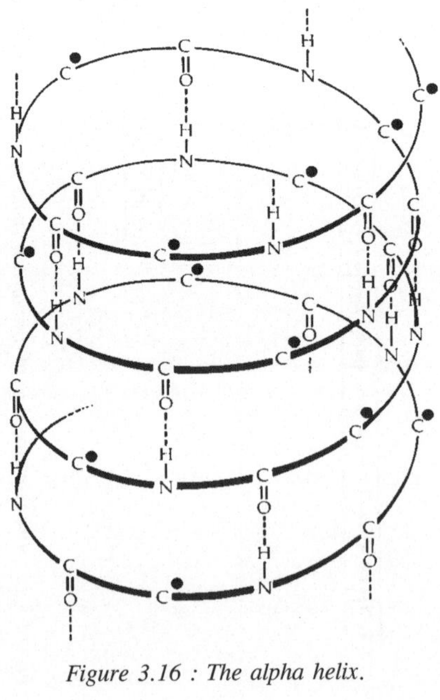

Figure 3.16 : The alpha helix.

Other forces, which involve the nature of the R groups, are also at work on the polypeptide chain, and these counteract the formation of the hydrogen bonds just described. For instance, an R group such as that of isoleucine is so bulky that it interrupts the turn of the helix, making the hydrogen bonding impossible.

Wherever a cysteine encounters another cysteine, a covalent bond may form, making a disulfide bridge that locks the molecule in that position. R groups with unlike charges are attracted to each other and those with like charges are mutually repelled. As the molecule is twisted and turned in solution, the hydrophobic R groups become clustered together in the interior of the molecule and the hydrophilic groups extend outward into the aqueous solution.

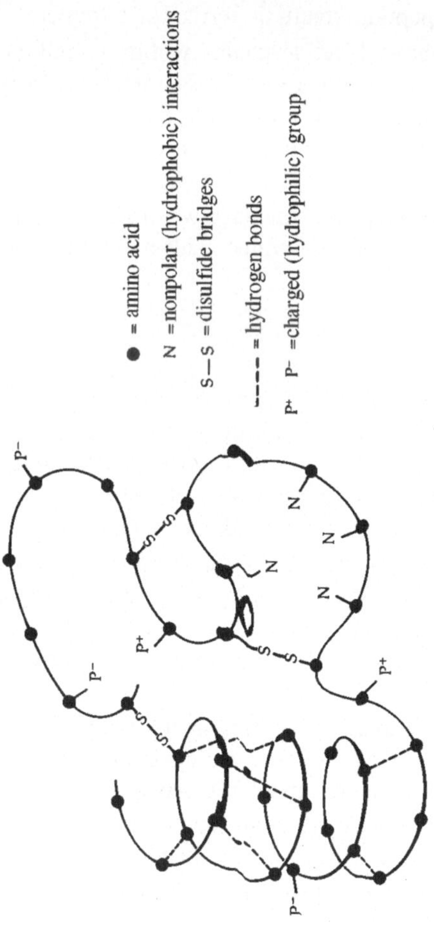

Figure 3.17 : (a) Bonds stabilizing the three-dimensional protein structure.

Hydrogen bonds form, linking together segments of the amino acid backbone. As a result of these interactions, many proteins take an intricately folded, globular shape, and these are known as *globular proteins*.

Figure elsewhere in this chapter indicates the various types of bonds that are involved in a globular structure. The intricate three-dimensional structure involving interactions among R groups is often referred to as *tertiary structure*.

Many proteins are composed of more than one polypeptide chain. The polypeptide chains are held together by hydrogen bonds, disulfide bridges, attractions between positive and negative charges, and hydrophobic forces. Such proteins are often called multimeric; a protein containing four polypeptide chains is termed a tetramer.

Often some of the polypetide chains within a multimeric protein are dissimilar. Hemoglobin, for example, is a tetramer; it is composed of four polypeptide chains, two of one kind (alpha) and two of another (beta). This level of organisation of proteins, which involves interaction of two or more polypeptides, is called a *quaternary structure*.

Note that the tertiary and quaternary structures depend on the primary structure-the sequence of amino acids-and on the local chemical environment.

Structural Proteins

Fibrous Proteins

In general, fibrous proteins have a regular, repeated sequence of amino acids and so a regular, repetitious structure. An example is collagen, which makes up about one-third of all the protein in vertebrates. The basic collagen molecule is composed of three very long polymers of amino acids-about 1,000 amino acids per chain.

These three polymers, which are made up of repeating groups of amino acids, are held together by hydrogen bonds linking amino acids of different chains in a tight coil. The molecules can coil so tightly because every third amino acid is glycine, the smallest of the amino acids.

Collagen performs many functions in the body. Consider a cow. Tendons, which link muscle to bone, are made up of collagen fibers in parallel bundles; thus arranged, they are very strong but do not stretch. The cow's hide, by contrast, is made up of collagen fibrils arranged in an interlacing network laid down in sheets.

Even its corneas-the transparent coverings of the eyeballs-are

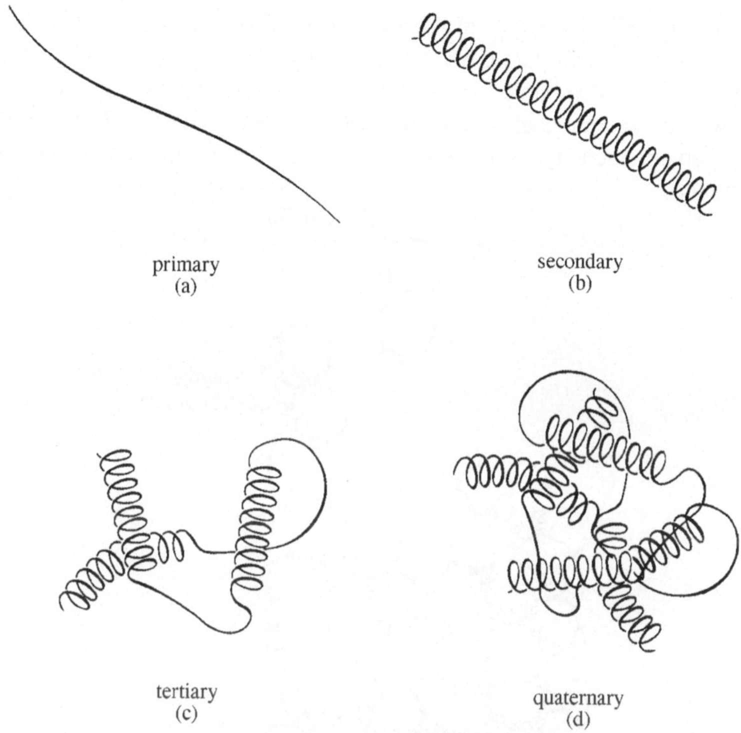

Figure 3.18 : The structures of protein.

composed of collagen. Boiling in water disperses the polymers of collagen into shorter chains, which we know as gelatin.

Other fibrous proteins include elastin, present in the elastic tissue of ligaments, silk, and keratin.

Structural Uses of Globular Proteins

Some structural proteins are globular. For example, microtubules, which function in a variety of ways inside the cell, are made up of globular proteins. They are long hollow tubes-so long that their entire length can seldom be traced in a single microscopic section.

They apparently act as internal skeletons, stiffening parts of the cell body. They also may serve as tracks along which substances can move inside the cell.

The formation of a new cellulose cell wall in a plant can be predicted by the appearance at the site of large numbers of microtubules; when cellulose fibrils are being laid down outside a plant cell membrane, as a cell wall forms or grows, it is possible to detect microtubules inside the cell aligned in the same direction as the fibrils outside.

Chemical analysis shows that each microtubule consists of a very large number of subunits, each of which is a globular protein made up of two polypeptide chains. The two polypeptides fit together because of their complementary configurations, forming approximately spherical subunits.

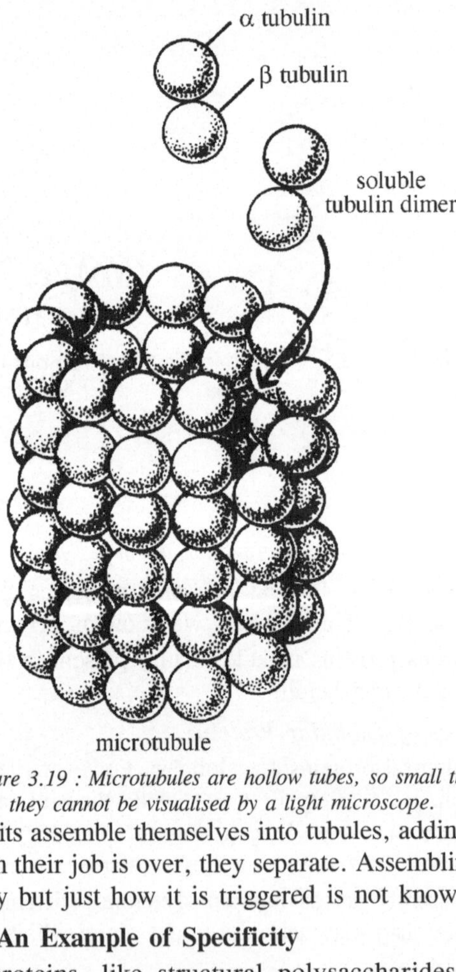

Figure 3.19 : Microtubules are hollow tubes, so small that they cannot be visualised by a light microscope.

The subunits assemble themselves into tubules, adding on length as required. When their job is over, they separate. Assembling requires an input of energy but just how it is triggered is not known.

Hemoglobin: An Example of Specificity

Fibrous proteins, like structural polysaccharides, are usually molecules with a relatively small variety of monomers in a repetitive sequence. Many proteins, by contrast, have extremely complex, irregular amino acid sequences, as complex and irregular as the sequence of letters in a sentence on this page. Just as these sentences make sense (if they do) because the letters are the right ones and in the right order, the proteins make sense, biologically speaking, because their amino acids are the right ones in the right order.

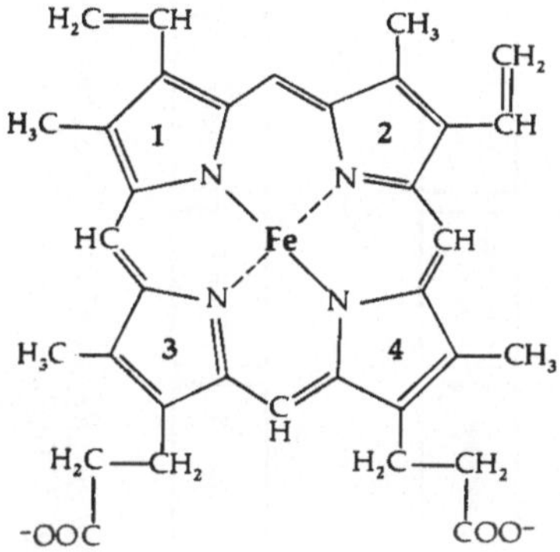

Figure 3.20 : The heme group of hemoglobin. It contains an iron atom (Fe) held in a porphyrin ring.

Hemoglobin, for example, has a quaternary structure that consists of four polypeptide chains, each of which is combined with an iron-containing molecule known as *heme*. In heme, an iron atom is held in the center of a ring of nitrogencontaining atoms known as a porphyrin ring.

Hemoglobin has two identical alpha chains and two identical beta chains, each about 150 amino acids long, for a total of about 600 amino acids in all. In man, hemoglobin molecules are manufactured and carried in the red blood cells. A mature red blood cell contains about 265 million molecules of hemoglobin.

These molecules possess the special property of being able to combine loosely with oxygen so that they can collect oxygen in the lungs and release it in the tissues.

Sickle cell anemia is a disease in which the hemoglobin molecules are defective. When oxygen is removed, the defective molecules change shape and combine with one another to form stiffened rodlike structures. Red cells containing large proportions of these molecules become stiff and deformed, taking on the characteristic sickle shape.

The deformed cells may clog the smallest blood vessels (capillaries), cutting off the local blood supply and resulting in anemia. The disease is usually painful and often fatal.

Analysis of the hemoglobin molecules of patients with sickle cell anemia reveals that the only difference between normal and sickle cell hemoglobin is that in a precise location in each beta chain, one glutamic

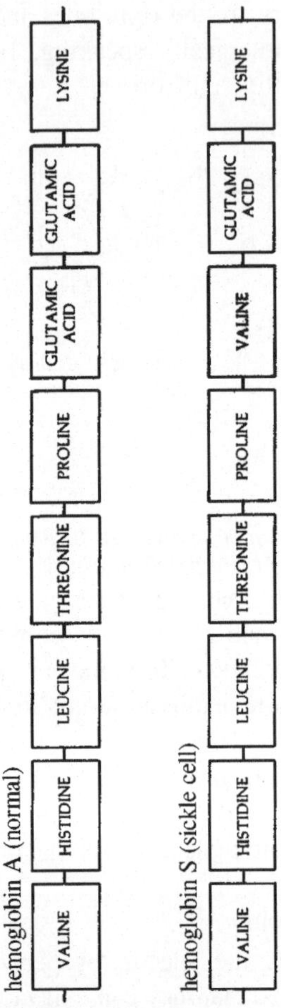

Figure 3.21 : An example of remarkable precision of the "language" of proteins. Portions of the beta chains of the hemolobin A (normal) molecule and the hemoglobin S (sickle cell) molecule are shown

acid is replaced by one valine. When one considers that this difference of two amino acids in a total of almost 600 is actually the difference between life and death, one begins to get an idea of the meaning of specificity and of the precision and the importance of the arrangement of amino acids in a precise sequence in a protein.

LEVELS OF ORGANISATION

In the last three chapters we have progressed from a brief consideration of subatomic particles to an examination of large proteins, among the most complex of all molecules. Although the neutrons, protons, and electrons of which atoms are composed are all the same, the elements differ greatly from one another. Mercury is a heavy metallic liquid, chlorine is a green gas, sulfur is a yellow powder, pure carbon can take the form of a hard solid-a diamond-and so on. The differences lie not in the nature of the subatomic particles, but rather in their number and arrangement-in their organisation.

And just as subatomic particles combine to form atoms, atoms, as we have seen, combine to form molecules. At each level of organisation, new properties appear.

Water, for instance, as we have seen, is not the sum of the properties of hydrogen and oxygen; it is something more and also something different. In a molecule such as hemoglobin, we see how amino acids, with their diverse properties, become organised into a polypeptide and how polypeptide chains combine in a new level of organisation, the quaternary structure of the complete molecule.

Only at this j level of organisation do the complex properties of the molecule emerge, and only l then can the molecule assume its function.

Living systems, as we noted earlier, obey the laws of physics and chemistry. Are we then "nothing but" a collection of atoms and molcules? There are recognisable differences between "life" and "nonlife." What is the basis of these differences? According to biologists, the differences are to be found not in the atoms and molecules themselves, but in their organisation.

4

BIOLOGICAL CATALYST

In the previous chapters, we have introduced you to the principal kinds of molecules found in living systems. In this chapter, we shall try to offer a glimpse of molecular dynamics. First we shall look at some general principles regarding the formation of molecules, and next we shall see how living systems build up and break down molecules, how they convert one kind to another, creating more of 'their own substance, and how they extract and harness the energy that drives these processes.

THE NATURE OF CHEMICAL REACTIONS

Let us look at a very simple example of a chemical reaction and consider what happens when two hydrogen atoms approach one another. For our purposes, a hydrogen atom is, simply, a positively charged proton and a negatively charged electron. When two hydrogen atoms approach one another, a variety of forces are set in motion.

First, as they come closer, the negative charges of the electrons repel the atoms from one another. As they come closer still, the two atoms encounter one another 's positive charges and are repelled. But there is a third force at work: The nucleus of the first atom attracts the electron of the second, and vice versa.

When the two nuclei are a certain distance (about 7.4 nanometers or 0.74×10^{-a} centimeter-in other words, a little less than a hundred millionth of a centimeter) apart from one another, these forces of repulsion and attraction are equalised. At this distance, the two electrons

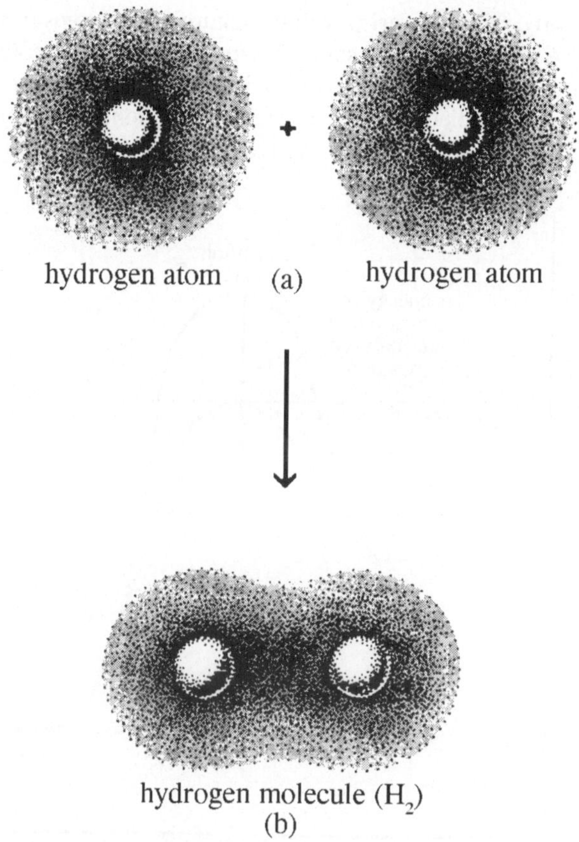

Figure 4.1 : (a) An individual atom has one electron in its first orbital. (b) When the nuclei of the two atoms are certain distance aprart, these forces are exactly balanced. The two electron shard qually btween the two nuclei.

are shared between the two nuclei, forming a strong covalent bond. This simple example illustrates two universal facts about chemical reactions:

1. All involve a change in the electron configurations of the atoms or molecules involved.
2. All require energy to make the transition between one stable electron configuration and another. This energy is known as the *energy of activation.*

Rates of Chemical Reactions

According to present concepts, atoms or molecules react with one another only when they collide with sufficient force to overcome the initial forces of repulsion.

The force required varies with the nature of the atoms or molecules; the more stable their initial state, the more forceful the collision must be. In any given group of atoms, it is likely that some proportion is moving with sufficient energy to cause a reaction to occur, but often this proportion is so small that the reaction, for all practical purposes, does not take place.

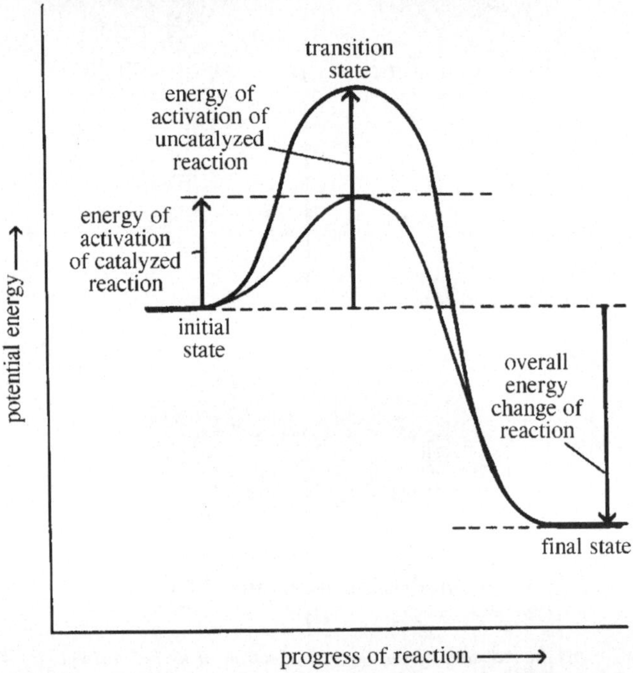

Figur 4.2 : Chemical reactions require an input of energy to get them started-analogous to the spark that lights a fire or the push that sends a boulder on its downhill course.

Reaction rates can be increased by increasing the likelihood of forceful collisions. One way to do this is to raise the temperature, thereby increasing the average velocity at which the atoms or molecules move and so increasing their likelihood of colliding with sufficient force.

Sometimes, as in the case of natural gas, a spark is all that is needed. Once the reaction begins, it liberates heat that is transferred to the other CH_4 molecules until all are moving rapidly enough to react almost simultaneously with explosive force. Driving a reaction by heat is a method commonly used in both chemical laboratories (for example, the familiar Bunsen burner) and industry.

A second way to increase the rate of collisions is to increase the number of reacting molecules (or to decrease the volume in which they move). Laboratories and chemical factories usually work with pure chemicals in high concentrations.

A third way is to use catalysts. Catalysts lower the energy of activation of a reaction. Metals, such as iron, nickel, and platinum, are commonly used as catalysts in industrial laboratories. Certain molecules apparently tend to cluster on the surfaces of such metals and so the likelihood of close encounters of the necessary kinds between the reactants is increased.

The metals, although they participate in the reactions, are not used up by them, and so they can be used over and over again.

Types of Reactions

Chemical reactions can be classified into a few general types. One type can be represented by the expression:

$$A + B \rightarrow AB$$

An example of this sort of reaction is the previously mentioned combination of hydrogen gas with oxygen gas to produce water:

$$2H_2 + O_2 \rightarrow 2H_2O$$

A reaction may also take the form of a dissociation:

$$AB \rightarrow A + B$$

For example, the equation above showing the formation of water can be reversed:

$$2H_2O \rightarrow 2H_2 + O_2$$

This means that water molecules yield hydrogen and oxygen gases. A reaction may also involve an exchange, taking the form:

$$AB + CD \rightarrow AD + CB$$

An example of such a reaction is the combination of hydrochloric acid (HCl) and sodium hydroxide (NaOH) to make table salt and water:

$$HCl + NaOH \rightarrow NaCl + H_2O$$

Oxidation-Reduction

The passing of an electron from one molecule to another is known as an oxidation-reduction (or redox) reaction. The loss of an electron is known as *oxidation,* and the compound that loses the electron is said to be oxidised. The reason electron loss is called oxidation is that oxygen, with its high electronegativity, is often the electron acceptor.

Reduction is, conversely, the gain of an electron. Oxidation and reduction take place simultaneously because an electron that is lost by the oxidised atom is accepted by another atom, which is then reduced. (The fact that reduction means a gain of an electron seems paradoxical and may make it hard to remember the distinction between the two terms. It may help to recall that gain of an electron *reduces* the charge of an atom or molecule.)

Redox reactions may involve only a solitary electron, as for instance when sodium loses an electron and becomes oxidised to Na^+, and chlorine gains an electron, thereby reducing its charge (Cl^-). Often the electron travels with a proton, so oxidation involves removal of hydrogen atoms and reduction the gain of hydrogen atoms. When glucose is burned (oxidised), hydrogen atoms are lost by the glucose molecule and gained by oxygen:

$$C_6H_{12}O_6 + 6O_2 \rightarrow 6CO_2 + 6H_2O$$

Chemical Equilibrium

Chemical reactions can go in either direction, as we have noted previously. When net change ceases, the reaction is said to be at equilibrium. In the reaction

$$A + B \rightleftharpoons C + D$$

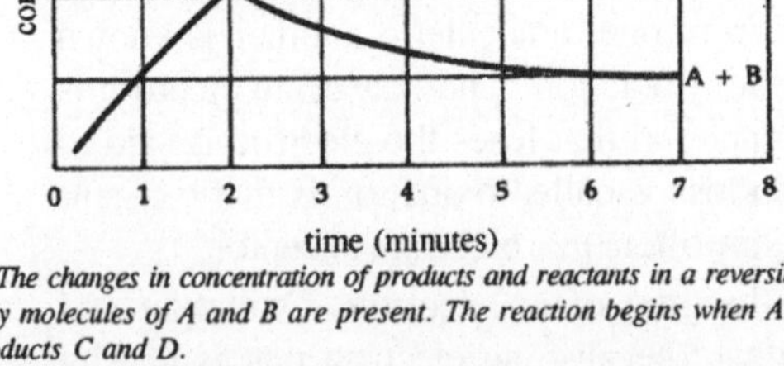

Figur 4.3 : The changes in concentration of products and reactants in a reversible reaction. At first, only molecules of A and B are present. The reaction begins when A and B start to yield products C and D.

the point of equilibrium is reached when as many molecules of C and D are being converted to molecules of A and B as molecules of A and B are being converted to molecules of C and D.

The concentration of reactants does not have to equal the concentration of products in order for equilibrium to be established;

only the rates of the forward and reverse reactions must be the same. Consider the reaction shown at the bottom of the facing page. The different lengths of the arrows indicate that at equilibrium there is more C + D present than A + B.

If only A and B molecules are present initially, the reaction occurs at first to the right, with A and B molecules converting into C and D molecules. Figure 4-3 shows the relative changes in concentration as the reaction continues. As C and D accumulate, the rate of the reverse reaction increases, and at the same time, the rate of the forward reaction decreases because of the decreasing concentrations of A and B.

At about minute 6, the rates of the forward and reverse reactions equalise and no further changes in concentration take place. The proportions of A + B and C + D will remain the same, but there will always be more C and D molecules in the system.

METABOLISM

In any living system, thousands of different chemical reactions take place, many of them simultaneously. The sum of all these reactions is referred to as *metabolism* (from the Greek *metabole,* meaning "change"). If we were merely to list the individual chemical reactions, it would be difficult indeed to understand a cell's metabolic activities. Fortunately, there are some guiding principles that lead one through the maze of cell metabolism.

First, virtually all the chemical reactions that take place in a cell involve enzymes-large protein molecules that play very specific roles. Second, biochemists are able to group these reactions in an ordered series of steps, commonly called a pathway; a pathway often has a dozen or more sequential reactions or steps. Each pathway serves a function in the overall life of the cell or organism.

Furthermore, certain pathways have many steps in common, for instance, those that are concerned with the synthesis of the different amino acids or the various nitrogenous bases. Some pathways converge; for example, the pathway by which fats are broken down to yield energy leads to the pathway by which glucose is broken down to yield energy.

Many living systems have pathways unique to them. Plant cells expend much of their energy building their cellulose walls, an activity not engaged in by animal cells. Red blood cells specialise in the synthesis of hemoglobin molecules, not made anywhere else in the animal body.

It is not surprising that the distinctive differences among cells and organisms are reflected not only in their forms and functions but also in their biochemistry. What is more surprising, however, is that much of the metabolism of even the most diverse of organisms is exceedingly similar; the differences in many of the metabolic pathways of humans, oak trees, mushrooms, and jellyfish are very slight. Some pathways are virtually universal, found in all living systems.

The magnitude of the chemical work carried out by a cell can be imagined if one recognises that, for the most part, the thousands of different molecules, large and small, found within a cell are synthesised there. The total of chemical reactions involved in synthesis is called *anabolism.*

Cells also are constantly involved in the breakdown of larger molecules; these activities are known, collectively, as *catabolism.* Catabolism serves two purposes: (1) It releases the energy for anabolism and other work of the cell, and (2) it serves as a source of raw materials for anabolic processes.

Not only do living systems carry out this multitude of chemical activities, but they do so under extraordinarily difficult conditions. Most of their chemical reactions are carried out within living cells, and in cells, not two or three but thousands of different kinds of molecules are intermingled.

Moreover, temperatures are not high. (Otherwise, many of the fragile structures on which life depends would be destroyed.) How is all this complex chemical work accomplished? The question can be answered in a single word: enzymes. Enzymes are the catalysts and regulators for all metabolic processes of living systems. If it were not for enzymes, biochemical reactions would take place so slowly that, for all practical purposes, they would not occur at all, and the activities we associate with life would cease to exist.

ENZYMES AS CATALYSTS

Enzymes are the catalysts of biological reactions. They differ from the catalysts previously described in that they are very selective in their action. A particular enzyme can generally catalyze reactions only between a very specific group of reactants, known as its substrate.

Otherwise, enzymes resemble the catalysts previously described in that they are not used up in the course of the reaction and so can be used over and over again. Enzymes also, as we shall see, appear to act in part by increasing the local concentrations of the reactants or substrate.

Enzymes enormously accelerate the rate at which reactions take place. For instance, the combination of carbon dioxide with water,

$$CO_2 + H_2O \rightleftharpoons \underset{\text{carbonic acid}}{H_2CO_3}$$

can take place spontaneously, as it does in the oceans. In the human body, however, this reaction is catalyzed by an enzyme, carbonic anhydrase, which is one of the fastest enzymes known, each enzyme molecule producing 10^5 (100,000) molecules of carbonic acid per second. The catalyzed reaction is 10^7 times faster than the uncatalyzed one.

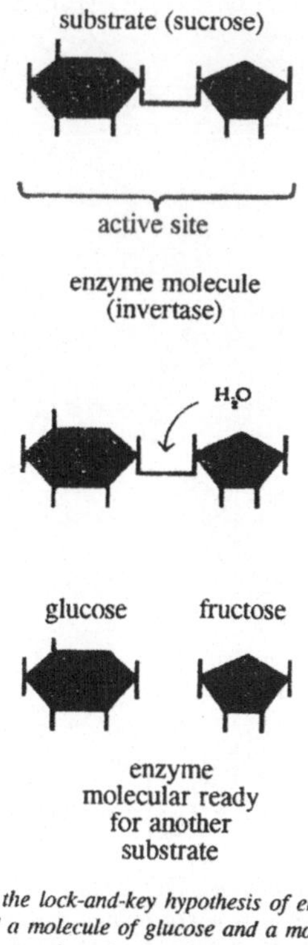

Figure 4.4 : A model of the lock-and-key hypothesis of enzyme action. Sucrose is hydrolyzed to yield a molecule of glucose and a molecule of fructose.

In animals, this reaction is essential in the transfer of carbon dioxide from the cells, where it is produced, to the bloodstream, which transports it to the lungs. (Note also another characteristic of enzymes-they usually have names ending in *ase.)*

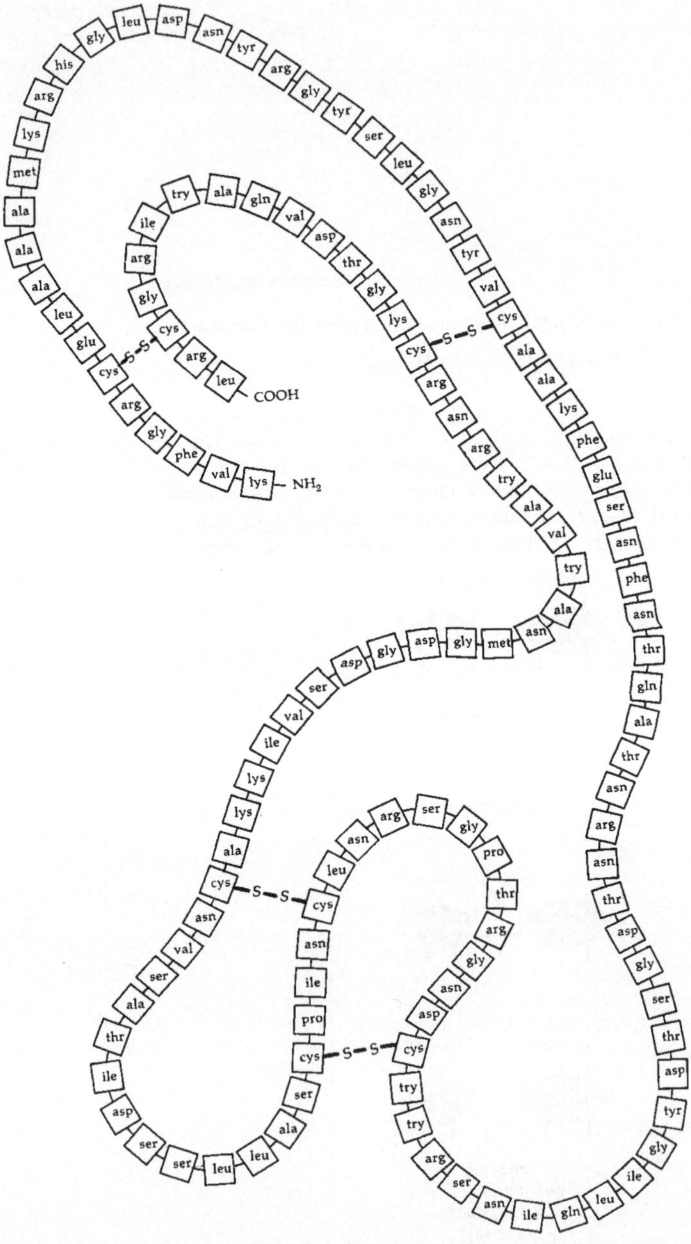

Figure 4.5: Primary structure of the enzyme lysozyme. This enzyme contains 129 amino acids, is found in many different types of animal cells.

STRUCTURE OF ENZYMES

Enzymes are large to very large, complex globular proteins consisting of one or more polypeptide chains. They are folded so as to form a groove or pocket into which the reacting molecule or molecules-the substrate-fit and where the reactions take place. This portion of the enzyme is known as the *active site*. The relationship between the active site and the substrate is very precise.

Emil Fischer, who postulated the existence of active sites in 1894, compared the relationship to that of a lock and a key. The active site, we know now, is a result of the very exact folding of the polypeptide chain.

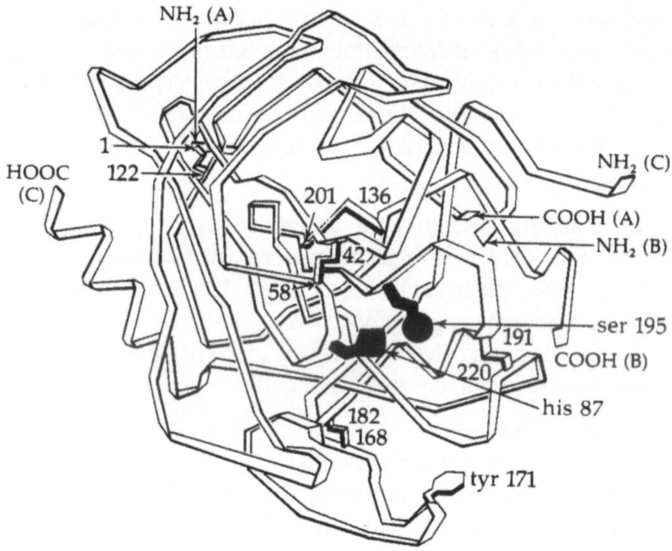

Figure 4.6 : Model of an enzyme. This enzyme (the digestive enzyme chymotrypsin) is composed of three polypeptide chains. The amino (NH_2) and carboxyl (COON) ends of each are labeled.

The active site not only has the right three-dimensional shape, but also it has exactly the right array of charged or uncharged, hydrophilic or hydrophobic areas on the binding surface. If a particular portion of the substrate has a negative charge, the corresponding feature on the active site has a positive charge, and so on. Thus the active site not only confines the substrate molecule but also orients it in the right direction.

The amino acids involved in the active site need not be adjacent to one another on the polypeptide chains. In fact, in an enzyme with quaternary structure, they may even be on different polypeptide chains, as-shown in Figure elsewhere in this chapter. They are _brought together at the active site by the precise folding of the molecule.

The Induced-Fit Hypothesis

Within the last several years, studies of enzyme structure have suggested that the binding between enzyme and substrate alters the conformation of the enzyme, thus inducing the close fit between the active site and the reactants. It is believed that this induced fit may put some strain on the reacting molecules and so further facilitate the reaction.

COFACTORS IN ENZYME ACTION

The catalytic activity of some enzymes appears to depend only upon the physical and chemical interactions between the amino acids of the active site and the substrate. Many enzymes, however, require additional nonprotein low-molecularweight substances in order to function. Such nonproteins that are essential for enzyme function are known as *cofactors*.

Ions as Cofactors

Certain ions are cofactors for particular enzymes. For example, the magnesium ion (Mg^{2+}) is required in all enzymatic reactions involving the transfer of a phosphate group from one molecule to another. Its two positive charges hold the negatively charged phosphate group in position. K^+, Ca^{2+}, and other ions play similar roles in other reactions. In some cases, ions serve to hold the protein together.

Coenzymes and Vitamins

Nonprotein organic molecules may also play a crucial role in enzyme-catalyzed reactions. Such molecules are called *coenzymes*. For example, in some oxidationreduction reactions, electrons-often traveling as a hydrogen ion with a pair of electrons-are passed to a molecule that serves as an electron acceptor.

There are several different electron acceptors in any given cell, each tailor-made to hold the electron at a slightly different energy level. As an example, let us look at just one, nicotinamide adenine dinucleotide (NAD^+). At first glance, NAD^+ looks complex and unfamiliar, but if you look at it more closely, you will find that you recognise most of its component parts.

The two units labeled ribose are five-carbon sugars. They are linked by two phosphate groups. One of the sugars is attached to the nitrogenous base adenine. The other is attached to another nitrogenous base, nicotinamide. (A nitrogenous base plus a sugar plus a phosphate

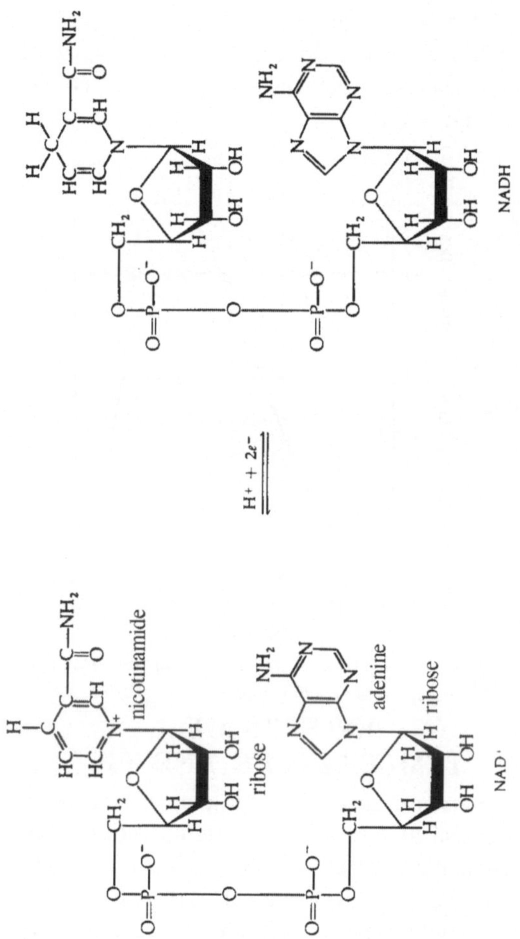

Figure 4.7 : Nicotinamide adenine dinucleotide (NAD) in its oxidised form, NAD^+, and its reduced form, NADH.

is called a *nucleotide,* and a molecule that contains two of them is called a dinucleotide. Watch out for nucleotides; they will return.)

The nicotinamide ring is the business end of NAD^+, the part that accepts the electrons. Nicotinamide is a vitamin, niacin. Vitamins are compounds required in small quantities that humans and other animals cannot synthesize themselves and so must obtain in their diets.

Thus we must eat foods containing niacin (which includes both nicotinamide and nicotinic acid but should not be confused with nicotine, found in tobacco). When nicotinamide is present, our cells can use it to make NAD^+. Many vitamins are coenzymes or parts of coenzymes.

Nicotinamide adenine dinucleotide, like other coenzymes, is

recycled. That is, NAD^+ is regenerated when NADH passes its electrons on to another electron acceptor. Thus, although this coenzyme is involved in many cellular reactions, the actual number of NAD^+ molecules required is relatively small.

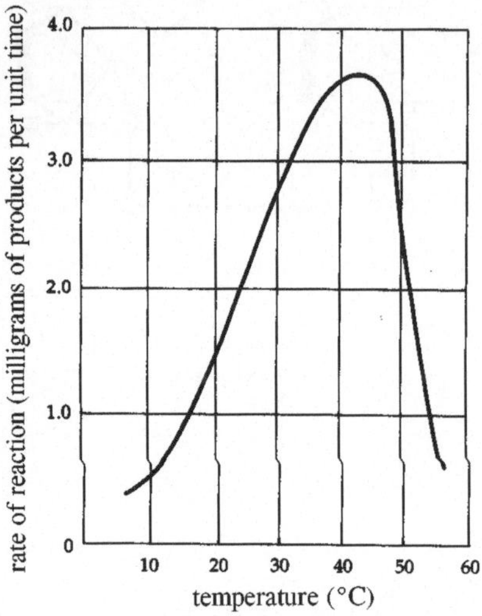

Figure 4.8 : The effect of temperature on the rate of an enzyme-controlled reaction. The concentrations of enzyme and reacting molecules (substrate) were kept constant.

EFFECTS OF TEMPERATURE AND PH

As we noted earlier, an increase in temperature increases the rate of uncatalyzed chemical reactions. This temperature effect also holds true for enzyme-catalyze(reactions-but only up to a point. As you can see in Figure elsewhere in this chapter, the rate of moss enzymatic reactions approximately doubles for each 10°C rise in temperature and then drops off very quickly at about 40°C.

The increase in reaction rate occur! because of the increased energy of the reactants; the decrease in the reaction rat(occurs as the enzyme molecule itself begins to move and vibrate, disrupting the hydrogen bonds and other relatively fragile forces that hold it together. A molecule that has lost its characteristic three-dimensional structure in this way is said to be *denatured.*

Some denatured enzymes regain their activity on being cooled, indicating that their polypeptide chains have regained their necessary shape. Others, however, are permanently tangled and inactivated. The pH of the surrounding solution also affects enzyme activity. The conformation of an enzyme depends, among other factors, on attractions and repulsions between negatively charged (acidic) and positively charged (basic) amino acids.

As the pH changes, these charges change, and so the shape of the enzyme changes until it is so drastically altered that it is no longer functional. More important, probably, the charges of the active site and substrate are changed so that the binding capacity is affected.

The optimum pH of one enzyme is not the same as that of another. The digestive enzyme pepsin, for example, works at the very low (highly acidic) pH of the stomach, in an environment where most other proteins would be permanently denatured.

ENZYMATIC PATHWAYS

Enzymes work in series-the pathways we referred to earlier.

$$\text{product 1} \xrightarrow{\text{enzyme 1}} \text{product 2} \xrightarrow{\text{enzyme 2}} \text{product 3} \xrightarrow{\text{enzyme 3}}$$

$$\text{product 4} \xrightarrow{\text{enzyme 4}} \text{product 5} \xrightarrow{\text{enzyme 5}} \text{end product}$$

As a consequence, compared to chemists in a laboratory, a living organism carries out its chemical activities with remarkable efficiency. First, there is little accumulation of waste products, since each tends to be used up in the next reaction along the pathway.

A second advantage of such sequential reactions can be understood readily if you remember the principle of reversible reactions. If product 2, for example, is used up (by being converted into product 3) almost as rapidly as it is formed, the reaction product 1 → product 2 can never reach equilibrium. If the eventual end product is also used up rapidly, the whole series of reactions will move toward completion.

A third advantage is that the groups of enzymes making up a common pathway can be segregated within the cell. Some are found in small vesicles, membranesurrounded sacs in the cytoplasm. Others are embedded in the membranes of specialised organelles.

ENZYME DEFICIENCIES

As with the hemoglobin molecule described in the previous chapter; slight variations in the amino acid sequence of an enzyme can have drastic effects on the function of the enzyme. A "mistake" involving any of the amino acids directly involved in the active site renders the enzyme less efficient or even completely inactive.

Changes in the rest of the molecule can be more or less important, depending on the extent to which they affect the tertiary or quaternary structure. For instance, one of the ways in which Siamese cats differ from their more common counterparts is that a particular enzyme, involved in controlling the synthesis of dark pigment for the coat, is especially sensitive to temperature.

It functions adequately in the cooler, peripheral areas of the body, such as the ears, nose, paws, and tip of the tail, but it becomes inactive in the warmer areas of the body. Cat fanciers who want their Siamese to be perfect specimens do not let them out in the winter because exposure to cold can make the entire coat turn darker.

Enzymes and Human Diseases

Enzyme deficiencies are the cause of many human diseases. One such was described in 1649:

The patient was a boy who passed black urine and who, at the age of fourteen years, was submitted to a drastic course of treatment which had for its aim the subduing of the fiery heat of his viscera, which

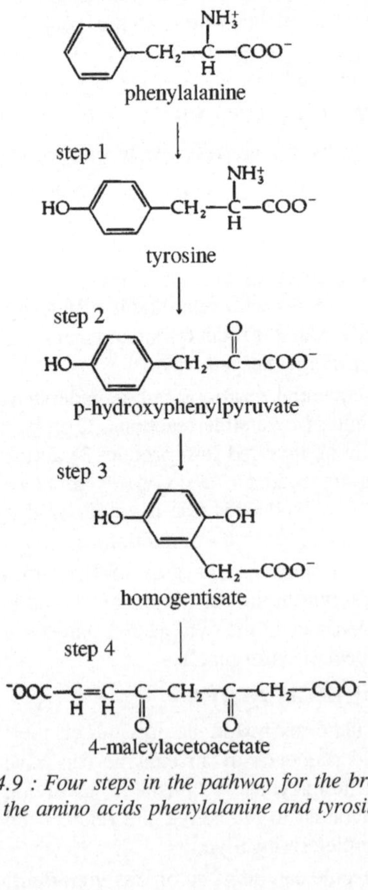

Figure 4.9 : Four steps in the pathway for the breakdown of the amino acids phenylalanine and tyrosine.

was supposed to bring about the condition in question by charring and blackening his bile.

Among the measures prescribed were bleedings, purgation, baths, a cold and watery diet and drugs galore. None of these had any obvious effect, and eventually the patient, who tired of the futile and superfluous therapy, resolved to let things take their natural course.

None of the predicted evils ensued, he married, begat a large family, and lived a long and healthy life, always passing urine black as ink. In 1902 the cause of this disease was identified by the physician Archibald Garrod. Alcaptonuria, as it came to be called, results from deficiencies in an enzyme that opens the ring structure (a benzene ring) at step 4 in the pathway of the breakdown of phenylalanine. As a consequence, the ring-containing compound homogentisate accumulates in the urine and, on exposure to air, oxidises, polymerizes, and turns black.

Figure 4.10 : An allosteric ("other shape") effector can bind to an enzyme and, by disrupting the bonds determining its tertiary structure, alter the active site. As a consequence, the enzyme may be altered so that it cannot interact with its substrate, as shown here, or it may be activated.

Unfortunately, not all enzyme deficiencies are so benign. Loss of function of another enzyme in this same pathway, the one that converts phenylalanine to tyrosine, produces phenylketonuria, which, if untreated, produces severe mental retardation and, in half of the cases, death by age 20.

REGULATION OF ENZYME ACTIVITY

Another remarkable feature of the metabolic activity of cells is the extent to which each cell regulates the synthesis of the products necessary to its well-being in the amounts and at the rates required, while avoiding overproduction, which would waste both energy and raw materials.

Temperature, as we have noted, affects enzymatic reactions, as does pH; some enzymes are usually found at a pH that is not their optimum, suggesting that this discrepancy may not be an evolutionary oversight but a way of damping enzyme activity. The availability of reactant molecules or of cofactors is a principal factor in limiting enzyme action, and most enzymes probably work at a rate well below their maximum for this reason.

Living systems also have more precise ways -of turning enzyme activity on and off. Some enzymes are produced only in an inactive form and, just when they are needed, are activated, usually by another-enzyme.

Pepsin, a digestive enzymes is controlled in this way-JA is synthesized by cells in the lining of the stomach in the form of pepsinogen, which contains 42 additional amino acids on the amino end of the molecule and is inactive. After pepsinogen is released into the stomach, a particular enzyme snips off these last 42 amino acids, converting pepsinogen to pepsin, the active form.

In this way, pepsin (and other digestive enzymes) are prevented from digesting the proteins in the cells in which they are synthesized. Once activated, these enzymes cannot again be deactivated, however.

Allosteric Interactions

An ingenious mechanism by which an enzyme may be temporarily activated or inactivated is known as *allosteric interaction.* Allosteric interactions occur among enzymes that have two binding sites, one the active site and another, into which a second molecule, known as an allosteric effector, fits. The binding of the effector changes the shape of the enzyme molecule and either activates or inactivates it.

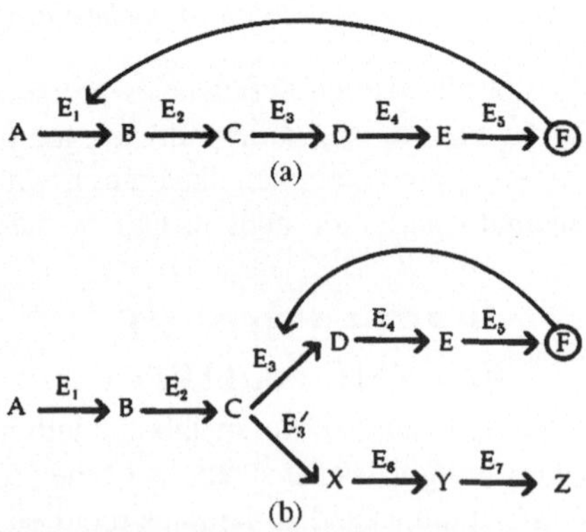

Figure 4.11 : Feedback inhibition.

Feedback Inhibition

Allosteric interactions are often involved in feedback inhibition, which is a common means of biological control. A familiar nonbiological example of feedback inhibition is a thermostat that turns off the furnace when the room temperature reaches a desired level. In feedback inhibition of enzymatic reactions, one of the products, usually the last in the series, acts as an effector, inhibiting the function of one of the enzymes, often the first in the series. Or, in a reaction that may take one of two directions, the effector may act to shunt the reactions along another pathway.

Competitive Inhibition

Some compounds inhibit enzyme activity by temporarily occupying the active site of the enzyme; regulation in this way is known as competitive inhibition, because the regulatory compound and the substrate compete for the active site. The result of the competition depends on how many of each kind of molecule are present. For example, in the reaction series

$$A \xrightarrow{E_1} B \xrightarrow{E_2} C \xrightarrow{E_3} D \xrightarrow{E_4} E \xrightarrow{E_5} F$$

the final product F might be rather similar in structure to product D. It could occupy the active site of enzyme E_4, preventing D, the normal substrate, from binding to the enzyme. As F was used up by the cell, the active site of enzyme E_4 would once more become available to D.

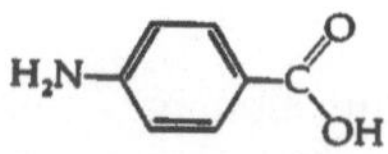

para-aminobenzoic acid (PABA)

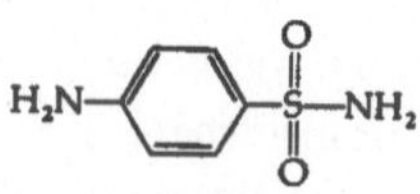

sulfanilamide

Figure 4.12 : Para-Aminobenzoic acid (PABA) is one of the compounds in the metabolic pathway to folic acid in bacterial cells.

Competitive inhibition probably does not play a large role in the normal life of a cell, but it is an important mechanism in the action of some drugs. For instance, bacteria can make the vitamin folic acid, which animal cells do not make (animals obtain folic acid from their food). One of the compounds in the metabolic pathway leading to folic acid is para-aminobenzoic acid.

Sulfanilamide, as you can see, has a structure very similar to PABA, so similar, in fact, that the enzyme involved in converting PABA to folic acid combines with the drug rather than with the PABA. Without folic acid, the bacterial cell dies, leaving the animal cell, which lacks this enzyme, unharmed.

Noncompetitive Inhibition

In noncompetitive inhibition, the inhibitory chemical, which need not resemble the substrate, binds with the enzyme either at the active

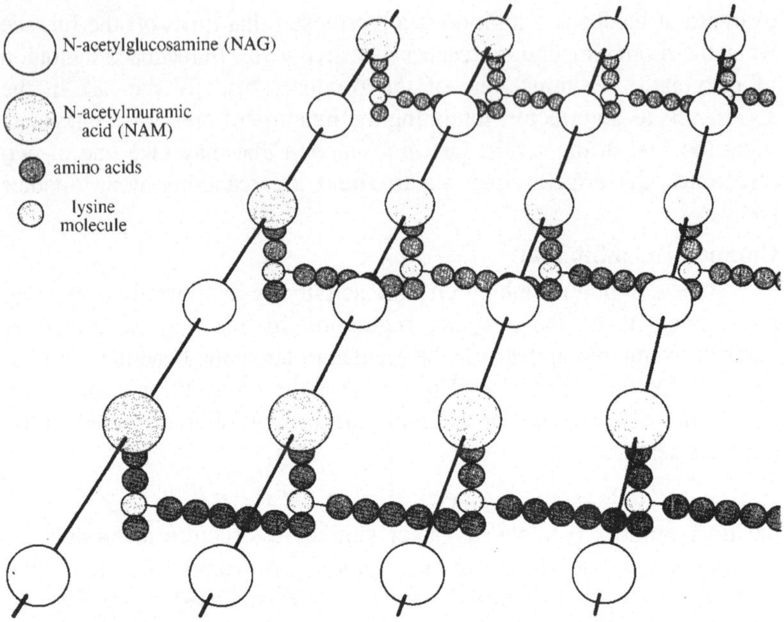

Figure 4.13 : The bacterial cell wall has polysaccharide backbones formed by alternating molecules of two sugars, NAG and NAM. The backbones (indicated by the thick black lines) are crosslinked by short peptide chains.

site or elsewhere in the molecule and prevents its functioning. Lead, for instance, forms covalent bonds with sulfhydryl (SH) groups. Many enzymes contain cysteine, which has a sulfhydryl group. The binding of lead to such enzymes permanently deactivates them, producing the symptoms associated with lead poisoning.

The most potent poisons known, including arsenic, the cyanides, mercury, and the nerve gases, all combine with and prevent the functioning of enzymes necessary for survival, as do many useful drugs.

Regulation at the Source

Many enzymes are broken down rapidly, characteristically by other enzymes. For such enzymes, a highly efficient means of enzyme regulation is to produce these large protein molecules only when they are needed. The way in which bacterial cells turn on and off their enzyme production at the source is described in some detail in other chapter.

THE ENERGY FACTOR : ATP

All of the biosynthetic activities of the cell (and many other activities as well) require energy. A large proportion of this energy is supplied by a single molecule, *adenosine triphosphate,* or ATP. ATP is the cell's

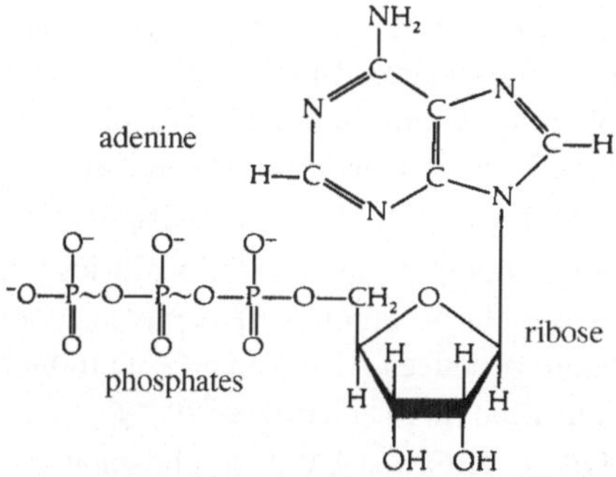

Figure 4.14 : Adenosine triphosphate (ATP) is the cell's chief energy currency. The bonds between the three phosphate groups in the molecule are important in ATP function.

chief energy currency. Glucose, glycogen, and starch are like money in the bank. ATP is like change in your pocket or a subway token.

At first glance, ATP, as shown in Figure elsewhere in this chapter, appears to be a complex molecule. As with NAD^+, you will find, however, that its component parts are familiar to you. It is made up of adenine, a five-carbon sugar known as ribose, and three phosphate groups.

These three phosphate groups with strong negative charges are covalently bonded to one another; this is an important feature in ATP function. To understand the role of ATP, we have to return briefly to the concept of the chemical bond and bond energies. A chemical bond is the total of the forces that hold the constituent atoms together in a molecule. Because a bond is a stable configuration, it takes energy to break an old bond and form a new one.

This energy is the energy of activation. Because of enzymes, which greatly reduce the energy of activation required, the reactions essential to life are able to proceed at an adequate rate. However, there is an important additional limitation on chemical reactions in living systems: The bond energies of the products must always be less than the bond energies of the reactants. (This is a variation on our previous statement that boulders will not roll uphill.) Following this statement to its logical conclusion, one might think that biosynthetic reactions could never take place.

Not true. Cells circumvent this requirement by *coupled reactions* in which energy-requiring chemical reactions are linked to energy-releasing reactions. The molecule that participates most frequently in such coupled reactions is ATP.

The internal structure of the ATP molecule makes it unusually suited to this role in living systems. In the laboratory, energy is released from the ATP molecule when the third phosphate is removed by hydrolysis, leaving ADP (adenosine diphosphate) and a phosphate:

$$ATP + H_2O \rightarrow ADP + \text{phosphate}$$

In the course of this reaction, about 7 kilocalories per mole of ATP are released, a relatively large amount of chemical energy. Removal. of the second phosphate produces AMP (adenosine monophosphate) and releases an equivalent amount of chemical energy.

$$ADP + H_2O \rightarrow AMP + \text{phosphate}$$

To indicate that relatively large amounts of chemical energy are involved, the covalent bonds linking these two phosphates to the rest of the molecule are often called high-energy bonds, symbolised by This term is somewhat misleading, however, because the energy released during the reaction does not arise entirely from the bond.

The difference in energy between reactants and products is due only in part to the energies in the bonds. It is also a result of a rearrangement of the orbitals of the ATP or ADP molecules.

The phosphate groups each carry negative charges and so tend to repel each other. When a phosphate group is removed, the molecule undergoes a change in electron configuration that results in a structure with less energy.

In living systems, ATP is also sometimes hydrolysed to ADP; ATP hydrolysis provides, for example, a rapid means for producing heat, as in an animal waking up from hibernation. Usually, however, the terminal phosphate group is not simply removed but is transferred to another molecule. (This addition of a phosphate group is known as phosphorylation; enzymes that catalyze such transfers are known as kinases.)

This reaction transfers some of the energy in the "high-energy" bond to the phosphorylated compound, which, thus energised, participates in the reaction.

For example, in the reaction,

$$A+B \rightarrow C+D$$

if the bond energies of A plus the bond energies of B were less than those of C plus D, the reaction would not take place. Chemists could drive the reaction by supplying outside energy, probably in the form of heat. The cell might handle it this way:

$$A + ATP \rightarrow A\text{-}P + ADP$$

The energy of the products is less than that of the reactants, so the reaction will take place. However, much of the ATP/ADP bond energy is conserved in the new compound A-phosphate, or A-P.

The next step in the reaction becomes:

$$A\text{-}P + B \rightarrow C + D + P$$

With the release of the phosphate from A, this second reaction also becomes one in which the energy of the products is less than the energy of the reactants and which, therefore, can take place.

Take, for instance, the formation of sucrose in sugarcane.

$$\text{glucose} + \text{fructose} \rightarrow \text{sucrose} + H_2O$$

In this reaction, the bond energy of the products is 5.5 kilocalories per mole greater than the bond energy of the reactants. However, the sugarcane plant couples this reaction to the breakdown of ATP:

$$\text{glucose} + \text{fructose} + 2ATP \rightarrow \text{sucrose} + 2ADP + 2P$$

Since the bond energy of 2 ADPs is about 14 kilocalories per mole less than the bond energy of 2 ATPs, the overall difference in products and reactants becomes 8.5 kilocalories per mole. The coupling of the two reactions permits sugarcane to form sucrose.

Where does the ATP come from? As we shall see, energy released in the cell's catabolic reactions, such as the breakdown of glucose, is used to "recharge" the ADP molecule. Thus the ATP/ADP system serves as a universal energy-exchange system, shuttling between energy-releasing reactions and energy-requiring ones.

One marvels at the process of evolution as exemplified by the intricate flower of an orchid, the shell of a chambered nautilus, or the opposable thumb and forefinger of the human hand. Remember that NAD, ATP, and indeed the place of each amino acid in a polypeptide chain are also the products of evolution and also, you must admit, quite marvelous. Perhaps even beautiful.

5

Photosynthesis in Plants

Over 300 years ago, the English physicist Sir Isaac Newton (1642-1727) separated visible light into a spectrum of colours by letting it pass through a prism. Then by passing the light through a second prism, he recombined the colours, producing white light once again. By this experiment, Newton showed that white light is actually made up of a number of different colours, ranging from violet at one end of the spectrum to red at the other.

Their separation is possible because light of different colours is bent at different angles in passing through the prism. Newton believed that light was a stream of particles (or, as he termed them, "corpuscles"), in part, because of its tendency to travel in a straight line.

In the nineteenth century, through the genius of James Clerk Maxwell, it became known that what we experience as light is in truth a very small part of a vast continuous spectrum of radiation, the electromagnetic spectrum. As Maxwell showed, all the radiations included in this spectrum act as if they travel in waves.

The wavelengths-that is, the distances from one peak to the next-range from those of gamma rays, which are measured in nanometers, to those of lowfrequency radio waves, which are measured in kilometers. Within the spectrum of visible light, red light has the longest wavelength, violet the shortest. Another feature that these radiations have in common is that, in a vacuum, they all travel at the same speed-300,000 kilometers per second.

By 1900, it had become clear, however, that the wave model of light was not adequate. The key observation, a very simple one, was made in 1888: When a zinc plate is exposed to ultraviolet light, it acquires a positive charge.

The metal, it was soon deduced, becomes positively charged because the light energy dislodges electrons, forcing them out of the metal atoms. Subsequently, it was discovered that this photoelectric effect, as it is called, can be produced in all metals.

Every metal has a critical wavelength for the effect; the light (visible or invisible) must be of that wavelength or a shorter wavelength for the effect to occur. With some metals, such as sodium, potassium, and selenium, the critical wavelength is within the spectrum of visible light, and as a consequence, visible light striking the metal can set up a moving stream of electrons (such a stream is an electric current).

Burglar alarms, exposure meters, television cameras, and the electric eyes that open doors for you at supermarkets or airline terminals all operate on this principle of turning light energy into electrical energy.

THE NATURE OF LIGHT

Now here is a problem. The wave model of light would lead you to predict that the brighter the light-that is, the stronger the beam-the greater the force with which the electrons would be dislodged. But as we have already seen, whether or not light can eject the electrons of a particular metal depends not on the brightness of the light but on its wavelength.

A very weak beam of the critical wavelength or a shorter wavelength is effective, while a stronger beam of a longer wavelength is not. Furthermore, as was shown in 1902, increasing the brightness of the light increases the number of electrons dislodged but not the velocity at which they are ejected from the metal. To increase the velocity, one must use a shorter wavelength of light.

Nor is it necessary for energy to be accumulated in the metal. With even a dim beam of a critical wavelength, electrons may be emitted the instant the light hits the metal.

To explain such phenomena, the particle model of light was resurrected by Albert Einstein in 1905. According to this model, light is composed of particles of energy called *photons*. The energy of a photon is not the same for all kinds of light but is, in fact, inversely proportional to the wavelength-the longer the wavelength, the lower the energy. Photons of violet light, for example, have almost twice the energy of photons of red light, the longest visible wavelength.

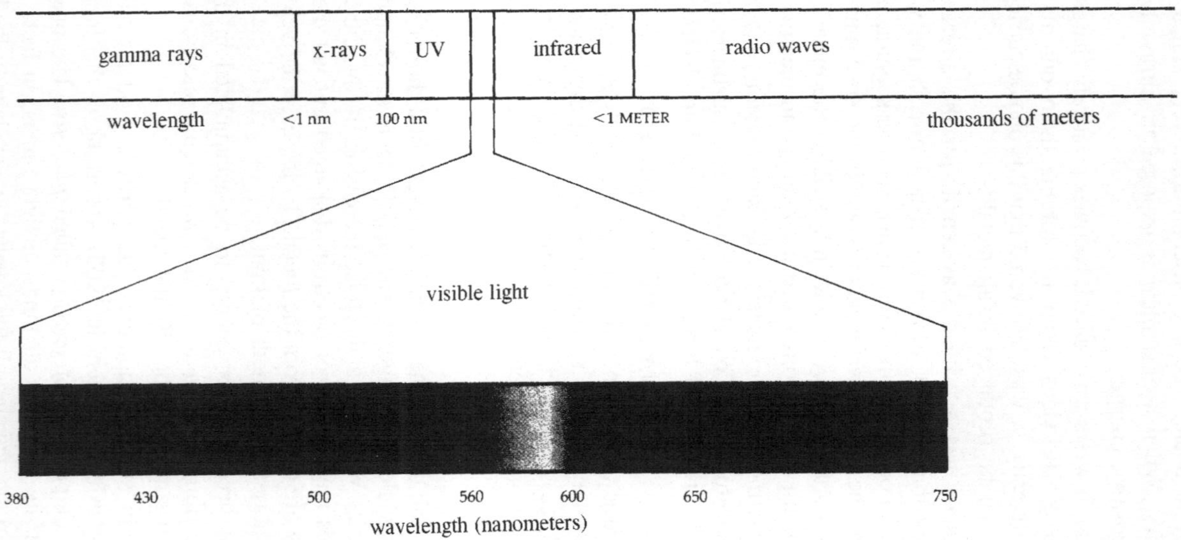

Figure 5.1 : Visible light is only a small portion of the vast electromagnetic spectrum. For the human eye, the visible spectrum ranges from violet light, which is made up of comparatively short rays, to red light, the longest visible rays.

The wave model of light permits physicists to describe certain aspects of its behaviour mathematically, and the photon model permits another set of mathematical calculations and predictions. These two models are no longer regarded as opposed to one another; rather, they are complementary, in the sense that both-or a totally new model-are required for a complete description of the phenomenon we know as light.

The Fitness of Light

Light, as Maxwell showed, is only a tiny band in a continuous spectrum. From the physicist's point of view, the difference between radiations we can see and radiations we cannot see-so dramatic to the human eye-is only a few nanometers of wavelength. Why does this particular small group of radiations, rather than some other, make the leaves grow and the flowers burst forth, cause the mating of fireflies and palolo worms, and when reflecting off the surface of the moon, excite the imagination of poets and lovers?

Why is it that this tiny portion of the electromagnetic spectrum is responsible for vision, for the rhythmic, day-night regulation of many biological activities, for the bending of plants toward the light, and also for photosynthesis, on which all life depends? Is it an amazing coincidence that all these biological activities are dependent on these same wavelengths?

George Wald of Harvard, one of the greatest living experts on the subject of light and life, says no. He thinks that if life exists elsewhere in the universe, it is probably dependent on this same fragment of the vast spectrum. Wald bases this conjecture on two points.

First, living things, as we have seen, are composed of large, complicated molecules held in special configurations and relationships to one another by hydrogen bonds and other weak bonds. Radiation of even slightly higher energies than the energy of violet light breaks these bonds and so disrupts the structure and function of the molecules. Radiations with wavelengths less than 200 nanometers drive electrons out of atoms.

Light of wavelengths longer than those of the visible band is absorbed by water, which makes up the great bulk of all living things on earth. When this light reaches molecules, its lower energies cause them to increase their motion (increasing heat) but do not trigger changes in their electron configurations.

Only those radiations within the range of visible light have the property of exciting molecules-that is, of moving electrons into higher-energy orbitals and so of producing chemical and, ultimately, biological changes. The second reason for the visible band of the electromagnetic spectrum being "chosen" by living things is that it, above all, is what is available. Most of the radiation reaching the earth from the sun is within this range.

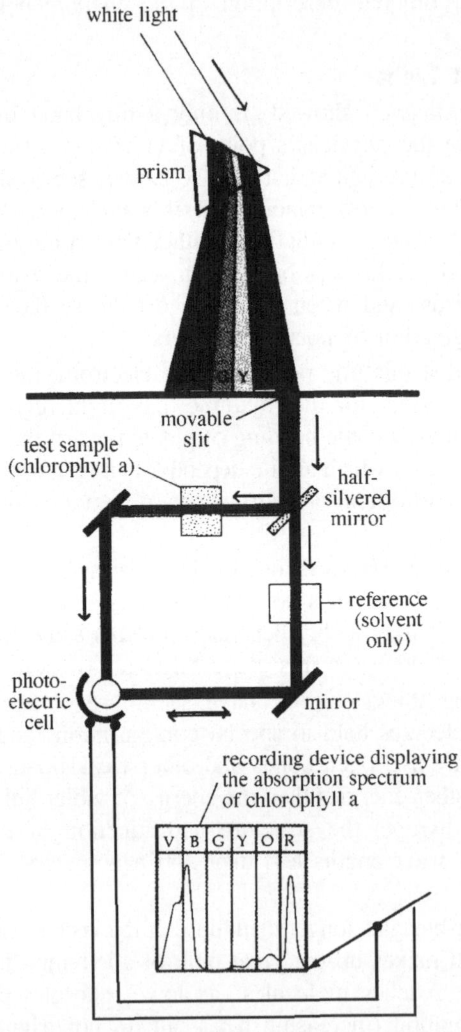

Figure 5.2 : The absorption spectrum of a pigment is measured with a spectrophotometer. This device directs a beam of light of each wavelength at the object to be analyzed and records what percentage of light of each wavelength is absorbed by the pigment sample as compared to a reference sample.

Higher-energy wavelengths are screened out by the oxygen and ozone high in the atmosphere. Much infrared radiation is screened out by water vapor and carbon dioxide before it reaches the earth's surface. This is an example of what has been termed "the fitness of the environment"; the suitability of the environment for life and that of life for the physical world are exquisitely interrelated. If they were not, life could not, of course, exist.

CHLOROPHYLL AND OTHER PIGMENTS

In order for light energy to be used by living systems, it must first be absorbed. A pigment is any substance that absorbs light. Some pigments absorb all wavelengths of light and so appear black. Some absorb only certain wavelengths, transmitting or reflecting the wavelengths they do not absorb.

Chlorophyll, the pigment that makes leaves green, absorbs light in the violet and blue wavelengths and also in the red; because it reflects green light, it appears green. Different pigments absorb light energy at different wavelengths. The absorption pattern of a pigment is known as the *absorption spectrum* of that substance.

Different groups of plants and algae use various pigments in photosynthesis. There are several different kinds of chlorophyll that vary slightly in their molecular structure. In plants, chlorophyll a is the pigment directly involved in the transformation of light energy to chemical energy.

Most photosynthetic cells also contain a second type of chlorophyll-in plants, it is chlorophyll *b* and *a* representative of another group of pigments called the carotenoids. One of the carotenoids found in plants is beta-carotene. The carotenoids are red, orange, or yellow pigments. In the green leaf, their colour is masked by the chlorophylls, which are more abundant.

In some tissues, however, such as those of a ripe tomato or the root of a carrot plant, the carotenoid colours predominate, as they do also when leaf cells stop synthesizing chlorophyll in the fall.

The other chlorophylls and the carotenoids are able to absorb light at wavelengths different from those absorbed by chlorophyll *a* and apparently can pass the energy on to chlorophyll *a,* thus extending the range of light available for photosynthesis. Whether or not a particular pigment can cause a chemical reaction depends not only on its structure but also on its relationship with neighboring molecules.

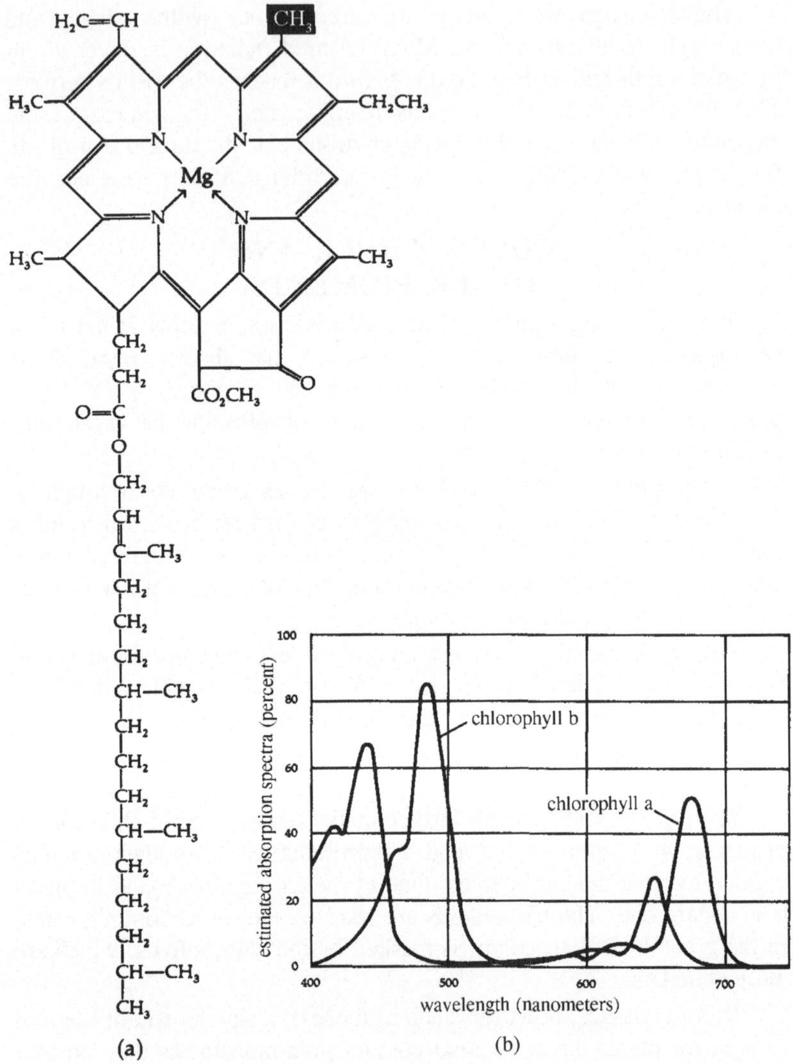

Figure 5.3 : (a) Chlorophyll a is a large molecule with a central atom of magnesium held in a porphyrin ring. (b) The estimated absorption spectra of chlorophyll a and chlorophyll b.

An *action spectrum* defines the relative effectiveness (per number of incident photons) of different wavelengths of light for light-requiring processes, such *as* photosynthesis, flowering, and phototropism (the bending of a plant toward light). Similarity between the absorption spectrum of a pigment and the action spectrum of a process is considered evidence that that particular pigment is responsible for that particular process. When pigments absorb light, electrons are boosted to a higher energy level. Three of the possible consequences are:

(1) The energy may be dissipated as heat;

(2) it may be re-emitted immediately as light energy of a longer wavelength, *a* phenomenon known as fluorescence;

(3) the energy may cause a chemical reaction, as happens in photosynthesis.

If chlorophyll molecules are isolated in a test tube and light is permitted to strike them, they fluoresce. In other words, the molecules absorb light energy, and the electrons are momentarily raised to a higher energy level and then fall back again to a lower one.

As they fall to a lower energy level, they release much of this energy as light. None of the light absorbed by isolated chlorophyll molecules is converted to any form of energy useful to living systems. Chlorophyll can convert light energy to chemical energy only when it is associated with certain proteins and embedded in a specialised membrane.

PHOTOSYNTHETIC MEMBRANES: THE THYLAKOID

The structural unit of photosynthesis is the *thylakoid,* which usually takes the form of a flattened sac or vesicle. In the photosynthetic prokaryotes, thylakoids may form a part of the cell membrane, or they may occur singly in the cytoplasm, or, as in the blue-green algae, they may be part of an elaborate internal membrane structure.

Chloroplasts

In eukaryotes, the thylakoids form a part of the internal membrane structure of specialised organelles, the chloroplasts. The alga *Chlamydomonas,* for instance, has a single very large chloroplast; the cell of a leaf characteristically has 40 to 50 chloroplasts, and there are often 500,000 chloroplasts per square millimeter of leaf surface.

Chloroplasts, like mitochondria, are surrounded by two outer membranes. The interior of the chloroplast is filled with a dense solution, the *stroma,* which (like the matrix of the mitochondrion) is different in composition from the material surrounding the organelles in the cytoplasm.

With the light microscope under high power, it is possible to see little spots of green within the chloroplasts of leaves. The early microscopists called these green specks *grana* ("grains"), and this term is still in use.

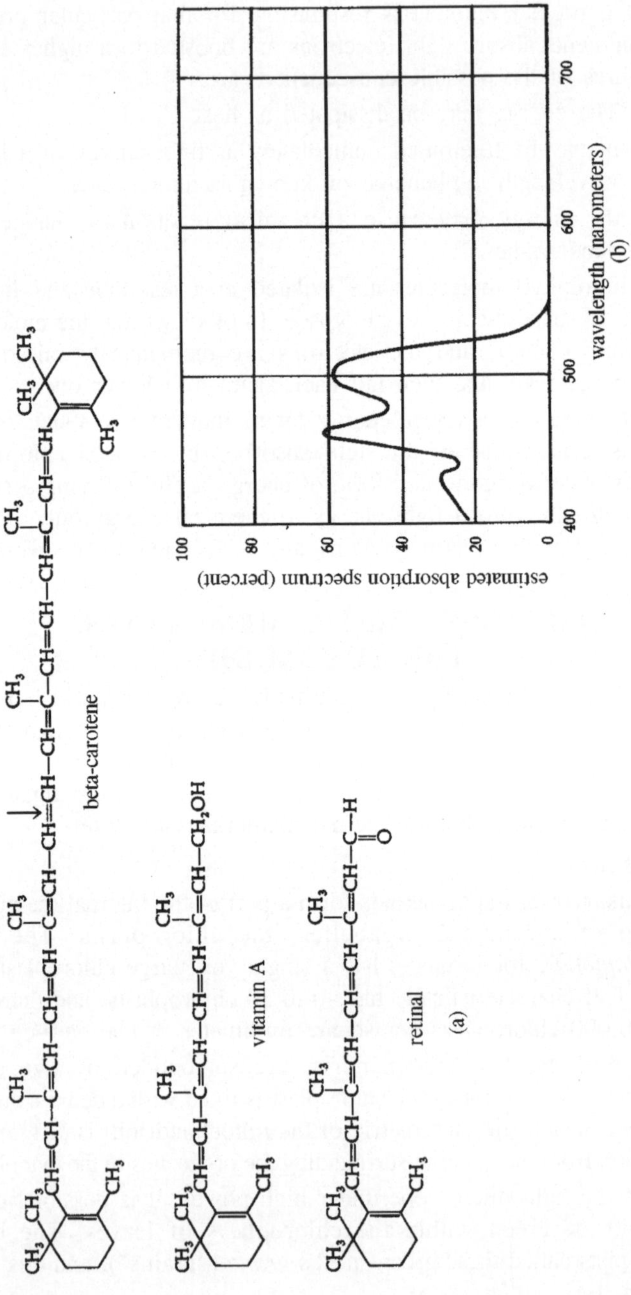

Figure 5.4 : (a) Related carotenoids. Cleavage of the beta-carotene molecule at the point indicated by teh arrow yields two molecules of vitamin A. (b) The estimated absorption spectrum of carotenoids in the chloroplast.

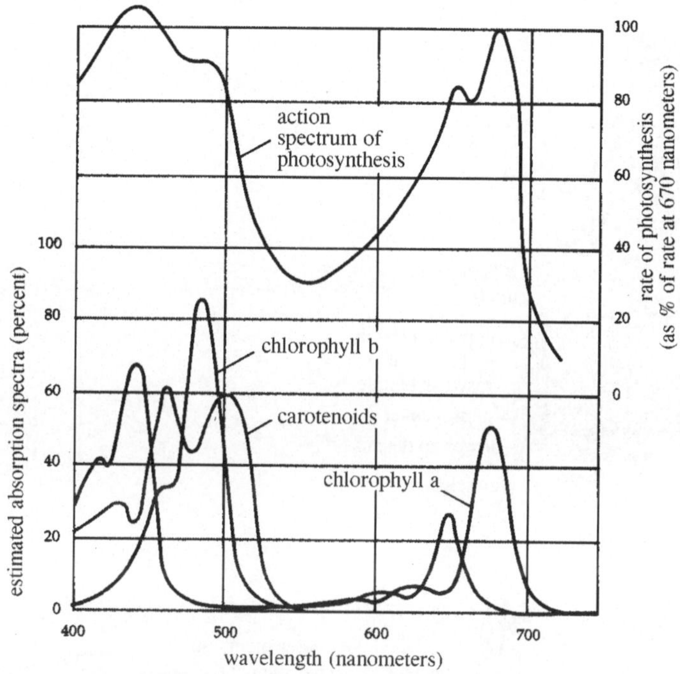

Figure 5.5 : The upper curves shows the action spectrum for photosynthesis and the lower curves, absorption spectra for chlorophyll a, chlorophyll b, and carotenoids in the chloroplast.

Under the electron microscope, it can be seen that the grana are stacks of thylakoids. Some of the thylakoid membranes have extensions that interconnect the grana through the stroma that separates them.

All the thylakoids in a chloroplast are oriented parallel to each other. Thus the whole chloroplast can swing toward the light, simultaneously aiming all of the millions of pigment molecules for optimum reception, as if they were a giant electromagnetic antenna (which, *of course, they are).*

THE LIGHT AND THE DARK REACTIONS

As we noted in other chapter of this book, it was discovered about 200 years ago that light is required for the process we now call photosynthesis. It is now known that photosynthesis actually takes place in two stages, only one of which requires light. Evidence for this two-stage mechanism was first presented in 1905 by the English plant physiologist F. F. Blackman, as the result of experiments in which he

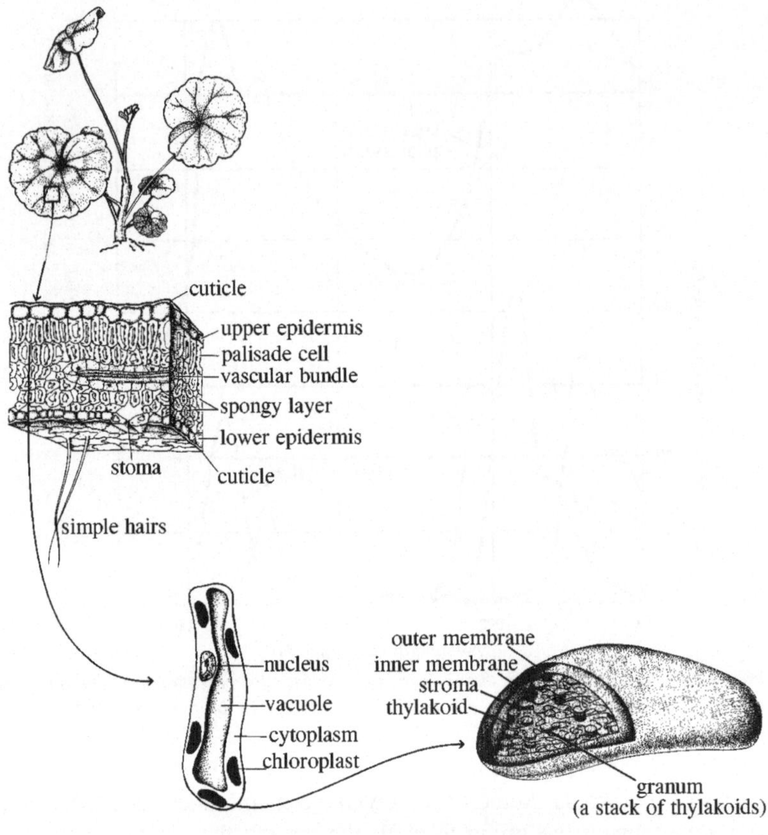

Figure 5.6: Journey into a chloroplast.

measured the rate of photosynthesis under varying conditions. Blackman first plotted the rate of photosynthesis at various light intensities.

In dim to moderate light, increasing the light intensity increased the rate of photosynthesis, but at higher intensities, a further increase in light intensity had no effect. He then studied the combined effects of light and temperature on photosynthesis. In dim light, an increase in temperature had no effect.

However, Blackman found that if he increased the light and also increased the temperature, the rate of photosynthesis was greatly accelerated. As the temperature increased above 30°C, the rate of photosynthesis slowed and finally the process ceased.

On the basis of these experiments, Blackman concluded that more than one set of reactions was involved in photosynthesis. First, there was a group of lightdependent reactions that were temperature-independent.

The rate of these reactions could be accelerated in the dim-to-moderate light range by increasing the amount of light, but it was not accelerated by increases in temperature. Second, there was a group of

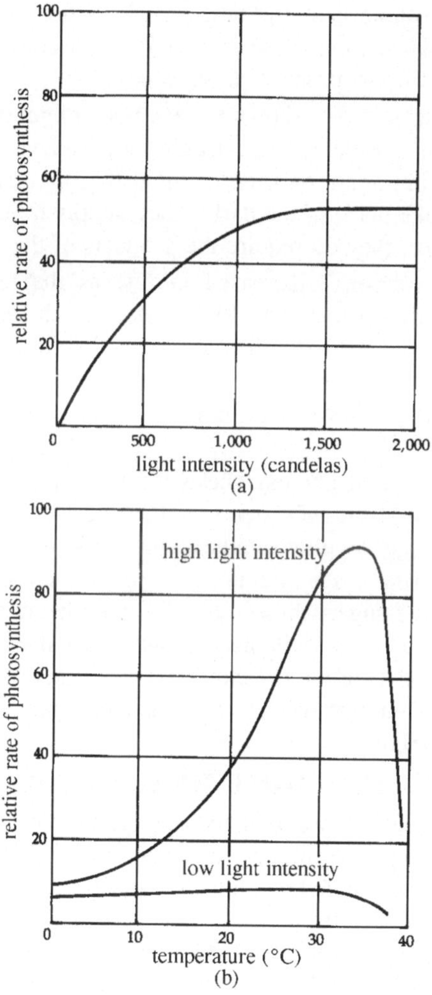

Figure 5.7 : (a) An increase in light intensity does not produce a corresponding increase in the rate of photosynthesis beyond about 1,200 candelas. A curve such as the one shown here indicates that some other factorknown as a rate-limiting factor-is involved in the process under study. (b) At a low intensity of light, an increase in temperature does not increase the rate of photosynthesis.

reactions that were dependent not on light but rather on temperature. Both sets of reactions seemed to be required for the process of photosynthesis.

Increasing the rate of only one set of reactions increased the rate of the entire process only to the point at which the second set of reactions began to hold back the first (that is, it became rate-limiting). Then it was necessary to increase the rate of the second set of reactions in order for the first to proceed unimpeded.

Photosynthesis was thus shown to have both a light-dependent stage, the socalled "light reactions," and a light-independent stage, the "dark reactions." It is important to keep in mind that the dark reactions do not necessarily take place in the dark. They simply do not require light as such. (However, they do require the products of the light reactions.)

The "dark reactions" increased in rate as the temperature was increased, but only up to about 30°C, after which the rate began to decrease. From this evidence it was concluded that these reactions were controlled by enzymes, since this is the way enzymes are expected to respond to temperature. This conclusion has since proved to be correct.

In the first stage of photosynthesis-the light reactions-light energy is used to form ATP from ADP and to reduce electron carrier molecules. In the second stage of photosynthesis-the dark reactions-the energy products of the first stage are used to reduce carbon from carbon dioxide to a simple sugar, thus converting the chemical energy of the carrier molecules to forms suitable for transport and storage and, at the same time, forming a carbon skeleton on which other organic molecules can be built. This binding of CO_2 into organic compounds is known as the *fixation* of carbon.

THE LIGHT REACTIONS

In the thylakoids, chlorophyll and other molecules are, according to the present model, packed into photosynthetic units. Each unit contains from 250 to 400 molecules of pigment, which serve as light-trapping antennae. Once a quantum of energy is absorbed by one of the antenna pigments, it is bounced around (like a hot potato) until it reaches a special form of chlorophyll *a,* which is the reaction center.

When this particular chlorophyll molecule absorbs the energy, an electron is boosted to a higher energy level from which it is transferred to another molecule, an electron acceptor. The chlorophyll molecule is thus oxidised (minus an electron) and positively charged.

The Photosystems

According to present evidence, there are two different kinds of photosynthetic units, each forming part of a different photosystem. In Photosystem I, the reactive chlorophyll *a* molecule is known as P_{700} because one of the peaks of its absorption spectrum is at 700 nanometers, a slightly longer wavelength than the usual chlorophyll a peak.

When P_{700} (P is for pigment) is oxidised, it bleaches, which is how

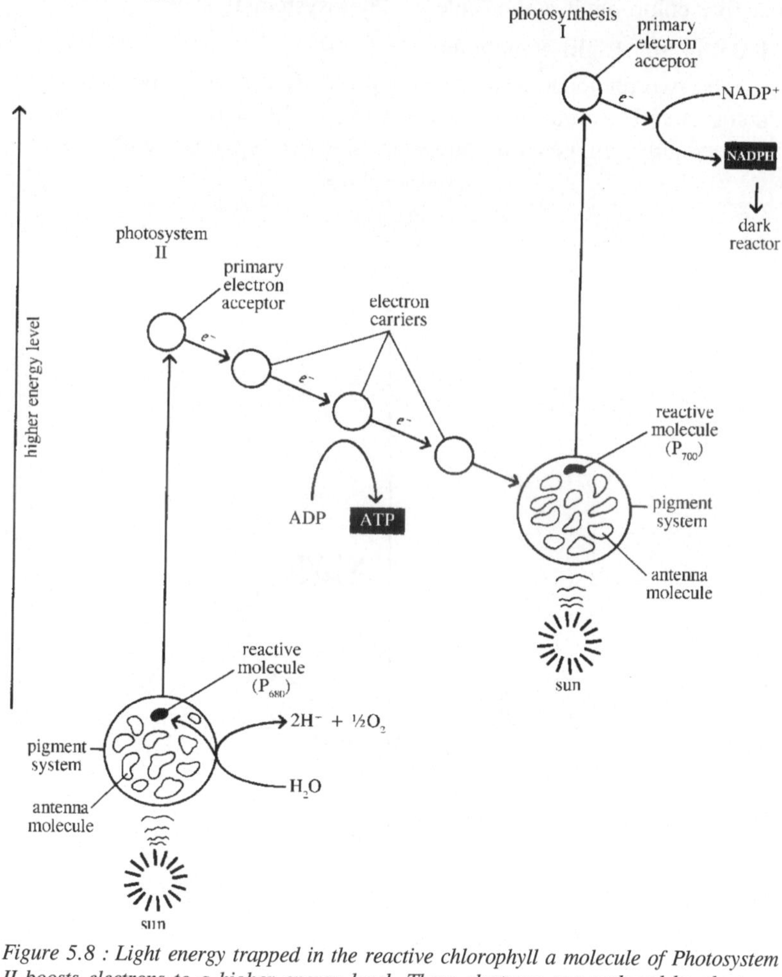

Figure 5.8 : Light energy trapped in the reactive chlorophyll a molecule of Photosystem II boosts electrons to a higher energy level. These electrons are replaced by electrons pulled away from water molecules, releasing protons and oxygen gas. The electrons are passed from the electron acceptor along an electron transport chain to a lower energy level, the reaction center of Photosystem I.

it was detected. No one has managed to isolate pure $P_{700.}$ Recent evidence indicates that P_{700} is not an unusual kind of chlorophyll but rather a dimer ("two-part") of two chlorophyll *a* molecules that has unusual properties because of its association with special proteins in the membrane and its position in relation to other molecules.

Photosystem II also contains a specialised chlorophyll *a* molecule, which passes its electron on to a different electron acceptor. The reactive chlorophyll a molecule of Photosystem II is P_{680}.

Model of the Light Reactions

The two photochemical systems probably evolved separately, with Photosystem I coming first. As we shall see, Photosystem I can operate independently. In general, however, the two systems work together

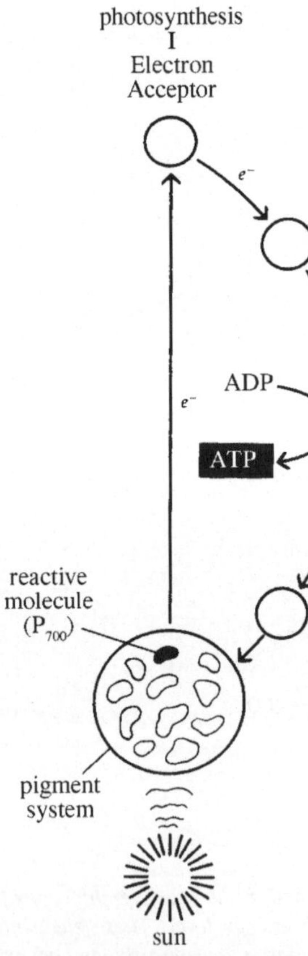

Figure 5.9 : Cyclic electron flow bypasses Photosystem TI and requires only Photosystem I. ATP is produced from ADP but oxygen is not released and NADP⁺ is not reduced.

simultaneously and continuously, as shown in Figure elsewhere in this chpater.

According to this model, light energy enters Photosystem II where it is trapped by the reactive chlorophyll molecule P_{680}. An electron is boosted to a higher energy level from which it is transferred to an electron acceptor molecule. The electrons then pass downhill along an electron transport chain to Photosystem I.

As the electrons pass along this transport chain, ATP is formed from ADP, probably via the same mechanism by which ATP is formed along the electron transport chain of the mitochondrion. This process is known as *photophosphorylation.*

Other events are taking place simultaneously:

1. The P_{680} chlorophyll molecule, as a result of having lost its electron, is avidly seeking a replacement. It finds it in the water molecule, which is thus dissociated into protons and oxygen gas.
2. Light energy is trapped in the reactive chlorophyll molecule (P_{700}) of Photosystem I. The molecule is oxidised, and an electron is passed to a primary electron acceptor from which it goes downhill to $NADP^+$.
3. The electron removed from the P_{700} molecule is replaced by the electron from Photosystem II.

Thus in the light there is a continuous flow of electrons from water to Photosystem II to Photosystem I to $NADP^+$.

The energy harvest from these steps is represented by an ATP molecule (whose formation releases a water molecule) and NADPH, which then becomes the chief source of energy for the reduction of carbon. To generate one molecule of NADPH, four photons must be absorbed, two by Photosystem II and two by Photosystem I.

In the words of Nobel laureate Albert Szent-Gyorgyi: "What drives life is ... a little electric current, kept up by the sunshine."

Cyclic Electron Flow

As we mentioned previously, there is also some evidence that Photosystem I can work independently. When this occurs, no NADPH is formed. In this process, called *cyclic electron flow,* electrons are boosted from P_{700} to an electron acceptor and from there pass downhill through a series of intermediates, including cytochromes, back into the reactive molecule. ATP is produced in the course of this passage. It is believed that the most primitive photosynthetic mechanisms did, indeed, work in this way, and this is apparently the way in which some prokaryotes carry out photosynthesis.

Also, eukaryotic cells are able to synthesize ATP by cyclic electron flow in the absence of $NADP^+$. However, O_2 is produced and carbon is reduced only if both systems are in operation.

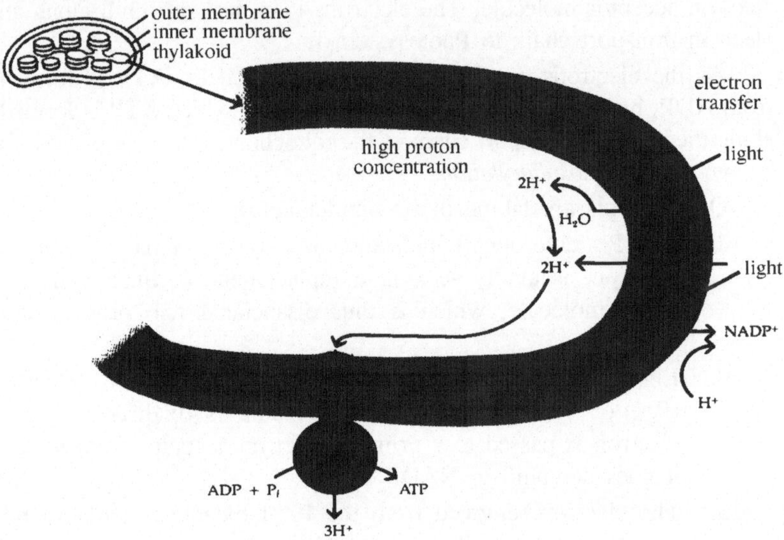

Figure 5.10 : The chemiosmotic model of photophosphorylation. According to this model, the energy of light creates a proton gradient across the thylakoid membrane. (In the chloroplast, however, in contrast to the mitochondrion, the protons are pumped inward.) As the protons flow outward, down the gradient, ADP is phosphorylated to ATP.

Photosynthetic Phosphorylation

We noted in the previous chapter that there are three current hypotheses for the mechanism of oxidative phosphorylation. These same three hypotheses also apply to photophosphorylation, and in the case of this latter process, there is much evidence supporting the chemiosmotic model.

When isolated chloroplasts are illuminated, they absorb protons from the medium in which they are suspended; when the light is turned off and electron flow stops, the protons slowly return from the chloroplasts to the medium.

Also, and most impressive, is the demonstration that an artificially produced proton gradient across the inner membranes of a chloroplast can drive the phosphorylation of ATP in the dark. The chemiosmotic model of photophosphorylation is shown in Figure elsewhere in this chapter.

Summary of the Light Reactions

The reactions that we have just described are the "light reactions" of photosynthesis. In -the course of these reactions, as we saw, light energy is converted to electrical energy-the flow of electrons-and the electrical energy is converted to chemical energy stored in the bonds of NADPH and ATP.

THE DARK REACTIONS

In the second stage of photosynthesis, the energy generated by the light reactions is I used to reduce carbon. Carbon is available to photosynthetic cells in the form of carbon dioxide. In algae, such as those seen in Figure elsewhere in this chapter, the carbon dioxide is

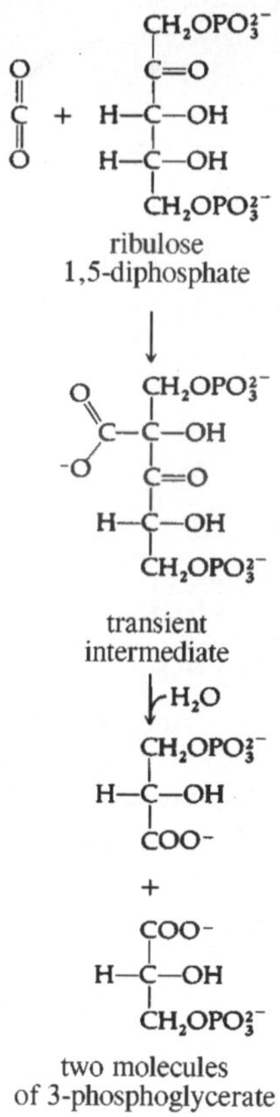

Figure 5.11 : Calvin and his collaborators briefly exposed photosynthesizing algae to radiactive carbon dioxide ($^{14}CO_2$). The radioactive carbon atom after 5 seconds of illumination was found almost entirely in the three-carbon compound phosphoglycerate.

dissolved in the surrounding water. In plants, carbon dioxide reaches the photosynthetic cells through specialised openings in leaves and green stems, called stomata.

The Calvin Cycle: The Three-Carbon Pathway

The reduction of carbon takes place in the stroma in a cycle called the Calvin cycle (named after its discoverer, Melvin Calvin). The Calvin cycle is analogous to the Krebs cycle in that, in each turn of the cycle, the starting compound is again regenerated. The starting (and ending) compound is a five-carbon sugar with two phosphates attached, ribulose diphosphate (RuDP).

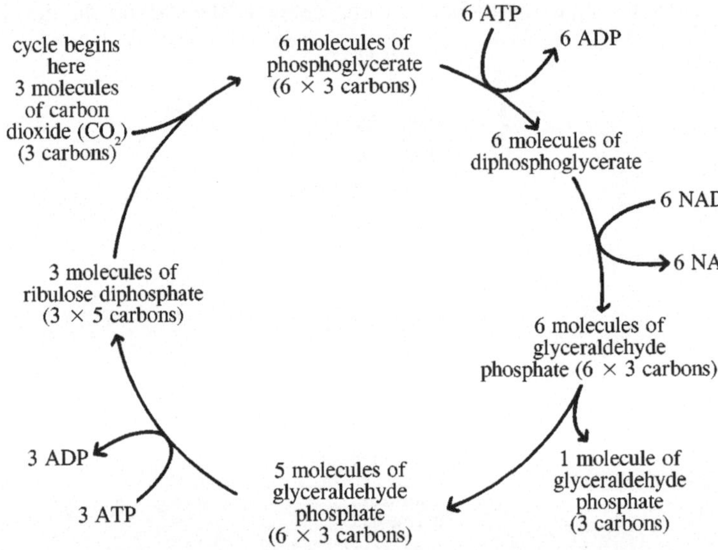

Figure 5.12 : Summary of the Calvin cycle. At each full "turn" of the cycle, one molecule of carbon dioxide enters the cycle. Three turns are summarised here.

The cycle begins when carbon dioxide enters the cycle and is bound to RuDP, which then splits to form two molecules of phosphoglycerate, or PGA. (Each PGA molecule contains three carbon atoms, hence the name, the three-carbon pathway.)

The enzyme catalyzing these crucial reactions (RuDP carboxylase) is very abundant in chloroplasts, making up more than 15 percent of the total chloroplast protein. (It is said to be the most abundant protein in the world.) This enzyme is located on the surface of the thylakoid membranes.

The complete cycle is diagrammed in Figure elsewhere in this chpater. As in the Krebs cycle, each step is regulated by a specific enzyme. At each full turn of the cycle, a molecule of carbon dioxide enters the cycle, is reduced, and a molecule of RuDP is regenerated.

Six revolutions of the cycle, with the introduction of six atoms of carbon, are necessary to produce a six-carbon sugar, such as glucose. The overall equation is

$$6RuDP + 6CO_2 + 18ATP + 12NADPH + 12H^+ + 12H_2O \rightarrow 6RuDP + glucose + 18P_i + 18ADP + 12NADP^+$$

The immediate product of the cycle itself is glyceraldehyde phosphate. This same sugar-phosphate is formed when the fructose diphosphate molecule is split at the fourth step in glycolysis.

The Four-Carbon Photosynthetic Pathway

The Calvin cycle is not the only carbon fixation pathway used in the dark reactions. In some plants, the first product of CO_2 fixation to be detected is not the threecarbon molecule phosphoglycerate, as it is in the Calvin cycle.

It is the four-carbon compound oxaloacetic acid. (Oxaloacetic acid, you may recall, is also an intermediate in the Krebs cycle.) Plants that

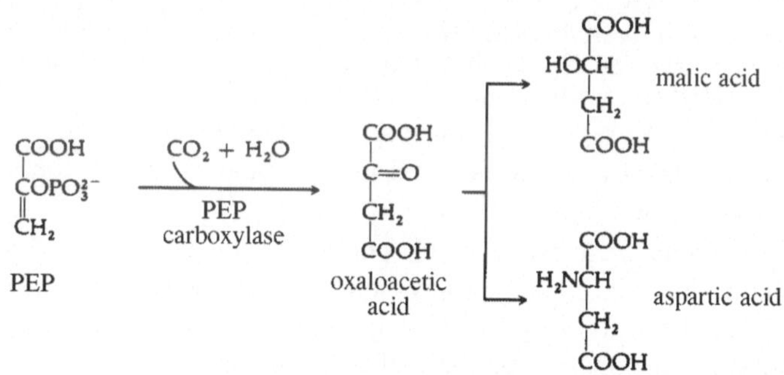

Figure 5.13 : Carbon dioxide fixation by the C_4 pathway. Carbon dioxide is incorporated into phosphoenolpyruvate (PEP) by the enzyme PEP carboxylase. The resulting oxaloacetic acid is converted either to malic acid or aspartic acid. These steps later will be reversed, releasing carbon dioxide for use in the Calvin cycle.

utilise this pathway, also known as the Hatch-Slack pathway, are commonly called C_4, or four-carbon plants, as distinct from the C_3 plants that use only the Calvin cycle.

The oxaloacetic acid is formed when carbon dioxide is bound to a compound known as phosphoenolpyruvate (PEP). This reaction is catalysed by the enzyme PEP carboxylase. The oxaloacetic acid is then reduced to malic acid or converted (with the addition of an amino group) to aspartic acid. These steps take place in mesophyll cells.

The next step is a surprise: The malic acid (or aspartic acid,

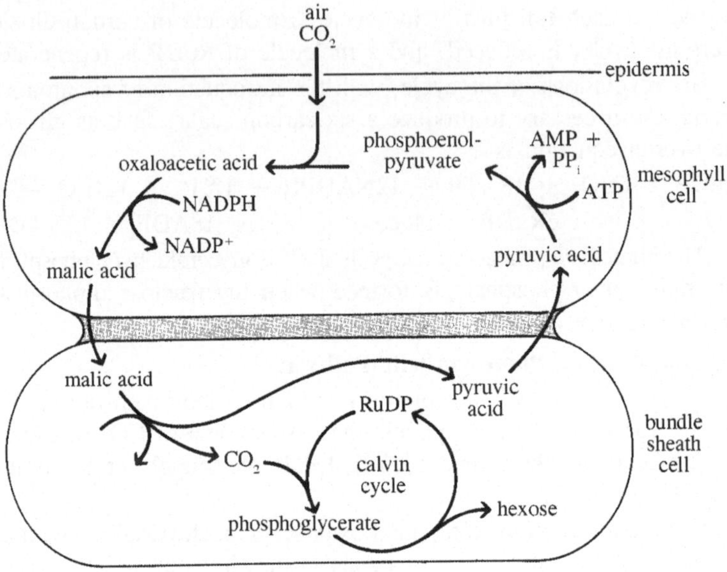

Figure 5.14 : A pathway for carbon fixation in C_4 plants. CO_2 is first fixed in mesophyll cells as oxaloacetic acid. It is then transported to bundle-sheath cells, where the carbon dioxide is released. The CO_2 thus formed enters the Calvin cycle. Pyruvic acid re turns to the mesophyll cell, where it is phosphorytated to PEP.

depending on the species) is transported to bundle-sheath cells where it is decarboxylated to yield CO_2 and pyruvic acid. The CO_2 then enters the Calvin cycle.

One might well ask why C_4 plants should have evolved such a seemingly clumsy and energetically expensive method of providing carbon dioxide to the Calvin cycle. This question can be answered only by considering the function of the leaf as a whole.

Carbon dioxide is not continuously available to the photosynthesizing cells. It enters the leaf by way of the stomata, specialised pores that open and close depending on, among other things, water stress.

PEP carboxylase has a higher CO_2 affinity than does RuDP carboxylase, so it keeps the CO_2 concentration lower within the leaf (that is, it fixes carbon dioxide faster, at low levels).

This maximises the gradient of carbon dioxide between the cells and the outside air. A higher gradient means the leaf will trap a larger fraction of the passing stream of carbon dioxide.

If the stomata must be closed much of the time, as in a hot, dry climate, the plant with C_4 metabolism will take up more carbon dioxide with each gasp (so to speak) than the plant that has only C_3 metabolism.

Hence, it is at a distinct advantage in drought-ridden areas.

The list of plants known to utilise the four-carbon pathway has grown to over 100 genera, at least a dozen of which have both C_3 and C_4 species. This pathway undoubtedly has arisen many times independently in the course of evolution. Sugarcane, corn, and sorghum are among the best-known C_4 plants.

Perhaps the most familiar example of the competitive capacity of C_4 plants is seen in lawns in the summertime. In most parts of the United States, lawns consist mainly of C_3 grasses such as Kentucky bluegrass and creeping bent.

In the summer, these dark green, fine-leaved grasses are often overwhelmed by rapidly growing crabgrass, which, to the dismay of the suburbanite, disfigures the lawn as its yellowish-green, broader-leaved plants slowly take over. Crabgrass, you will not be surprised to hear, is a C_4 plant.

THE PRODUCTS OF PHOTOSYNTHESIS

The three-carbon sugar produced by the Calvin cycle may seem an insignificant reward, both for all the enzymatic activity on the part of the cell and for our own intellectual stress. However, this molecule and those derived from it provide (1) the energy source for all living systems, and (2) the basic carbon skeleton for all organic molecules. Carbon has been fixed-that is, it has been brought from the inorganic world into the organic one.

Molecules of glyceraldehyde phosphate may flow into a variety of different metabolic pathways, depending on the activities and requirements of the cell. Often they are built up to glucose or fructose, following a sequence that is in many of its steps the reverse of the glycolysis sequence described in the previous chapter. (At some steps, the reactions are simply reversed and the enzymes are the same : Other steps-the highly exergonic ones of the downhill sequence-are bypassed.); Plant cells use these six-carbon sugars to make starch and cellulose for their own 3 purposes and sucrose for export.

Animal cells store them as glycogen. All cells use sugars, including glyceraldehyde phosphate and glucose, as the starting point for the manufacture of other carbohydrates, fats and other lipids, and, with the addition of nitrogen, amino acids and nitrogenous bases. Finally, as we saw in the preceding chapter, the carbon fixed in photosynthesis is the source of ATP energy for heterotrophic cells.

6

TAXONOMIC FEATURES

The universe was perhaps 15 billion years old, cosmologists calculate, when the star that is our sun came into being. According to current hypotheses, it formed, like other stars, from an accumulation of particles of dust and hydrogen and helium gases whirling in space among the older stars.

The immense cloud that was to become the sun condensed gradually as the hydrogen and helium atoms were pulled toward one another by the force of gravity, falling into the center of the cloud and gathering speed as they fell.

As the cluster grew denser, the atoms moved faster and faster. More and more atoms collided with each other, and the gas in the cloud became hotter and hotter. As the temperature rose, the collisions became increasingly violent until the hydrogen atoms collided with such force that their nuclei fused, forming helium and releasing nuclear energy.

This thermonuclear reaction is still going on at the heart of the sun and is the source of the energy radiated from its glowing surface. The planets, according to current theory, formed from the remaining gas and dust moving around the newly formed star. At first, particles would have collected at random, but as each mass grew larger, other particles began to be attracted by the gravity of the largest masses.

The whirling dust and forming spheres continued to revolve around the sun until finally each planet had swept its own path clean, picking up loose matter like a giant snowball. The orbit nearest the sun was swept by Mercury, the next by Venus, the third by earth, the fourth by Mars, and so on out to Neptune and Pluto, the most distant of the planets. The planets, including earth, are calculated to have come into being about 4.6 billion years ago.

THE EARTH AND THE BIOSPHERE

During the time earth and the other planets were being formed, the release of energy from radioactive materials kept their interiors very hot. When earth was still so hot that it was mostly liquid, the heavier materials collected in a dense core whose diameter is about half that of the planet. As soon as the supply of stellar dust, stones, and larger rocks was exhausted, the planet ceased to grow.

As earth's surface cooled, an outer crust, a skin as thin by comparison as the skin of an apple, was formed. The oldest known rocks in this layer are about 3.98 billion years old.

Only 50 kilometers below its surface, the earth is still hot-a small fraction of it is even still molten. We see evidence of this in the occasional volcanic eruption that forces lava, which is molten rock, through weak points in the earth's skin, or in the geyser, which spews up boiling water that has trickled down to the earth's interior.

The biosphere is the part of the planet within which life exists. It forms a thin film on the outermost layer, extending only about 8 or 10 kilometers up into the atmosphere and about as far down into the depths of the sea.

Why on Earth?

In our solar system, earth among all the planets seems most favoured for the production of life. A major factor is that earth is neither too close nor too distant from the sun. The chemical reactions on which life-any form of life-depends virtually cease at very low temperatures. At high temperatures, complex chemical compounds are too unstable for life to form or survive.

Earth's size and mass are also important factors. Planets much smaller than earth do not have enough gravitational pull to hold a protective atmosphere, and any planet much larger than earth is likely to have so dense an atmosphere that light from the sun cannot reach its surface.

THE BEGINNING OF LIFE

Darwin believed that it would probably be impossible ever to look back down that long corridor of time and reconstruct life's beginnings.

Until very recently, the earliest fossils known were those of the Cambrian period, a mere 600 million years ago, and for a long time after the publication of *The Origin of Species*, biologists regarded the earliest events in the history of life as chapters that would probably remain forever closed.

Two scientific developments, however, have greatly improved our long-distance vision. One was the formulation of a testable hypothesis about the events preceding life's origins; the second was the discovery of cells more than 3 billion years old.

The testable hypothesis was offered by the Russian biochemist A. I. Oparin. According to Oparin, the appearance of life was preceded by a long period of what is sometimes called chemical evolution.

During this period, which occupied almost a third of the earth's history, there was little or no free oxygen in the atmosphere surrounding the earth, and the oxygen that was present existed mainly in the form of water vapor.

The atmosphere was a reducing one-an atmosphere that abounded in hydrogen gas, methane (CH_4), ammonia (NH_3), and other carbonhydrogen gases. As we have seen, combinations of these four elements available in the primitive atmosphere-hydrogen, oxygen, carbon, and nitrogen-make up j more than 95 percent of living tissues.

Energy was required to break apart the simple gases of the atmosphere and re-form them into organic molecules. And energy abounded on the *young* earth. There was heat energy, both boiling (moist) heat and baking (dry) heat.

Water vapor spewed out of the primitive seas, cooled in the upper atmosphere, collected into clouds, fell back on the crust of the earth, and steamed up again. Violent rainstorms were accompanied by lightning, which provided electrical energy. The sun bombarded the earth's surface with high-energy particles and ultraviolet light, and radioactive elements within the earth released their energy into the atmosphere.

Oparin hypothesized that under such conditions organic molecules were formed and collected in a thin soup in the earth's seas and lakes. Some of these molecules might have become locally more concentrated by the drying up of a lake or by the adhesion of the molecules to a solid surface. (Oparin published his small monograph in 1922, but at that time biochemists were so convinced by Pasteur's demonstrations disproving spontaneous generation-page 224—that the scientific community ignored his ideas.)

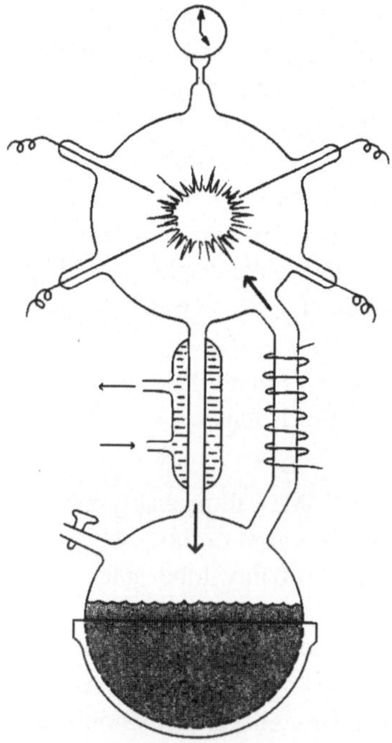

Figure 6.1 : Conditions believed to exist on primitive earth are siumulated in this apparatus. Methane and ammonia are contiunously circulated between a lower "ocean," which is heated, and an upper "atmosphere," through which an electric discharge is transmitted.

In the 1950s, Oparins hypothesis was tested in the laboratory by Stanley Miller, then a graduate student at the University of Chicago. Miller showed that under conditions simulating those believed to have been present some 3 to 4 billion years ago, amino acids are produced from hydrogen gas, ammonia, methane, and water vapor.

Miller's experiments have now been repeated many times in other laboratories. With various modifications in the experimental conditions, almost all of the common amino acids have been produced and also purines, pyrimidines, ribose, and nucleotides.

As the concentrations of such molecules increased, it is not difficult to imagine that they would have assembled themselves in aggregates, held together by hydrophobic interactions, hydrogen bonds, and other weak forces.

The most stable of the chemical combinations would have tended to survive, and hence a form of natural selection played a role in chemical evolution as well as in the biological evolution that was to follow.

At some stage in chemical evolution, a boundary or membrane formed around such an aggregate of macromolecules, permitting it to lead a separate existence from its external environment. What was enclosed in that boundary membrane? A catalytic protein? A self-replicating nucleic acid? Such questions lead directly to the mystery of the origin of the genetic code.

As far as we can see, there is no underlying molecular logic to the code, no reason why a particular triplet should specify one amino acid rather than another. Did the code come into being purely by chance? It would appear so.

All we know for sure is that all living systems are the descendants of these tiny metabolizing droplets.

The First Cells

When did life begin? We will probably never be able to answer this question because it depends first on how we define life and, second, on finding chemical traces probably long since erased. We can establish some sort of time scale, however, owing to the discovery little more than a decade ago of microfossils in flintlike rocks, called chert, in South Africa.

The fossils, whose structure is visible only by electron microscopy, resemble present-day bacteria and blue-green algae. The rocks in which they were found, according to radioactive dating, are 3.4 billion years old. Thus life began very early, perhaps in the first billion years of earth's history.

The Evolution of Energy Systems

Although both heterotrophs and autotrophs are represented among the earliest microfossils, it is logical to postulate that the first living cell was an extreme heterotroph. It probably possessed few enzymes, compared with a modern cell, and so was capable of only a few anabolic reactions. It would have had to find most of the molecules it required in Oparin s organic soup.

As the primitive prokaryotic heterotrophs increased in number, according to this hypothesis, they began to use up the complex molecules on which their existence depended and which had taken millions of years to accumulate. Competition began.

Under the pressure of this competition, cells that could make efficient use of the limited energy sources now available were more likely to survive than cells that could not. In the course of time, cells evolved that were able to synthesize organic molecules out of simple inorganic materials. Without the evolution of these autotrophs, life on earth would soon have come to an end.

The most successful of the autotrophs were those that evolved a system for making direct use of the sun's energy-the process of photosynthesis. With the advent of photosynthesis, the flow of energy in the biosphere came to assume its modern form: Radiant energy channeled through photosynthetic autotrophs to other forms of life.

With the evolution of photosynthetic cells that produced oxygen, the atmosphere slowly began to change. As a result of photosynthesis, the concentration of oxygen in the atmosphere rose to 1 percent about 600 to 1,000 million years ago and to 10 percent only about 400 million years ago.

The present concentration of 21 percent oxygen has been created and is maintained by photosynthesis. The accumulation of oxygen in the air made possible, in turn, the evolution of organisms that produced most of their chemical energy by cellular respiration.

According to this hypothesis, in terms of energy production, anaerobic glycolysis came first, followed by photosynthesis and finally, as oxygen accumulated, by respiration. The genetic code was determined and the pathways of glycolysis, respiration, and photosynthesis were established in nearly their present form long before the appearance of any eukaryotic cells.

THE EVOLUTION OF EUKARYOTES

The microfossil record indicates that the eukaryotes probably evolved about 1.6 billion years ago. Eukaryotes, as we saw in Section 1, are distinguished from prokaryotes by their larger size, the separation of nucleus from cytoplasm by a nuclear envelope, the organisation of their DNA, and their complex organelles, among which are chloroplasts and mitochondria.

The step from prokaryotes to the first eukaryotes was one of the big evolutionary transitions, second only to the origin of life. The question of how it came about is a matter of current and lively discussion. One interesting hypothesis is that larger, more complex cells evolved partly as a result of certain prokaryotes' taking up residence inside other cells. (Such a close association between two organisms of different species is known as symbiosis.)

As oxygen gas began slowly to accumulate in the atmosphere, those bacteria that were able to convert to the use of oxygen in ATP production gained a strong advantage, and so such forms began to prosper and increase. Some of these evolved into modern forms of bacteria. Others, according to this theory, became symbionts within larger cells and evolved into mitochondria.

Several lines of evidence support the hypothesis that mitochondria are descended from specialised bacteria: Mitochondria contain their own DNA, and this DNA is present in a single, continuous ("circular") molecule, like the DNA of bacteria; many of the same enzymes contained in the cell membranes of bacteria are found in mitochondrial membranes.

The ribosomes of mitochondria resemble those of bacteria both in their size (they are smaller than those of eukaryotic cells) and in some details of their chemical composition; mitochondria appear to be produced only by other mitochondria, which divide within their host cell. (However, to make the situation more complex, there is nowhere near enough DNA in mitochondria to code for all the mitochondrial proteins. Host-cell DNA is also required for mitochondrial structures.)

We know little about the original cells in which these bacteria first set up housekeeping-or, indeed, if they actually existed. But if they did exist, they probably had no means of using oxygen for cellular respiration and so were dependent entirely on anaerobic fermentation as an energy-releasing process, which, as we have seen, is relatively inefficient.

Cells with respiratory assistants would have been more efficient than those lacking them and so would have outreproduced them.

In an analogous fashion, photosynthetic prokaryotes ingested by larger, nonphotosynthetic cells are believed to be the forerunners of chloroplasts. By this symbiosis, the smaller cells gained nutrients and protection, and the larger cells were given a new energy source.

This hypothesis accounts for the presence in eukaryotic cells of complex organelles not found in the far simpler prokaryotes. It gains support from the fact that many modern organisms contain intracellular symbiotic bacteria and algae, indicating that such associations are not difficult to establish.

Modern one-celled eukaryotes-the protists-are a very diverse group, most of which probably bear little or no resemblance to the first eukaryotic cells.

The multicellular organisms are all eukaryotes. The major groups-the fungi, the plants, and the animals—are believed each to have originated from *one* (and possibly more) separate types of one-celled eukaryotes.

There is no fossil evidence of their origins. The first fossils of

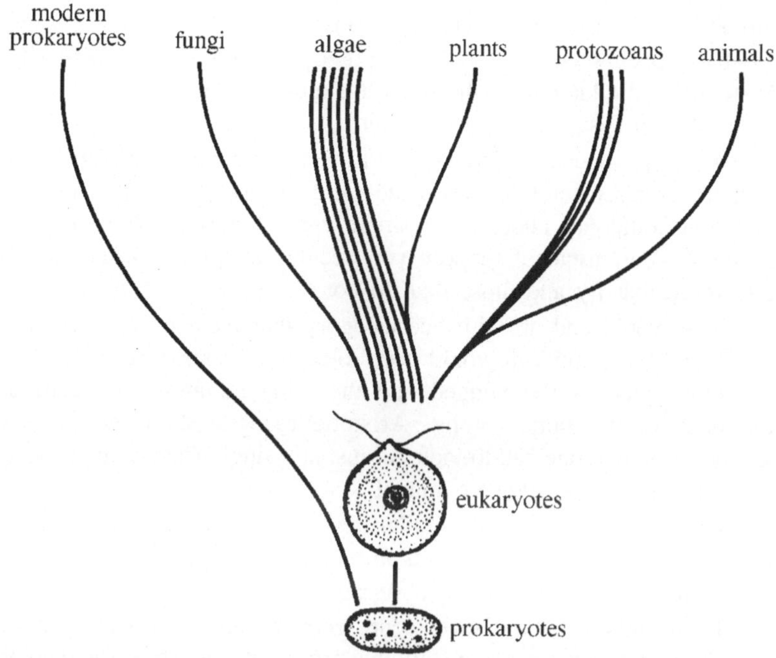

Figure 6.2 : Possible evolutionary relationships among the major groups of organisms. According to these hypotheses, the fungi, the various phyla of eukaryotic algae, and the modern protozoans evolved separately from single celled eukaryotes.

multicellular organisms are found in sediments a mere 0.6 billion years old, and their diversity and complexity indicate that eukaryotes had been in existence for millions of years.

The history of evolution from this time forward is summarised in Table elsewhere in this chapter. Some aspects will be covered in more detail in the chapters that follow.

As you can see in Figure elsewhere in this chpater, members of the human species appeared only very recently in the evolutionary timetable.

If we measure out the history of the earth on a 24-hour time scale, the oldest known fossils appeared at 6 A.M., the oldest eukaryotes between 4 and 5 P.M., the first multicellular organisms between 8 and 9 P.M., and *Homo sapiens* in the last 30 seconds at 11:59:30 P.M.

CLASSIFICATION OF ORGANISMS

As late arrivals on the evolutionary scene, we humans are confronted with a bewildering variety of living things. As many as 5 million different kinds of organisms share the biosphere. For thousands of years, we have been trying to find order and meaning in this diversity. Systematists are biologists who study this order, and taxonomists arrange organisms in systems of classification.

Aristotle is generally considered to be among the first to have tried to group organisms in ways that made sense. He recognised, for example, that you could not choose any single characteristic as the basis for grouping. For instance, suppose you decided to group all the animals into those that fly and those that do not.

You would end up with one category that included most insects, birds, and bats, and you would have to separate some obviously close relations, such as the winged and the wingless ants that occur as members of the same colony. Aristotle recognised, as do modern taxonomists, that one had to look not just at a single feature but at many characteristics of a plant or animal.

On the basis of overall similarities and differences, an organism could be placed with other forms in increasingly restricted categories: vertebrate, bird, duck, mallard, for example.

In the middle of the seventeenth century, an English clergyman, John Ray, set out to catalog all the organisms in the world and to arrange them systematically. He was the first to use the word *species* to describe a kind of organism.

A species, according to Ray, was made up of organisms that were morphologically the same-from *morphe,* meaning "shape" in Greek-and that could reproduce their own kind.

Ray cataloged all the plants in the vicinity of Cambridge, the first complete catalog of one locality ever to be made. Then, traveling through England and the Continent, he worked his way, astonishingly, through all the plants that he could learn about (almost 19,000) and the birds, the fishes, and the four-footed animals.

At the time of Ray, and for a number of years thereafter, plants and animals were designated by cumbersome phrase names, or polynomials. These polynomials were brief descriptive phrases concerning the plant or animal to which they were applied.

The first word in the polynomial had come, by the close of the seventeenth century, to designate the *genus* (plural, *genera),* an inclusive group of similar species. Thus, the numerous kinds of roses were grouped in the genus *Rosa,* many butterflies in the genus *Papilio,* and cats and catlike animals in the genus *Felis.*

THE BINOMIAL SYSTEM

The system of naming living things was simplified by the eighteenth-century Swedish professor, physician, and naturalist, Carolus Linnaeus. (Linnaeus was born Carl von Linne but latinized his name in the scholarly fashion of his time.) His ambition was to classify all the known kinds of plants and animals according to their genera.

In 1753, he published a two-volume work, *Species Plantarum* ("the kinds of plants"), which contained brief analytical descriptions of every species of plant known to European science. Although he used the polynomial designations and regarded them as the proper names for species, he made an important innovation.

In the margin of his book, opposite the "proper" name of each species, Linnaeus entered a single word, which, together with the generic name, formed a convenient "shorthand" designation for the species. In the book, catnip, which had previously been designated by the polynomial *Nepeta floribus interrupte spicatus pedunculatis ("Nepeta* with flowers in an interrupted pedunculate spike"), was described under *Nepeta,* and *cataria* was put in the margin, making it *Nepeta cataria,* which is its name today.

The convenience of this system was quickly recognised, and Linnaeus and subsequent authors soon replaced all "proper" names with "shorthand" ones. This binomial ("two-name") system is still used today. A species name, as we have seen, consists of two parts-the generic name and the specific epithet (adjective or modifier).

However, a genus name may be written alone when one is referring to members of the entire group of species making up that genus, such as *Drosophila* or *Paramecium.*

A specific epithet is meaningless when written alone, however, because many different species in different genera may have the same specific epithet. The domestic dog is *Canis familiaris,* for instance; *familiaris* is a commonly used specific epithet and by itself would not identify any organism.

For this reason, the specific epithet is always preceded by the genus name, or, in a context where no ambiguity is possible, the genus name may be abbreviated to its initial letter. Thus *Canis familiaris* may be designated *C. familiaris.*

WHAT IS A SPECIES?

Species in Latin simply means "kind," and so species, in the simplest sense, are the different kinds of organisms. A more technical definition of species is "a group of interbreeding organisms that do not ordinarily breed with members of other groups." This definition conforms to common sense. If one species interbred freely with other species, it would no longer represent a distinct kind of organism.

This definition, although useful for animals, is not so useful for other organisms, such as some bacteria and protists that do not breed at all, as far as is known, and for some plants in which fertile crossings can take place among very different kinds of plants.

A profound change occurred in the concept of species with the acceptance of evolutionary theory. Rather than being the immutable, ideal form conceived by Linnaeus, a species is now seen to change constantly in both time and space.

However, even though a precise definition of species is elusive, the term is understandable in a practical way. For instance, anthropologists point out that primitive peoples, particularly hunter-gatherers, are able to recognise, distinguish, and name great numbers of the organisms with which they come in contact.

What these people, operating on a practical level, recognise as a "kind"-something different enough to have its own name-almost always coincides with what scientists recognise as a "species." So despite the inability of experts always to agree upon a definition (or the organism to conform to one), the species is a clear and useful reality.

OTHER TAXONOMIC GROUPS

Scientists before Linnaeus recognised the plant, animal, and mineral kingdoms, and the *kingdom* is still the major category used in biological classification. Between the level of genus and the level of kingdom, however, Linnaeus and subsequent taxonomists have added a number of categories.

Thus, genera are grouped into *families*, families into *orders*, orders into *classes*, and classes into *phyla*. These categories may be subdivided or aggregated into a number of less important ones, such as subgenera and superfamilies.

The groups that are placed in the categories are known as *taxa* (singular, taxon. Thus, in Table elsewhere in this chapter, Plantae and Animalia are taxa within the category of kingdom, and Angiospermae and Mammalia are taxa having the categorical rank of class. By convention, generic and specific names are written in italics, while the names of families, orders, classes, and other taxa whose categories rank above the genus level are not, although they are capitalised.

Table elsewhere in this chapter shows the classification of two different types of organisms. Note how much information we have about a plant or animal if we know its classification. Indexing this information is one of the chief functions of a classification scheme.

Table 6.1 : Biological Classifications.

Red Maple *(Acer rubrum)*

Category	*Taxon*	*Characteristics*
Kingdom	Plantae	Organisms that usually have rigid cell walls and usually possess chlorophyll
Subkingdom	Embryophyta	Plants forming embryos
Phylum	Tracheophyta	Vascular plants
Subphylum	Pterophytina	Generally large, conspicuous leaves, complex vascular pattern
Class	Angiospermae	Flowering plants, seed enclosed in ovary
Subclass	Dicotyledoneae	Embryo with two seed leaves (cotyledons)
Order	Sapindales	Soapberry order; trees and shrubs
Family	Aceraceae	Maple family; trees of temperate regions
Genus	*Acer*	Maples and box elder
Species	*Acer rubrum*	Red maple

Man *(Homo sapiens)*

Category	*Taxon*	*Characteristics*
Kingdom	Animalia	Multicellular organisms requiring organic plant and animal substances for food
Phylum	Chordata	Animals with notochord, dorsal hollow nerve cord, gills in pharynx at some stage of life cycle
Subphylum	Vertebrata	Spinal cord enclosed in a vertebral column, body basically segmented, skull enclosing brain
Superclass	Tetrapoda	Land vertebrates, four-limbed
Class	Mammalia	Young nourished by milk glands, skin with hair or fur, body cavity divided by diaphragm, red corpuscles without nuclei, high body temperature

Category	*Taxon*	*Characteristics*
Order	Primates	Tree dwellers or their descendants, usually with fingers and flat nails, sense of smell reduced
Family	Hominidae	Flat face, eyes forward, colour vision, upright, bipedal locomotion, with hands and feet differently specialised
Genus	*Homo*	Large brain, speech, long childhood
Species	*Homo sapiens*	Prominent chin, high forehead, sparse body hair

TAXONOMY AND EVOLUTION

To Linnaeus and his immediate successors, taxonomic classification was a revelation of grand, unchanging design. When evolutionary theory came to be the dominant ordering principle in the biological sciences, systematics, as the science of taxonomy is called, took on a new meaning. The goal is to classify organisms in a way that reflects their evolutionary history.

Thus species are groups that have diverged only recently, genera share more distant ancestors, and so on. A major problem is that all species alive today are equally modern; none is an ancestor of any other. So the degrees of similarity and differences among modern forms may or may not represent the closeness of relationship.

Traditionally, taxonomy has depended on morphological criteria-the arrangement of parts and the external appearance of the organism. Recently, increased knowledge of cellular biochemistry is leading to greater reliance on biochemical criteria, such as the composition of the cell membrane and the cell wall or the use of certain anabolic or catabolic pathways.

The bacteria are a particularly difficult group, taxonomically speaking, because their forms are variable and their evolutionary histories are, to a large extent, unknown. Now studies are being made using hybridizing techniques to reveal the extent of differences and similarities among the DNAs of certain bacterial groups. The use of genotype rather than phenotype as a basis for classification probably represents the taxonomic ideal, not soon to be obtained but clearly the solution to many problems.

A QUESTION OF KINGDOMS

In Linnaeus's time, as we mentioned, it was thought that there were three kingdoms-animals, plants, and minerals-and until very recently it was popular to classify every living thing as either an animal or a plant. Animals were organisms that moved, ate things, and breathed, and their limbs and organs and bodies grew to a certain size and then stopped growing.

Plants were organisms that did not move, eat, or breathe, and that grew indefinitely. Thus the fungi, algae, and bacteria were grouped with the plants, and the protozoans-one-celled organisms that ate and moved-were classified with the animals.

In the twentieth century, new data began to emerge. This was partly a result of improvements in the light microscope and, subsequently, the development of the electron microscope, and partly because of the application of biochemical techniques to studies of differences and similarities among organisms.

As a result, the number of groups recognised as constituting different kingdoms has increased as biological knowledge has accumulated. The most recent proposals recommend five kingdoms: Prokaryotae, Protista, Fungi, Plantae, and Animalia. In Appendix C, the major groups of organisms are classified within these five kingdoms.

Other systems group the eukaryotic algae and the fungi with the plants, ending up with three kingdoms: prokaryotes, plants, and animals. Some retain the two-kingdom classification system: plants and animals.

In truth, no system is really satisfactory. For instance, at the one-celled level of life, there are no useful criteria for separating plants from animals. Two species of single-celled, motile organisms may be almost identical in most respects, except that one has chloroplasts and the other does not.

In some cases, the one that has chloroplasts can lose them from time to time and still continue to survive and reproduce indefinitely. Yet in a plant-animal division based on the capacity for photosynthesis, these two closely related forms are separated at the level of kingdom.

On the other hand, as we shall see in other chapter of this book, there is a clear evolutionary sequence, with modern, living representatives, leading from certain one-celled algae to the flowering plants. So if we group all of the one-celled eukaryotes together-the protists-as we do in this text, we break up what would appear to be a clear evolutionary line leading to the plants.

Whether organisms are classified in two, three, or five kingdoms, however, their species designations are not affected, nor are most of the other categories in which they are classified.

7

DIVERSITY OF PROKARYOTES

In the next three chapters, we are going to describe the three kingdoms comprising the microorganisms: the prokaryotes, the protists, and the fungi. Although they are dissimilar in many important ways, and many algae and fungi are quite large, they are conventionally studied together in the science known as microbiology.

Viruses will also be described briefly in this chapter. Although they do not fit comfortably in any of the taxa of living systems, they too are traditionally a part of microbiology.

The prokaryotes are the oldest and most abundant group of organisms in the world. About 1,600 species have been described. They are the smallest cellular organisms; a single gram (about $^1/_{28}$ of an ounce) of fertile soil can contain as many as 2½ billion individuals.

The success of the prokaryotes, biologically speaking, is undoubtedly due to their rapid rate of cell division and their great metabolic versatility. Growing under optimum conditions, a population can double in size every 20 or 30 minutes. Prokaryotes can survive in many environments that support no other form of life.

They have been found in the icy wastes of Antarctica, the near-boiling waters of natural hot springs, and even in the dark depths of the ocean. Some bacteria are among the very few modern organisms that can survive without free oxygen, obtaining their energy by anaerobic glycolysis. Oxygen is lethal to some types (obligate anaerobes), whereas others can exist with or without oxygen (facultative anaerobes).

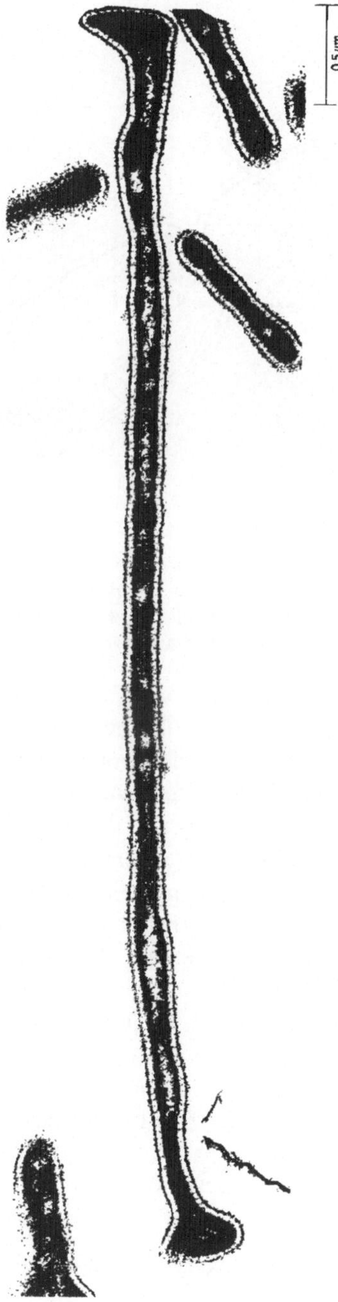

Figure 7.1 : Thermophilic bacteria thrive at 92°C, a temperature close to the boiling point of water. This electron micrograph shows a single long filamentous type and several short rodlike types.

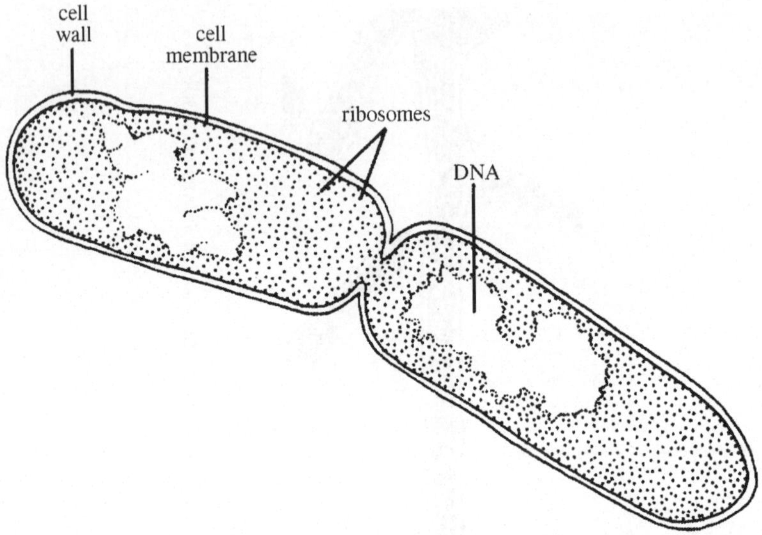

Figure 7.2 : Cells of Escherichia coli, a modern prokaryote that is a common inhabitant of the human digestive tract. The DNA is in the less dense (lighter-appearing) material in the center of each cell. The most dense small bodies in the cytoplasm are ribosomes. The two cells in the center have just finished dividing and have not yet separated completely.

A few prokaryotes can form thick-walled, dry spores. These spores are inactive, resistant forms that enable the cells to survive for long periods of time without water or nutrients or in conditions of extreme heat or cold. They may stay dormant for years, and some remain viable even when boiled in water for as long as 2 hours.

From the ecological point of view, prokaryotes are important as decomposers, breaking down organic material to a form in which it can be used by plants. They also play a major role in the process known as nitrogen fixation, by which nitrogen gas (N_2) is reduced to ammonia (NH_3) or ammonium (NH_4^+).

Although nitrogen is abundant in the atmosphere, no eukaryotes are able to use atmospheric nitrogen, and so the crucial first step in the incorporation of nitrogen into organic compounds depends largely on a few species of prokaryotes, some free-living and some in symbiotic association with plants. Some forms are photosynthetic, and some few are both photosynthetic and nitrogen-fixing.

THE PROKARYOTIC CELL

The essential features of a prokaryotic cell were outlined in Chapter

5 and are reviewed in Figure elsewhere in this chapter. The cell shown here is the familiar *Escherichia coli*, one of the eubacteria. The eubacteria, in general, and *E. coli*, in particular, are the best studied of the prokaryotes.

The Cytoplasm

The cytoplasm of prokaryotes is relatively unstructured. Except for the blue-green "algae," the cytoplasm is not divided or compartmentalised by membranes and does not contain any membrane-bound organelles. The most prominent feature within the cytoplasm is the chromosome.

All prokaryotic chromosomes analyzed so far have proved to be one single, continuous ("circular") molecule of DNA. In addition, a prokaryotic cell may contain one or more plasmids.

The cytoplasm often has a fine granular appearance due to its many ribosomes. These are somewhat smaller than eukaryotic ribosomes but have the same general shape.

The Cell Membrane

The membrane surrounding a prokaryotic cell is similar in chemical composition to that of a eukaryotic cell but, with the exception of the mycoplasma (the smallest free-living cells known), it lacks cholesterol or other steroids.

In the aerobic prokaryotes, the cell membrane incorporates the electron transport system found in the mitochondrial membrane of eukaryotic cells, and in one group of photosynthetic prokaryotes (the purple bacteria), the sites of photosynthesis are found in the outer membrane.

In the purple bacteria and in aerobes with large energy requirements, the membrane is often extensively convoluted, with folds extending into the interior. These, of course, greatly increase the working surface of the membrane. The membrane appears to contain specific attachment sites (called mesosomes) for the DNA molecules; these sites are believed to play a role in ensuring the separation of the duplicate chromosomes at cell division.

The Cell Wall

Almost all prokaryotes are surrounded by a cell wall, which ranges from 5 to 80 nanometers in diameter and gives the different types their characteristic shapes. Many prokaryotes have rigid walls, some have flexible walls, and only the mycoplasma have no cell walls at all.

Because most bacterial cells are hypertonic in relation to their environment, they would burst without their walls. (The mycoplasma live as intracellular parasites in an isotonic environment.)

Chemical Structure of the Cell Wall

The cell walls of prokaryotes are complex and contain many kinds of molecules not present in eukaryotes. The walls of prokaryotic cells contain complex polymers known as peptidoglycans, which are primarily responsible for the mechanical strength of the wall.

In addition, in some prokaryotes, large molecules of lipopolysaccharide are deposited over the peptidoglycan layer. Bacterial cell walls that lack the lipopolysaccharide layer combine firmly with such dyes as gentian violet, and those in which it is present do not.

Those that combine with the dyes are known as gram-positive, whereas the others are gram-negative, after Hans Christian Gram, the Danish microbiologist who discovered this distinction. Gram staining is widely used as a basis for classifying bacteria, since it reflects a fundamental difference in the architecture of the cell wall.

This architecture in turn affects various other characteristics of the bacteria, such as their patterns of susceptibility to antibiotics. Gram-positive bacteria are more susceptible to most antibiotics than are gram-negative bacteria.

They are also more susceptible to lysozyme, an enzyme found in nasal secretions, saliva, and other body fluids, which digests the cell walls of bacteria. In certain bacteria, a gluey polysaccharide capsule, which is secreted by the bacterium, is present outside the cell wall. The function of the capsule is not entirely clear, but its presence is associated with pathogenic activity in certain organisms.

For example, as shown in Figure elsewhere in this chapter, the encapsulated form of *Diplococcus pneumoniae* is virulent, whereas the nonencapsulated form is generally nonvirulent. It appears that the capsule interferes with phagocytosis by host white blood cells.

Flagella and Pili

Some types of bacteria have long, slender extensions, known as flagella and pili. Bacterial flagella, as we noted in other chapter of this book, are made up of monomers of protein known as flagellin, which are assembled in chains and wound around a hollow central core.

The flagella of different species differ slightly in diameter (12 to 18 nanometers), probably due to slight differences in the composition of their flagellin.

Electron microscopy has recently revealed that bacterial flagella are anchored into the cell wall and membranes by a fascinatingly complicated assembly. The filament (the helix of flagellin monomers

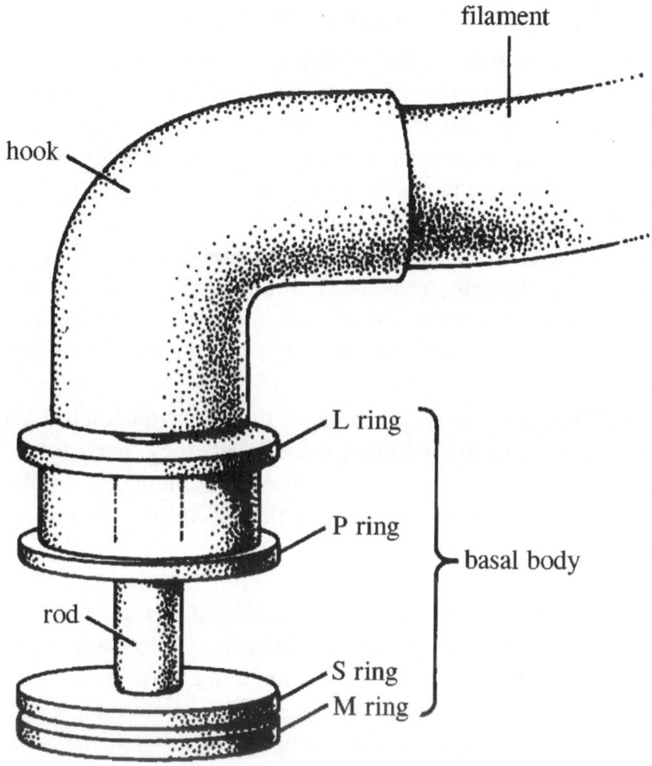

Figure 7.3 : Diagramof a flagellum from E. coli. The basal body, which serves to anchor the flagellyum to the cell wall and the cell membrane, cosists of several rings surrounding a rod.

with its hollow core) terminates in a hook made up of a different protein. The hook is inserted into a basal body that consists of a rod and, in gram-negative bacteria, two pairs of rings, one pair of which is embedded in the cell wall and one pair in the cell membrane. In gram-positive bacteria, only the inner pair of rings is present.

Pili (singular, pilus) are assembled from protein monomers in much the same way that the filaments of flagella are. (You will not be surprised to learn that the protein is called pilin.) They are rigid, cylindrical rods that extend out from the cell, sometimes to a considerable distance. They are shorter and thinner than flagella and are often present in large numbers (hundreds on a single cell).

They serve to attach bacteria to a food source, to the surface of a liquid (where oxygen is present), or, in the case of conjugating bacteria, to one another.

DIVERSITY OF FORM

The oldest method of identifying microorganisms is by their physical appearance. The shape of individual prokaryotes is a result, as we noted previously, of their cell wall. In addition, different types of bacteria have characteristic patterns of growth, producing colonies that also have a distinctive shape, and many forms have sheaths or other coatings outside their cell walls.

The eubacteria, or true bacteria, for example, may have any one of four forms. Straight, rod-shaped forms like E. coli are known as *bacilli;* spherical ones are called *cocci;* long, spiral rods are called *spirilla;* and short, curved rods, probably incomplete spirals, are called *vibrios*.

Cocci may stick together in pairs after division (diplococci), they may occur in clusters (staphylococci), or they may form chains (streptococci). One bacterium that causes pneumonia is a diplococcus, while the staphylococci are responsible for many serious infections characterised by boils or abscesses.

Rod-shaped bacilli usually separate after cell division. When they do remain together, they spread out end to end in filaments, since they always divide in the same plane (transversely). Because these filaments are funguslike in appearance, the combining form *myco-* (from the Greek word for "fungus") is often a part of the name of these organisms. *Mycobacterium tuberculosis,* for example, the cause of tuberculosis, is a rod-shaped bacillus that forms a filamentous, funguslike growth.

Spirochetes are among the easiest microorganisms to identify. They are very long (5 to 500 micrometers) and slender (about 0.5 micrometer in diameter) and have an unusual structure, known as an axial filament, attached at each end of the cell.

Axial filaments have now been shown to contain two fibrils, identical to flagella, in their structure, and so they are recognised as modified flagella. They are wrapped around the cell between the cell membrane and the delicate wall, with the fibrils of each filament overlapping at the middle of the cell.

Rickettsia, another type of prokaryote distinguishable by its form, is shown in Figure elsewhere in this chpater.

TYPES OF MOTILITY

Prokaryotes move in a variety of ways, all of which are more or less mysterious. Flagella beat with a rotary movement. The flagella are so fine and the beat so fast, the motion of the flagellum itself cannot be seen. (The flagella of *Spirillum serpens*, for instance, are reported to have been clocked at 2,400 rpm.) Ingenious methods have been devised by which the cells can be tethered in place by the flagella.

As a result, the cells rotate instead of the flagella, and the rotational movement can be observed. The basal end of the flagella, with its complex structure, apparently acts as a motor, perhaps running on chemiosmotic power.

Another characteristic form of movement for some bacteria is gliding. Gliding requires attachment to a solid surface and the secretion of some sort of slime or mucus along which the cells slide. It has been suggested that cytoplasmic streaming may play a role in imparting motility to these cells, but so far the mechanism remains unknown.

Spirochetes move by a corkscrew motion caused, apparently, by contractions of the axial filament.

REPRODUCTION AND RESTING FORMS

Most prokaryotes reproduce by simple cell division, also called binary fission. In some forms, reproduction is by budding or by the breaking off of fragments of the cell. As they multiply, these prokaryotes, barring mutations, produce clones of genetically identical cells.

Genetic recombinations take place as a result of conjugation, transformation, transduction, and exchanges of plasmids. It is not known how common such genetic recombinations are in nature or whether or not they occur in all types of prokaryotes.

Many prokaryotes have the capacity to form spores, which are dormant, resting cells. Again, the process has been studied most extensively in the rod-shaped eubacteria. It occurs characteristically when a population of cells, growing very rapidly, has begun to use up its food supply.

Each cell, at the beginning of sporulation (spore formation), contains two duplicate chromosomes. A cell membrane grows around one of the chromosomes, separating it from the rest of the cell, which then engulfs the newly formed cell (as in phagocytosis). Thus the spore-to-be is ' now surrounded by two membranes, its own and that of the larger cell (this series i of events is shown in Figure elsewhere in this chpater).

A spore coat containing a unique peptidoglycan forms around this smaller cell. Covered by an outer layer of proteins composed largely of hydrophobic amino acids, this peptidoglycan is completely different from that present in the bacterial cell wall. The spore remains in this

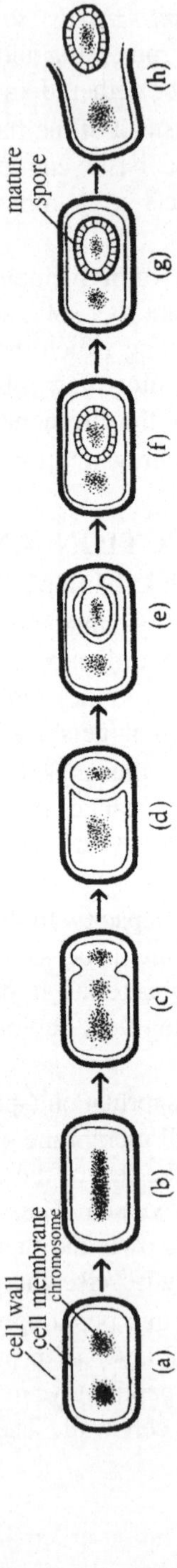

Figure 7.4 : Endospore formation in Bacillus cereus.

protected state until appropriate events trigger its germination. Germination takes place rapidly, with the uptake of water, the dissolution of the spore coat, and the formation of a new cell wall. Genetic studies of the spore-making *Bacillus subtilis* indicate that some 50 genes, clustered in about five segments of the chromosome, are involved in spore production.

The myxobacteria, a type of gliding bacteria, form fruiting bodies, which are brightly coloured collections of spores and slime large enough to be seen by the unaided eye.

Spore formation greatly increases the capacity of prokaryotic cells to survive. The spores of *Clostridium botulinum,* for instance, the bacterium that causes botulism, are not destroyed by boiling for several hours.

PROKARYOTIC NUTRITION

Heterotrophs

Most prokaryotes are heterotrophs; most types feed on dead organic matter. Bacteria and other microorganisms are responsible for the decay and recycling of organic material in the soil. Typically, different groups of bacteria play different, specific roles-such as the digestion of cellulose, starches, or other polysaccharides, or the hydrolysis of specific peptide bonds, or the breakdown of amino acids.

Because of their high degree of nutritional specialisation, prokaryotes are able to live in large numbers in the same small area with reduced competition and, indeed, with mutual assistance, as the activities of one group make food molecules available to another group.

These combined activities release the nutrients and make them available to plants and, through plants, to animals. Thus, they are an essential part of ecological systems.

Some heterotrophic bacteria are symbionts. Some of these are parasites that break down organic material in the bodies of living organisms. The disease-causing (pathogenic) bacteria belong to this group, as do a number of other nonpathogenic forms.

Some of the symbiotic bacteria have little effect on their hosts, and some are actually beneficial. Cows and other ruminants can digest cellulose only because their stomachs contain bacteria and certain symbiotic protozoans.

Our own intestines contain a number of types of generally harmless bacteria (including *E. coli*). Some supply vitamin K, which is necessary for blood clotting. Others prevent us from developing serious infections.

When the normal bacterial inhabitants of the human intestinal tract are destroyed-as can happen, for example, following prolonged antibiotic therapy-our tissues are much more vulnerable to disease-causing microorganisms.

One group of very small bacteria, members of the genus *Bdellovibrio* (from *bdello,* the Greek word for leech) are parasites on other bacteria. They make a hole in the host cell wall and multiply between the wall and the membrane, digesting the host cell as they multiply.

Chemoautotrophs

Chemoautotrophic prokaryotes obtain their energy from the oxidation of inorganic compounds. Only prokaryotes are able to use inorganic compounds as an energy source.

Certain chemosynthetic bacteria are essential components of the nitrogen cycle, the process by which nitrogen compounds are cycled and recycled through ecosystems. One group oxidises ammonia or ammonium (derived from the breakdown of organic materials, the activities of nitrogen-fixing prokaryotes, or, to a minor extent, from lightning or volcanic activities).

The products of this reaction are nitrite (NO_2) and energy. Another group oxidises nitrites, producing nitrate (NO_3) and energy. Nitrate is the form in which nitrogen moves from the soil into the roots of plants.

Sulfur is also required by plants for amino acid synthesis. Like nitrogen, it is converted to the form in which it is taken up by plant roots by the activities of chemoautotrophic bacteria that oxidise elemental sulfur to sulfate:

$$2S + 2H_2O + 3O_2 \rightarrow 2H_2SO_4$$

Other sulfur bacteria, such as *Thiothrix* and *Beggiatoa,* obtain energy by oxidising hydrogen sulfide.

These important biogeochernical cycles and the roles of microorganisms in them will be discussed further in other chapter of this book.

Photosynthetic Prokaryotes

Among the eubacteria are three photosynthetic forms: the green sulfur bacteria, the purple sulfur bacteria, and the purple nonsulfur bacteria. (The colours of the third group may actually range from purple to red or brown.)

The chlorophyll found in the green sulfur bacteria, chiorobium chlorophyll, is chemically similar to chlorophyll *a*. The chlorophyll found in the two groups of purple bacteria is bacteriochlorophyll, which differs chemically in several details from chlorophyll *a* and is a pale blue-gray. The colours of the purple bacteria are due to the presence of several different yellow and red carotenoids, which function as accessory pigments.

In the photosynthetic sulfur bacteria, as we noted in other chapter of this book, the sulfur compounds are the electron doctors, playing the same role in bacterial photosynthesis that water does in photosynthesis in eukaryotes.

$$CO_2 + 2H_2S \xrightarrow{\text{light}} (CH_2O) + H_2O + 2S$$

Photosynthesis by eubacteria is carried out anaerobically, and it never results in the production of molecular oxygen (O_2). However, in all species except the methanogens, carbon is fixed by means of the Calvin cycle.

In the nonsulfur photosynthetic bacteria, other compounds, including alcohols, fatty acids, and a variety of other organic substances, serve as electron donors for the photosynthetic reaction.

THE BLUE-GREEN "ALGAE"

The blue-green "algae" are essentially bacteria, members of the gliding group. Unlike other prokaryotes, they contain chlorophyll a, which is also found in all photosynthetic eukaryotes. They have several kinds of accessory pigments, including xanthophyll, which is a yellow carotenoid, and several other carotenoids. (Carotenoids can also be found in photosynthetic eukaryotes and in some other bacteria.)

The cells of blue-green algae may also contain one or two pigments known as phycobilins: phycocyanin, a blue pigment, which is always present, and phycoerythrin, a red one, which is often present. Chlorophyll and the accessory pigments are not enclosed in chloroplasts, as they are in plant cells, but are part of a membrane system distributed in the peripheral portion of the cell.

Cells of the blue-greens, as with many other prokaryotes, have an outer polysaccharide sheath, or coating. The outer sheath is often deeply pigmented, particularly in species that spread up onto the land; the colours include a light golden yellow, brown, red, emerald green, blue, violet, and blue-black.

In addition, the carotenoids and phycobilins modify the colour of the cells in which they occur. Thus, not only are they not algae, but only about half of the known species are actually blue-green. Indeed, the Red Sea was so named because of the dense concentrations, or "blooms," of red-pigmented blue-green algae that float on its surface.

Some species of blue-green algae are capable of nitrogen fixation.

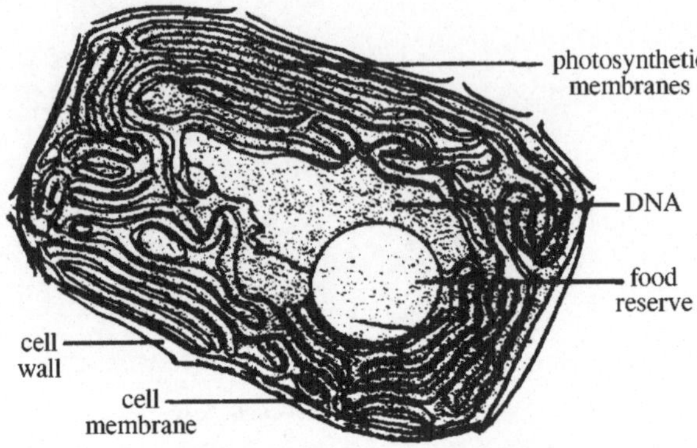

Figure 7.5 : Electron micrograph of the blue-green alga Anabaena cylindrica.

The photosynthetic, nitrogen-fixing blue-green algae have gone the farthest along the pathway to independence hypothesized for prokaryote evolution. They have the simplest nutritional requirements of any living thing, needing only N_2 and CO_2 which are always present in the atmosphere, a few minerals, and water.

The ecological importance of the blue-green algae appears to be less than that of the nitrogen-fixing bacteria, at least for agriculture. However, in Southeast Asia, rice can be grown on the same land for years without the addition of fertilisers because of the rich growth of nitrogen-fixing blue-green algae in the rice paddies.

Because of their nutritional independence, the blue-green algae are able to colonise bare areas of rock and soil. A dramatic example of such colonization was seen on the island of Krakatoa in Indonesia, which was denuded of all visible plant life by its cataclysmic volcanic explosion of 1883.

Filamentous blue-green algae were the first living things to appear on the pumice and volcanic ash; within a few years they had formed a dark-green gelatinous growth. The layer of blue-green algae eventually became thick enough to provide a substrate for the growth of higher plants. It is very probable that the blue-green algae were similarly the first colonisers of land in the course of biological evolution.

VIRUSES

Viruses do not fit easily into any of the traditional kingdoms of living organisms, and the problem of categorising them is made even more difficult by the fact that there is doubt about whether or not they should be considered living.

Structure of Viruses

In size, viruses range from about 17 nanometers (a hemoglobin molecule is 6.4 nanometers in diameter) to about 300 nanometers, larger than small bacteria. The larger ones are at the limits of resolution of the light microscope.

Viruses are made up of nucleic acid, either DNA or RNA, enclosed in a protein coat. The protein coat determines the specificity of the virus; a cell can be infected by a virus only if that type of cell has a receptor site for the virus protein.

Thus cold viruses infect cells in the mucous membranes of the respiratory tract; measles and chicken pox infect skin cells; and polio infects the upper respiratory tract, the intestinal lining, and sometimes nerve cells. Even bacteria, as we noted in Section 3, have their own set of specific viruses, the bacteriophages.

In some virus infections, the protein coat is left outside the cell; in others, the intact virus enters the cell, but once inside, the protein is destroyed by enzymes. The DNA of a DNA-containing virus serves as a template for more viral DNA and also for messenger RNA, which codes for viral enzymes, viral coat protein, and probably, at least in some cases, repressors and other regulatory chemicals.

The virus uses the equipment of the host cell, including ribosomes, transfer RNA molecules, amino acids, and nucleotides. Many viruses use host enzymes as well as those coded for by their own nucleic acids, and some break up host DNA and recycle the nucleotides as viral DNA.

In the case of the RNA viruses, the viral RNA not only serves as a template for more RNA but also acts directly as messenger RNA. As we noted in other chapter of this book, viral RNA can also serve as a template for viral DNA. This phenomenon of reverse transcription is observed almost exclusively with cancer-causing viruses.

Virus particles are assembled within the host cell. They then leave the cell, often lysing the membrane. Some viruses, such as influenza virus, bud off from the host cell membrane and, in so doing, become wrapped in fragments of it. Each new viral particle is capable of setting up a new infective cycle in an uninfected cell.

Origin of Viruses

Are viruses very simple forms of life? Can they give us clues to the nature of a precellular living system of which no fossil is likely to remain? As information increases on the nature of viruses and, in

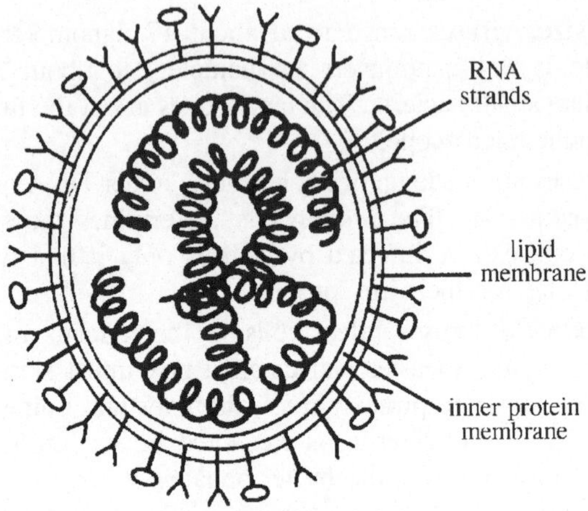

(a)

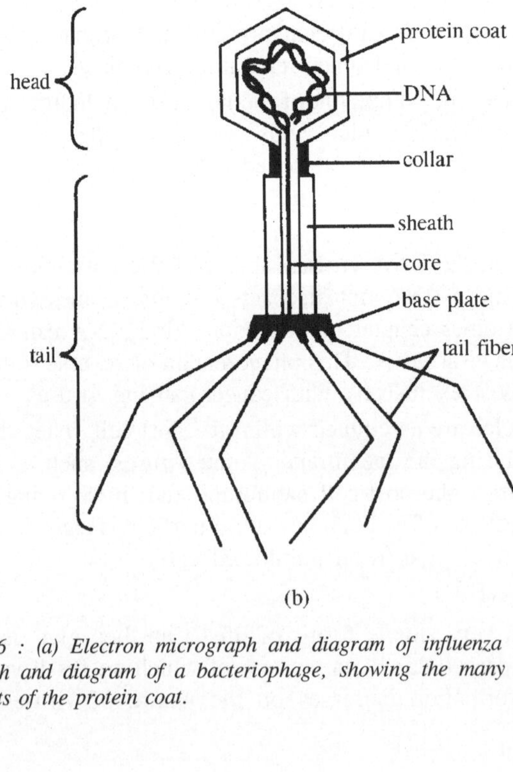

(b)

Figure 7.6 : (a) Electron micrograph and diagram of influenza virus. (b) Electron micrograph and diagram of a bacteriophage, showing the many different structural components of the protein coat.

particular, of their relationships with host cells, this interpretation of viral origins seems less and less likely. Viruses are able to reproduce and to make their protein coats only because they are capable of commandeering the enzymes and other metabolic machinery of the host cell.

Without this machinery, they are as inert as any other macromolecule, lifeless by many criteria. It seems more likely that viruses are cellular fragments that have set up a partially independent existence. S. E. Luria has called viruses "bits of heredity looking for a chromosome."

MICROORGANISM AND HUMAN ECOLOGY

Symbiosis

Symbiosis ("living together") is a close and permanent association between organisms of different species. There are three types of symbiotic relationships. If the relationship is beneficial to both species, it is called *mutualism.* If one species benefits from the association while one is neither harmed nor benefited, it is called commensalism.

If one species benefits and the other is harmed, the relationship is known as *parasitism.* Microorganisms and human beings are often symbionts. When the microorganisms are parasites, they are said to be pathogenic-diseasecausing. The lines of demarcation between the different categories of symbiosis are not clearcut.

A bacterium such as *E. coli,* which lives in the lower intestine, may be commensal, depending on its host for food and shelter and neither helping nor harming. If it produces a needed vitamin or digestive enzyme, the relationship is then mutualistic. If it gets in the bloodstream and causes septicemia (blood poisoning), it is a parasite and a pathogen.

Evolutionary success is measured, as we noted, in terms of surviving progeny. A parasite that destroys its host is less likely to be successful by the evolutionary criterion than one that enjoys a long and comfortable relationship with its protector. Disease is likely to be the result of a sudden change in the parasite, in the host, or in their relationship.

For instant- many persons harbor small numbers of *Mycobacterium tuberculosis* without any symptoms of disease; however, factors such as malnutrition, fatigue, or other diseases may weaken host defenses so that the signs of tuberculosis appear. Similarly, herpes simplex, the virus that causes "cold sores," may remain latent for months or years at a time, with the lesion appearing only in response to some change in the condition of the host.

How Microbes Cause Disease

The pathogenic effects of microbes are produced in a variety of ways. The viruses, as we have seen, enter particular types of cells and often destroy them. Bacteria may produce cell destruction also.

Frequently, however, the effects we recognise as disease are caused not by the direct action of the pathogens but by toxins, or poisons, produced by them. For instance, diphtheria is caused by a bacillus, *Corynebacterium diphtheriae*. The organisms are inhaled and establish infection in the upper respiratory tract.

They do not invade the bloodstream, but the powerful toxin they produce does. (This toxin is made only when the bacterium is harboring a particular prophage.) The toxin is absorbed by the body cells. Under the influence of the toxin, an enzyme involved in the assembly of activated amino acids into polypeptides becomes irreversibly bound to a fragment of NAD^+. The cells can no longer make proteins and so can no longer function.

Some diseases are the result of the body's reaction to the pathogen. In pneumonia caused by *Streptococcus pneumoniae,* the infection causes a tremendous outpouring of fluid and cells into the air sacs of the lungs, thus interfering with respiration. The symptoms caused by fungus infections of the skin similarly result from inflammatory responses.

A single disease agent can cause a variety of diseases. Skin infections *of Streptococcus pyogenes* cause the disease known as impetigo. Throat infections by the same bacteria are the familiar strep throat.

Throat infections with strains of the bacteria that produce toxins (again as a result of a bacteriophage) are known as scarlet fever. Among the persons with untreated strep throat or scarlet fever, about 0.5 percent develop rheumatic fever, which is characterised by inflammatory changes in the joints, heart, and other tissues, apparently as a result of reactions involving the body's own immune system. Conversely, many agents may cause the same symptoms; the "common cold" can result from infection with any one of a large number of viruses.

Prevention and Control of Infectious Disease

Although microorganisms were first seen and depicted with remarkable accuracy by Antony van Leeuwenhoek in the late seventeenth century, they were not generally recognised as a cause of disease until 100 years ago.

The relationship was made clear by the work of Louis Pasteur on disease in silkworms and by Robert Koch, who studied anthrax in sheep and tuberculosis in humans. Recognition of microbes as disease agents opened the way to control measures, among the most important of which were the introduction of sterile procedures in hospitals.

Among the agents spreading bacterial infection were physicians, surgeons, nurses, and hospitals. Childbed fever, for example, once a leading cause of sickness and death among young women, was transmitted almost exclusively by physicians who carried streptococci from patient to patient on their hands or unsterilised instruments.

The battlefields of World War II were the proving grounds for new antimicrobial drugs, such as sulfa and penicillin. These drugs made possible not only treatment of wounds but also the widespread and often life-saving use of major surgery as a treatment for cancer and other diseases. Ironically, with the advent of strains of bacteria resistant to these drugs and endemic in hospitals, the latter are once more becoming reservoirs of serious bacterial diseases.

Even more important than improvement in medical practices was the institution of public health measures, for example, the eradication of fleas, lice, mosquitoes, and other agents that carry disease; disposal of sewage and other wastes; protection of public water supplies; pasteurization of milk; quarantine; and other procedures.

Not long ago, for instance, infant mortality during the first years of life was often as high as 50 percent in some localities owing to infant diarrhea caused by contaminated milk and water.

Many infectious diseases can be prevented by immunization, a practice that dates back to 1796. Observing that persons who had cowpox, a mild disease, did not develop smallpox, Edward Jenner boldly undertook to inoculate healthy people with cowpox. (Cowpox is called vaccinia and hence immunization came to be called vaccination.) We know now that vaccination is effective because the protein coat of the vaccinia virus is similar enough to that of the smallpox virus to stimulate the production of antibodies effective against both viruses.

Immunization procedures have now been developed against a large number of diseases including mumps, measles, German measles, and polio (all virus-caused) and diphtheria, whooping cough, and tetanus (all bacteria-caused). They involve stimulation of the immune system either with a related microorganism (as in smallpox or tuberculosis), with a killed strain (as in the Salk vaccine or typhus vaccine), or with a strain attenuated (weakened) by adaptation to another host (oral polio vaccine, measles, German measles).

In 1935, sulfanilamide, the first of the new "wonder drugs" for the control of bacterial infection, was discovered in Germany, and in 1940 the effects of penicillin were reported from England. Penicillin was the first-discovered antibiotic-by definition, a chemical that is produced by a living organism and is capable of inhibiting the growth of microorganisms.

Many antibiotics are produced by bacteria, especially the actinomycetes; some are formed by fungi. Many, including penicillin, can now be synthesized in the laboratory.

The tremendous decrease in deaths from infectious disease over the last decades is a chief cause of the present population explosion.

8

DIVERSITY OF PROTISTS

The protists are all eukaryotic. Most are unicellular, and those that are not have relatively simple multicellular structures. Apart from these two characteristics, they are an extremely diverse group of organisms. The kingdom includes heterotrophs, among them a number of parasitic forms; photosynthetic autotrophs; and a few versatile organisms that are both heterotrophic and photosynthetic.

Protists are far from simple. Indeed among one major phylum, the Protozoa, are found probably the most complex of all cells, with an astonishing variety of highly specialised structures. That single cells should be so complex is actually not surprising.

Among the protists, each cell is a self-sufficient organism, as capable of meeting all of the requirements of living as a complex, multicellular organism. As their complexity reminds us, modern protists-that is, all protists alive today-are not beginnings. They are in themselves the end products of millions of years of evolution.

Those that have not changed much in that time-amoebas might be an example-have survived over the millennia because they are exquisitely adapted to the environment in which they live. It is all a question of how one measures evolutionary success.

There are eight major phyla of Protista, six of which are algae. Biologists generally agree (1) that the protists represent a number of quite different evolutionary lines, and (2) that all other eukaryotic organisms-fungi, plants, and animals-originated from primitive protists.

PHYLUM PROTOZOA

The Protozoa-"first animals"—are one-celled heterotrophs. Classification of the Protozoa into three of their four major groups is based upon their characteristically different methods of locomotion:

(1) by flagellar movement (the zooflagellates"animal flagellates"- or mastigophores),

(2) by pseudopodia (the sarcodines), and

(3) by ciliary movements (the ciliates).

The fourth major group, the sporozoans, are nonmotile during the major phases of their lives and all are parasites.

Protozoa usually reproduce asexually, by mitosis. Many also have sexual cycles, involving meiosis and the fusion of gametes, or *syngamy*. (Syngamy in animals is usually referred to as fertilization.) The fusion of gametes results in a diploid *(2n)* zygote.

The zygote is often a thick-walled, resistant resting cell, formed during periods of cold or drought. Some protozoa, notably the ciliates, have a special type of sexuality involving exchanges of genetic material between individuals.

Table 8.1: The Kingdom Protista.

Phylum Protozoa	Unicellular heterotrophs, including flagellates (mastigophores), amoeba-like organisms (sarcodines), ciliates, and sporozoans
Phylum Euglenophyta	Euglena and related algae, all unicellular, mostly freshwater
Phylum Chrysophyta	Diatoms and related algae, all unicellular, mostly marine
Phylum Pyrrophyta	Dinoflagellates and related algae, all unicellular, marine and freshwater
Phylum Chlorophyta	Green algae, including unicellular, colonial, and multicellular forms; mostly freshwater
Phylum Phaeophyta	Brown algae, including the kelps, all multicellular, almost all marine
Phylum Rhodophyta	Red algae, all multicellular, mostly marine
Phylum Gymnomycota	Slime molds

Class Mastigophora

The zooflagellates are regarded as the most primitive of the Protozoa. They are thought to have been derived from photosynthetic flagellated cells, such as *Euglena,* that lost their chloroplasts. Almost all of the smaller cells have one or two flagella, and larger cells frequently have many flagella. These flagella have the characteristic 9 + 2 structure. The zooflagellates multiply asexually by mitosis and cell division, and, in some forms, sexually, by syngamy.

They generally have no outer wall, and some are able to form pseudopodia, temporary extensions of the cell body that are used in locomotion and in engulfing food particles. Most are free-living, but some are parasitic.

The latter include *Trypanosoma* gambiense, a flagellate that causes African sleeping sickness, and members of the genus *Trichonympha,* complex and beautiful flagellates that live as symbionts in the digestive tracts of termites, where they digest the wood ingested by the termite.

Class Sarcodina

The sarcodines include amoebas and their relatives. They have no coat or wall outside their cell membranes and generally move and feed by the formation of pseudopodia. They take their name from the word "sarcode," coined in the early nineteenth century to describe the "simple, glutinous, and homogeneous jelly" of which, at one time, simple cells were thought to be composed.

Despite their uncomplicated appearance, they are complex cells and are even capable of some complex behaviour patterns, as when sensing and pursuing prey organisms.

Sarcodines are thought to have originated from mastigophores; some sarcodines may develop flagella during particular stages of their life cycle or under particular environmental conditions. They are found in both fresh water and salt water. Some are parasites, such as those that cause amoebic dysentery.

Reproduction may be asexual or sexual. Asexual reproduction takes place by cell division accompanied by mitosis in which the nuclear envelope usually does not break down. In sexual reproduction, the cells, which are diploid, undergo meiosis, forming gametes, which then fuse to form zygotes.

Many of the sarcodines have outer shells, often brightly coloured. Some, like *Arcella,* secrete a hard, keratinlike material, while others, like *Difflugia,* exude a sticky organic substance upon which forms a sort of haphazard mosaic made up of specks of sand and bits of the discarded shells of other minute creatures.

Such shells presumably evolved as defenses against predators. Some, the "sun animals," resemble pincushions, with fine pseudopodia stiffened with microtubules radiating from their bodies. *Actinospherium,* the protozoan shown in Figure elsewhere in this chapter, may reach as much as a millimeter in diameter and may sometimes be seen as a tiny white speck floating on the surface of a pond.

Other sarcodines, the Foraminifera, have snail-like shells and live in the sea. Their shells are made of calcium carbonate, extracted from the sea water. The white cliffs of Dover and similar chalky deposits throughout the world are the result of the long accumulation of these discarded shells.

The shells of the Foraminifera have been accumulating on the ocean bottom for millions of years, and in many areas, as a result of geologic changes, thick deposits of their skeletons (the foraminiferan ooze) can be found on the surface of the land or under later rock formations.

Since the skeletons have evolved over this long period of time, it is possible to date a particular stratum by the type of Foraminifera that it contains, a fact that has proved of immense practical value in locating oil-bearing strata in Texas, Oklahoma, and many other oil-rich areas.

Class Ciliophora

The ciliophores, or ciliates, are the most highly specialised and complicated of the Protozoa, and indeed probably represent the most complex of all living cells. They are believed to have been derived from primitive mastigophores, which, traveling in the opposite evolutionary direction from the sarcodines, developed elaborate ciliary systems.

They are characterised by 9 + 2 cilia. In some species, the cilia adhere to each other in rows, forming brushlike structures called membranelles or clumps of cilia called cirri, which can be used for walking or jumping.

Cilia, membranelles, and cirri move in a coordinated fashion, although the way in which they are coordinated is not understood. Some ciliates also have myonemes, contractile threads. All have a complex skin, the cortex, which includes the cell membrane. In some groups, the cortex contains small barbs known as trichocysts, which are discharged when the cell is stimulated in certain ways.

The ciliates have another unusual feature: They have two kinds of nuclei, micronuclei and macronuclei. One or more of each kind is present in all cells. They also have a complex system for exchange of genetic information, in which cells conjugate and the micronuclei undergo meiosis.

Cells then exchange haploid micronuclei that fuse, so that each cell has a new diploid micronucleus, which then divides. The old macronucleus

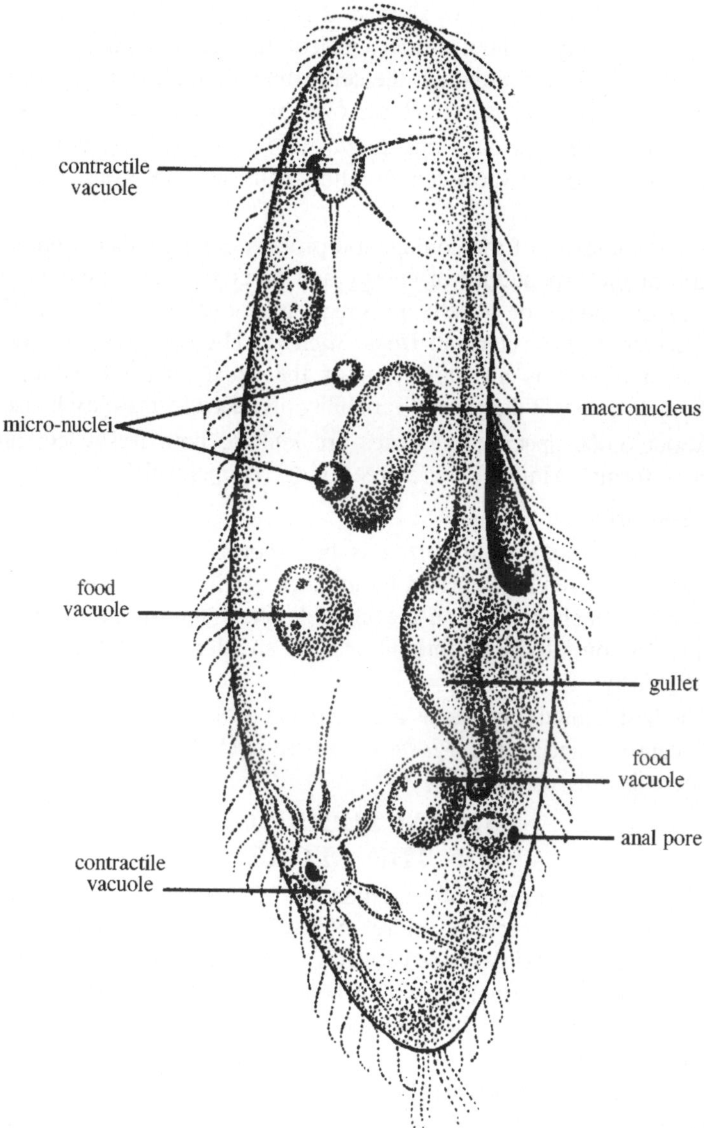

Figure 8.1 : Drawing of a Paramecium, a ciliate.

dissolves, and a new macronucleus develops from one of the new micronuclei. The macronucleus in certain ciliates contains 50 to 100 times as much DNA as the micronucleus and so is believed to represent multiple copies of it.

This view is supported by the fact that, in many ciliates, a cell can survive indefinitely without a micronucleus if even a small portion of a macronucleus is left, although the cell cannot conjugate. However, it cannot live without a macronucleus, even if it has a micronucleus.

The macronucleus does not divide mitotically but is apportioned approximately equally between dividing cells as they constrict and separate.

The complexity of the conjugation process among ciliates reminds us again of the expenditure of energy and other resources involved in effecting exchanges of genetic information among individuals of the same species, from bacteria to *Homo sapiens*. The high biological cost of these activities is an indication of the great survival value, in evolutionary terms, of the genetic variability produced by these exchanges.

About 6,000 species of ciliates are known, both freshwater and saltwater forms. Almost all are free-living (nonparasitic).

Class Sporozoa

The fourth class of Protozoa is the Sporozoa, all of which are parasitic. They are characterised by the lack of cilia or flagella in adult forms and by their complex life cycles. A single sporozoan undergoes multiple fission, dividing into numerous smaller cells (the spores) simultaneously.

The best known sporozoans are members of the genus *Plasmodium,* which cause malaria. The *Plasmodium* life cycle is shown in Figure elsewhere in this chapter.

CHARACTERISTICS OF THE ALGAE

Among the eukaryotic algae, a number of distinct lines had evolved by the early Paleozoic era, more than 450 million years ago. The approximately 22,000 described species now in existence are grouped into six phyla. The term "algae" has been abandoned as a formal term in modern classification, because the various groups are not directly related to one another.

Three of these phyla—the Euglenophyta, the Chrysophyta, and the Pyrrophyta-consist almost entirely of unicellular organisms. The other three phyla-Chlorophyta, Rhodophyta, and Phaeophyta-include groups that are multicellular. Nearly all members of these phyla are photosynthetic.

In general, they all have a relatively simple structure, which may be a single cell, a filament of cells, a plate of cells, or a solid body

Table 8.2 : Comparative Summary of Characteristics in the Six Major Phyla of Eukaryotic Algae

Phylum	*Number of Species*	*Photosynthetic Pigments*	*Food Reserve*	*Flagella*	*Cell Wall Component*	*Remarks*
Euglenophyta (euglenoids)	800	Chlorophyll *a* and *b*, c arotenoids	Paramylum and fats	1, 2, or 3 per cell, apical	No cell wall	All unicellular, most freshwater; sexual reproduction unknown
Chrysophyta (golden-brown algae and diatoms)	6,000-10,000	Chlorophyll *a*, and often c, carotenoids, including fucoxanthin	Leucosin and oils	1 or 2, apical, equal or unequal	Pectic compounds with siliceous material	Most marine
Pyrrophyta (dinoflagellates)	1,100	Chlorophyll *a* and c, carotenoids	Starch and oils	2, lateral	Cellulose	Marine and fresh water; sexual reproduction rare
Chlorophyta (green algae)	7,000	Chlorophyll *a* and *b*, c arotenoids	Starch identical	Usually 2 per cell,	Cellulose	Mostly fresh water, but some marine

(Table Contd.)

Phylum	Number of Species	Photosynthetic Pigments	Food Reserve	Flagella	Cell Wall Component	Remarks
Phaeophyta (brown algae)	1,500	Chlorophyll *a* and c, carotenoids, including fucoxanthin	Laminarin and fats	2, lateral, in reproductive only	Cellulose and cells algin	Almost all marine, flourish in cold ocean waters
Rhodophyta (red algae)	4,000	Chlorophyll *a*, carotenoids, phycobilins, chlorophyll *d* in some	Floridean starch	None	Cellulose, pectic materials common, xylan in *Porphyra*	Mostly marine, some freshwater; complex sexual cycle; many species tropical

more or less comparable to that found in the vascular plants. The cell walls of algae, in general, have a cellulose matrix, often with massive amounts of other polysaccharides that give certain algae a mucilaginous consistency.

When algal cells divide, the cell membranes generally pinch inward from the margin of the cell (furrowing), just as in animals, fungi, and protozoa. However, cell plates, like those of plants, are formed during cell division in one brown alga and a few green algae. Most algal cells-except those of the red algaehave centrioles.

The phyla of algae differ from one another widely in the nature of their flagella (when present) and in their biochemical characteristics, especially with respect to differences in pigmentation, nature of reserve food, and cell wall components.

The names of some phyla are derived from the colours of the predominant accessory pigments, which mask the bright green of the chlorophylls. A wide variety of carotenoids is found in the algae. The xanthophylls are yellowishbrown carotenoids; the xanthophyll fucoxanthin gives the brown algae their characteristic colour and name.

It is also found in the golden-brown algae and diatoms (phylum Chrysophyta). The red algae (Rhodophyta) owe their colours to several kinds of phycobilins, accessory pigments that, unlike the carotenoids, are water-soluble. In the green algae the colour of the chlorophylls is usually not masked by accessory pigments.

The diversity of pigments present in the chloroplasts of the various phyla of algae suggests that (1) various types of oxygenproducing prokaryotes were in existence prior to the development of eukaryotic cells, and (2) the various phyla of algae may have evolved as a result of the establishment of symbiotic relationships with different photosynthetic prokaryotes, which then evolved into modern chloroplasts.

A rich diversity of storage products is found in the different phyla

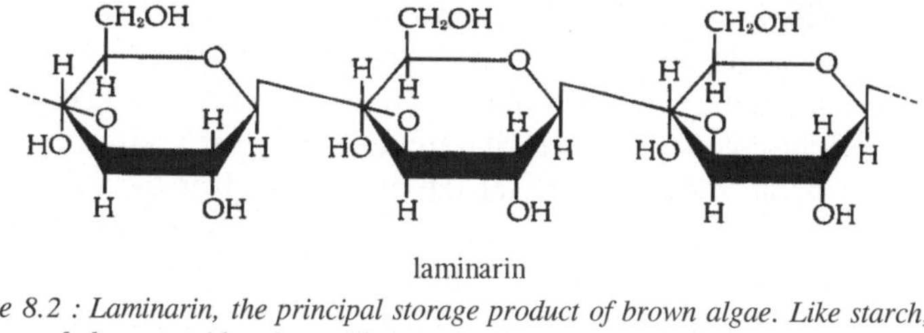

laminarin

Figure 8.2 : Laminarin, the principal storage product of brown algae. Like starch, it is made up of glucose residues but unlike starch, there are only about 15 to 30 glucose units per molecule, and their linkage is different.

of algae, with most having distinctive carbohydrate food reserves, often in addition to lipids. The green algae and dinoflagellates store their carbohydrates as starch, as do vascular plants. In the brown algae, another glucose polymer, laminarin, takes the place of starch. The carbohydrate reserves of the red algae are biochemically similar to starch.

Unicellular Algae

These minute photosynthesizing cells are usually found floating near the surface of the oceans and inland waters. Together with small invertebrates and immature forms of larger animals they form the *plankton* (from *planktos,* the Greek word for wanderer). Each cell is a totally self-sufficient individual, dependent only on light from the sun and carbon dioxide and minerals from the water that surrounds it.

These cells may live in colonies, and sometimes the cells of a single colony may be attached to one another as the gliding bacteria, for instance, are held together by such sticky secretions, but there is no division of labor among the cells. There are, as we noted, three principal phyla of these unicellular forms.

Phylum Euglenophyta

Euglenophyta is a small group of unicellular organisms (about 800 species), most of which are found in fresh water. They are named for the genus *Euglena,* the most common of the group. Characteristically, they have one or two flagella. Their chloroplasts contain chlorophylls *a* and *b* like those of plants.

They store their food as paramylum, an unusual polysaccharide found almost exclusively in this group. The cells lack a cell wall but have a flexible series of protein strips, which make up the pellicle, inside the cell membrane. They reproduce asexually, dividing longitudinally to form two new cells that are mirror images of one another.

The cells are complex. *Euglena is* characteristically an elongated cell with a single nucleus, two flagella (one of which is small and inactive), and numerous small emerald-green chloroplasts that give the cell its bright colour. The flagella are attached at the base of a flask-shaped opening, the reservoir, at the anterior end of the cell.

Emptying into the reservoir is the contractile vacuole, which collects excess water from all parts of the cell and discharges it into the reservoir. Unlike the stiff walls of the cells of plants, the flexible pellicle permits *Euglena* to change its shape, providing an alternative

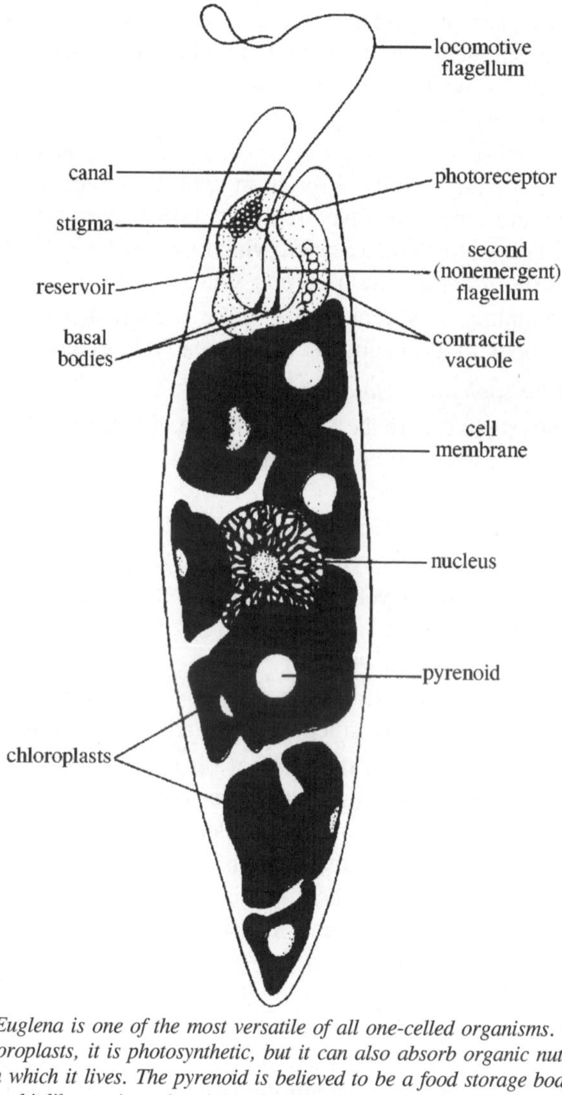

Figure 8.3 : Euglena is one of the most versatile of all one-celled organisms. Containing numerous chloroplasts, it is photosynthetic, but it can also absorb organic nutrients from the medium in which it lives. The pyrenoid is believed to be a food storage body. Euglena moves by the whiplike motion of a single flagellum.

means of locomotion-wriggling-for mud-dwelling forms. Only a few other photosynthetic organisms have contractile vacuoles, which are common features among the protozoans.

If one leaves a culture of *Euglena* near a sunny window, a clearly visible green cloud will form in the water, and this will move as the light changes. *Euglena is* probably able to orient with respect to light because of a pair of special structures: the stigma, or eyespot, which is a patch of pigment, and an underlying photoreceptor. The exact way in which these function is not known.

Some nonphotosynthetic protists-members of the genus *Peranema,* for example-closely resemble *Euglena* but lack chloroplasts. In fact, if some strains of *Euglena* are kept at an appropriate temperature and in a rich medium, the cells may replicate faster than the chloroplasts, producing nonphotosynthetic cells, which can survive indefinitely in a suitable medium containing a carbon source.

It is tempting to speculate that some modern heterotrophs' arose from autotrophs in an analogous manner early in evolutionary history.

Phylum Chrysophyta: "Golden" Algae

The chrysophytes are the "golden" algae. There are 6,000 to 10,000 species, most of which are diatoms. Members of this group have several identifying characteristics:

(1) Their photosynthetic pigments are chlorophyll *a* and chlorophyll c, which closely resembles the chlorophyll *b* of plants;

(2) they contain a yellow-brown carotenoid, fucoxanthin, which functions as an accessory pigment and gives them their characteristic colour;

(3) their cell walls, which contain no cellulose, are often impregnated with silicon compounds and thus are very rigid;

(4) they store food in the form of oil rather than starch. Because of these oil reserves, fresh water containing large numbers of these algae may have an unpleasant oily taste, as may fish caught in such waters. It has, in fact, been suggested that golden algae might be a potential source of oil for fuel. They are a major component of plankton.

Diatoms are enclosed in a fine double shell, the two halves of which fit together, one on top of the other, like a carved pillbox. Electron microscopy has shown that the fine tracings in diatom shells actually represent minute, intricately shaped pores or passageways connecting the protoplasm within the cell to the exterior environment.

The piled-up silicon shells of diatoms, which have collected over millions of years, form the fine, crumbly substance known as "diatomaceous earth," used as an abrasive in silver polish and toothpaste and for filtering and insulating materials.

Some other members of the phylum lack cell walls and are amoeboid. Except for the presence of chloroplasts, the amoeboid cells are indistinguishable from amoeboid protozoans (the sarcodines), and the two groups may be closely related. Reproduction usually takes place by mitosis, but zygotes are sometimes formed. Diatoms are diploid, except for the gametes.

Phylum Pyrrophyta: "Fire" Algae

The Pyrrophyta is also largely composed of single-celled algae, the dinoflagellates ("spinning flagellates"), of which about 1,000 different species are known, almost all of them marine forms. Like the diatoms, they are important components of the phytoplankton. Other members of the phylum are heterotrophs clearly related to the photosynthetic forms.

The dinoflagellates usually have two flagella that beat within grooves: one encircling the body like a belt and a second lying perpendicular to the first. The beating of the flagella in their respective grooves causes the cells to spin like tops as they move through the water.

Many of the dinoflagellates are bizarre in appearance, with a stiff cellulose wall (theca), which often looks like a strange helmet or an ancient coat of armor.

These dinoflagellates are often red in colour (hence the name of the phylum), and the infamous red tides, in which thousands of fish die, are caused by great blooms of red dinoflagellates. The poison in these red tides has been traced to one species of armored dinoflagellate, *Gonyaulax catanella*. It is such an extraordinarily powerful nerve toxin that 1 gram of it would be enough to kill 5 million mice in 15 minutes.

Blooms of *Gonyaulax catanella* appear regularly on the Pacific Coast and the Gulf of Mexico and have recently been reported off the New England coast. Mussels ingest the algae and concentrate the poison; the mussels then become dangerous for consumption by vertebrates. Many dinoflagellates are bioluminescent.

Multicellular Algae

The multicellular algae are adapted to living in shallow waters and along the shores. Here the waters are usually richer in nutrients, leached from the land or swept up in currents from the deeper waters. Living conditions are otherwise often more difficult, however. Along a rocky shore, for instance, multicellular algae-the seaweeds-are subject to great fluctuations of humidity, temperature, salinity, and light; to the pounding of the surf; and to the abrasive action of sand particles churned up by the waves.

Life close to the shore is also more crowded and competitive. Under these pressures, different groups of algae become specialists at exploiting particular areas along the tidal shores. The result is the zonation of life forms visible in many coastal areas.

Phylum Chlorophyta: Green Algae

The green algae are the most diverse of all the algae, comprising at least 7,000 species. Although most green algae are aquatic, others occur in a wide variety of habitats, including the melting surface of snow, as green patches on tree trunks, and as symbionts in lichens, protozoans, and invertebrates.

Of the aquatic species, a few groups are entirely marine, but the great majority are found in fresh water. Many green algae are microscopic. *Chlamydomonas*, visible only as a fleck of green under the light microscope, is a chlorophyte. Some of the marine forms are large; *Codium magnum* in the Gulf of Mexico, for example, sometimes attains a breadth of 25 centimeters and a length of more than 8 meters.

Some forms, such as *Valonia,* have many nuclei within a common cytoplasm. This type of organisation is neither truly unicellular nor multicellular but is known as *coenocytic,* pronounced see-no-sit-ik (from the Greek *koinos,* "shared in common"). The Fungi, as we shall see, are almost completely coenocytic.

The chlorophytes are of interest to students of evolution because, whereas the three phyla previously discussed contain only unicellular forms and the members of the two phyla that follow are strictly multicellular, the Chlorophyta have members of both types.

The Volvocine Line

One pathway leading to increased complexity is called the volvocine line, after one of its more spectacular members, *Volvox*. It is based on the cohesion of Chlamydomonas-like cells in motile colonies. Cellular colonies differ from multicellular organisms in that in colonies, the individual cells preserve a high degree of independent function.

The cells are connected by cytoplasmic strands, which integrate the colony sufficiently that it may be regarded as a single organism. The simplest member of the volvocine line is *Gonium*. The Gonium colony consists of 4 to 32 separate cells (depending on the species) arranged in a shield-shaped disk.

The flagella of each cell beat separately, pulling the entire colony forward. Each cell in Gonium divides to produce an entire new colony. A closely related colonial organism is *Pandorina,* which consists of 16 or 32 cells in a tightly packed ovoid or ellipsoid shape. The colony is polar, that is, one end is different from the other: The eyespots are larger in the cells at one pole of the colony. Each cell has two flagella, and because all the flagella point outward, *Pandorina* rolls through the water like a ball.

When the cells attain their maximum size, the colony sinks to the bottom, and each of the cells divides to form a daughter colony. The parent colony then breaks open like Pandora's box (which suggested its name), releasing new daughter colonies.

Volvox, from which the group gets its name, is a hollow sphere that is made up, according to species, of a single layer of 500 to 50,000 tiny biflagellate cells. The flagella of each cell beat in such a way as to turn the entire colony around its axis, spinning it majestically through the water.

Volvox orients its anterior end toward the light but moves away from light that is too strong. Most of the cells are vegetative and do not take part in reproduction. For reasons that are not entirely understood, only some of the cells of the lower hemisphere can form daughter colonies; in other words, there is some specialisation of function.

These cells, which appear identical to others in the young colony, become larger, greener, and morphologically distinct as the colony matures. Then they enlarge and divide, forming new spheres of hundreds or thousands of cells. Daughter colonies remain inside the mother colony until the mother colony eventually breaks apart.

Thus, in these four extant genera of chlorophytes, *Chlamydomonas, Gonium, Pandorina,* and *Volvox,* there is a steady progression in size and complexity and also a trend toward specialisation of function.

The plants are believed to have originated among the Chlorophyta. Evidence for this theory includes the fact that both the chlorophytes and all plants, but no other groups of algae, contain chlorophylls *a* and b and beta-carotene as their photosynthetic pigments and store their foods as starch. All also have cell walls of cellulose.

The chlorophytes will be discussed further in other chapter of this book, in relation to plant evolution.

Phylum Phaeophyta: Brown Algae

The brown algae are the principal seaweeds of temperate and polar regions. An almost exclusively marine group, they dominate the rocky shores throughout the cooler regions of the world, and some, like the kelps, often form extensive beds offshore.

One species of brown alga, *Sargassum nitans,* is a major component of the dense floating masses of seaweeds that cover the Sargasso Sea, an area of more than 5 million square kilometers, reaching from the Bahamas to the Azores.

The brown algae contain chlorophylls *a* and c and fucoxanthin, as do the Chrysophyta. They differ from most plants in that they store their food as an unusual polysaccharide (laminarin), or sometimes as oil, but never as starch, as do green algae and plants. Their cell walls contain cellulose.

The brown algae are often very large, and many have a variety of specialised tissues. Some of the giant kelps are nearly 60 meters long;

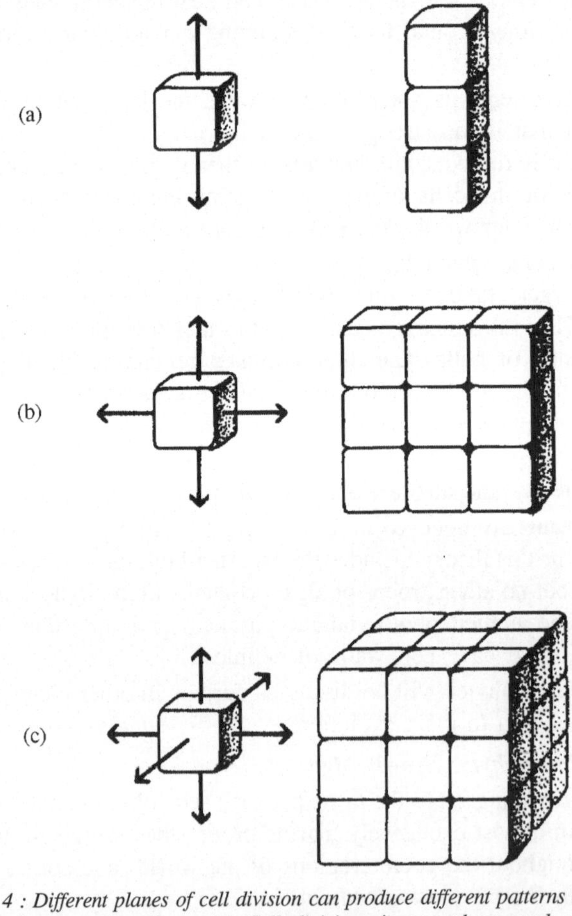

Figure 8.4 : Different planes of cell division can produce different patterns of growth, all represented among the algae. (a) Cell divisions in one plane produce a filament. (b) Divisions in two planes produce a one-celled layer. (c) Divisions in three planes produce a three-dimensional solid body. The arrows indicate the direction of growth.

these are annuals, reaching their full size in a single season. The body of an alga (or a plant) that is multicellular, but relatively unspecialised, is known as a *thallus*. In some kelps, the thallus is well differentiated into *holdfast ("root"), stipe* ("stalk"), and *blade ("leaf")*.

The words are put into quotation marks because, although the corresponding parts of the alga superficially resemble the organs of plants, they are not really comparable in their internal organisation. However, the kelps have strands of elongated conducting cells in the center of the stipe that are similar to the cells that conduct sugars in the vascular plants.

Carbohydrates produced in the blades, which are exposed to sunlight, are thus transported to the stipe and holdfast, which may be far below the surface of the water. There are no modern unicellular forms in this group, except for the gametes. Sperm and spore cells are often flagellated.

Phylum Rhodophyta: Red Algae

The red algae are most commonly found in warm marine waters; they make up the other principal group of large seaweeds. The red algae contain chlorophylls *a* and *d,* carotenoids, and also certain phycobilins, which give them their distinctive colours. (Phycobilins and chlorophyll a are also found in the blue-green "algae," and it is believed that the modern blue-greens and the chloroplasts of the red algae are related.)

Most of the seaweeds of the world are red algae, of which there are some 4,000 species. Less than 2 percent are freshwater forms. Red algae usually grow attached to rocks and other algae; there are no large red algae capable of prolonged life in the floating state, like the sargasso weed of the Sargasso Sea. (They die when floating because the water must pass over them for adequate gas exchange; without it, they suffocate.)

As you would expect from their red colour, which indicates that they absorb blue light, some grow at greater depths than other algae; they have been found attached 175 meters below the ocean surface in the clear water of the tropics. Although some are several meters long, red algae never attain the size of the largest of the brown algae. They have a reproductive pattern in which neither of the gametes is motile; the male is carried to the fixed female reproductive cell by the movement of the water. They are one of the few groups of organisms that have no flagellated cells; they also lack centrioles.

PHYLUM GYMNOMYCOTA: SLIME MOLDS

The slime molds are a group of curious organisms classified with the protists-although some of them are multicellular in some stages-because of their similarity to protozoans, especially the amoebas. Two main groups (classes) are known, the plasmodial slime molds (Myxomycetes) and the cellular slime molds (Acrasiomycetes).

Most slime molds live in cool, shady, moist places in the woods-on decaying logs, dead leaves, or other damp organic matter. One of the common species *(Physarum cinereum),* however, is sometimes found creeping across city lawns. The plasmodia come in a variety of colours and can be spectacularly beautiful.

The function of the pigments is not known with certainty, but they are probably photoreceptors because only slime molds with pigmented plasmodia require light for spore production.

During their nonreproductive stages, the Myxomycetes, or "true" slime molds, are thin, streaming masses of protoplasm, which creep along in amoeboid fashion. As one of these plasmodia travels, it engulfs bacteria, yeast, fungal spores, and small particles of decayed plant and animal matter, which it digests.

It may grow to weigh as much as 50 grams or more, and, since slime molds are spread thinly, this mass can cover an area more than a meter in diameter. The plasmodium is coenocytic, and as it grows, the nuclei divide repeatedly and, in the early stages, synchronously.

Plasmodial growth continues as long as an adequate food supply and moisture are available. When either of these is in short supply, the plasmodium separates into many mounds of protoplasm, each of which develops into a mature sporangium (a structure in which spores develop) borne at the tip of a stalk.

Meiosis takes place and cell walls form around the individual haploid nuclei to produce spores, which are resistant resting forms. The spores germinate under favourable conditions, and each spore, depending on the species, produces one to four haploid, flagellated cells. Some of these cells fuse to form a zygote, from which a new plasmodium develops.

The life cycle of an Acrasiomycetes, or cellular slime mold, is shown on page 121. These slime molds also begin as amoebalike organisms but differ from the plasmodial slime molds in that the amoebas, on swarming together, do not lose their cell membranes but retain their identity as individual cells.

9

Diversity of Fungi

The fungi are a group of organisms so unlike any others that, although they were long classified with the plants, it has come to seem appropriate to assign them to a separate kingdom. Except for some one-celled forms, such as the yeasts, the fungi are basically coenocytic organisms composed of masses of filaments.

A fungal filament is called a *hypha,* and all the hyphae of a single organism are collectively called a *mycelium.* The mycelium may appear as a mass on the surface of the nutrient or may be hidden beneath the surface. A fungus is essentially a multinucleate mass of cytoplasm enclosed within a rigid, much-branched system of tubes (the hyphae). The cytoplasm, organelles, and nuclei flow within those tubes.

A mycelium normally arises by the germination and outgrowth of a single cell, with growth taking place only at the tips of hyphae. The complex, spore-producing structures of fungi, such as mushrooms, are tightly packed hyphae.

In most groups of fungi, the cell walls are composed primarily of chitin, a polysaccharide that is never found in the kingdom Plantae (it is, however, the principal component of the exoskeletons-the hard outer coverings-of insects).

In some groups, the hyphae are septate-divided by cell walls-but the walls, or septa, are perforated, and the cytoplasm and even the nuclei are able to flow through the septa. Only the reproductive structures are separated by cell membranes.

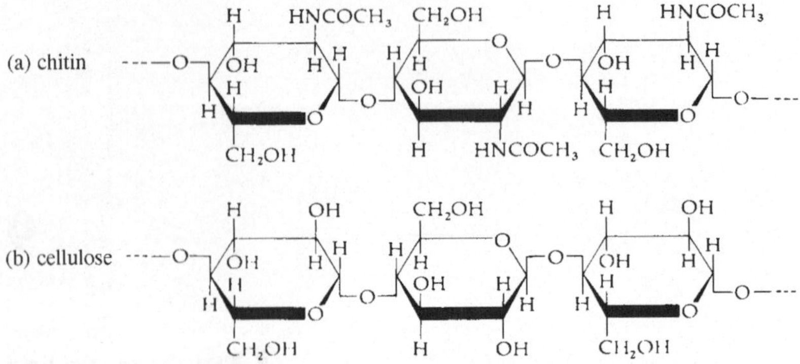

Figure 9.1 : Fungal cell walls characteristically contain chitin (a) rather than cellulose (b), the polysaccharide found in the cell walls of plants. Chitin resembles cellulose in that it is tough, inflexible, and insoluble in water. As you can see, they are also structurally very similar; in chitin, the hydroxyl (OH) group in the 2 position is replaced by a nitrogen-containing group.

All fungi are heterotrophs with a highly characteristic means of nutrition. Because of their filamentous form, each fungal cell is no more than a few micrometers from the soil, water, or other substance in which the fungus lives, and is separated from it only by a thin cell wall. Because of their rigid walls, fungi are unable to engulf small microorganisms or other particles.

They obtain food by absorbing dissolved inorganic and organic materials. Typically a fungus will secrete digestive enzymes onto a food source and then absorb the smaller molecules released.

The only motile cells of fungi are reproductive cells which may travel through water or air. Growth of the mycelium substitutes for motility, bringing the organism into contact with new food sources and different mating strains.

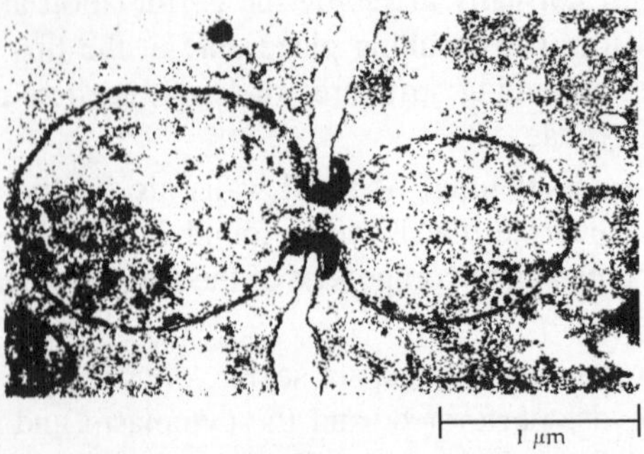

Figure 9.2 : The perforated cross wall of a fungus showing a nucleus in the perforation. The fungus is Neurospora crassa, the red bread mold.

Under favourable conditions, a fungus can expand very rapidly, as evidenced by the overnight appearance of a lawnful of mushrooms, produced by the sudden transport of material from the underground mycelium into the fruiting bodies, or mushrooms.

The fungi, together with the bacteria, are the principal decomposers of the world. As we shall see in other section, their activities are as vital to the continued survival of higher forms of life as are those of the food producers.

Some are also destructive; they may interfere with human activities by attacking our foodstuffs, our domestic plants and animals, our shelter, our clothing, and even our persons.

REPRODUCTION IN THE FUNGI

Fungi reproduce both asexually and sexually. Asexual reproduction takes place either by the fragmentation of the mycelium (with each fragment becoming a new individual) or by the production of spores. In some of the fungi, spores are produced in reproductive structures called *sporangia,* and are borne on specialised hyphae called *sporangiophores.* Spores are often, but not necessarily, resting forms, surrounded by a tough, resistant wall.

They are able to survive during periods of lack of water and extreme temperatures. Some airborne spores are very small and so can remain suspended in the air for long periods and be carried for great distances. Often the sporangia are raised above the mycelium by the sporangiophores; thus the spores are easily caught up and transported by air currents.

The bright colours and powdery textures associated with many particular types of molds are produced by the spores.

Sexual reproduction can occur in a variety of ways: (1) by fusion of gametes, (2) by penetration of a gamete into a specialised reproductive structure called a *ganwtangium,* or (3) by fusion of gametangia.

Sometimes the fusion of fungal hyphae is not followed immediately by the fusion of nuclei. Thus strains of fungi may exist with two genetically distinct kinds of nuclei operating simultaneously. Such a combination, known as *dikaryosis, is* found uniquely among the higher fungi (Ascomycetes and Basidiomycetes).

PHYLUM MYCOTA

The kingdom Fungi consists of only one phylum, Mycota, which is divided into five principal classes: Oomycetes, Zygomycetes, Ascomycetes, Basidiomycetes, and Fungi Imperfecti.

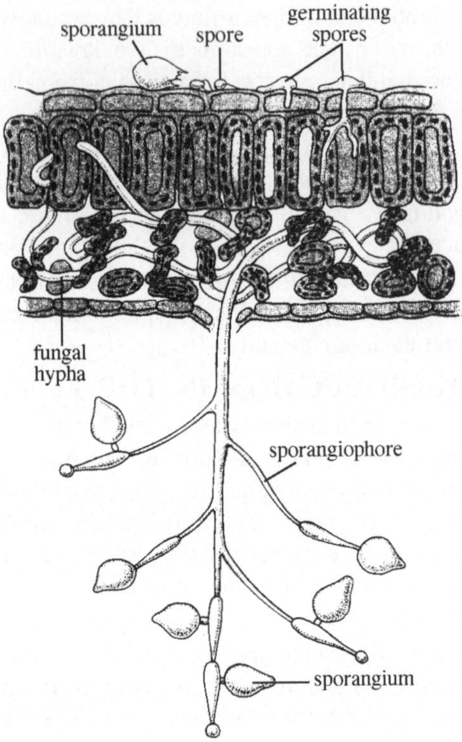

Figure 9.3 : Phytophthora infestans, cause of potato blight. Infection begins when an airborne sporangium alights on a leaf, releasing spores that move about in the film of water on the leaf's surface.

Class Oomycetes

The oomycetes are also known as the water molds because many of them are aquatic. They are the only group of fungi that produce flagellated, swimming spores. Even the terrestrial forms produce swimming spores that require free water.

Most oomycetes are saprobes, living on dead organic matter. Some forms are parasitic and pathogenic, however, and, as mycologist C. J. Alexopoulos has said, "At least two of them have had a hand-or should we say a hypha!—in shaping the economic history of an important portion of mankind."

The first of these is *Phytophthora infestans* (*phytophthora* literally means "plant destroyer"), the cause of the "late blight" of potatoes, which produced the great potato famines in Ireland. The second economically important member of this group is *Plasmopara viticola,* the cause of downy mildew of grapes. This mildew threatened the entire French wine industry during the latter part of the nineteenth century.

The oomycetes derive their name from *oion,* the Greek word for "egg." They are the only group of fungi in which the gametes are clearly male (sperm) and female (egg). They are also the only group of fungi with cellulose rather than chitin in their cell walls. Sperm and eggs, each of which are borne in their own type of gametangia, fuse to produce a zygote.

Class Zygomycetes

The zygomycetes are terrestrial fungi, most of which live in the soil, feeding on dead plant or animal matter. Some are parasites of plants, insects, or small soil animals. Unlike oomycetes, they produce no flagellated spores at any stage of the life cycle. In sexual reproduction, they produce zygospores, which are thickwalled, resistant spores that develop from a zygote.

One of the most common members of this class is *Rhizopus stolonifer,* the black bread mold. Infection begins when a spore germinates on the surface of bread, fruit, or some other organic matter and forms hyphae. Some of the hyphae extend rootlike anchoring structures, called *rhizoids.* The rhizoids secrete digestive enzymes and absorb dissolved organic materials. Other specialised hyphae, the sporangiophores, push up into the air, and sporangia form on their tips. As the

sporangia mature, they become black, giving the mold its characteristic colour. They eventually break open, releasing numerous airborne spores, each of which can germinate to produce a new mycelium.

Sexual reproduction in *Rhizopus* occurs when the specialised hyphae of two different mating strains meet and fuse, attracted toward one another by hormones that diffuse in the form of gases. The two strains are designated plus (+) and minus (-), since there are no morphological differences between them on which to base male and female designations.

Septa, or cross walls, form behind the tips of the touching hyphae; the two tip cells thus formed are gametangia, one containing numerous + nuclei, the other containing numerous - nuclei. Two gametangia fuse, and the two types of nuclei then fuse, producing a diploid nucleus. The resulting multinucleate cell, the zygote, then forms a hard, warty wall and becomes dormant.

During this dormant stage, it can survive periods of extreme heat or cold or desiccation. At the end of dormancy, only one diploid nucleus remains, and this undergoes meiosis when the zygote germinates. Only one of the four nuclei produced by meiosis generally survives. It commonly

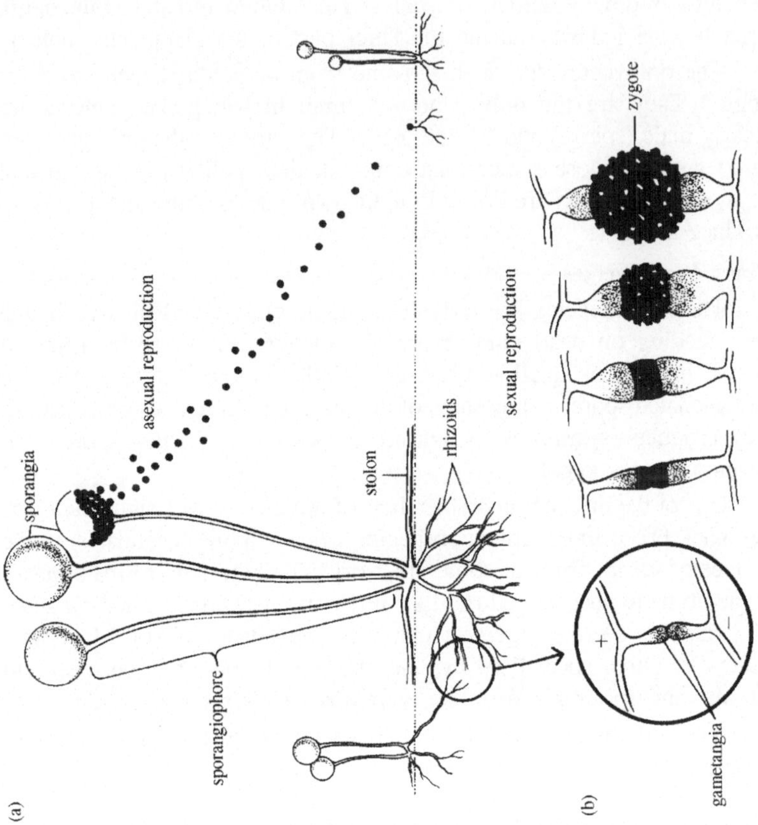

Figure 9.4 : Asexual and sexual reproduction in Rhizopus. The mold consists of branched hyphae, including rhizoids, which anchor the mycelium; stolons, which run aboveground; and sporangiophores.

gives rise to a sporangiophore, from which airborne spores are released.

Class Ascomycetes

The ascomycetes are the largest class of fungi (about 30,000 species), including the yeasts and powdery mildews, many of the common black and blue-green molds, and the morels and truffles prized by gourmets.

Members of this group of fungi are the cause of many plant diseases, such as chestnut blight and Dutch elm disease, and are the source of many of the antibiotics. The red bread mold *Neurospora,* which played a major role in the history of modern genetics, is an ascomycete.

In ascomycetes, the hyphae are divided by cross walls, or septa, unlike the hyphae of the oomycetes and most zygomycetes. Each compartment generally contains a separate nucleus, but the septa have pores in them through which the cytoplasm and the nuclei can move. Spores are formed sexually and asexually.

Asexual spores are formed either singly or in chains at the tip of a specialised hypha. They are characteristically very fine and so are often called *conidia,* from the Greek word for "dust."

Sexual reproduction always involves the formation of an *ascus* ("little sac"), a structure that is characteristic of the group. Ascus formation is preceded by the fusion of hyphae of different mating strains to form a dikaryon. The nuclei form pairs that divide synchronously as the hypha grows. Eventually some of the nuclei fuse; this is the only truly diploid stage in the life cycle.

The diploid nuclei immediately undergo meiosis, producing four haploid nuclei, which then divide mitotically, producing eight haploid nuclei. Each of these nuclei becomes surrounded by a tough wall; a mature ascus contains eight of these spores (ascospores). In most ascomycetes, the ascus becomes turgid at maturity and finally bursts, releasing its ascospores explosively into the air.

Single-celled ascomycetes are known as yeasts. They are characteristically small, oval cells that reproduce by budding. Many yeasts are adapted to environments with high sugar content, such as the nectar of flowers or the surface of fruits and, as we noted in other chapter of this book, they are responsible for the fermentation of fruit juice to wine.

Many members of this class are plant parasites. Ergot, for instance, one of the most famous fungus-produced diseases, is caused by *Claviceps purpurea,* a parasite of rye. Although ergot seldom causes serious damage to a crop of rye, it is dangerous because a small amount mixed with rye grains is enough to cause severe illness among domestic animals or among the people who eat bread made with the flour.

Ergotism is often accompanied by gangrene, nervous spasms, psychotic delusions, and convulsions. It occurred frequently during the Middle Ages, when it was known as St. Anthony's fire. In one epidemic in the year 994, more than 40,000 people died. Ergot, which causes muscles to contract and blood vessels to constrict,

has various medical uses. It is also the initial source for the psychedelic drug lysergic acid diethylamide (LSD).

Class Basidiomycetes

The most familiar basidiomycetes are mushrooms. The mushroom,

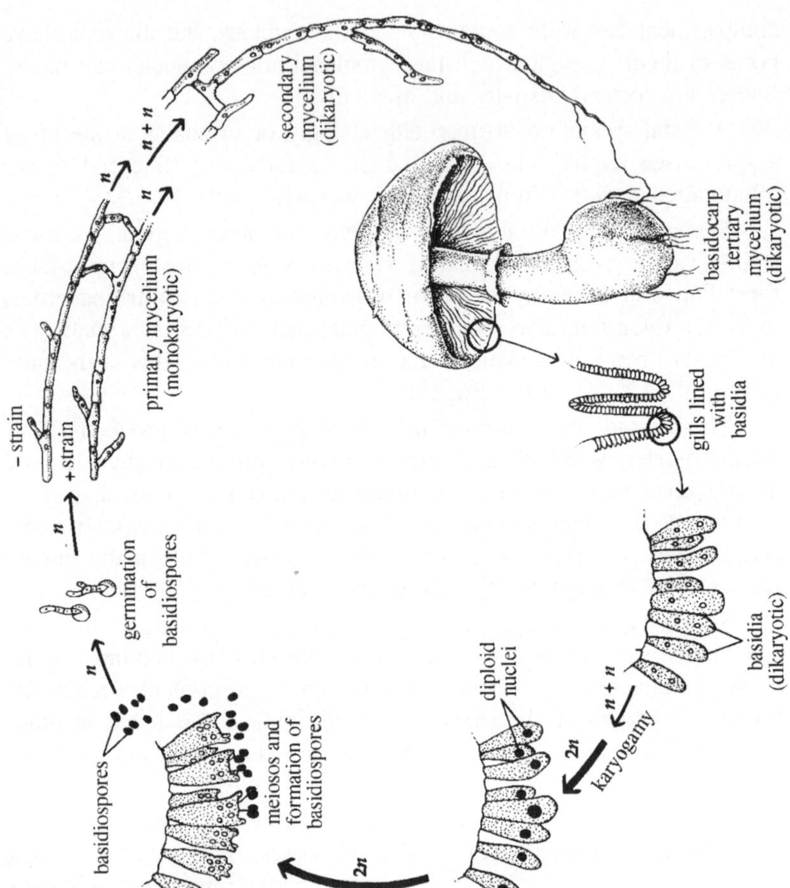

Figure 9.5 : Life cycle of a basidiomycete.

which is the spore-producing body, is composed of masses of tightly packed hyphae. The mycelium from which the mushrooms are produced forms a diffuse mat, which may grow as large as 35 meters in diameter. Mushrooms usually form at the outer edges, where the mycelium grows most actively, since this is the area in which there is the freshest nutritive material.

As a consequence, the mushrooms will appear in rings, and as the mycelium grows, the ring becomes larger and larger in diameter. Such circles of mushrooms, which might appear in a meadow overnight, were known in European folk legends as "fairy rings." They can make such a rapid appearance because most of the production of new protoplasm takes place underground, in the mycelium. The protoplasm then streams into the new hyphae of the fruiting body as it forms aboveground.

The basidiomycetes have hyphae subdivided by perforated septa. Sexual reproduction is initiated by the fusion of haploid hyphae to form a dikaryon. The dikaryon may persist for years, forming an elaborate mycelium. Eventually, some of the nuclei fuse to form diploid nuclei that immediately undergo meiosis.

Fusion and meiosis always take place in a specialised hypha called a *basidium* (from the Greek word for "club"). The spores (basidiospores) are formed externally on the basidium. Many of the larger basidiomycetes seem to have lost the capacity to produce asexual spores.

The best-known mushrooms belong to the group known as the gill fungi, which includes *Agaricus campestris,* the common field mushroom. Varieties of this species are the only mushrooms it has been possible to cultivate commercially. The gill fungi also include most of the known poisonous mushrooms.

Mushrooms of the genus *Amanita* are the most highly poisonous of all mushrooms; even one bite of the white *Amanita verna,* the "destroying angel," can be fatal. Some species of toxic mushrooms, such as *Psilocibe mexicana* (the source of psilocybin), are eaten for their hallucinogenic effects.

The spores of the gill mushrooms are found in the furrows, or "gills," under the cap. If you cut off the cap of a mature mushroom and place it on a piece of white paper, it will release fine spores that will trace out a negative copy of the gill structure. The spores, which come in a variety of colours, are a useful means of identifying various mushrooms.

Other types of basidiomycetes include puffballs (a few of which are a meter in diameter), earthstars, stinkhorns, and the parasitic rusts and smuts, some of which cause severe losses among cereal crops.

The Fungi Imperfecti

This class includes fungi in which sexual reproduction is unknown, either because it has disappeared or because it has not been observed. Also included in this class for convenience are certain other closely related fungi whose sexual stages are known. Taxonomists refer to groups like this as "waste baskets" because species are included here only because they do not fit in other taxa.

Among the Fungi Imperfecti are parasites that cause diseases of plants and animals. The most common human diseases caused by this

Table 9.1 : Major Classes of Fungi.

Class	*No. of Species*	*Examples*	*Distinctive Characteristics*	*Diseases*	*Economic Uses*
Oomycetes	Several hundred	Potato blight fungus	Some aquatic; flagellated spores; formation of eggs and sperm in special gametangia; cell walls contain cellulose	Blights and mildews of plants, fish infections	None
Zygomycetes	Several hundred	Black bread mold	Formation of zygospores (tough, resistant spores resulting from a fusion of gametangia); no flagellated cells	Few	None
Ascomycetes	30,000	Neurospora, yeasts, morels, truffles	Formation of fine asexual spores (conidia); sexual spores in asci; hyphae divided by perforated septa; dikaryons; no flagellated cells	Powdery mildews of fruits, chestnut blight, Dutch elm disease, ergot	Food (morels, truffles), wine, beer, bread making (yeasts)
Basidiomycetes	25,000	Toadstools, mushrooms	Sexual spores in basidia; hyphae divided by perforated septa; dikaryons; no flagellated cells	Rusts, smuts	Food (mushrooms)

(Table contd.)

Class	*No. of Species*	*Examples*	*Distinctive Characteristics*	*Diseases*	*Economic Uses*
Fungi Imperfecti	25,000	Penicillium	Fungi with no known sexual cycles; no flagellated cells	Ringworm, thrush	Cheeses, antibiotics

group are infections of the skin and mucous membranes, such as ringworm (including "athlete's foot") and thrush. A few are of economic importance due to the part they play in the production of certain cheeses (Roquefort and Camembert, for example) and of antibiotics, including penicillin.

THE LICHENS

A lichen is a combination of a specific fungus and an alga. The organisms resulting from these combinations are very different from either the alga or the fungus growing alone, as are the physiological conditions under which the lichen can survive. The lichens are widespread in nature. They occur from arid desert regions to the Arctic and grow on bare soil, tree trunks, sun-baked rocks, fence posts, and windswept alpine peaks all over the world. They are often the first colonists of bare rocky areas.

Lichens do not need an organic food source, as do their component fungi, and unlike free-living algae, they can remain alive even when desiccated. They require only light, air, and a few minerals. They apparently absorb some minerals from their substrate (this is suggested by the fact that particular species are characteristically found on specific kinds of rocks or soil or tree trunks), but minerals reach the plant primarily through the air and in rainfall. Because lichens rapidly absorb substances from rainwater, they are particularly susceptible to airborne toxic compounds. Thus, the presence or absence of lichens is a sensitive index of air pollution.

The algae found in lichens also occur as free-living species, whereas the lichen fungi are generally found in nature only in the lichens. For these reasons, lichens are generally classified according to the species of the fungal complement.

There are about 17,000 species of lichens-that is, of lichen fungi. Most are ascomycetes or Fungi Imperfecti, although a few are basidiomycetes. Algae from some 30 different genera are found in symbiotic combination with these fungi.

Lichens reproduce most commonly by the breaking off of fragments containing both fungal hyphae and algae. New lichens are formed by the capture of an alga by a fungus. Sometimes the alga is destroyed by the fungus, in which case the fungus also dies. If it survives, a lichen is produced.

10

Evolution of Plants

Plants are multicellular photosynthetic organisms adapted for life on land. As usual there are a few exceptions to this simple statement. Some plants-such as Indian pipe and dodder-in the course of evolution have become parasites and are no longer photosynthetic. Others, such as the water fern *Marsilea,* have returned to an aquatic existence; however, like whales and porpoises, these plants bear the unmistakable traces of an ancestral sojourn on the land.

As we have noted, all plants appear to have arisen from a group of the green algae (Chlorophyta). There are several lines of evidence leading to this conclusion. Some of the clues are biochemical: Like the plants, the green algae contain *chlorophylls a* and *b* as their photosynthetic pigments; they accumulate their food as starch; and their cell walls contain cellulose.

Additional evidence is found in their pattern of cytokinesis. In almost all other organisms, division of the cytoplasm takes place by constriction and pinching off of the cell membrane. In plants and in a few species of green algae, the cytoplasm is divided by the formation of a cell plate at the equator of the spindle. (Cell-plate formation is also seen in one species of brown algae, but this alga does not contain chlorophyll *b* or store its food as starch.)

Finally, all multicellular green algae have a life cycle characterised by alternation of generations, which is also found in all plants. As we described in other chapter, in this type of life cycle, a diploid, spore-

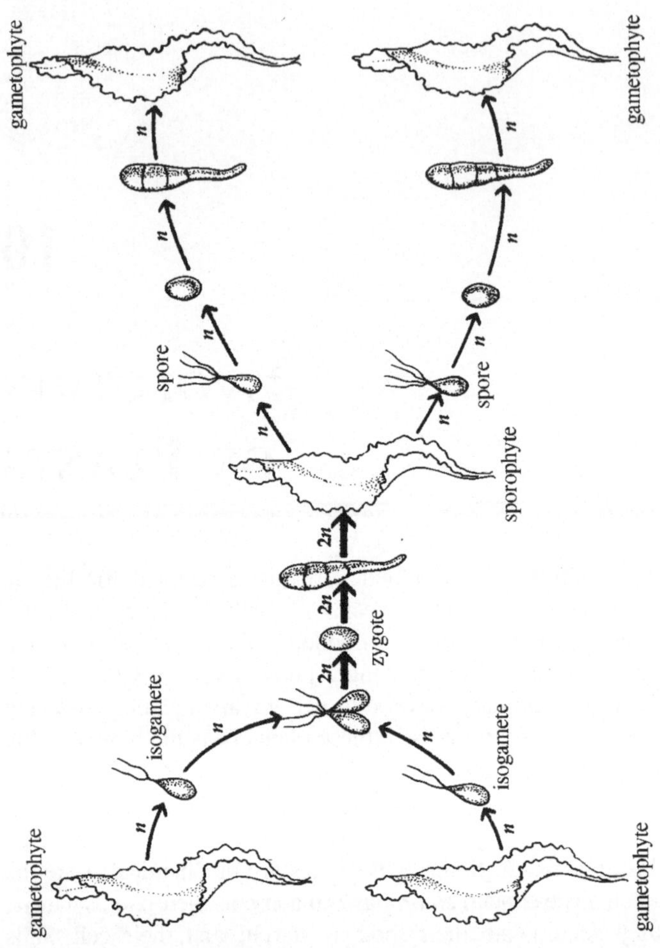

Figure 10.1 : In the sea lettuce, Ulva, we can see the reproductive pattern known as alternation of generations, in which one generation produces spores, the other gametes. The haploid (n) gametophyte produces haploid isogametes, and the gametes fuse to form a diploid (2n) zygote.

producing generation alternates with a haploid, gamete-producing generation. The plant that produces gametes is known as the *gametophyte,* the gamete-producing plant. The individual cells of this plant are haploid *(n)* and so are the gametes it produces.

The gametes fuse to form a diploid (2n) zygote. The zygote develops into a plant in which all the cells are diploid. This plant is known as the *sporophyte,* the spore-producing plant. Spores, which are produced by meiosis, are always haploid.

Among plants, spores differ from gametes in that when a spore germinates it forms a new organism, while a gamete must first unite with another gamete before further development occurs. The gametophyte

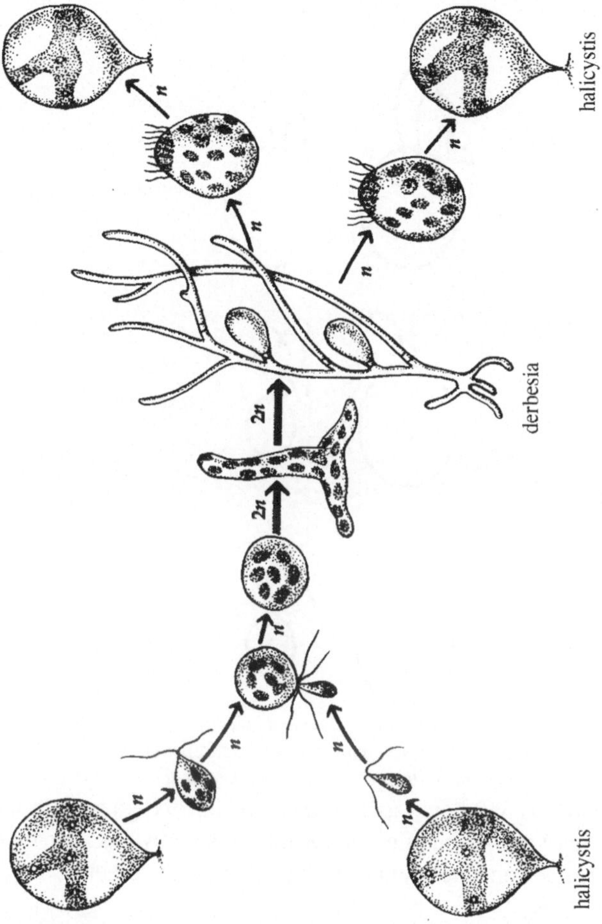

Figure 10.2 : In some algae the alternating generations are so different that they once were believed to be different genera. At one time, the gametophyte of the Valonia-like alga shown here was called Halicystis and the sporophyte Derbesia.

and the sporophyte are always genetically different, since one is composed of haploid cells and the other of diploid cells.

In some chlorophytes, such as the sea lettuce *Ulva*, the two generations look alike. In other green algae, the sporophyte and the gametophyte do not resemble one another, and the generations are said to be heteromorphic. In fact, in some cases, the two generations of the same alga were once considered to be two entirely different species until the organism was studied in the laboratory.

Figure elsewhere in this chapter shows such an alga-a large coenocytic alga like *Valonia-which* was called *Derbesia* in its sporophyte *(2n)* form and *Halicystis* in its gametophyte (n) form.

The gametes may be identical in size and structure, as they are in

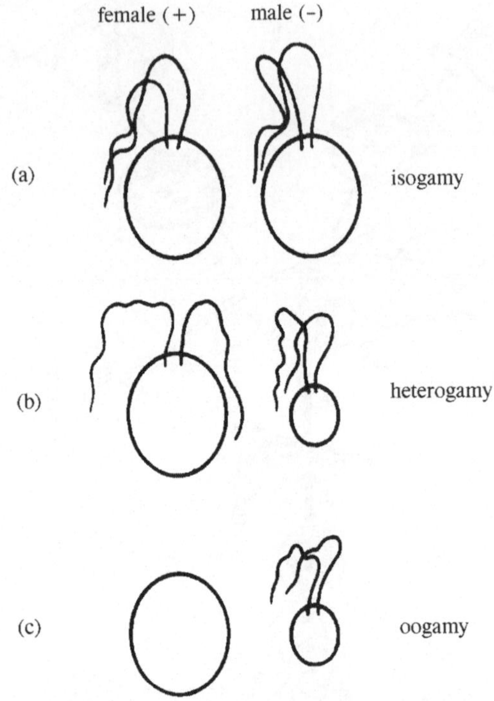

Figure 10.3 : Evolution of sex. (a) Isogamy. The gametes are similar in size and shape. (b) Heterogamy. One gamete, conventionally termed male, is smaller than the other. (c) Oogamy. One gamete, usually the smaller, is motile, and the other is not.

Ulva; this condition is known as *isogamy*. When one gamete is larger than another, but both are motile, the condition is known as *heterogamy,* as in *Derbesia*. When one gamete is motile and the other is not, the condition is *oogamy*.

An individual that produces gametes that are nonmotile and (usually, though not always) larger is known as female, and this is where sexual differentiation, with its mixed blessings and many complications, all began. All plants are oogamous and heteromorphic.

THE TRANSITION TO LAND

Water was the first life zone for living things. Land was the next life zone, and air was the third. We are now beginning the occupation of a possible fourth life zone, outer space.

The second life zone, the land, offered a wealth of advantages to plants. Light was abundant from daylight to dusk, unfiltered by the turbulent water. Carbon dioxide, needed for photosynthesis, was plentiful in the atmosphere, as was oxygen by this time, and both circulated much more freely in air than in water. And there was a great abundance of unoccupied space, as compared with the shorelines, now teeming with life.

Terrestrial existence presented some major difficulties, however. First and foremost-and still the principal problem for many plants-is water loss and desiccation. Water is freely available to every cell of a green alga, but the major source of water for plants is beneath the ground.

No light is available there for photosynthesis, however, and so the belowground parts of a plant are, in essence, heterotrophic, depending on the aboveground photosynthetic plant parts for organic molecules. The modem plant represents a collection of solutions to and compromises with these problems.

ADAPTATIONS TO LAND

One of the principal adaptations to land, which apparently occurred early in plant evolution, was the development of a fatty protective cuticle, which reduces water loss from the aboveground portions of the plant. The stomata, openings that permit the gas exchange necessary for photosynthesis, are a related adaptation.

Another adaptation related to the hazard of water loss was the development of multicellular reproductive organs with a protective layer of sterile (nonreproductive) cells around the gametangia. These gametangia are called *archegonia* if they give rise to egg cells and *antheridia* if they give rise to sperm.

Among algae the zygote leads an independent existence. In plants, the zygote and embryo are retained within the female gametangium, and the embryo and young sporophyte are protected during their early development.

The presence of lignin in the cell walls is another feature that appeared early in plant evolution. Lignin stiffens the cell walls so they are better able to support the plant body.

As past evolutionary events are reconstructed, it is apparent that these developments took place before the plants diverged into the two separate lines, represented today by: (1) Bryophyta, a small phylum that includes the mosses, hornworts, and liverworts, and (2) Tracheophyta, the vascular plants, a large phylum that includes all of the dominant modern plants.

The principal difference between the bryophytes and the tracheophytes

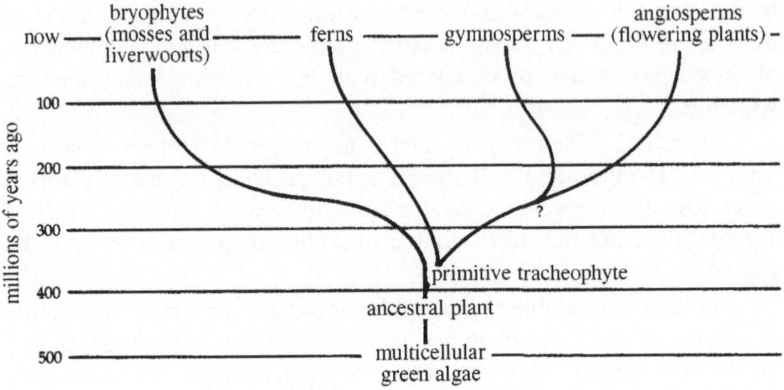

Figure 10.4 : Evolution of plants.

is that the tracheophytes have a well-developed vascular system that transports water, minerals, sugars, and other nutrients.

Table 10.1 : The Bryophytes
(*Land Plants without True Vascular Systems*)

No. of Class	*Common Name*	*Species*
Hepaticae	Liverworts	9,000
Anthocerotae	Hornworts	100
Musci	Mosses	14,500

According to this evidence, the bryophytes and the vascular plants diverged long ago. The oldest fossils of vascular plants are from the Silurian period, which ended some 400 million years ago. The bryophytes first appear in the fossil record in the Devonian period, more than 350 million years ago. These ancient fossils are quite similar to bryophytes living today.

PHYLUM BRYOPHYTA: MOSSES, HORNWORTS, AND LIVERWORTS

Lacking water-gathering roots and specialised vascular tissues, the bryophytes absorb moisture through aboveground structures. As a consequence, they grow most successfully in moist, shady places and in bogs.

Some of them, like sphagnum (peat moss), are able to absorb and hold large amounts of water, so that they in effect maintain a watery existence even on land. Most bryophytes are tropical, but some species occur in temperate regions, and a few even reach the Arctic and Antarctic.

In the damp environments frequented by the bryophytes, individual cells can absorb water and nutrients directly from the air or by diffusion from nearby cells. (Thus, like lichens, they are sensitive indices of air pollution.) These plants do not have any stiff supporting structures to hold them erect, and, in general, they have no conducting cells to transport water up the plant body. As a consequence, many of them are very small, and even the largest reach little more than 30 centimeters above the ground.

Bryophytes have motile sperm; free water is necessary for the completion of their sexual cycle, because the sperm swim to the egg. Thus the bryophytes are not completely adapted to land.

The bryophytes do have some special structural adaptations to a terrestrial existence. They have small leaflike structures in which photosynthesis take place, and, as in the tracheophytes, the body of the

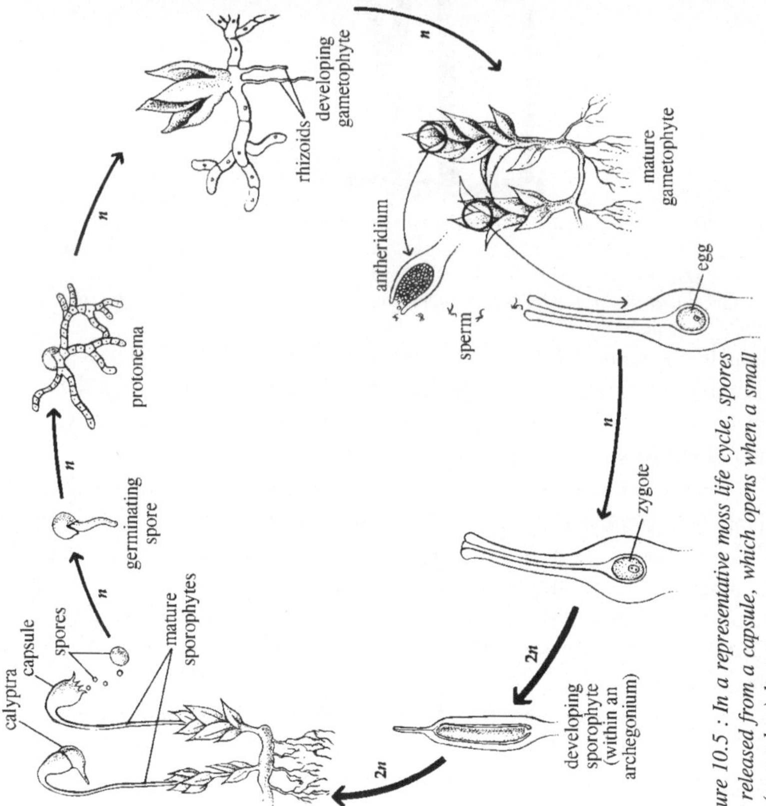

Figure 10.5 : In a representative moss life cycle, spores are released from a capsule, which opens when a small lid (operculum) bursts.

Figure 10.6 : Rhynia major, one of the earliest known vascular plants. It lacked leaves and roots. Its aerial stems, which were photosynthetic, were attached to an underground stem, or rhizome. The aerial stems were covered with a cuticle and contained stomata. The dark structures at the tips of the stems are sporangia, which released the spores by splitting longitudinally.

plant is specialised for support and food storage. Thus the bryophytes resemble other plants far more than they do the algae, although they are not usually classified as "higher plants" and do not seem to have been their ancestors.

The bryophytes do not have roots. In the mosses, the individual plants (gametophytes) grow up like branches from a network of horizontal filaments known as protonemata (singular, protonema). Each moss plant is attached to the substrate by means of elongate single cells called rhizoids. A single moss plant may sprawl over a considerable area, but most liverworts are so small that they are noticeable only to a keen observer.

In both mosses and liverworts, small leaflike structures lack the specialised tissues of the leaves of higher plants and are only one or a few cell layers thick. Moss leaves are believed to have evolved separately from "true" leaves.

Bryophyte Reproduction

In the bryophytes, unlike any tracheophytes, the gametophyte (the haploid form, you will recall) is often larger than the sporophyte. The antheridia and archegonia are borne on the gametophyte. When sufficient moisture is present, the sperm, which are biflagellate, are released and swim to the archegonium, to which they are attracted chemically. Fusion of sperm and egg takes place within the archegonium.

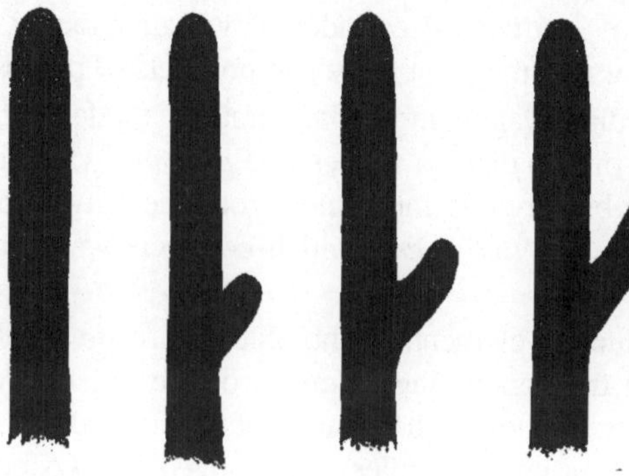

evolution of microphylls

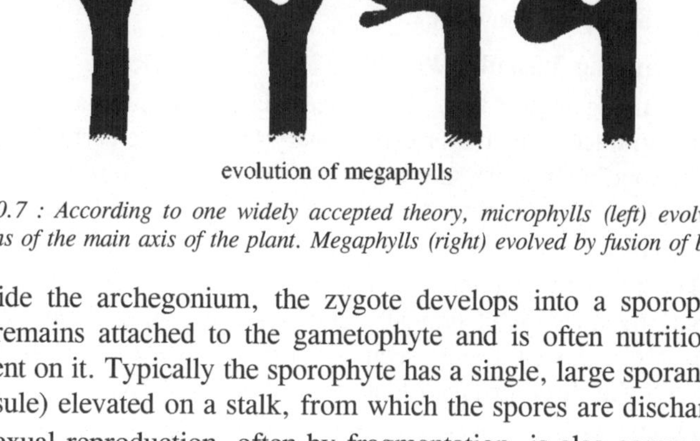

evolution of megaphylls

Figure 10.7 : According to one widely accepted theory, microphylls (left) evolved as outgrowths of the main axis of the plant. Megaphylls (right) evolved by fusion of branch systems.

Inside the archegonium, the zygote develops into a sporophyte, which remains attached to the gametophyte and is often nutritionally dependent on it. Typically the sporophyte has a single, large sporangium (or capsule) elevated on a stalk, from which the spores are discharged.

Asexual reproduction, often by fragmentation, is also common. A moss life cycle is shown in Figure elsewhere in this chapter.

PHYLUM TRACHEOPHYTA: THE VASCULAR PLANTS

Rhynia major is an example of the earliest known vascular plants, dating back some 400 million years ago. As you can see, it does not look much like any modern vascular plant and, indeed, is much more primitive in appearance than a bryophyte.

However, it differs from all bryophytes in one important respect: Within its stem is a central cylinder of vascular tissue, specialised for conducting water up the plant body and products of photosynthesis down.

The vascular system in *Rhynia,* and in modern tracheophytes as well, consists of two distinct tissues: the *phloem,* which conducts sugars and other soluble organic molecules from the leaves to other parts of the plant body, and the *xylem,* which conducts water and minerals up from the roots.

The conducting elements of the phloem are *sieve cells* or *sieve-tube elements,* and the conducting elements of the xylem are *tracheids* and *vessel elements*. In stems, the strands of xylem and phloem are side by side, either in vascular bundles or arranged in two concentric layers (cylinders), in which one tissue (typically the phloem) appears outside the other.

Rhynia major and its relatives are now extinct, as are some other subphyla of vascular plants.

Three groups of vascular plants still have living representatives. Two of the groups are small: the Lycophytina (club mosses) and the Sphenophytina (horsetails). The third group, the Pterophytina, a very large subphylum, includes all the major groups of plants: ferns, gymnosperms, and flowering plants.

Trends among Vascular Plants

Beginning with a very simple vascular plant, such as *Rhynia,* it is possible to trace some major evolutionary trends. One early development was the root, a structure specialised for the absorption of water. Another was the leaf. Two distinct types of leaves evolved, the microphyll and the megaphyll.

The microphyll contains only a single strand of vascular tissue, whereas the megaphyll typically contains a complex system of veins. These two types of leaves seem clearly to have evolved in different ways. Of the three groups of modern plants, the Lycophytina and the Sphenophytina have microphylls and the Pterophytina have megaphylls.

A third evolutionary trend is the development of increasingly complex and efficient vascular systems. A fourth trend is seen in the reduction of the gametophyte. In all vascular plants, the gametophyte is smaller than the sporophyte.

However, in the more primitive tracheophytes, the gametophyte is separate and nutritionally independent, whereas in the more recently evolved forms, it has been reduced to microscopic size and dependency status.

Also related to the reproductive cycle is the trend toward heterospory. The earliest vascular plants produced only one kind of spore (homospory) in one kind of sporangium. Upon germination, such spores produce gametophytes on which both antheridia and archegonia form.

In plants that are heterosporous, two different kinds of gametophytes develop; one bearing archegonia and the other, antheridia. (As the gametophytes become reduced, archegonia and antheridia decrease in size until, in the most highly evolved gymnosperms and in the angiosperms, they disappear.)

The final and perhaps the most significant innovation was the seed. The seed is, in effect, the sporangium, outside of which is one or two layers of tissue, the integument, and inside of which is the spore. The spore germinates to form the female gametophyte, in which an egg cell differentiates and becomes an embryonic sporophyte-"three generations under one roof."

The sporangium with its integument and contents is called the *ovule,* and it is the mature ovule that is properly known as the seed. The earliest known seeds were fossilized in late Devonian deposits some 350 million years ago.

All of these developments will be discussed in greater detail in the pages that follow.

Class Filicinae: Ferns

Ferns are vascular plants that can usually be distinguished from most other plants by their large, feathery leaves, which, in most species, unroll from base to tip during growth. The sporangia commonly are on the undersurface of the leaves or, sometimes, on specialised leaves. Spore-bearing leaves are called *sporophylls.* As we shall see, the carpels and stamens of flowers are also sporophylls.

According to the fossil record, ferns first appeared almost 400 million years ago, and they are still relatively abundant. Most of the 11,000 living species are found in the tropics, but some occur in temperate and even arid regions. Because they have flagellated sperm and need free water for fertilization, those species growing in arid regions exploit the seasonal occurrence of water for sexual reproduction.

The stems of ferns are anatomically simple compared with those of gymnosperms and angiosperms, and are often reduced to a creeping underground stem (rhizome). Although ferns do not exhibit secondary growth-the type of growth that results in increase of girth and formation of bark and woody tissue-some grow very tall. For instance, *Cyathea australis,* a tree fern found on Norfolk Island in the South Pacific, sometimes reaches 28 meters in height.

The leaves of ferns are usually finely divided into pinnae; these divided leaves spread widely and so collect more light, and apparently they are thus adapted to growing on the forest floor in diffused light. The sporangia develop on the lower surface of sporophylls, which may resemble the other green leaves on the plant or may be nonphotosynthetic stalks (modified leaves).

The sporangia commonly occur in small clusters known as sori (singular, sorus). In the ferns, as in all the vascular plants, the predominant plant form is the sporophyte. The gametophyte of the homosporous ferns begins development as a small algalike filament of cells, each filled with chloroplasts, and then develops into a flat structure, often only one layer of cells in thickness.

Although this gametophyte is small, it is nutritionally independent, as is the sporophyte. All but a few genera are homosporous, and the single gametophyte produces both antheridia and archegonia. The sperm are coiled and multiflagellate. The life cycle of a fern is shown elsewhere in this chapter.

Gymnosperms

The humid Paleozoic era was the age when the earth's coal deposits were formed from lush vegetation that sank so swiftly into the warm, marshy soil that there was no chance for much of it to decompose. At the close of this era, in the Permian period, 225 to 280 million years ago, there were worldwide changes of climate, with the advent of widespread glaciers and drought.

The amphibians gave way to the scaly-skinned reptiles, which may have been better suited to the harsher climate. Under similar selective pressures, plants began to evolve specialised structures that enabled them to survive during periods when no water was available.

It was during the Permian period that the gymnosperms-the naked-seed plants-evolved. There are four groups of gymnosperms with living representatives, three small groups (the cycads, the ginkgos, and the Gnetinae) and one large and familiar group (the conifers).

The Seed

The seed is a protective structure in which the embryonic plant can lie dormant until conditions become favourable for its survival. Thus, in its function, it parallels the spores of bacteria or the resistant zygotes of the freshwater algae.

In structure it is far more elaborate, however. A seed includes the embryo (the young, dormant sporophyte), a store of nutritive tissue, and an outer protective coat.

To understand the evolution of the seed it is necessary to return for a moment to the life cycle, or alternation of generations, found in all the vascular plants, and foreshadowed in the green algae. In the green algae, the two generations, sporophyte and gametophyte, are independent. In most ferns, the gametophytes, although still independent, are usually smaller than the sporophytes.

In the seed plants, the gametophytic generation is reduced still further and is totally dependent on the sporophyte. All gymnosperms are heterosporous, producing both male and female gametophytes.

The female gametophyte develops on the mother sporophyte within the ovule. Within the female gametophyte, one or more egg cells are formed. Sperm cells develop in another gametophyte, also protected and nourished by a sporophyte. They are carried to the female gametophyte and fertilise the eggs developing there.

The zygote develops into an embryo. Following fertilization, the ovule enlarges and its outer surface hardens, forming a protective cover around the embryo and the gametophyte tissue in which the embryo is embedded. This complex is released as the seed.

Let us look at a specific example, the formation of a pine seed. A pine tree has two types of cones, which produce the two types of spores. The small "male" cones resemble those of club mosses, but on the large "female" cones, the scales that bear the ovules are much thicker and tougher than the sporophylls of the male cones.

In the male cones, specialised cells inside the sporangia undergo meiosis to produce haploid spores. Each spore differentiates into a microscopic, windborne pollen grain, an immature male gametophyte. The wind is an unreliable messenger, disseminating the pollen grains at random, and wind-pollinated plants characteristically produce pollen in great quantities.

Fertilization

Within the ovules of the female cones, a second type of spore is formed by meiosis. (Spores that give rise to female gametophytes are often referred to as megaspores, as distinct from microspores, from which male gametophytes arise.) Of the four spore cells produced within the ovule by each meiotic sequence, three disintegrate and the remaining one forms a tiny gametophyte.

This haploid gametophyte grows within the cone and develops two or more archegonia, each of which contains a single egg cell. The development from the spore into the gametophyte with its egg cells may take many months-slightly more than a year, for example, in some common pines. The ripening ovule secretes a sticky liquid.

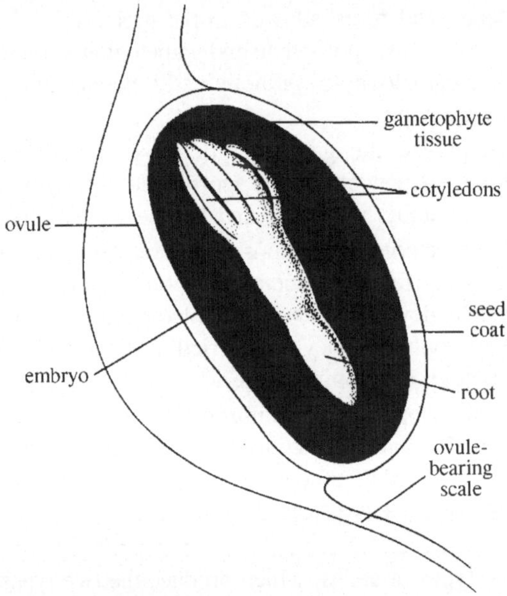

Figure 10.8 : Pine seed. The outer layers of the ovule have hardened into a seed coat, enclosing the female gametophyte and the embryo, which now consists of an embryonic root, the radicle, and a number of embryonic leaves, the cotyledons.

When the cones become dusted with pollen, some of the pollen sifts down between the cone scales and comes into contact with the liquid. Pollen grains, caught in the sticky liquid, are drawn to the ovule as the liquid dries.

Here the pollen grain develops into a mature gametophyte. The male gametophyte produces two nonmotile cells, the male gametes, or sperm. These are carried toward the egg within the pollen tube, which is produced by the male gametophyte and which grows through the tissues of the ovule.

Because the drought-resistant pollen is blown to the ovule of the female cones by the wind, and the sperm are carried to the egg by the pollen tube, the pines and other conifers are not dependent on free water for fertilization. Thus they are able to reproduce sexually when (and where) ferns and bryophytes cannot.

Following fertilization, the zygote begins to divide and forms the embryo. As the ovule matures, its outer walls harden into a seed coat, enclosing both the embryo and the female gametophyte (the latter provides food for the embryo when the seed germinates). After the cone matures, it releases its seeds. In most conifers the seeds are winged and are spread widely by the wind.

Figure elsewhere in this chapter shows a cross section of a pine seed. The seed coat and the wing on which the seed is carried arise from the hardened outer layers of the ovule, derived from the mother sporophyte.

The next layer represents the body of the gametophyte; swollen and packed with stored food reserves, it grows and displaces the original sporophyte tissue. The inner core is the embryo with its many *cotyledons,* the embryonic leaves, which will appear as the first leaves of the shoot of the new sporophyte when the seed germinates. The lower part of the embryo, the radicle, will form the root.

The seed was in existence by the close of the Carboniferous period, and according to the fossil record, some of the fernlike plants and even some of the club mosses had seedlike structures.

But it was not until the close of the Permian period, at the end of the Paleozoic era (some 225 million years ago), when the land became colder and drier, that plants that had seeds gained a major evolutionary advantage and the seed plants became the dominant plants of the land.

The Conifer Leaf

Another feature commonly associated with conifers, although not with all gymnosperms, is their needlelike leaf. Figure elsewhere in this chapter shows a cross section of a pine leaf, which may be 10 or more centimeters long but only 1 to 3 millimeters in diameter. In the center you can see veins, the vascular transport system, which carries water in one set of conducting cells (the tracheids) and sugars in another (the sieve cells).

Outside the veins are parenchyma cells in which photosynthesis takes place. The ducts on the facing sides of the needles carry resin, a substance that is released if the plant is wounded and may serve to close the break, The outside layer of cells (epidermis) is porous but very hard. The needlelike leaf, despite its slender form, is a megaphyll. It is well adapted to long periods of low humidity, such as in northern winters, and to moisture-losing, sandy soils.

One or both of those are characteristic of many regions in which modern conifers are abundant. (In areas with more available water in the air or soil, they cannot usually compete with angiosperms.)

Class Angiospermae: Flowering Plants

It is believed that the angiosperms evolved from a now-extinct group of gymnosperms. They appear in the fossil record suddenly and in abundance during the Cretaceous period, about 100 million years ago, as the dinosaurs were vanishing. Numerous angiosperm genera appeared suddenly at that time, and many of these seem to have been very similar to our modern plants.

According to Daniel Axelrod, a paleobotanist at the University of California, angiosperms probably arose long before this time, during the Permian period. They are likely to have originated on the less fertile hills and uplands of tropical areas, the richer lowlands being crowded with ferns, gymnosperms, and lycopods.

Once established, they spread into the lowlands, where they soon became the dominant plant forms and were deposited as fossils. During this mid-Cretaceous period, the climate of the earth was warmer and more uniform than it is at present, and by the end of the Cretaceous period, much of the land was covered with a rich forest of angiosperms, reaching almost as far north as the Arctic Circle.

About 250,000 different species of angiosperms are known. Just listing them, one after another, would require a book twice the length of this one. They dominate the tropical and temperate regions of the world.

The angiosperms include not only the plants with conspicuous flowers but also most of the great trees, the oak, the willow, the elm, the maple, and the birch; all the fruits, vegetables, nuts, and herbs; the cactus and the coconut; and all the corn, wheat, rice, and other grains and grasses that are the staples of the human diet and the basis of agricultural economy all over the world.

Angiosperms, like other vascular plants, contain chlorophylls *a* and b and betacarotene, and have megaphylls, stomata, and a cuticle impervious to water. The modern forms have a more highly evolved vascular system than is found in other groups. They also have two new, interrelated structures that distinguish them from all other plants: the flower and the fruit.

The Flower

Figure elsewhere in this chapter is a diagram of a simple flower. The central structure is the *carpel,* the female reproductive structure.* The carpel is believed to be a modified leaf, which, in the course of evolution, enfolded in such a way that the ovule is attached to its inner surface.

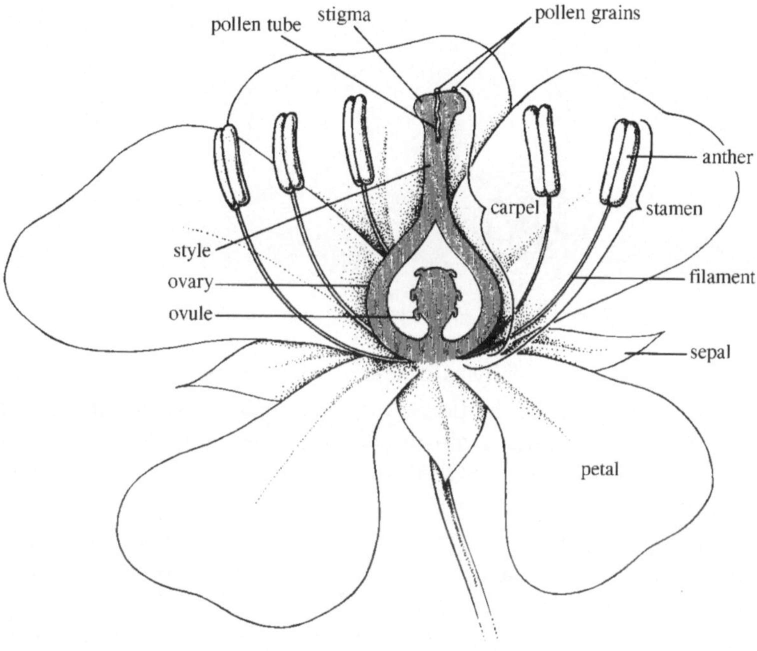

Figure 10.9 : Structure of a flower.
The sex organs are shown in the figure.

A single carpel may contain one or more ovules, and a single flower one or more carpels. The carpels may be separate (blackberry) or fused (tomato and apple). The swollen base of the carpel or carpels is the *ovary.* Within the ovary is the ovule, or ovules, in which the female gametophyte develops.

The tip of the carpel or carpels has become specialised as a *stigma,* a sticky surface to which pollen grains adhere. The stigma and ovary are connected by a slender column of tissue, the *style.*

The pollen grains (immature male gametophytes) develop in the *stamen,* which, like the carpel, is the evolutionary descendant of a sporophyll. It consists of the *anther,* which is a group of sporangia in

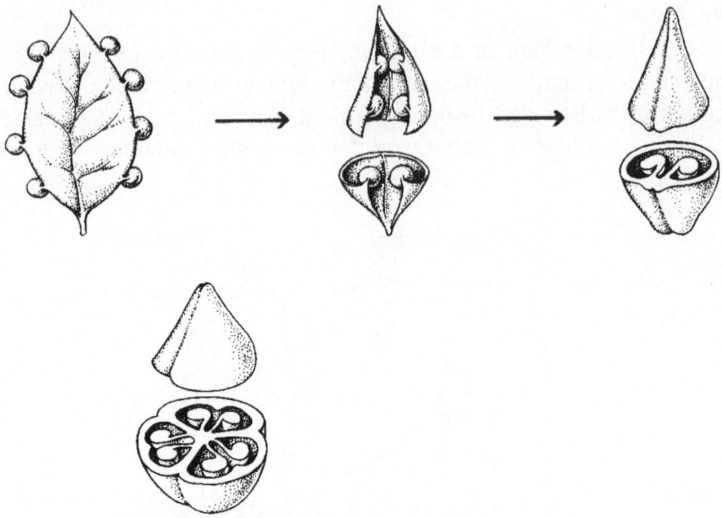

Figure 10.10 : Presumed evolutionary development of simple and compound ovaries.

which the male gametophytes develop, and a supporting *filament*.

The other parts of the flower are specialised to attract insects and other pollinators. Pollen grains produced in the anthers are carried to the stigma of (usually) another flower, where they germinate, developing pollen tubes that grow down through the style toward the ovule.

The sperm cells are carried by the pollen tubes to the female gametophyte. This gametophyte typically consists of only eight cells, one of which is the egg cell. It is fertilised by a sperm cell, giving rise to an embryo sporophyte. (The extraordinary phenomenon of double fertilization is described elsewhere in this chapter.)

Evolution of the Flower

The flower evolved as a device by which plants induce animals to transport their pollen, and hence sperm, to the egg cells. The most primitive flowers are believed to have resembled the modern hepatica, shown in Figure elsewhere in this chapter, which has numerous floral parts, each clearly separate from the other.

By comparing this type of flower with some of the more specialised ones, such as a composite or an orchid, it is possible to see four main trends in flower evolution, as listed on the next page.

1. Reduction in number of floral parts. Most specialised flowers have few stamens and few carpels, and these are present in a definite number, depending on the species.

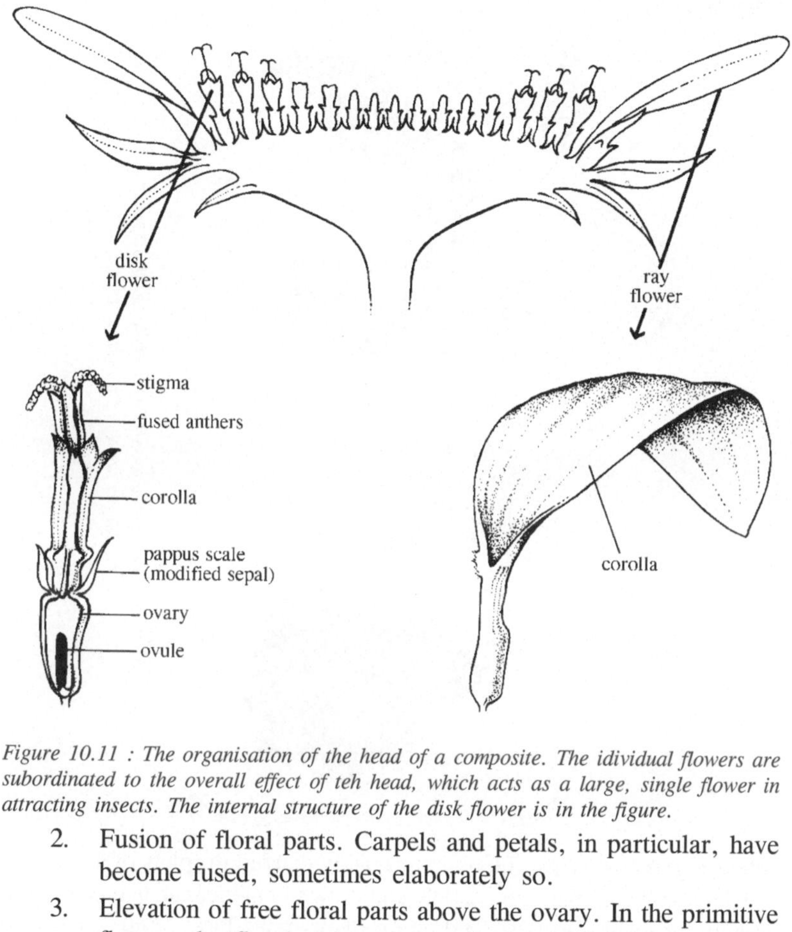

Figure 10.11 : The organisation of the head of a composite. The idividual flowers are subordinated to the overall effect of teh head, which acts as a large, single flower in attracting insects. The internal structure of the disk flower is in the figure.

2. Fusion of floral parts. Carpels and petals, in particular, have become fused, sometimes elaborately so.
3. Elevation of free floral parts above the ovary. In the primitive flower, the floral parts arise at the base of the ovary. Such ovaries are said to be superior. In the more advanced flowers, the free portions of the floral parts are above the ovary; this is an important adaptation by which the ovules are protected from foraging insects. Such ovaries are said to be inferior.
4. Changes in symmetry. The radial symmetry of the primitive flower has given way, in more advanced flowers, to bilaterally symmetrical forms.

The Agents of Evolution

The early gymnosperms from which the angiosperms evolved were probably wind-pollinated, as are modern gymnosperms. And, as in the

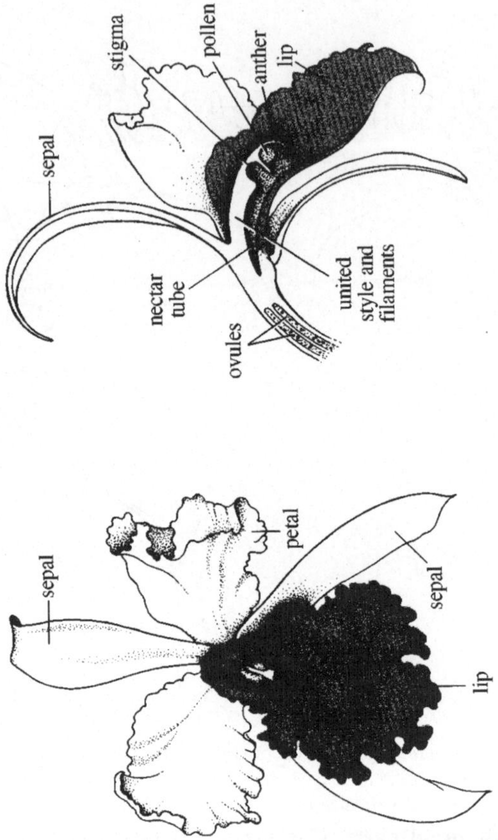

Figure 10.12 : Orchidaceae, with about 20,000 species, is the larges family of flowering plants.

modern gymnosperms, the ovule probably exuded droplets of sticky sap in which pollen grains were caught and drawn to the female gametophytes. Insects, probably beetles, feeding on plants must have come across the protein-rich pollen grains and the sticky, sugary droplets. As they began to depend on these new-found food supplies, they inadvertently carried pollen from plant to plant.

Beetle pollination must have been more efficient than wind pollination for some plant species because, clearly, selection began to favour those plants that had insect pollinators. The more attractive the plants were to the beetles, the more frequently they would be visited and the more seeds they would produce.

Any chance variations that made the visits more frequent or that made pollination more efficient thus offered immediate advantages; more seeds would be formed, and more offspring would survive. Nectaries

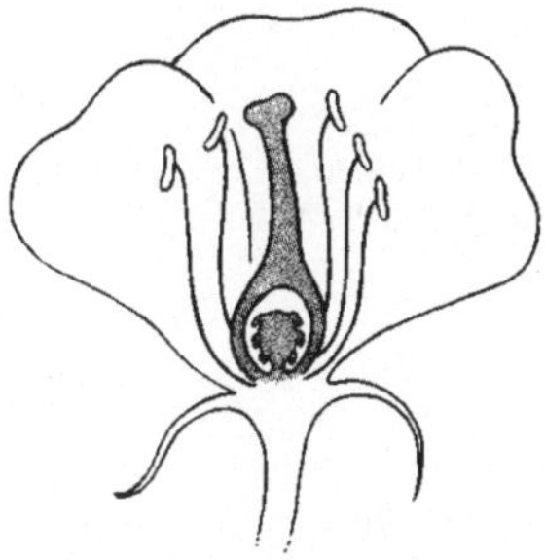

superior

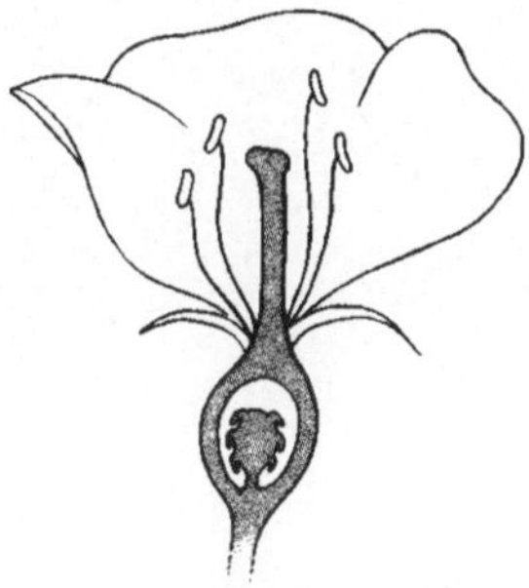

inferior

Figure 10.13 : (a) Superior and (b) inferior ovaries. In flowers with superior ovaries, the floral parts are attached below the ovaries. In flowers with inferior ovaries, the floral parts are attached above, and the ovaries are protected.

(nectar-secreting organs) evolved, which lured the pollinators. Plants developed white or brightly coloured flowers that called attention to the nectar and other food supplies.

The carpel, originally a leaf-shaped structure, became folded on itself, enclosing and protecting the ovule from hungry pollinators. By the beginning of the Cenozoic era, some 65 million years ago, the first bees, wasps, butterflies, and moths had appeared.

These are long-tongued insects for which flowers are often the only source of nutrition for the adult forms. From this time on, flowers and certain insect groups had a profound influence on one anther's history, each shaping the other as they evolved together.

A flower that attracts only a few kinds of animal visitors and attracts them regularly has an advantage over flowers visited by more promiscuous pollinators: Its pollen is less likely to be wasted on a plant of another species.

In turn, it is an advantage for the insect to have a "private" food supply that is relatively inaccessible to competing insects. Most of the

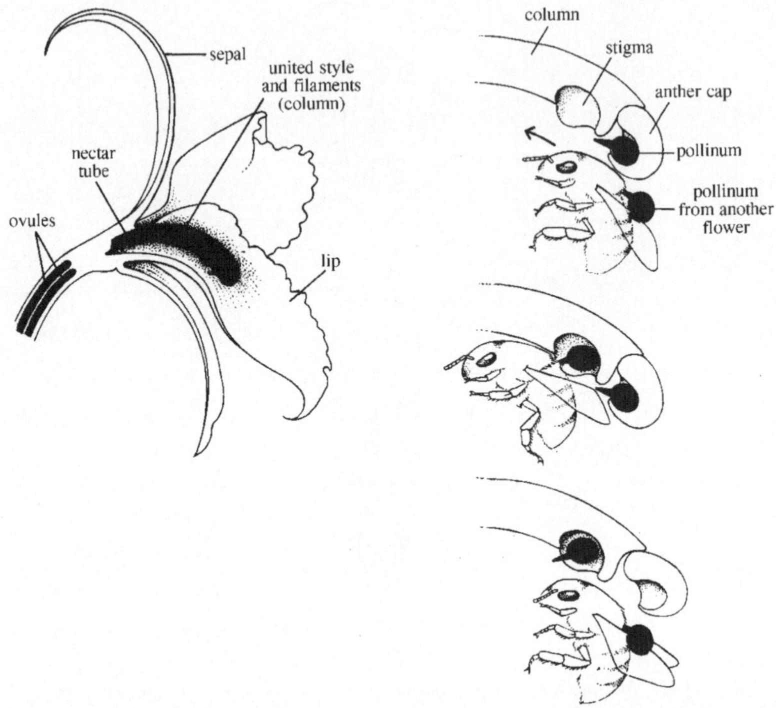

Figure 10.14 : Orchid pollen is bound together in a mass, called a pollinium, which contains a sticky extension that attaches the pollinium to the pollinating insect.

distinctive features of modern flowers are special adaptations that encourage regular visits (constancy) by particular pollinators. The varied colours and odours allow sensory recognition by pollinators. The diverse shapes such as deep nectaries and complex landing platforms that are found, for example, in orchids, snapdragons, and irises, represent ways of excluding indiscriminate pollinators.

Dispersal of Fruits and Seeds

Following fertilization in the angiosperm, the ovary develops into the fruit. Fruits are adaptations for seed dispersal. Many edible fleshy fruits become brightly coloured as they ripen, attracting the attention of birds and mammals.

The seeds within the fruits pass through the digestive tract hours later and are often deposited some distance away. In some species the seed coat's exposure to digestive juices or bile is a prerequisite for germination. The seeds themselves may be toxic, as in apples, discouraging animals from grinding up and digesting the seeds.

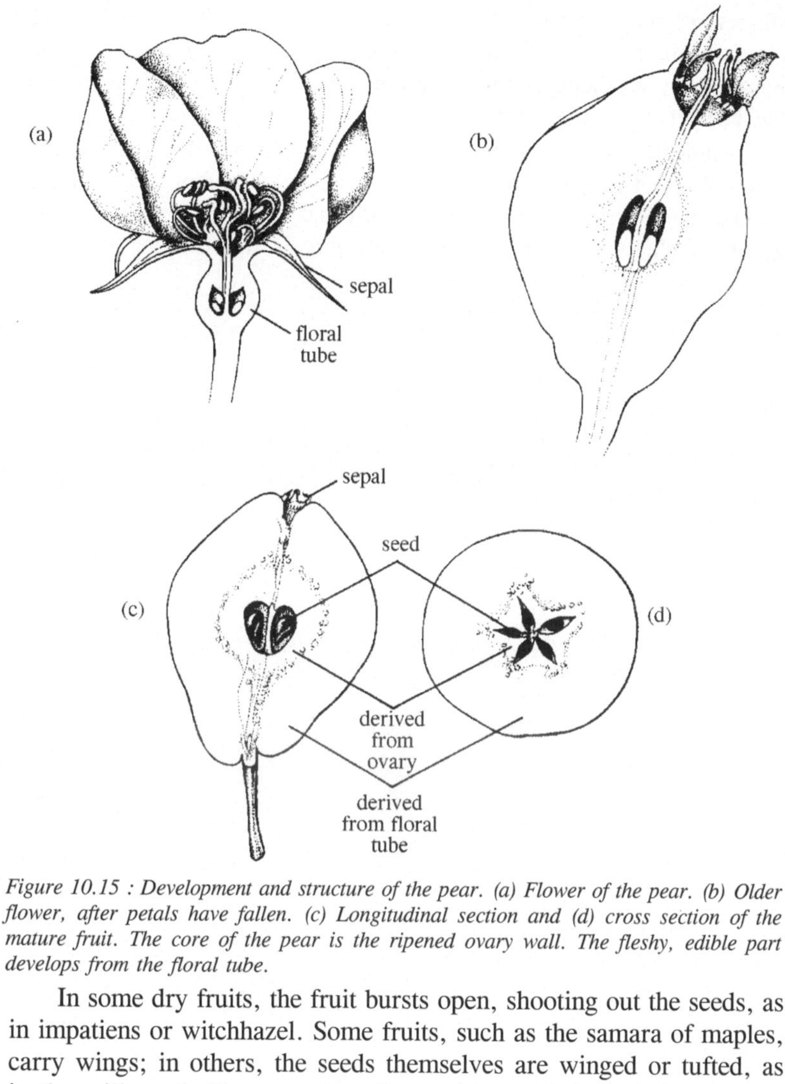

Figure 10.15 : Development and structure of the pear. (a) Flower of the pear. (b) Older flower, after petals have fallen. (c) Longitudinal section and (d) cross section of the mature fruit. The core of the pear is the ripened ovary wall. The fleshy, edible part develops from the floral tube.

In some dry fruits, the fruit bursts open, shooting out the seeds, as in impatiens or witchhazel. Some fruits, such as the samara of maples, carry wings; in others, the seeds themselves are winged or tufted, as in the milkweed. Some species of geranium send forth their seeds by a sort of slingshot.

Burrs are dry fruits that adhere to fur, feathers, or clothing and so are carried by involuntary porters to far-off fields and meadows. In the tumbleweed, the whole plant is blown across open country, with fruits opening and scattering the seeds as they go. The many extraordinary means of seed dispersal are another major reason for the evolutionary success of angiosperms. Angiosperms differ from the other vascular plants in their more efficient conducting systems, their flowers, which increase the efficiency of fertilization, and their fruits, which increase the efficiency of distribution.

Angiosperms represent the most successful of all plants in terms of numbers of individuals, numbers of species, and their effects on the existence of other organisms. The anatomy and physiology of this dominant group of plants will be explored elsewhere in this chapter.

11

LOWER ANIMALS

Animals are many-celled heterotrophs. They depend directly or indirectly for their nourishment on photosynthetic autotrophs-algae or plants. Most digest their food in an internal cavity, and most store food as glycogen or fat. Their cells do not have walls. Most move by means of contractile cells (muscle cells) containing characteristic proteins. Reproduction is usually sexual.

As adults, most are fixed in size and shape, in contrast to plants, in which growth often continues for the lifetime of the organism. The higher animals-the arthropods and the vertebrates—are the most complex of all organisms, with many kinds of specialised tissues, including elaborate sensory and neuromotor mechanisms not found in any of the other kingdoms.

For most of us, animal means mammal, and mammals are, in fact, the chief focus of attention in other section. However, the mammals, or even the vertebrates as a whole, represent only a small fraction of the animal kingdom. More than 90 percent of the different species of animals are invertebrates-that is, animals without backbones and most of these are insects. Indeed, the enormous variety displayed by the invertebrates is partly why they are so endlessly fascinating to study. They are, in addition, of great ecological importance; the insects, for example, have long challenged human dominance of the earth.

Finally, and perhaps most important, the invertebrates, confronted with the same biological problems that we face, demonstrate a spectrum of ingenious solutions. In this way, they illuminate the essential nature of these problems and so help us to understand and evaluate the solutions arrived at by mammals.

THE SOURCES OF DIVERSITY

In other chapter of this book, we commented upon the tremendous versatility of the prokaryotes, as exemplified by the wide range of environments they inhabit and the many ways in which they satisfy their energy requirements.

Among the invertebrates, we see, on a slightly different scale, this same pattern of adaptation to many different ways of life. Thus, for instance, on a single coral head, only a meter or two in diameter, one finds a dazzling array of different forms-sponges, jellyfish, starfish, sea urchins, anemones, and the coral animals themselves.

Similarly, to take terrestrial examples, a single spadeful of soil turns up earthworms, pillbugs, spiders, nematodes, and various other tiny animals; and the branch of a single tree may harbor a dozen different kinds of insects. Given the relentless force of natural selection, why do not the larger ones crowd out the smaller? Why are not the "lower" animals replaced by "higher' animals with superior strength or intelligence?

Darwin, again, offered the answer: The different organisms, he noted, "occupy different positions in the economy of nature." Each has been shaped by the long process of evolution to occupy a different niche in the environment. Natural selection has worked not to make one "superior" to the other but to continuously adapt the different forms to different ways of life.

This process of adaptation, of course, continues. Every species, including our own, is a traveler through time, caught for only an instant in the present.

THE SOURCES OF CONTINUITY

Through the patterns of diversity, there is a strong theme of continuity. One reason is simply that of "descent." We are all related; not only are we made of the same atoms and molecules and even macromolecules, but from *E. coli* to elephant, we even share many of the same enzymes.

Although the evolutionary relationships between us and the invertebrates are obscure, we can read into them traces of our own biological beginnings. In the twitch of a tiny segment of an earthworm's artery, we sense the echo of our own heartbeat.

Second, all organisms face the same set of problems. These problems can best be defined by recalling that an organism is a cell or group of cells. A primary need is to supply the cell or cells with, first of all, a source of energy. Also, most cells-on this planet, at least-require water, oxygen, a source of nitrogen, fixed carbon (in the case of heterotrophs), and a few ions.

Another requirement is to eliminate wastes, including excess carbon dioxide, nitrogenous wastes from the breakdown of amino acids, and, in some cases, excess water. Cells that live individual or colonial lives in a watery environment can solve these problems in relatively simple ways, but as organisms get larger, thicker, and more complex, the problem of servicing each individual cell becomes correspondingly more complicated.

Another set of problems that a multicellular organism must solve in order to exist arises from the fact that it is more than just a group of cells. It is, in fact, a complex society of cells, in which the needs of each individual cell are subordinated to the needs of the society. In a population of *Paramecium,* the organisms have common requirements, but each is in competition with the others.

In a society of even a few thousand cells—a small crustacean, for instance-the individual cells are dependent on the existence of the group and are organised in a system of mutual cooperation. The second group of problems faced by organisms, therefore, relates to the organisation or integration of activities.

Hormones are one of the chief means of integration in both plants and animals. In the animals, another, more rapid integrating mechanism has evolved: the nervous system, by which the organism keeps in touch with its environment and coordinates its own activities.

A QUESTION OF SIZE

At this point, one might well ask: Considering the problems faced by larger organisms, why did larger animals evolve? What selective advantages do the multicellular, more complex animals have as compared with the smaller ones? Some answers to these questions are obvious and simple.

Larger animals are, in general, more likely to eat than be eaten. Larger organisms, especially those that live underwater or on land, are generally able to travel faster and farther than small ones, and this is an advantage.

A small ciliate, for instance, might starve only a few centimeters from a food supply. On the other hand, its requirements are very modest.

Perhaps even more important, however, than mobility and edibility is what the French physiologist Claude Bernard called the *milieu interieur,* the internal environment of the animal, as distinct from the external environment that surrounds it.

A single-celled organism is as cold or as hot and as wet or as dry as its surroundings, whereas a larger animal is more independent and, to some extent, controls the environment in which its cellular society lives. Control of the internal environment is more readily achieved by the many-celled animal because of the simple surface-to-volume geometry we noted in other chapter.

Exchanges between a cell and its surroundings take place across a cell's available surface area. This is a principal reason why a cell, which depends for its existence on the exchange of substances with its environment, cannot be very large.

On the other hand, since it may be advantageous to conserve certain substances, such as water and heat, an organism may be better off, within limits of weight and mobility, if its relative surface area is reduced. One-celled animals can live successfully only in water or as parasites in the bodies of other organisms, which amounts to the same thing.

Many-celled animals can live not only in water but also on land, in the sky, and even, as we are now beginning to discover, in outer space-which is a logical extension of an old evolutionary trend. In this chapter, we shall discuss the so-called lower invertebrates and some that must clearly be considered higher, such as the clever and highly emotional octopus.

The chapter that follows deals with the insects and other arthropods and, briefly, with the vertebrates. There are almost 30 phyla of invertebrates. Of these, we are going to discuss relatively few, concentrating on the largest phyla and those of particular biological interest.

PHYLUM PORIFERA: SPONGES

Sponges seem to have had a different origin from other members of the animal kingdom and to have traveled a solitary evolutionary route. For this reason, they are often classified in a subkingdom of their own, the Parazoa ("alongside of animals").

In fact, until the eighteenth century, the sponges were classified as plant-animals ("zoophytes") since they are all sessile (attached to a substrate) during their adult life. Sponges are found on ocean floors throughout the world. Most live along the coasts in shallow water, but

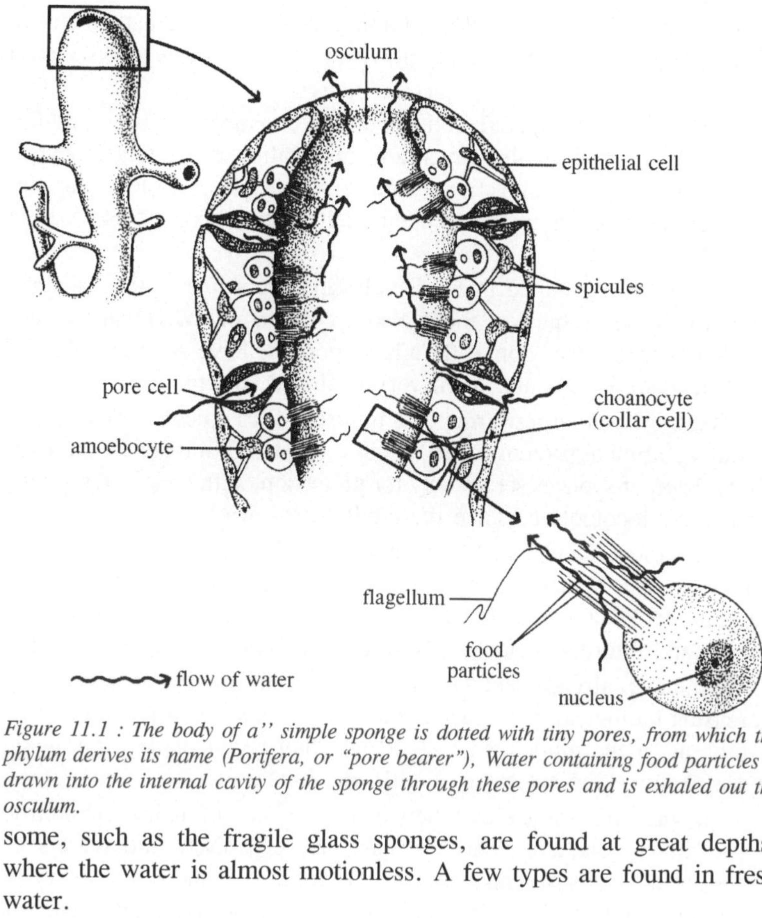

Figure 11.1 : The body of a'' simple sponge is dotted with tiny pores, from which the phylum derives its name (Porifera, or "pore bearer"), Water containing food particles is drawn into the internal cavity of the sponge through these pores and is exhaled out the osculum.

some, such as the fragile glass sponges, are found at great depths, where the water is almost motionless. A few types are found in fresh water.

A sponge is essentially a water-filtering system, made up of one or more chambers through which water is driven by the action of numerous flagellated cells. Sponges are made up of a relatively few cell types, the most characteristic of which are the choanocytes, or collar cells, the flagellated cells that line the interior cavity of the sponge.

Similar cells, the choanoflagellates, are found among the ciliated protozoans, and it is possible that the sponges arose from such organisms. All of a sponge's digestive processes are carried out intracellularly; hence, even a giant sponge-and some stand taller than a person-can eat nothing larger than microscopic food particles.

The outer surface of the sponge is covered with epithelial cells. Among these epithelial cells are cells that contract in response to touch or to irritating chemicals, and in so doing, close up pores and channels. Each cell acts as an individual, however; there is little coordination among them.

Between the epithelial cells and the choanocytes is a middle, jellylike layer, and in this layer are amoebalike cells, amoebocytes, which carry out various functions. Some amoebocytes carry food particles from the choanocytes to the epithelial cells. Amoebocytes also secrete skeletal materials.

Sponges are grouped into three classes, according to their skeletal structure. In some species, the skeleton consists of individual spicules of calcium carbonate. Some, the glass sponges, have spicules of silica fused in a continuous and often very beautiful structure.

The third and largest group has unfused silica spicules, or a tough, fibrous keratinlike protein called spongin, or a combination of the two. The skeleton of sponges serves only for protection, stiffening, and support, but not for locomotion, since the adult forms are sessile.

The sponge shown in Figure elsewhere in this chapter is a small and simple one. In larger sponges, the body plan, although it is essentially the same, looks far more complex. These sponges have greatly increased feeding and filtering surfaces, owing to their highly folded body walls.

We have already encountered this evolutionary strategem for increasing biological work surfaces at the cellular level—as in the inner membrane of the mitochondrion-and we shall be encountering it again as we examine the structure of gills and lungs.

Sponges are somewhere between a colony of cells and a true multicellular organism. The cells are not organised into tissues or organs; each leads an independent existence. Yet there is a form of recognition among the cells that holds them together and organises them.

If the sponge Microciona prolifera is squeezed through a fine sieve or a piece of cheesecloth, the body of the sponge is separated into individual cells and small clumps of cells. Within an hour, the isolated sponge cells begin to reaggregate, and as these aggregations get larger, canals, flagellated chambers, and other characteristics of the body organisation of the sponge begin to appear.

This phenomenon has been used as a model for the analysis of cell adhesion, recognition, and differentiation, all of which are basic biological features of development in higher organisms.

Most kinds of sponges are hermaphroditic; that is, they have male and female reproductive organs in the same individual. Gametes appear

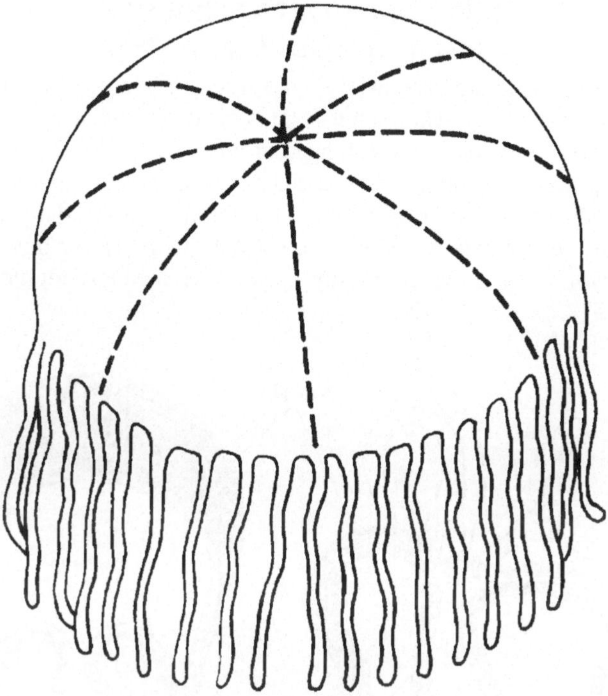

Figure 11.2 : In organisms with radial symmetry, any plane through the animal that passes through the central axis divides the body into halves that are mirror images of one another.

to arise from an enlarged amoebocyte, but there are reports that choanocytes can also form gametes. A sperm enters another sponge in a current of water.

It is captured by a choanocyte and transferred to an amoebocyte, which then transfers it to a ripe egg (a method of fertilisation unique to the sponges). The fertilised egg develops into a ciliated, free-swimming larva. After a short life among the plankton, the larva settles and becomes sessile.

Sponges also reproduce asexually, either by fragments that break off from the parent animal, or by gemmules, aggregations of amoebalike cells within a hard, protective outer layer. Production of such resistant forms is found, in general, only among freshwater organisms.

In the ocean, conditions are relatively unchanging, but the freshwater environment is much harsher. Invertebrates that live in fresh water are more likely to have protected embryonic forms than even closely related marine species.

PHYLUM COELENTERATA: POLYPS AND JELLYFISH

The coelenterates are a large and often strikingly beautiful group of aquatic organisms. Their adult-form is generally radially symmetrical; that is, their body parts are arranged around a central axis, like spokes around a hub. As you can see in figure elsewhere in this chapter, the basic body plan is a simple one: The animal is essentially a hollow container, which may be either vase-shaped, the *polyp,* or bowl-shaped, the *medusa.* The polyp is usually sessile; the medusa, motile.

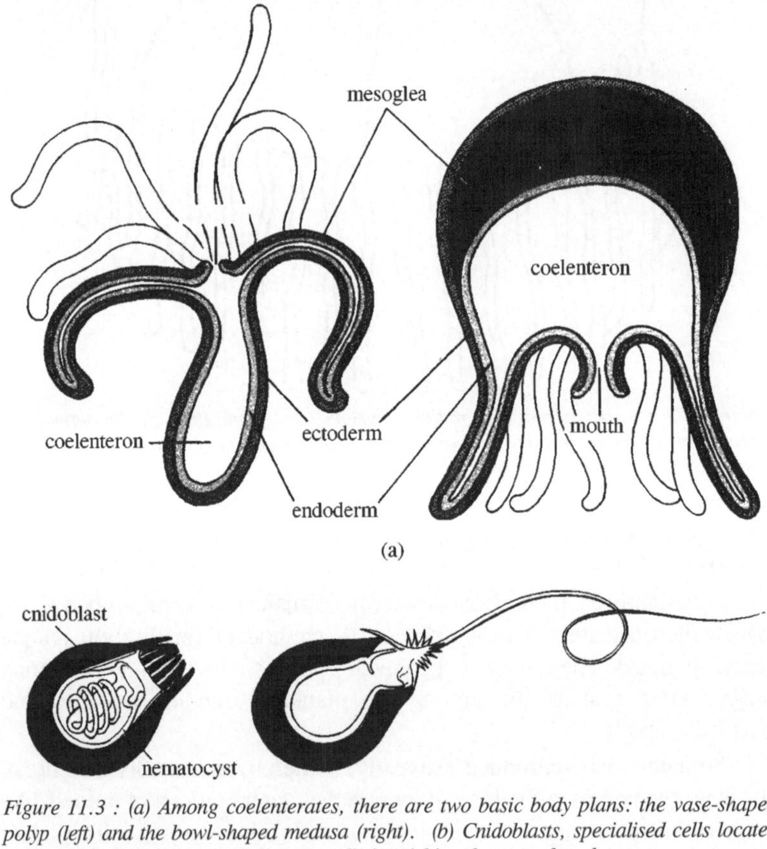

Figure 11.3 : (a) Among coelenterates, there are two basic body plans: the vase-shaped polyp (left) and the bowl-shaped medusa (right). (b) Cnidoblasts, specialised cells located in the tentacles and body wall, are a distinguishing feature of coelenterates.

Both consist of two layers of tissue: *ectoderm* and *endoderm* (from the Greek *ektos,* "outer," and *endon,* "inner," plus *derma,* "skin"). Between the two layers is a gelatinous filling, the *mesoglea* ("middle jelly"), which is made of a collagenlike material. In the polyp form,

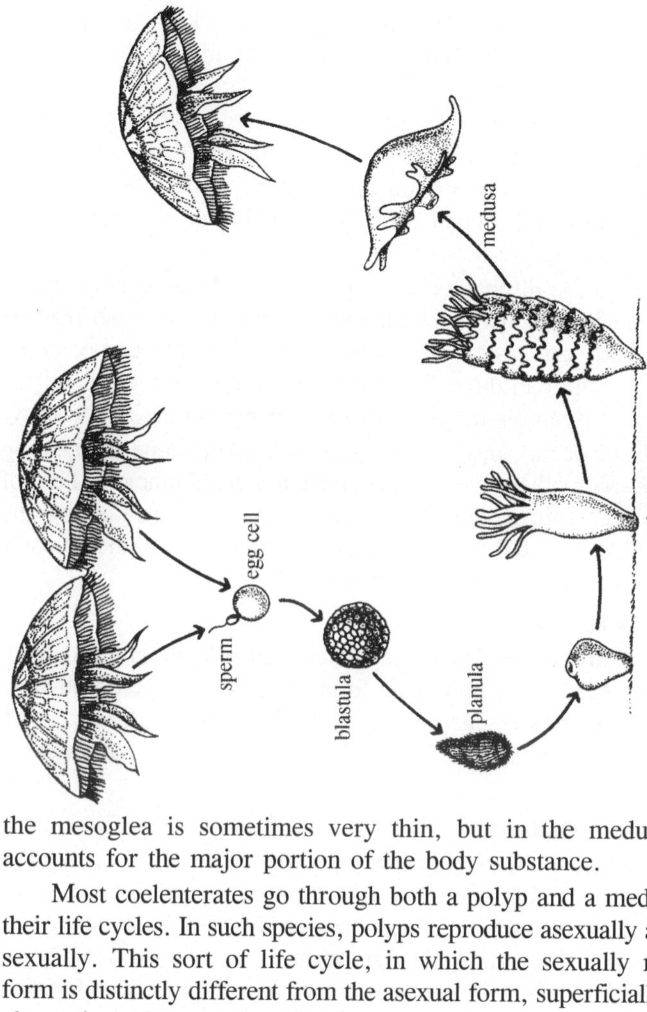

Figure 11.4 : The life cycle of the coelenterate Aurelia. Sperm and egg cells are released from adult medusas into the surrounding water. Fertilization takes place, and the resulting zygote develops first into a hollow sphere of cells, the blastula, and then elongates and becomes a ciliated larva called a planula.

the mesoglea is sometimes very thin, but in the medusa, it often accounts for the major portion of the body substance.

Most coelenterates go through both a polyp and a medusa stage in their life cycles. In such species, polyps reproduce asexually and medusas sexually. This sort of life cycle, in which the sexually reproductive form is distinctly different from the asexual form, superficially resembles alternation of generations in plants.

There is, however, no alternation between haploid and diploid forms as there is in plants; the only haploid forms are the gametes.

Another distinctive feature of the animals in this phylum is the *coelenteron,* a digestive cavity with only one opening. Within this cavity, enzymes are released that break down food, partially digesting it extracellularly, as our own food is digested within the stomach and intestinal tract.

The food particles are then taken up by the cells lining the cavity;

they complete the digestive process and pass the products on to the other cells of the animal. Inedible remains are ejected from the single opening.

A third distinctive feature of coelenterates is the *cnidoblast*. Coelenterates are carnivores. They capture their prey by means of tentacles that form a circle around the "mouth." These tentacles are armed with cnidoblasts, special cells that contain nematocysts (thread capsules).

Nematocysts are discharged in response to a chemical stimulus or touch. The nematocyst threads, which are often poisonous and may be sticky or barbed, can lasso prey, harpoon it, or paralyze it-or some useful combination of all three. The toxin apparently produces paralysis by attacking the lipoproteins of the nerve cell membrane of the prey.

Cnidoblasts occur only in this phylum, with some interesting exceptions. Certain other invertebrates, including nudibranchs (a kind of mollusk) and flatworms, can eat coelenterates without triggering the nematocysts. The nematocysts then migrate to the surface of the predator and can be fired in their new host's defense.

Classes of Coelenterates

There are three major classes of coelenterates: Hydrozoa, in which the polyp is usually the dominant form; Scyphozoa, predominantly medusoid, exemplified by the common jellyfish; and Anthozoa, which includes the sea anemones and the reef-building corals, and has only the polyp.

Class Hydrozoa: Hydra

One of the most thoroughly studied of the coelenterates is *Hydra,* which is a small, common freshwater form, convenient to keep in the laboratory. Figure elsewhere in this chapter shows a small section of the body wall of *Hydra*. The ectoderm is composed largely of epitheliomuscular cells, which perform a covering, protective function and also serve as muscle tissue.

Each cell has contractile fibers, myonemes, at its base and so can contract individually, like the contractile epithelial cells of the sponge. The endoderm is mostly made up of cells concerned with digestion; these cells also contain contractile fibers.

In *Hydra*, as in other polyps, the contractile fibrils of the ectoderm attach lengthwise to the mesoglea and the fibrils of the endoderm cells attach transversely, so the body walls can stretch or bulge, depending on which group is stimulated.

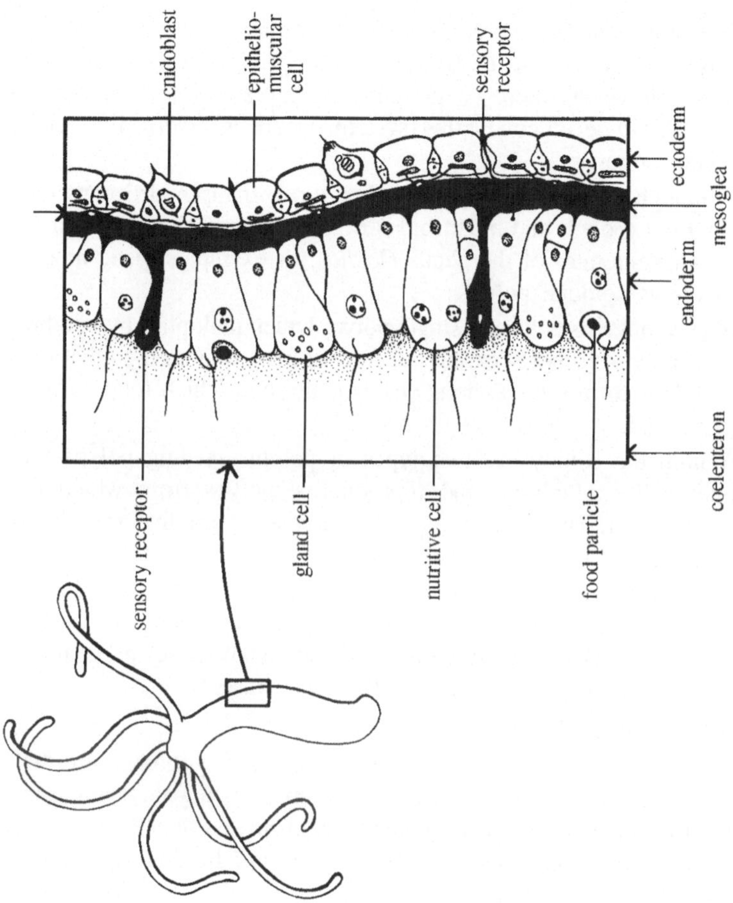

Figure 11.5 : The structure of the body wall of Hydra.

In addition to cnidoblasts and epitheliomuscular cells, which are independent effectors-cells that both receive and respond to stimuli-Hydra contain two other types of nerve cells: sensory receptor cells and cells connected into a network, the nerve net.

Sensory receptor cells are more sensitive than other epithelial cells to chemical and mechanical stimuli, and when stimulated they transmit their impulses to an adjacent cell or cells. The adjacent cell may be simply an epitheliomuscular cell, an effector, which then responds.

Note that this system is one step more complicated than the epitheliomuscular cell or cnidoblast, which acts as both receptor and effector. The nerve net, a loose connection of nerve cells lying at the base of the epithelial layers, is the simplest example of a nervous system that links an entire organism into a functional whole. It coordinates the muscular contractions of *Hydra,* making possible a wide variety of activities. However, there is no center of operations for the nervous system. This type of conducting system occurs in *Hydra* and certain other coelenterates.

Although *Hydra* has only the polyp form, many hydrozoans have both hydroid (polyp) and medusoid forms at different times in their life cycles. Coelenterates of the genus *Obelia,* for example, spend most of their lives as colonial polyps.

The colony arises from a single polyp, which multiplies by budding. The new polyps do not separate but remain interconnected so that their body cavities form a continuous channel, through which food particles are circulated.

Within the colony are two types of polyps: feeding polyps with tentacles and cnidoblasts, and reproductive polyps from which tiny medusas bud off. These medusas produce eggs or sperm that are released into the water and fuse to form zygotes.

Thus colonial polyps, with their division of labor between feeding and reproductive forms, are very like a single organism. Such a high degree of specialisation of structure and function among social organisms is seen in other phyla only among the social insects.

Class Scyphozoa: Jellyfish

A second major class of coelenterates is Scyphozoa, or "cup animals," in which the medusa form is dominant. Scyphozoans, more commonly known as jellyfish, range in size from less than 2 centimeters in diameter up to animals 4 meters across and trailing tentacles 10 meters long.

In the adult animal, the mesoglea is so firm that a large, freshly beached jellyfish can easily support the weight of a human being. The mesoglea of some jellyfish is filled with wandering, amoebalike cells, which serve to transport food from the nutritive cells of the endoderm. Unlike *Hydra,* scyphozoans have true muscle cells; these underlie the ectoderm, contracting rhythmically to propel the medusa through the water.

Nervous System of Medusa

In the medusa, there are concentrations of nerve cells in the margin of the bell. These nerve cells connect with fibers innervating (providing the nerve supply for) the tentacles, the musculature, and the sense organs.

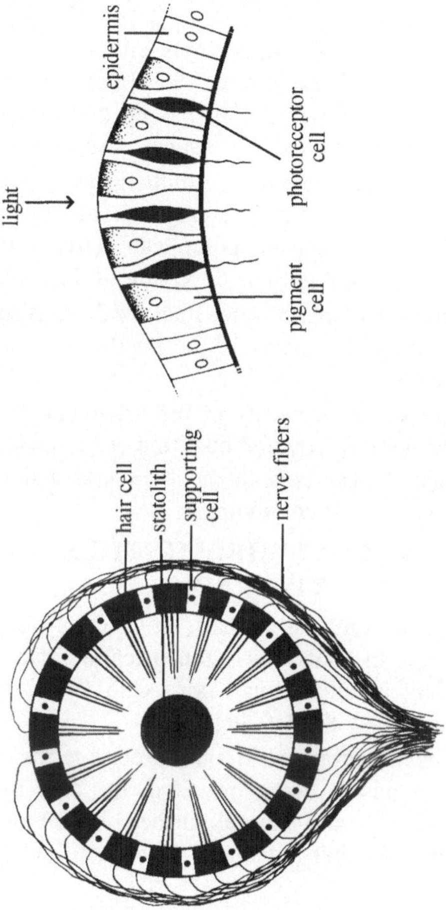

Figure 11.6 : (a) The statocyst is a specialised receptor organ that orients the jellyfish with respect to gravity. When the bell tilts, gravity pulls the statolith, a grain of hardened calcium salts, down against the hair cells. This stimulates the nerve fibers and signals the animal to right itself. (b) Eyespot (ocellus), the simplest type of photoreceptor organ. Ocelli of this sort are found among coelenterates.

The bell margin is liberally supplied with sensory receptor cells sensitive to mechanical and chemical stimuli. In addition, the jellyfish has two types of true sense organs: statocysts and light-sensitive ocelli.

Statocysts are specialised receptor organs that provide information by which an animal can orient itself with respect to gravity. The statocyst, which seems to have been one of the first special sensory organs to have appeared in the course of evolution, has persisted apparently unchanged to the present day, appearing in many animal phyla.

Ocelli, which may have evolved even earlier, are groups of pigment cells and photoreceptor cells. They are typically located at the bases of the tentacles.

Class Anthozoa

Anthozoans ("flower animals")-the corals and sea anemones-are members of a class of coelenterates that, like *Hydra,* have lost the medusa stage. They differ from *Hydra* in having a gullet lined with epidermis and a coelenteron divided by vertical partitions.

In most corals, which are colonies of anthozoans, the epidermal cells secrete protective outer walls, usually of calcium carbonate (limestone), into which each delicate polyp can retreat. The coral-forming polyps are the most ecologically important of the coelenterates.

The 2,000-kilometer-long Great Barrier Reef off the northeast shores of Australia, and the Marshall Islands in the Pacific are examples of coral-created land masses.

A coral reef is composed primarily of the accumulated limestone skeletons of coral coelenterates, covered by a thin crust occupied by the living colonial animals. A reef is both the structural and nutritional basis of the complex coral reef community.

PHYLUM PLATYHELMINTHES: FLATWORMS

The flatworms are the simplest animals, in terms of body plan, to show bilateral symmetry. In bilaterally symmetrical animals, the body plan is organised along a longitudinal axis, with the right half an approximate mirror image of the left half.

It also has a top and a bottom or, in more precise terms (applicable even when it is turned upside down or, as in the case of humans, standing upright), a dorsal and a ventral surface. Like most bilateral organisms, the flatworm also has a distinct "*headness*" and "*tailness,*" anterior and posterior.

Having one end that goes first-cephalization-is characteristic of actively moving animals. In such animals, many of the sensory cells are also collected into the anterior end. With the aggregation of sensory cells, there came a concomitant gathering of nerve cells; this gathering is a forerunner of the brain.

Flatworms have three distinct tissue layers-ectoderm, mesoderm, and endoderm-characteristic of all animals above the coelenterate level of organisation.

Moreover, not only are their tissues specialised for various functions, but also two or more types of tissue cells may combine to form organs-for example, the muscular pharynx. Thus, while sponges are made up of aggregations of cells and coelenterates are largely limited to the tissue level of organisation, flatworms can be said to exemplify the organ level of complexity. There are three classes of flatworms: the free-living turbellaria and two parasitic forms, flukes and tapeworms.

The flatworms are believed by some zoologists to have evolved from the coelenterates (or, perhaps, vice versa), not by way of either adult form, however, but from the ciliated larval form.

Others are persuaded that the flatworms had independent origins among the ciliates. Still another group maintains that they are degenerate annelids. It is unlikely that this matter will soon be resolved.

The Planarian

The free-living flatworms form a large and varied group, and we shall single out just one for examination, the freshwater planarian. The ectoderm of the planarian is made up of cuboid epithelial cells, many of which are ciliated, particularly those on the ventral surface.

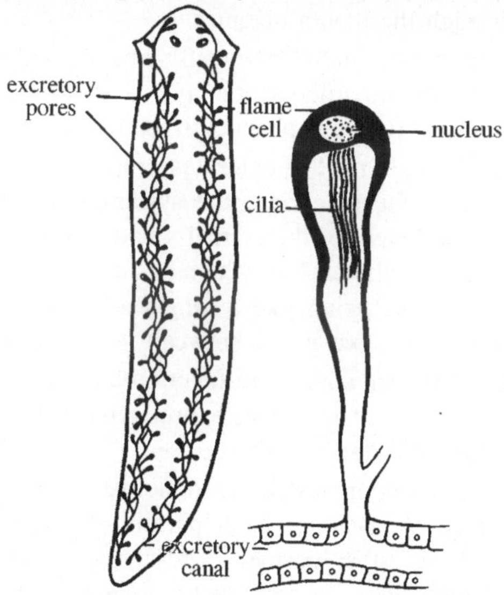

Figure 11.7 : Flatworms have a tubular excretory system. The system usually consists of two or more branching tubules running the length of the body.

Ventral ectodermal cells secrete mucus, which provides traction for the planarian as it moves by means of its cilia along its own slime trail. Planarians are among the largest animals that can use cilia for locomotion.

The cilia in larger species are usually employed for moving water or other substances along the surface of the animal, as in the human respiratory tract, rather than for propelling the animal.

The planarian has an endoderm composed largely of amoeboid cells, which, although they are phagocytic, are not wandering cells like the amoebocytes of the jellyfish. Between the ectoderm and the phagocytic endoderm is a *mesoderm,* or middle tissue layer.

In planarians, as in all other groups to follow, the muscle cells and the principal organ systems are of mesodermal origin.

The planarian, like the coelenterates, has a digestive cavity (gut) with only one opening, located on the ventral surface. This digestive cavity has three main branches, which is why planarians are placed in the order of flatworms known as Tricladida.

Like other flatworms, the planarian is carnivorous. It eats either dead meat or slow-moving animals it can fasten itself to or subdue by sitting on, such as smaller planarians. It feeds by means of a muscular tube, the pharynx, which is free at one end. The free end can be stretched out through the mouth opening.

Muscular contractions in the tube cause strong sucking movements, which tear the meat into microscopic bits and draw them into the internal cavity, where they are phagocytized by the endodermal cells.

Unlike the sponges or coelenterates, most flatworms have an excretory system. In the planarian, the system is a network of fine tubules that runs the length of the animal's body. Side branches of the tubules contain flame cells, each of which has a hollow center in which a tuft of cilia beats, flickering like a tongue of flame, moving water along the tubules to the exit pores between the epidermal cells.

The flame-cell system appears to function largely to regulate water balance; most of the metabolic waste products probably diffuse out through the ectoderm or the endoderm.

Planarians have a complicated reproductive system. The eggs are fertilised internally. At mating, each partner deposits sperm in the copulatory sac of the other partner. These sperm then travel along special tubes, the *oviducts*, to fertilise the eggs as they become ripe.

As we mentioned earlier, organisms like planarians, in which both types of gametes are produced by one individual, are known as hermaphrodites (from Hermes and Aphrodite).

Solitary, slow-moving animals, such as earthworms and snails, are often hermaphrodites; these animals may seldom encounter another adult member of the species, but every such encounter can result in a mating. Some types of hermaphroditic animals can fertilise themselves, although they do not usually do so if another individual is present.

The Planarian Nervous System

The evolution of bilateral symmetry brought with it marked changes in the organisation of the nervous system as well as of other systems. Even among primitive flatworms, the neurons (nerve cells) are not dispersed in a loose network, as in *Hydra,* but are instead condensed into longitudinal cords.

In the planarians, this condensation is carried further, and there are only two main conducting channels, one on each side of the flat, ribbonlike body. These channels carry impulses to and from the aggregation of nerve cells in the anterior end of the body. Such aggregations of nerve cell bodies are known as *ganglia* (singular, ganglion).

The ocelli of the planarian are usually inverted pigment cups. They have no lenses, and they cannot form an image. However, they can distinguish light from dark and can tell the direction from which the light is coming.

Planarians are photonegative; if you shine a light on a dish of planarians from the side, they will move steadily away from the source of light.

Among the epithelial cells are receptor cells sensitive to certain chemicals and to touch. The head region in particular is rich in *chemoreceptors.* If you place a small piece of fresh liver in the culture water so that its juices diffuse through the medium, the planarians will raise their heads off the bottom and, if they have not eaten recently, will lope directly and rapidly (on a planarian scale) toward the meat, to which they then attach themselves to feed.

The animal locates the food source by repeatedly turning toward the side on which it receives the stimulus more strongly until the stimulus is equal on both sides of its head. If the chemoreceptor cells are removed from one side of the head, the animal will turn constantly toward the intact side.

Planarians, with their simple nervous systems, their capacity to react to a variety of stimuli, and their powers of regeneration, have been the subject of a number of experiments. In one group, planarians trained to avoid electric shock were fed to untrained planarians.

The result, it was claimed, was that the untrained planarians that had eaten the trained ones behaved as if they had been trained. These experiments, still not verified, on the "transfer of training by cannibalism" led to a great deal of controversy in the 1960s and also, as you might expect, to a number of suggestions for more meaningful student-teacher relationships.

Tapeworms and Flukes

Phylum Platyhelminthes includes also the tapeworms and the trematodes (flukes), parasitic forms that can cause serious and sometimes fatal diseases among vertebrates. Members of both of these parasitic classes have a tough outer layer of cells that is resistant to digestive fluids and, usually, suckers or hooks on their anterior ends by which they fasten to their victims.

Trematodes feed through a mouth, but the tapeworms, which have no mouths, digestive cavities, or digestive enzymes, merely hang on and absorb predigested food molecules through their skin. Tapeworms are found in the intestines of many vertebrates, including humans, and may grow as long as 5 or 6 meters.

They cause illness not only by encroaching on the food supply but also by producing wastes and by obstructing the intestinal tract. The most common human tapeworm, the beef tapeworm, infects people who eat the undercooked flesh of cattle that have eaten fodder contaminated by human feces containing tapeworm segments.

All parasites, including parasitic flatworms, are believed to have originated as free-living forms and to have lost certain tissues and organs (such as the digestive tract) as a secondary effect of their parasitic existence, while developing adaptations of advantage to the parasitic way of life. Such adaptations also often include a complex life cycle.

PHYLUM RHYNCHOCOELA: RIBBON WORMS

The ribbon worms (sometimes called nemertines), although a small phylum, are of special interest to biologists attempting to reconstruct the evolution of the invertebrates. They appear to be closely related to the flatworms, but with an important difference: They have a one-way digestive tract beginning with a mouth and ending with an anus.

This is a far more efficient arrangement than the one-opening digestive system of the coelenterates and flatworms. In the one-way tract, food moves assembly-line fashion, with the consequent possibilities (1) that eating can be continuous and (2) that various segments of the tract can become specialised for different stages of digestion. The ribbon worms also have a circulatory system, usually consisting of one dorsal and two lateral blood vessels that carry the colourless blood.

This phylum is called Rhynchocoela ("beak" plus "hollow") because these worms are characterised by a long, retractile, slime-covered tube (proboscis). The proboscis, sometimes armed with a barb, seizes prey and draws it to the mouth where it is engulfed. Some inject a paralyzing poison into their prey.

PHYLUM NEMATODA: ROUNDWORMS

The number of species of roundworms (nematodes) has been variously estimated as low as 10,000 and as high as 400,000 to 500,000. Most are free-living, microscopic forms. It has been estimated that a spadeful of good garden soil usually contains about a million nematodes. Some are parasites; most species of plants and animals are parasitised by at least one species of nematodes.

Humans are hosts to about 50 species, including hookworms, pinworms, and *Trichinella.* The latter causes trichinosis, which is transmitted by eating uncooked or undercooked pork, a single gram of which may contain 3,000 cysts (resting forms) of *Trichinella.* Ingestion of only a few hundred of these cysts can be fatal to human beings.

Nematodes have a three-layered body plan and a tubular gut with a mouth and an anus. They are unsegmented and are covered by a thick, continuous cuticle, which is molted periodically as they grow.

An interesting, and unique, feature of nematode construction is the absence of circular muscles. The contraction of the longitudinal muscles acting against the tough, elastic cuticle gives the worm its characteristic whipping movement in water. The sexes are usually separate.

Nematodes may have evolved from early Platyhelminthes, possessing, as they do, a three-layered body plan without a true coelom. They have, however, what is known as a pseudocoelom, a body cavity that is between the endoderm and the mesoderm and lacks the epithelial lining of a true coelom.

Six other minor (in terms of species and numbers) phyla, mostly small, wormlike animals, have body plans based on the pseudocoelom, but Nematoda is the only major pseudocoelomate phylum.

PHYLUM ANNELIDA : SEGMENTED WORMS

This phylum includes almost 9,000 different species of marine, freshwater, and soil worms, including the familiar earthworm. The term annelid means "ringed" and refers to the most distinctive feature of this group, which is the division of the body into segments, visible as rings on the outside and with partitions on the inside.

This segmented pattern is found in a modified form in higher animals, too, such as dragonflies, millipedes, and lobsters, which are thought to have evolved from the same ancestors that gave rise to modern annelids.

The annelids have a three-layered body plan, a tubular gut, and a well-developed circulatory system that transports oxygen (diffused through the skin or through fleshy extensions of the skin) and food molecules (from the gut) to all parts of the body.

The excretory system is made up of specialised paired tubules, nephridia, which occur in each segment of the body except the head. Annelids have a nervous system and a number of special sense cells, including touch cells, taste receptors, light-sensitive cells, and cells concerned with the detection of moisture. Some also have well-developed eyes and sensory antennae.

In the flatworms and ribbon worms, the mesoderm is packed solid with muscle and other tissues, but in the annelids there is a fluid-filled cavity, the *coelom*, (pronounced see-loam) in this middle layer. (Note that the term coelom, although it sounds similar to coelenteron and comes from the same Greek root, meaning "cavity," refers quite specifically to a cavity *within* the mesoderm, whereas the coelenteron is a digestive cavity lined by endoderm.)

Within the coelom, the gut-lined with an epithelium-is suspended by double layers of mesoderm known as mesenteries. The fluid in the coelom constitutes a hydrostatic skeleton for the annelid, stiffening the body in somewhat the same way water pressure stiffens and distends a fire hose.

The muscles of the earthworm work against this hydrostatic skeleton much as our muscles work against our bony skeleton. Although the opening of a cavity within the mesoderm may seem less dramatic than other evolutionary innovations, it is extremely important.

Within such a space, organ systems can bend, twist, and fold back on themselves, increasing their functional surface areas and filling, emptying, and sliding past one another, surrounded by lubricating coelomic fluid. Consider the human lung, constantly expanding and contracting in the chest cavity, or the 6 or 7 meters of coiled human intestine; neither of these could have evolved until the coelom made room for them.

Earthworms

The earthworm is the most familiar of the annelids. Figure elsewhere in this chapter shows a portion of the body of an earthworm. Note how the body is compartmented into regular segments. Most of these segments, particularly the central and posterior ones, are identical, each exactly

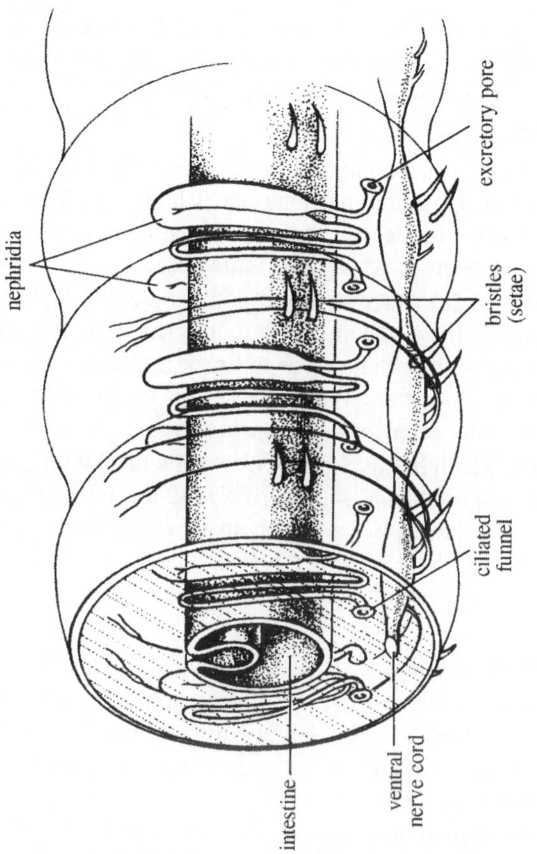

Figure 11.8 : Three segments of the earthworm, an annelid. On each segment are four pairs of bristles, which are extended and retracted by special muscles. These are used by the worm to anchor one part of its body while it moves another part forward.

like the one before and the one after. Each identical segment contains four pairs of bristles, or *setae*; two *nephridia,* excretory tubules that pick up waste materials from the body fluids and excrete them through pores on the ventral surface of the worm; four sets of nerves branching off from the central nerve cord running along the ventral surface; a portion of digestive tract; and a left and right coelomic cavity.

The chief exceptions to this rule of segmented structure are found in the most forward segments. In these, sensory cells, a cluster of nerve cells (ganglia), and specialised areas of the digestive, circulatory, and reproductive systems are found.

The tubelike body is wrapped in two sets of muscles, one set running longitudinally and the other encircling the segments. When the earthworm moves, it anchors some of its segments by its setae, and the circular muscles of the segments anterior to the anchored segments contract, thus extending its body forward. Then its forward setae take hold, and the longitudinal muscles contract while the posterior anchor is released, drawing the posterior segments forward.

Digestion in Earthworms

The digestive tract of the earthworm is a long, straight tube. The mouth leads into a strong, muscular pharynx, which acts like a suction pump, drawing in decaying leaves and other organic matter, as well as dirt, from which organic materials are extracted.

The earthworm makes burrows in the earth by passing such material through its digestive tract and depositing it outside in the form of castings, a ceaseless activity that serves to break up, enrich, and aerate the soil. The narrow section of tube posterior to the pharynx, the *esophagus*, leads to the crop, where food is stored.

In the gizzard, which has thick, muscular walls lined with protective cuticle, the food is ground up with the help of the ever-present soil particles. The rest of the digestive tract is made up of a long intestine, which has a large fold along its upper surface that increases its surface area. The intestinal epithelium consists of enzyme-secreting cells and ciliated absorptive cells.

Circulation in Earthworms

In the protists and in the smaller and simpler animals, food molecules and oxygen are supplied to cells largely by diffusion, aided by the movement of external fluids and, sometimes, as we saw in coelenterates, by wandering, amoeboid cells.

A circulatory system that propels extracellular fluid around the body solves the problem of providing each cell with a more direct and rapid line of supply.

The circulatory system of the earthworm is composed of longitudinal vessels running the entire length of the worm, one dorsal and several ventral. The largest ventral vessel underlies the intestinal tract, collecting nutrients from it and distributing them by means of many small branches to all the tissues of the body and to the three smaller ventral vessels that surround the nerve cord and nourish it.

Numerous small capillaries in each segment carry blood from the ventral vessels through the tissues to the dorsal vessel. Also in each segment are larger parietal ("along the wall") vessels transporting blood from the subneural vessels to the dorsal vessel. Fluids collected in this way from all over the animal's body are fed into the muscular dorsal vessel, which propels the blood forward.

Connecting the dorsal and ventral vessels, and so completing the circuit, are five pairs of hearts, muscular pumping areas in the blood vessels. Their irregular contractions force the blood down to the ventral vessels and also forward to the vessels that supply the more anterior segments.

Both the hearts and the dorsal vessel have valves that prevent backflow. Note that the blood flows entirely through vessels. Such a system is known as a closed circulatory system. Evolution of a closed circulatory system, in effect, added a new compartment to the body plan and, in so doing, made possible a degree of control, not previously feasible, over the content of the circulating body fluid.

Excretory System of Earthworms

The excretory system consists of pairs of tubules, the nephridia; one pair for each segment. Each nephridium consists of a long, convoluted tubule that terminates in a ciliated funnel opening into the coelomic cavity of the anteriorly adjacent segment.

Coelomic fluid is carried into the funnel by the beating of the cilia and is excreted through an outer pore. As the fluid makes its way through the long tubule, water, sugar, salts, and other needed materials are returned to the coelomic fluid through the walls of the tubule, while other materials are absorbed into the tubule for excretion.

Thus the excretory system is concerned not only with the problem of water balance, as are the contractile vacuoles of *Paramecium* and the flame cells of planarians, but also with the homeostatic regulation of the chemical composition of the body fluids.

Thus, in effect, one segment monitors and regulates this aspect of the physiology of its neighboring segment-a neat trick for integrating the animal as a whole.

Respiration in Earthworms

The earthworm has no special respiratory organs; respiration takes place by simple diffusion through the body surface. The gases of the atmosphere dissolve in the liquid film on the surface of the earthworm's body, which is kept moist by secreted mucus and excreted water.

Oxygen travels inward by diffusion, since the surface film, exposed to the oxygen-rich atmosphere, contains more oxygen than does the blood in the network of capillaries just underlying the body surface. The oxygen is consumed by body cells as the blood circulates.

Carbon dioxide moves out to the surface film and then into the air by the same principle. In fact, all gas exchange in animals, whether the organism is land-dwelling or water-dwelling, takes place across moist membranes.

Nervous System in Earthworms

The earthworm has a variety of sensory cells. It has touch cells, or *mechanoreceptors*. These contain tactile hairs, which, when stimulated, trigger a nerve impulse. Patches of these hair cells are found on each segment of the earthworm. The hairs probably also respond to vibrations in the ground, to which the earthworm is very sensitive.

The earthworm does not have ocelli-as one might expect, since it lives most of its life in complete darkness-but it does have light-sensitive cells. Such cells are more abundant in its anterior and posterior segments, the parts of its body most likely to be outside of the burrow.

These cells are not responsive to light in the red portion of the spectrum, a fact exploited by anglers who search for worms in the dark using red-lensed flashlights.

Among the earthworm's most sensitive cells are those that detect moisture. The cells are located on its first few segments. If an earthworm emerging from its burrow encounters a dry spot, it swings from side to side until it finds dampness; failing that, it retreats.

However, when the anterior segments are anesthetised, the earthworm will crawl over dry ground. The animal also appears to have taste cells. In the laboratory, worms can be shown to select, for example, celery in preference to cabbage leaves and cabbage leaves in preference to carrots.

Each segment of the worm is supplied by nerves that receive impulses from sensory cells and by nerves that cause muscles to contract. The cell bodies for these nerves are grouped together in clusters (ganglia). The movements of each segment are directed by a pair of ganglia.

Movement in each segment is triggered by movement in the adjacent anterior segment; thus a headless earthworm can move in a coordinated manner. However, an earthworm without its cerebral ganglia moves ceaselessly; in other words, cephalic ganglia modulate activity.

There are also, as in planarians, conducting channels made up of nerve fibers bound together in bundles, like cables, which run lengthwise through the body. These nerve fibers are gathered together in a double nerve cord that runs along the ventral surface of the body.

The nerve cords contain fast-conducting fibers that make it possible for the earthworm to contract its entire body very quickly, withdrawing into its burrow when disturbed.

Reproduction in Earthworms

Earthworms are hermaphrodites. Two earthworms, held together by mucous secretions from the clitellum (a special collection of glandular cells), exchange sperm and separate. Two or three days later, the clitellum forms a second mucous sheath surrounded by an outer, tougher protective layer of chitin.

This sheath is pushed forward along the animal by muscular movements of its body. As it passes over the female gonopores, it picks up a collection of mature eggs, and then, continuing forward, it picks up the sperm deposited in the spermathecas.

Once the mucous band is slipped over the head of the worm, its sides pinch together, enclosing the now fertilised eggs in a small capsule from which the infants hatch.

Other Annelids

Other annelids resemble the earthworm in that they are cylindrical worms divided into a series of similar segments, and they have a complex circulatory system of blood vessels, a main ventral nerve trunk, a complete digestive tube, and a coelom.

The phylum is usually divided into three principal classes: Oligochaeta, Polychaeta, and Hirudinea. Oligochaeta is the group that includes the earthworms and related freshwater species. The polychaetes, which are marine animals, differ from the earthworms and other oligochaetes in a number of ways.

The most striking difference is that they typically have a variety of appendages, including tentacles, antennae, and specialised mouthparts. Each segment contains two fleshy extensions, parapodia, which function in locomotion and also, because they contain many blood vessels, are important in gas exchange.

Many polychaetes live in elaborately fashioned tubes constructed in the mud or sand of the ocean bottom. Usually the sexes are separate, fertilization is external, and the larvae are freeswimming. Hirudinea are the leeches, which have flattened, often tapered, bodies with a sucker at each end.

Bloodsucking leeches attach themselves to their hosts by their posterior sucker, and then, with their anterior sucker, either slit the host's skin with their sharp jaws or digest an opening through the skin by means of enzymes. Finally, they secrete a special chemical (hirudin) into the host's blood to prevent it from coagulating.

PHYLUM MOLLUSCA: MOLLUSKS

The mollusks constitute one of the largest phyla of animals, both in numbers of species and in numbers of individuals. They are characterised by soft bodies within a hard, calcium-containing shell, although in some forms the shell has been lost in the course of evolution, as in slugs and octopuses, or greatly reduced in size and internalised, as in squids.

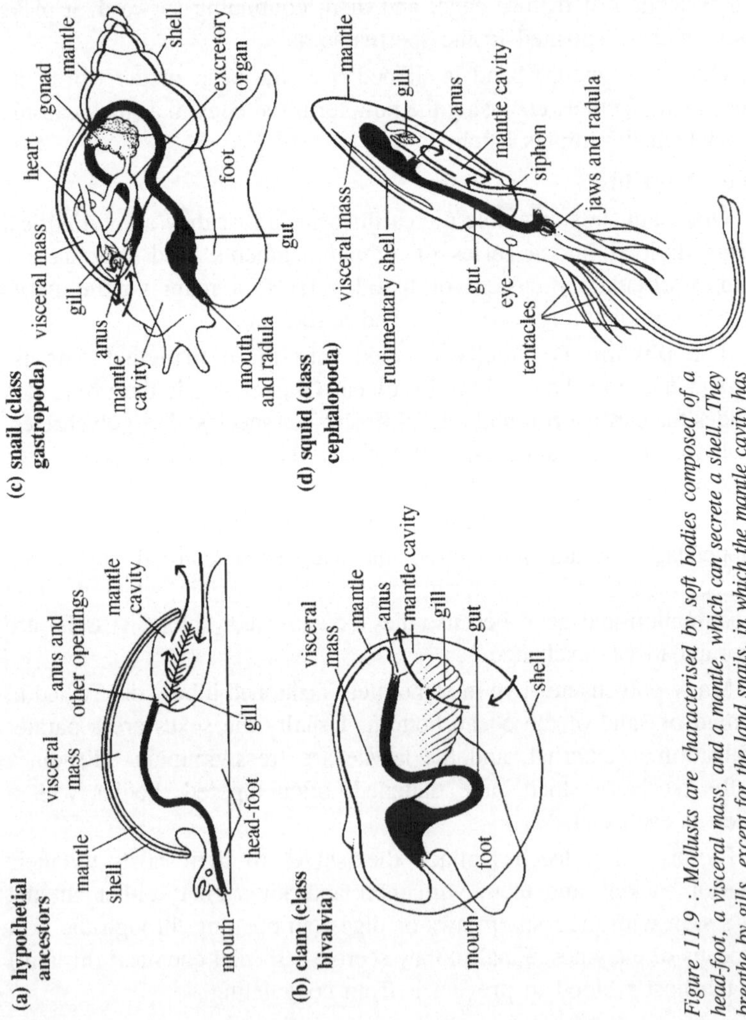

Figure 11.9 : Mollusks are characterised by soft bodies composed of a head-foot, a visceral mass, and a mantle, which can secrete a shell. They breathe by gills, except for the land snails, in which the mantle cavity has been modified for air breathing.

There are three major classes of mollusks: (1) the gastropods, such as the snails, whose shells are generally in one piece; (2) the bivalves, including the clams, oysters, and mussels, which have two shells joined by a hinge ligament; and (3) the cephalopods, the most active and most intelligent of the mollusks, including the cuttlefish, squids, and octopuses.

The basic molluscan body plan is shown in figure elsewhere in this chpater. As you can see, this hypothetical animal was bilaterally symmetrical and segmented.

Among modern mollusks, only the chitons, a relatively small group, bear any obvious resemblance to the archetypal model, but modern mollusks, although diverse in size and shape, all have the same fundamental body plan.

There are three distinct body zones: a head-foot, which contains both the sensory and the motor organs; a visceral mass, which contains the organs of digestion, excretion, and reproduction; and a mantle, which hangs over and enfolds the visceral mass and which secretes the shell.

The mantle cavity, a space between the mantle and the visceral mass, houses the gills; the digestive, excretory, and reproductive systems discharge into it. Water sweeps into the mantle cavity (propelled in the bivalves by cilia on the gills), passing through the gills and aerating them. It then passes by the nephridia, gonopores, and rectum, which are always downstream from the gills.

Water leaving the mantle cavity carries excreta and, in season, gametes. The digestive tract is far more convoluted and so provides more working surface than that of the annelids.

In all mollusks, the digestive tract is extensively ciliated, with many different working areas. Food is taken up by the cells lining the digestive glands arising from the stomach and the anterior intestine, and then is passed into the blood.

A characteristic organ of the mollusk, found only in this phylum, and in all classes except the bivalves, is the radula, a tooth-bearing strap of movable pieces of chitinous tissue covering the tongue.

The radula apparatus, which operates with a rhythmic back-and-forth movement, serves both to scrape off algae and other food materials and also to convey them backward to the digestive tract. It is also used in combat.

Mollusks, as we noted previously, have gills. To understand the basic plan of gill structure and function, it is necessary only to recall the moist epidermis of the earthworm, through which oxygen diffuses, and the blood vessel lying close beneath it, which transports the oxygen to other parts of the body. A gill is a structure with an increased amount of surface area, through which gases can diffuse, and a rich blood supply for transport of these gases.

Oxygen diffuses inward, along the gradient, because the cells of the animal have removed oxygen from the bloodstream by cellular respiration. Carbon dioxide, produced by cellular respiration, diffuses outward.

Mollusks have three-chambered hearts; two of the chambers (atria) collect oxygenated blood from the gills, and the third (the ventricle) pumps it to the oxygen-depleted tissue.

Except for the cephalopods, mollusks have what is known as an open circulation; that is, the blood does not circulate entirely within vessels-as it does in the earthworm, for example-but is oxygenated, pumped through the heart, and released directly into spaces in the tissues from which it returns, deoxygenated, to the gills and then to the heart.

Such a blood-filled space is known as a hemocoel ("blood cavity"). Cephalopods, which are extremely active animals, have accessory hearts that propel blood into the gills, and a closed circulatory system.

Class Bivalvia

In the bivalves, the two-shelled mollusks, the body has become flattened between the two shells, and "*headness*" has generally disappeared. The bivalves are sometimes called Pelecypoda-"hatchet foot"—because the muscular foot is often highly developed in this group.

A clam, using its "*hatchet foot*," can dig itself into sand or mud with remarkable speed. However, the bivalves are largely sessile forms, and many of them secrete strong strands of protein by which they anchor themselves to rocks.

Most bivalves are filter-feeding herbivores; they live largely on microscopic algae. Their gills, which are large and elaborate, collect food particles.

Water is circulated through the sievelike gills by the beating of gill cilia. Small organisms and particles of food are trapped in mucus on the gill surface and swept toward the mouth by the cilia; the gills also sort particles by size, rejecting sand and other larger particles.

The shells are held together and opened at the hinge by a strong ligament and are drawn closed by one or two large muscles connecting the two shells.

Throughout the molluscan phylum, there is a wide range of development of the nervous system. The bivalves have three pairs of ganglia of approximately equal size-cerebral, visceral, and pedal (supplying the foot)-and two long pairs of nerve cords interconnecting them.

They have statocysts, usually located near the pedal ganglia, and sensory cells for discrimination of touch, chemical changes, and light. The scallop has quite complex eyes; a single individual may have a hundred or more eyes located among the tentacles on the fringe of the mantle.

The lens of this eye cannot focus on images, however, so it does not appear to serve for more than the detection of light and dark and movement.

Class Gastropoda

The gastropods, which include the snails, whelks, periwinkles, abalones, and slugs, are the largest group of mollusks. They have either a single shell or, as a secondary evolutionary development, no shell. Another feature common to all members of this group, as compared with the ancestral mollusk, is that all of them have undergone torsion.

In other words, the internal organs, the shell, and the mantle have been twisted 180° so that in the modern animal, the mouth and anus and also the gills share the same comparatively small mantle cavity, now pointing forward instead of toward the rear.

Third, the stomach and digestive gland have become twisted upward into a spirally coiled visceral mass. In response to this displacement and consequent crowding of the internal organs, the gill and nephridium of the right side have been lost in many species.

In some close relatives of the snails, such as the slugs, the digestive tract has become straightened out again by another course of evolutionary events, in which the shell was lost but the missing organs were not regained.

Land-dwelling snails do not have gills but the area in their mantle cavities once occupied by gills is rich in blood vessels, and the snail's blood is oxygenated there.

Some snails that were once land dwellers have returned to the water, but they have not regained gills. Instead, they must bob up to the surface at regular intervals to entrap a fresh bubble of air in their mantle cavities.

Thus the mantle cavity has, in effect, become a lung. Moreover, as with all lungs, the opening is reduced to retard evaporation. Gastropods, which lead a more mobile, active existence than bivalves, have a ganglionated nervous system with as many as six pairs of ganglia connected by nerve cords.

There is a concentration of nerve cells at the anterior end of the animal, where the tentacles, which have chemoreceptors and touch receptors, and the eyes are located. In some of the animals, the eyes are quite highly developed in structure; they appear, however, to function largely in the detection of changes in light intensity, like the eyes of the scallop.

Class Cephalopoda

The cephalopods (the "head-foots") are the most highly developed mollusks. The large head has conspicuous eyes and a central mouth surrounded by arms, some 70 or 80 in the chambered nautilus, 10 in the squid, and 8 in the octopus.

The nautilus, as the only modem shelled cephalopod, offers an indication of some of the steps by which this class disposed of the shell entirely. The animal occupies only the outermost portion of its elaborate and beautiful shell, the rest of which serves as a flotation chamber.

In the squid and its relative, the cuttlefish, the shell has become an internal stiffening support, and in the octopus, it is lacking entirely.

The octopus body seldom reaches more than 30 centimeters in diameter (except on the late late show), but giant squids sometimes attain sea-monster proportions. One caught in the Atlantic some hundred years ago was 15 meters long, not counting the tentacles, and was estimated to weigh 2 tons.

Freedom from the external shell has given the mantle more flexibility. The most obvious effect of this is the jet propulsion by which cephalopods dart through the water. Usually, water taken into the mantle cavity bathes the gills and is then expelled slowly through a tube-shaped structure, the siphon; but when the cephalopod is hunting or being hunted, it can contract the mantle cavity forcibly and suddenly, thereby squirting out a sudden jet of water.

Contraction of the mantlecavity muscles usually shoots the animal backward, head last, but the squid and the octopus can turn the siphon in almost any direction they choose. In addition to the siphon, cephalopods have sacs from which they can release a dark fluid that forms a cloud, concealing their retreat and confusing their enemies.

These coloured fluids were at one time a chief source of commercial

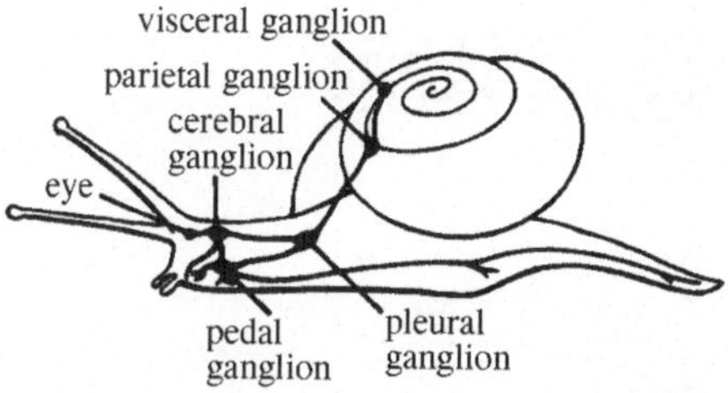

Figure 11.10 : The ganglionated nervous system of a gastropod. Each dot represents a pair of ganglia, each innervating a different segment of the body. The cerebral ganglia supply the tentacles and eyes; the pleural ganglia, the mantle; the pedal ganglia, the foot muscles; and so on.

inks. *Sepia is* the name of the genus of cuttlefish from which a brown ink used to be obtained.

The cephalopods have well-developed brains, composed of many groups of ganglia, in keeping with their highly developed sensory systems and their lively, predatory behaviour. These large brains are covered with cartilaginous cases.

The rapid responses of the cephalopods are made possible by a bundle of giant nerve fibers that control the muscles of the mantle. Many of the studies on conduction of the nerve impulse are made with the giant axon of the squid, which is large enough to permit the insertion of an electrode.

Evolutionary Affinities of the Mollusks

Although the annelids and the mollusks are quite different in their basic body plans, there are some similarities between them that seem to suggest evolutionary links. One of these is the trochophore larva. Many of the annelids (the oligochaetes and hirudineans excepted) have this very distinct larval form.

Most marine mollusks (except the cephalopods) also pass through a trochophore stage in their development. Until fairly recently, the lack of unequivocal traces of segmentation in the mollusks seemed to argue against the evidence of close affinity provided by the trochophore.

In the 1950s, however, 10 living specimens of *Neopilina,* a genus of mollusks previously known only from Cambrian fossils, were dredged from a deep ocean trench off the coast of Costa Rica. *Neopilina,* which is little more than 2.5 centimeters long, resembles a combination of gastropod and chiton, with a single large shell but five pairs of gills, five pairs of retractor muscles, and six pairs of nephridia, all arranged in what seems to be a distinctly segmental pattern.

A third link between mollusks and annelids is the pattern of

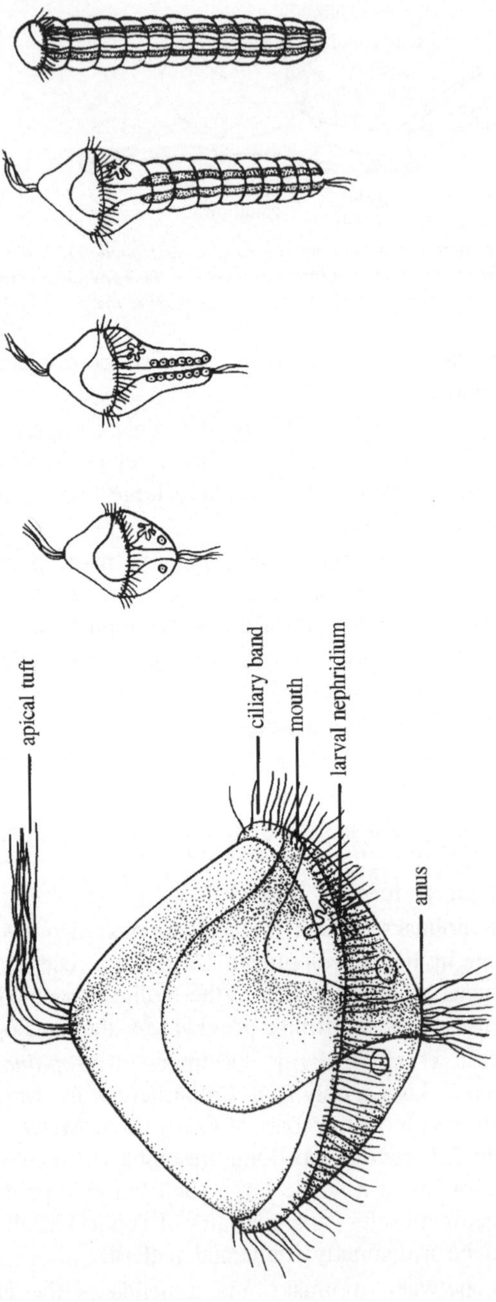

Figure 11.11 : How the annelid trochophore develops into a segmented worm. The process begins with the elongation of the lower part of the trochophore. The elongated region then becomes constricted into segments, which soon develop bristles. The apical tuft disappears, and the upper part of the trochophore becomes the head. The worm will continue to grow throughout its lifetime by adding new segments just in front of its rear segment.

embryonic development-protostomes vs. deuterostomes-which we shall discuss further at the end of this chapter.

PHYLUM ECHINODERMATA: STARFISH

The starfish and its relatives are known as echinoderms, or "spiny skins." Adult echinoderms are radially symmetrical, like most coelenterates, although the symmetry is imperfect with some traces of bilaterality in the adults and with bilaterally symmetrical larvae.

Starfish

The most familiar of the echinoderms is the starfish, whose body consists of a central disk from which radiate a number of arms. Most starfish have five arms, which was the ancestral number, but some have more.

A starfish has no head, and any arm may lead in its sluggish, creeping movements along the sea bottom. The central disk contains a mouth on the ventral surface, above which is the stomach. Like all echinoderms, the starfish has an interior skeleton that typically bears projecting spines, the characteristic from which the phylum derives its name.

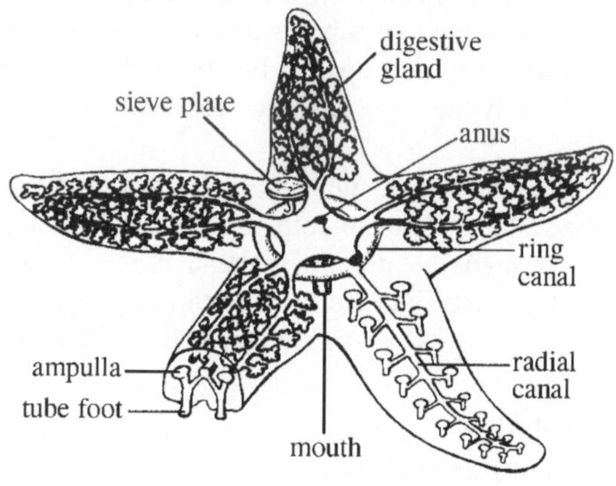

Figure 11.12 : The water vascular system of the starfish is its means of locomotion.

The skeleton is made up of tiny, separate calcium-containing plates held together by the skin tissues and-by muscles. Each arm contains a pair of digestive glands and also a nerve cord, with an eyespot at the end.

These latter are the only sensory organs, strictly speaking, of the starfish, but the epidermis contains thousands of neurosensory cells (as many as 70,000 per square millimeter) concerned with touch and chemoreception. Each arm also has its own pair of gonads, which open directly to the exterior through small pores.

The circulatory system consists of a series of channels within the coelomic cavity. Respiration is accomplished by many small fingerlike projections, the skin gills, which are protected by spines. Amoeboid cells circulate in the coelomic fluid, picking up the wastes and then escaping through the thin walls of the skin gills, where they are pinched off and ejected.

The water vascular, or hydraulic, system is a unique feature of the phylum. Each arm of a starfish contains two or more rows of water-filled tube feet. These tube feet are interconnected by a central ring and radial canals. Water filling the soft, hollow tubes makes them rigid enough to walk on.

Each tube foot connects with a rounded muscular sac, the ampulla. When the ampulla contracts, the water is forced under pressure through a valve into the tube foot; this extends the foot, which attaches to the substrate by its sucker. When the muscles at the base of the tube feet contract, the animal is pulled forward.

If the tube feet are planted on a hard surface, such as a rock or a clam shell, the collection of tubes will exert enough suction to pull the starfish forward or to pull apart a bivalve mollusk, a feat that will be appreciated by anyone who has ever tried to open an oyster or a clam.

When attacking bivalves, which are its staple diet, the starfish everts its stomach through its mouth opening and then squeezes the stomach tissue through the minute space that the starfish has made between the bivalve shells. The stomach tissues can insinuate themselves through a slit as narrow as 0.1 millimeter and begin to digest the soft tissue of the prey.

Echinoderm Evolution

The echinoderms are believed to have evolved from an ancestral, bilateral, mobile form that settled down to a sessile life, and then became radially symmetrical. The sea lilies represent this second hypothetical stage.

In the third evolutionary stage, some of the animals, as represented by the starfish and sea urchins, became mobile again. Following this line of reasoning, one might expect an eventual return to bilateral symmetry in this group, and, in fact, this is seen to some extent in the soft, elongated bodies of sea cucumbers.

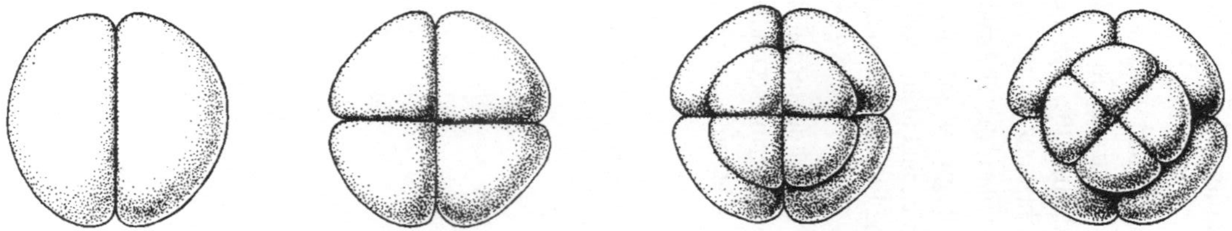

Figure 11.13 : Egg cleavages, showing radial and spiral patterns at the third cleavage. Radial cleavage occurs in deuterostomes (echinoderms and chordates); spiral cleavage occurs in protostomes (mollusks, annelids, and arthropods).

The ancestral bilateral form, like most other hypothetical ancestors, was wormlike. It had a coelom and a one-way digestive tract. However, it differed from the ancestor of the mollusks and annelids in what zoologists consider a very fundamental way, its early embryonic development.

Among mollusks, annelids, and also arthropods, the early cell divisions of the zygote are spiral, occurring in a plane oblique to the long axis of the egg. In the echinoderms, the cleavage pattern is radial, parallel to and at right angles to the axis of the egg.

The second difference appears when the embryo becomes a hollow sphere of cells. In the embryos of both groups, an opening, the blastopore, appears. Among the mollusks, annelids, and arthropods, the mouth (stoma) of the animal develops at or near the blastopore, and this group is called the protostomes—"first the mouth."

In the echinoderms, which are called deuterostomes, the anus forms at or near the blastopore and the mouth forms secondarily. The chordates, the phylum to which we vertebrates belong, share these characteristics with the echinoderms.

12

HIGHER ANIMALS

This chapter will be concerned chiefly with the arthropods, the largest by far of all the phyla. Almost 1 million species of insects and other arthropods have been classified to date, and estimates of the total number are as high as 10 million. As to the number of individuals, it has been calculated that, of insects alone, as many as 10^{18}—a billion billion-are alive at any one time.

It has been estimated that over every square kilometer in the temperate zone there are, at certain seasons, some 20 million individual arthropods, layered in the atmosphere, like plankton.

At the end of this chapter, we shall discuss the evolution of the Chordata, a much smaller phylum. This latter discussion will serve as an introduction to other section of this book, which deals principally with the human species and other chordates.

PHYLUM ARTHROPODA

The arthropods, "joint-footed" animals, include such creatures as the crustaceans (crabs and lobsters), arachnids (spiders, ticks, mites, and scorpions), and insects; the latter constitute by far the largest group. Despite the huge size and diversity of the arthropod phylum, there are a number of features shared by all the members of this group.

CHARACTERISTICS OF THE ARTHROPODS

The Exoskeleton

First, all arthropods have an articulated (jointed) exoskeleton. This exoskeleton, or cuticle, is secreted by the underlying epidermis and is attached to it; it is made up of an outer waxy layer, composed of lipoprotein, and a middle horny layer and an inner flexible one, both composed principally of chitin. The exoskeleton not only covers the surface of the animal but also extends inward at both ends of the digestive tract and, in insects, lines the tracheae (breathing tubes) as well.

Muscles are attached to the various segments of the exoskeleton, just as they are attached to the various bones of the endoskeleton in vertebrates. When the muscles contract, the exoskeleton moves at its joints, rather than restricting the animal to moving inside of it, as with the shelled mollusks.

The cuticle may form a veritable coat of armor, as it does in beetles and in some of the crustaceans (in which it is often infiltrated with calcium salts), but at the joints it is flexible and thin, permitting free movement. It serves as protection against predators, and it is waterproof, keeping exterior water out and interior water in. It is used for food grinders in the foregut, for wings, and for tactile hairs. Cuticle even forms the lens of the arthropod eye.

The exoskeleton has certain disadvantages. It does not grow (as the bony vertebrate endoskeleton does) and so it must be discarded and re-formed many times as the animal grows and develops. Molting is dangerous; the newly molted animal is soft and hence particularly vulnerable to predators and, in the case of terrestrial forms, subject to water loss.

Many arthropods go into hiding until their new cuticle has hardened. Molting is also costly in terms of metabolic expenditures (although a number of insects and some freshwater crustaceans limit their losses by thriftily eating the old exoskeleton).

The fact that the exoskeleton is waterproof made possible the evolution of terrestrial forms among the arthropods. The arthropods are the only major invertebrate phylum with many species adapted to life on land in nonmoist habitats.

Other Arthropod Characteristics

All arthropods are segmented, a characteristic that suggests a common ancestry with the annelids. In some of the arthropods the segments have become fused, forming a head, a thorax (sometimes fused with the head to form a cephalothorax), and an abdomen.

But the basic segmented pattern is often still clearly evident in the immature stages (witness the caterpillar) and can be discerned in the adult by examination of the appendages, the musculature, and the nervous system. Arthropods have a large number of jointed appendages. Especially among the insects and crustaceans, these appendages constitute a kit of highly specialised tools, including jaws, gills, poison fangs, tongs, egg depositors, sucking tubes, claws, antennae, paddles, and pincers.

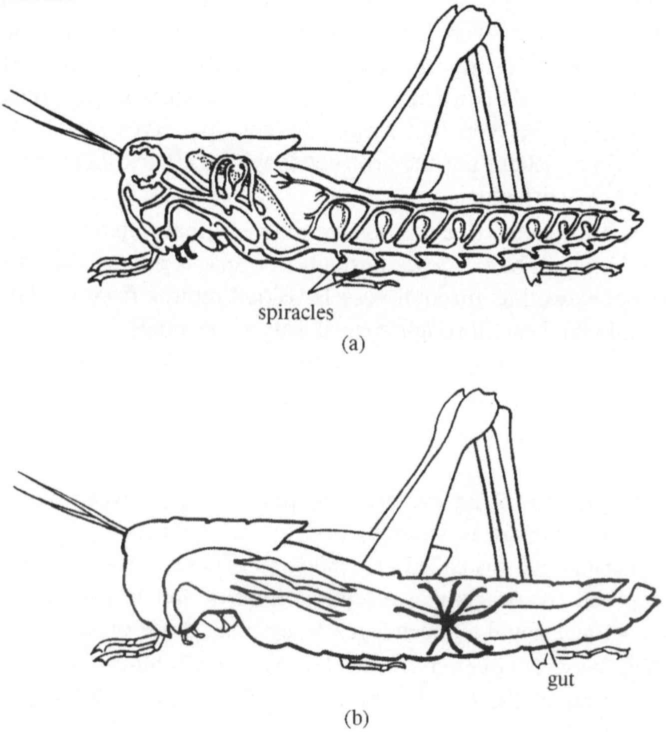

Figure 12.1 : (a) Respiration by means of a system of internal tubes (called tracheae) is found only among arthropods. Tracheae are usually branched, like those shown here, and open to the outside by spiracles that may be closed to conserve water. (b) Malpighian tubules represent another exclusively arthropod characteristic, although like tracheae, they are not found in all classes.

The insects and some other terrestrial forms have unusual means of respiration, consisting of a system of cuticle-lined air ducts (tracheae) that pipe air directly into various parts of the body. Air flow is regulated by the opening and closing of special pores (spiracles) on the exoskeleton.

Terrestrial arthropods, such as spiders, that do not have tracheae have book lungs, structures that are also unique to this phylum. Excretion in terrestrial forms is by means of tubes (called Malpighian tubules) attached to and emptying into the midgut or hindgut. They absorb wastes from the body cavities. Respiration by tracheae, book lungs, or book gills and excretion by Malpighian tubules are found only in arthropods (although not all arthropods have these features).

Arthropods also share a number of characteristics, besides segmentation, with the annelids. Like them, they are bilaterally symmetrical, three-layered, and have a tubular mouth-to-anus gut. They have a coelom, as do the annelids, but the arthropod coelom is markedly reduced, consisting only of the cavities of the gonads and the nephridia. (As you will recall, the coelom serves as a hydrostatic skeleton in annelids, but the arthropods with their exoskeletons require less internal stiffening.)

The arthropods, like the bivalve mollusks, have an open circulatory system in which blood flows through free spaces among the tissues-the hemocoel-as well as through vessels. Blood returns from the hemocoel to the tubular heart through special valved openings.

An open blood system creates little in the way of turgor pressure, which accounts for the general squashiness of the internal organs of insects compared with the firmness, for example, of the vertebrate kidney.

The premise of an evolutionary relationship between the annelids and the arthropods is strengthened by the existence of a group of caterpillar-like worms called Onychophora. These worms have nephridia and reproductive tracts that resemble those of annelids but a heart and hemocoel and jawlike appendages resembling those of arthropods.

The body is covered with a thin cuticle of chitin; however, there are no joints in the cuticle, which is soft enough so that it bends as the animal moves.

The Arthropod Nervous System

Arthropods have a ladderlike nervous system, with a double chain of segmental ganglia running along the ventral surface. The double chains part to encircle the esophagus, ending in a pair of dorsal ganglia. The dorsal ganglia are enough larger than the other ganglia to be called a brain.

However, many arthropod activities are controlled at the segmental level, as in annelids. For example, members of a number of species can move, eat, and carry on other functions normally, even after the brain is removed. In fact, in the arthropods generally, the brain appears to act not so much as a stimulator of the action of the animal but as an inhibitor, as in the earthworm.

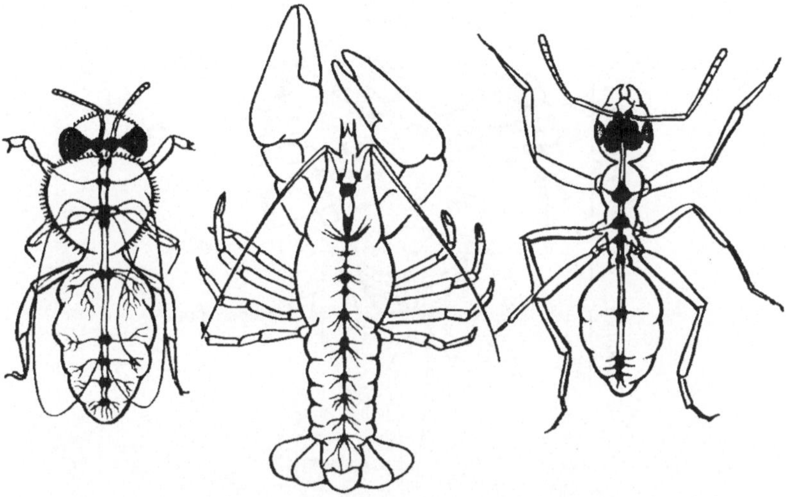

Figure 12.2 : Arthropod nervous systems: a bee, a crayfish, and an ant.

The grasshopper, for example, can walk, jump, or fly with its brain removed; indeed, the brainless grasshopper responds to the slightest stimulus by jumping or flying. The extreme consequences of this releasing of inhibition can be seen in the praying mantis.

Mantises are carnivorous and cannibalistic, and the female, being larger than the male, frequently captures her mate and, grasping him with her forelegs, begins to eat him, head first. This decapitation results in the release of strong motor activities by which the headless male struggles loose from the grasp of the female, mounts her, and mates with her.

The headless male is more likely to copulate than an intact male; investigators seeking to breed mantises have found that males of strains that do not mate readily in captivity will often do so after decapitation.

SUBDIVISIONS OF THE PHYLUM

The arthropods are often classified in two subphyla, the Mandibulata and the Chelicerata, which can be clearly distinguished by even an inexperienced eye. There are conspicuous differences in the appendages. The most anterior appendages in the mandibulates (insects, crustaceans) are *antennae,* one or two pairs, and the next are *mandibles* (jaws).

The chelicerates, which include horseshoe crabs, sea spiders, and arachnids (spiders, mites, scorpions, and their relatives), have no antennae and no true mandibles. Their first pair of appendages consist

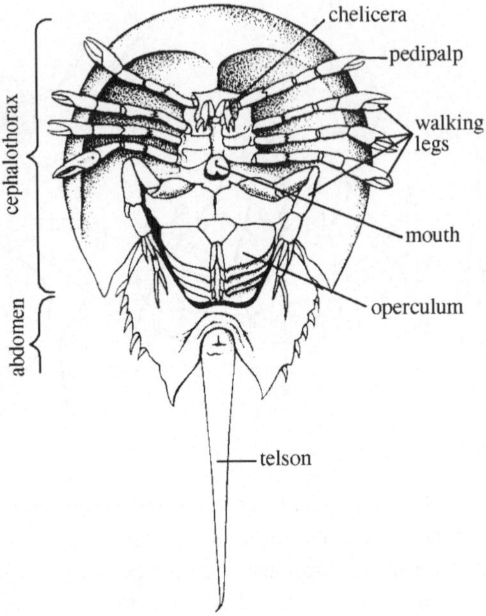

Figure 12.3 : Because the body of the horseshoe crab is largely covered with a heavy shield, or carapace, its segmented body plan is only evident from the underside. The operculum is a flat, movable plate that covers and protects the book gills dorsal to it. Horseshoe crabs are often called living fossils because their remarkably similar ancestors date back to the Cambrian period. There are now only five living species.

of *chelicerae* (singular, chelicera), which usually take the form of pincers or fangs. In spiders, ducts from a pair of poison glands lead through the chelicerae, which are sharp and pointed and are used for biting and paralyzing prey.

Chelicerates may have book lungs or book gills; these structures, which are not present in mandibulates, derive their name from their resemblance to the leaves of a partially opened book.

Each of these subphyla are, in turn, divided into several classes. The three largest classes are the crustaceans, the insects (both mandibulates), and the arachnids (chelicerates). Smaller classes include the horseshoe crab and sea spiders (xiphosurans), which are chelicerates, and the centipedes and millipedes, which are mandibulates.

Class Crustacea

The crustaceans include crabs, crayfish, lobsters, barnacles, shrimp, prawns, *Daphnia* (water fleas), and a number of smaller forms found largely in freshwater and marine plankton, as well as some terrestrial forms such as the familiar pillbugs or sowbugs. Crustaceans are mandibulates. They differ from the insects, which are also mandibulates, in that they have legs or leglike appendages on the abdomen as well as the thorax, and have two pairs of antennae as compared to the insects' one.

Lobster

Figure elsewhere in this chapter shows the structure of a lobster, a representative crustacean. A crayfish, which is a freshwater form, differs morphologically from the lobster only in minor respects.

The lobster has 20 segments, the first 13 of which are united on the dorsal side in a combined head and thorax, or cephalothorax. A heavy shield, or carapace, arises from the head and covers the thorax. Carapaces are common among crustaceans.

The abdomen consists of six distinct segments. (To lobster eaters, the abdomen is the "tail," but to biologists, the designation "tail" is usually reserved for areas of the body posterior to the anus.)

The various appendages have special functions. The antennae, of which there are two pairs, are sensory. The mandibles, or jaws, are used for crushing food; like all arthropod jaws, they move laterally, opening and closing from side to side like a pair of ice tongs rather than up and down like the jaws of vertebrates.

The maxillae and the maxillipeds serve chiefly to collect food, mince it, and pass it on to the mouth. The laws are unequal in size in the full-grown lobster; the larger claw is used for defense and for crushing food, and the smaller claw, which has the sharper teeth, seizes and tears the prey.

The first two pairs of walking legs have small pincers, which can also seize prey. The last pair of walking legs also serves to clean the abdominal appendages. The flattened posterior appendages are used, like flippers, for swimming. The claws and abdomen are filled almost entirely with the large striated muscles many of us enjoy eating. These muscles are extremely powerful.

A lobster can snap its "tail" ventrally with enough force to shoot backward through the water, and a large lobster can shatter the shell of a clam or oyster with its crushing claw. Any one of its appendages can be regenerated over a series of molts if lost, and a lobster will often drop off (automize) a claw or leg that is held by a predator, in order to escape. Severely damaged legs are also automised, reducing blood loss.

The anterior and posterior regions of the digestive tract, the foregut and hindgut, are lined with cuticle. As a consequence, most of the

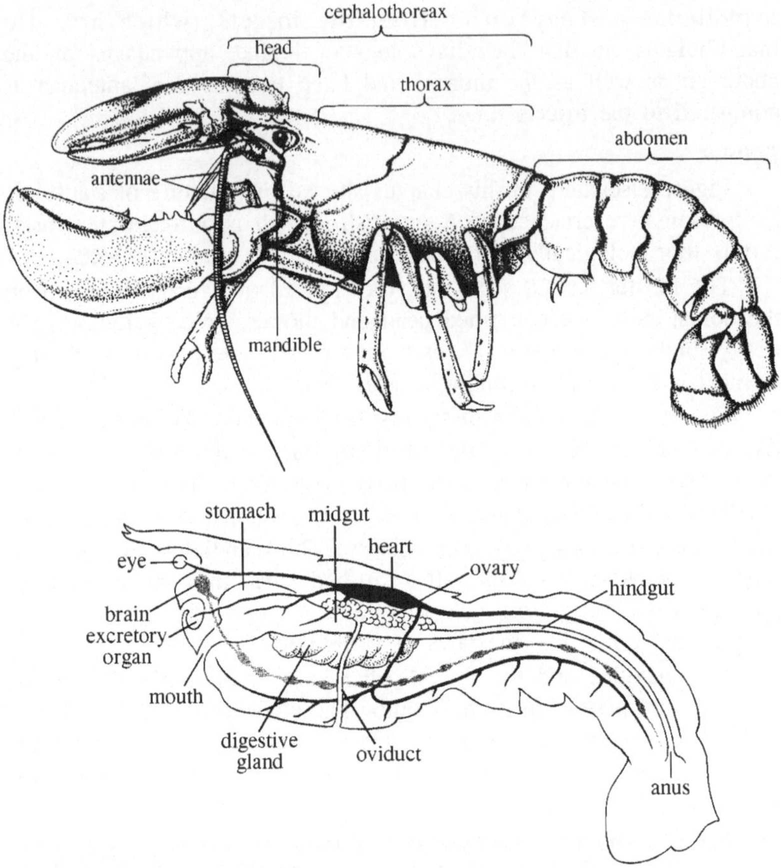

Figure 12.4 : A representative crustacean, the American lobster, Homarus americanus. The lobster has 19 pairs of appendages, including antennae, mouth parts, and legs specialised for feeding, walking, and swimming.

food is absorbed through the midgut and through the cells of the large digestive gland, an appendage of the midgut.

Respiration is accomplished by the flow of water over 20 pairs of feathery gills attached to the bases of the legs. A pair of nephridia is located in the head; wastes extracted from the blood are collected into a bladder and excreted from a pore at the base of each of the second antennae. Fertilization is external; the sperm, which are deposited near the female gonopores, fertilize the eggs as they are laid, and the fertilised eggs cling by means of a sticky secretion to the swimmerets of the female until they hatch.

Terrestrial Crustaceans

Unlike other arthropod groups, almost all crustaceans are aquatic; some crabs, however, are amphibious or terrestrial. Amphibious crabs continue to breathe with gills, carrying around water in their thoracic cavities with which to keep the gills wet and aerating the water through holes in their exoskeletons.

The true land crab has lost the gill structures and instead has an area of highly vascularised epithelial tissue through which oxygen is exchanged. The land snail, you will recall, solved the respiratory problems involved in the transition from water to land in an analogous way.

Class Arachnida

The arachnids, which include spiders, ticks, mites, scorpions, and daddy longlegs, are chelicerates. In this class, the first pair of appendages, the chelicerae, which are usually sharp and fanglike, are used for biting and paralyzing prey by the injection of a poison.

The second pair are the pedipalps, which, in scorpions, for example, are used for handling and tearing food. Male spiders also use pedipalps to transfer semen to the female. Arachnids have four pairs of walking legs.

Spiders, like most arachnids, live on a completely liquid diet. All are predatory. The prey is bitten and often paralyzed by the chelicerae, and then enzymes from the midgut are poured out over the torn tissues to produce a partially digested broth.

The liquefied tissues of the prey are pumped into the stomach by the muscular pharynx, where digestion is completed and the juices absorbed. Arachnids respire by means of tracheae or book lungs, or both. Book lungs are a series of leaflike plates within a chitin-lined chamber into which air is drawn and expelled by muscular actidn.

On the posterior portion of the spider's abdominal surface is a cluster of spinnerets, fingerlike organs from which a fluid protein exudes that polymerizes into silk as it is exposed to air.

Silk is used not only for the variety of prey-snaring webs made by the different species but for a number of other purposes as well, such as a drop line, on which the spider can make a defensive dive, draglines for marking a course, gossamer threads for ballooning, hinges for trap doors, an egg case, lining for a burrow, the shroud of a victim, or a wrapping for an edible offering presented to the female of certain species by the courting male.

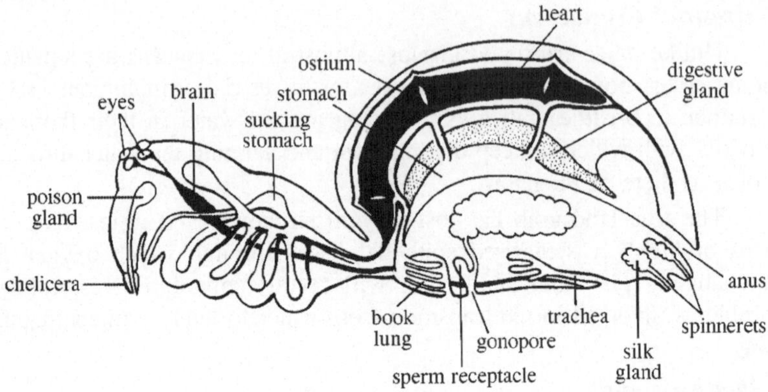

Figure 12.5 : A spider, an arachnid. Ducts from the poison gland open at or near the tips of the chelicerae. The flow of poison is voluntarily controlled by the spider. Only a few spiders are dangerous to human beings; perhaps the most dangerous are member of the species shown here, the black widow.

Most spiders can spin several kinds and thicknesses of silk. Webs are species-specific, and web-building is a genetically programmed behaviour.

Class Insecta

The insects constitute the largest class, by far, of the arthropods. In fact, there are more species of insects than of all other animals combined. More than 700,000 are known.

Insects are the only invertebrates capable of flight. When insects began to fly-more than 240 million years ago-they were able to move into and exploit a life zone almost totally unoccupied by any other form of animal life. In terms both of numbers of species and of individuals, they are the dominant organisms of this planet.

Insect Characteristics

Figure elsewhere in this chapter shows a grasshopper. Here you can see many of the characteristic features of insects: three main divisions—the head, the thorax, and the abdomen; three pairs of legs; one pair of antennae; and a set of mouthparts similar to those of the lobster.

In the more primitive insects, such as the grasshopper, the mouthparts are used for handling and masticating food, but in the more highly specialised groups, the mouthparts are often modified into sucking, piercing, slicing, or sponging organs. Some are exquisitely adapted to draw in nectar from the deep, tubular nectaries of specialised flowers.

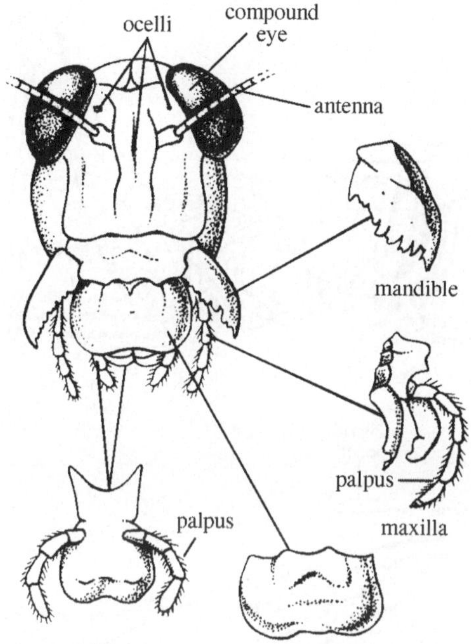

Figure 12.6: Mouthparts of a grasshopper.

Most adult insects have two pairs of wings made up of light, strong sheets of chitin; the veins in the wings are chitinous tubules that serve primarily for strengthening. In some entire orders, such as fleas and lice, wings are totally lost, returning the insect to the condition of its wingless ancestors. Other species may have short, nonfunctional wings in one or both sexes.

There are more than 20 orders of insects, of which we shall briefly describe four examples: Diptera, Lepidoptera, Hymenoptera, and Coleoptera. The Diptera ("two-winged") include the familiar flies, gnats, and mosquitoes. The Lepidoptera ("scale wings") are the moths and the butterflies.

Hymenoptera ("membranewinged") include ants, wasps, and bees, many species of which are social. The Coleoptera ("shield-winged") are the beetles, most of which have a pair of hard protective forewings, which pivot forward out of the way during flight, and a pair of membranous hindwings used for flying. Of the more than 700,000 classified insects, at least 275,000 species are beetles.

Digestive and Respiratory Systems

The foregut and hindgut of the insect digestive tract are lined

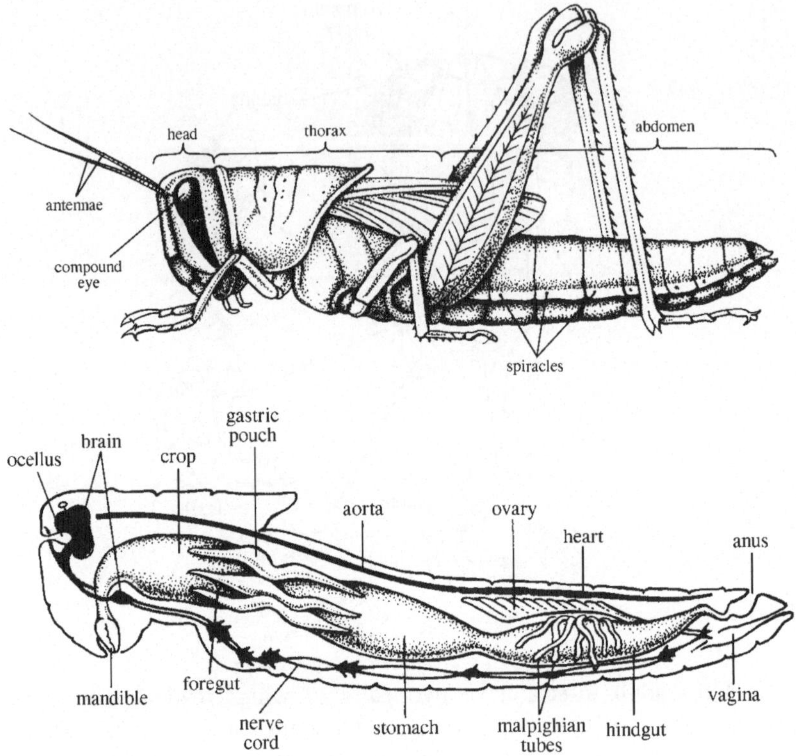

Figure 12.7 : In the grasshopper, an insect, the head consists of six fused segments that have appendages specialised for tasting and biting. The spiracles in the abdomen open into a network of chitin-lined tubules through which air circulates to various tissues of the body, This sort of tubular breathing system is found only among insects and some other land-dwelling arthropods. Excretion takes place by Malpighian tubules that empty into the hindgut.

with chitin. Salivary gland fluids are carried with food into the crop, where digestion begins. The stomach, or midgut, which lies mainly in the abdomen, is the chief organ of absorption.

Insects have digestive enzymes as specialised as their mouthparts; the structure of the enzymes depends on whether the insect dines on blood, seeds, other insects, eggs, flour, cereal, glue, wood, paper, or your woolen clothes. Excretion is carried out through Malpighian tubules.

In the grasshopper and many other insects, the nitrogenous and other wastes are eliminated in the form of nearly dry crystals of uric acid, an adaptation that promotes water conservation.

The respiratory system consists of a network of chitin-lined tubules through which air circulates to the various tissues of the body, supplying each cell directly. Muscular movements of the animal's body improve the internal circulation of air. The amount of incoming air and also the degree of water loss is regulated by the opening and closing of the spiracles.

Metamorphosis

Growing insects change not only in size but often in form, a phenomenon known as metamorphosis. The extent of change varies. In some species, the young, although sexually immature, looks like a small adult; it grows larger by a series of molts until it reaches full size.

In others, like the grasshopper, the newly hatched young are wingless but may gain wingpads in later immature stages; otherwise they are similar to the adult. These immature, nonreproductive forms are known as *nymphs*. Almost 90 percent of the insects, however, undergo a complete metamorphosis, in which adults are drastically different from their immature forms.

The immature feeding forms are all correctly referred to as *larvae,* although they are also commonly known as caterpillars, grubs, or maggots, depending on the different species. Following the larval period, the insect undergoing complete metamorphosis enters an immobile pupal stage within which extensive remodeling of the organism occurs.

The adult (sexually mature) insect emerges from the pupa. Both eggs and pupae (which are nonfeeding) can endure lengthy cold or dry seasons.

The insect that undergoes complete metamorphosis exists in four different forms in the course of its life history. The first form is the egg and the embryo. The second form is the larva, the animal that hatches from the egg; larvae eat and grow.

In many larvae, such as those of flies, growth takes place not by an increase in the number of cells, as in most animals, but by an increase in the size of the cells, in somewhat the same way that growth takes place in certain plant tissues. During the course of its growth, the larva molts a characteristic number of times-twice in the fruit fly, for example.

The stages between molts are known as *instars*. Then, when the larva is full-grown, it molts to form the pupa. During this outwardly lifeless pupal stage, many of the larval cells break down, and entirely new groups of cells, set aside in the embryo, begin to proliferate, using the degenerating larval tissue as a culture medium. These groups of cells are known as imaginal discs since they form the imago, the adult insect, which, according to Aristotle, is the perfect form or ideal image that the immature form is "seeking to express." These imaginal discs develop into the complicated structures of the adult.

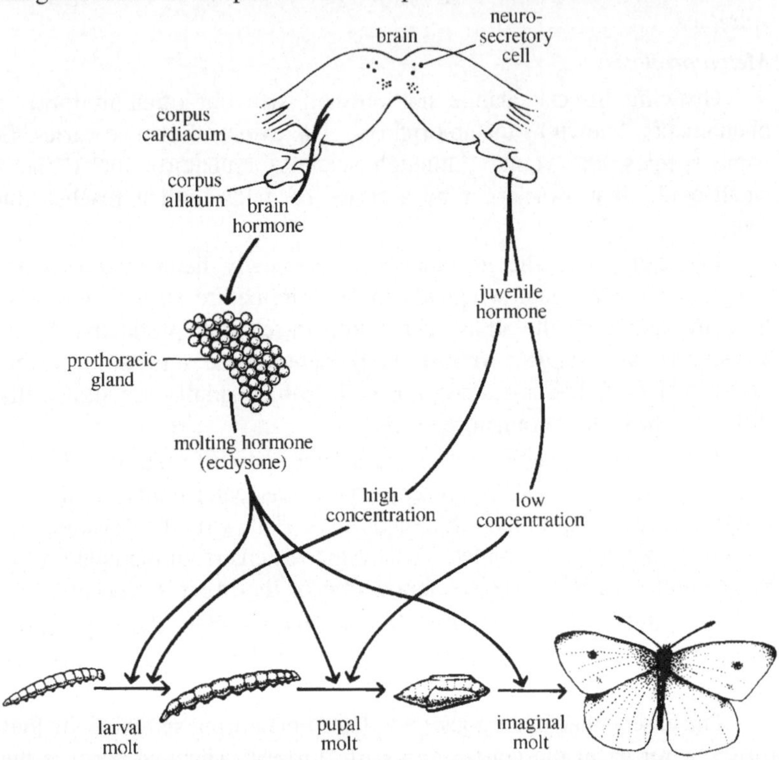

Figure 12.8 : Molting is under hormonal control. In insects, a hormone (brain hormone) produced by neurosecretory cells in the brain and released from corpora cardiaca stimulates the prothoracic gland, which, in turn, produces molting hormone (ecdysone).

Molting and metamorphosis are under hormonal control. Like many hormonecontrolled processes, they are the end result of an interplay of several hormones: brain hormone, molting hormone (ecdysone), and juvenile hormone.

At intervals during larval growth, brain hormone, produced by neurosecretory cells in the brain, is released into the blood. It stimulates the release, in turn, of molting hormone from a gland in the thorax.

The molting hormone stimulates not only molting but also the formation of a pupa and the development of adult structures. The latter are held in check, however, by a third hormone, the juvenile hormone. Only when the production of juvenile hormone declines, in later larval life, can metamorphosis to the adult form take place.

REASONS FOR ARTHROPOD SUCCESS

Among all the invertebrates, why are the arthropods, in general, and the insects, in particular, so spectacularly successful? One important reason is undoubtedly the nature of the exoskeleton, which waterproofs, provides protection, and makes possible the evolution of the many finely articulated appendages characteristic of this phylum.

A second reason, which applies especially to insects, is the high specificity of diet and other requirements of each species. As a consequence, many different species can live in a single small environment-in a few cubic centimeters of soil, on a small plant, or on or within the egg or body of a single animal—without competing with one another.

The varied and highly specialised mouthparts are a reflection of this specificity of diet. Among the insects with complete metamorphosis, even the larvae of a species do not compete with the adults for food and for the same territory.

A third reason for the success of the insects, as we mentioned previously, is their capacity for flight, which gives them an extraordinary mobility, in three dimensions.

A fourth reason for success is undoubtedly the arthropod nervous system, with its fine control over the various appendages and the many extraordinarily sensitive sensory organs found in great diversity throughout the phylum.

The rest of this discussion deals with sensory perception among arthropods, especially insects, and some examples of arthropod behaviour. The social behaviour of bees is described in other chapter of this book.

Arthropod Senses and Behaviour

Vision: The Compound Eye

The most conspicuous sensory organ of the arthropods is the compound eye, which is an evolutionary development characteristic of this one phylum. The basic structural unit of this eye is the *ommatidium.* A dragonfly has some 30,000 ommatidia. Each ommatidium is covered by a cornea, usually with a round or hexagonal surface; these are visible under low-power magnification as individual facets of the eye.

Underlying the cornea is a group of eight retinular cells surrounded by pigment cells. The light-sensitive portion of the ommatidium is the *rhabdom,* which is the central core of the ommatidium.

Nerve fibers carry the stimulus from each ommatidium to the brain. The pigment cells prevent light from traveling from one ommatidium to another. An ommatidium is much larger than a vertebrate photoreceptor, and so there are far fewer in an equivalent space. Hence, the image has less resolution, like a newspaper picture under high magnification.

Although the compound eye is deficient in acuity, offering less detail than the vertebrate eye, it is better for detecting motion because each ommatidium is stimulated separately and so has a separate visual field. Also, each ommatidium responds to stimuli more rapidly than does a vertebrate photoreceptor. Ability to detect motion can be measured accurately in the laboratory by testing a phenomenon known as flicker fusion.

In this test, a light is flicked on and off with increasing rapidity until the observer sees the flicker as a continuous beam. The beam is perceived as continuous because stimulation of any retinal cell persists for a brief period even after the stimulus disappears.

So, in effect, the flicker-fusion test is a measurement of how quickly the photoreceptor cell recovers from one stimulus and becomes sensitive to another. It is possible to test flicker-fusion rates in animals by training experiments in which the animal learns to associate a flickering light with a reward (usually food) and a steady beam with no reward, or vice versa. Such tests have proved that the compound eye greatly exceeds the camera eye of vertebrates in this respect.

A bee would see in clear outline a moving figure that we would see as blurred, and if the bee went to the movies, the film seen by us as a continuous picture would jerk along from frame to frame for the bee.

The ability to perceive motion is extremely important for an insect since it must be able to make out objects when it is flying at high speed (which, as far as the visual apparatus is concerned, presents the same problems as following a moving object).

In addition to, or instead of, compound eyes, many of the arthropods possess simple eyes, or ocelli, which seem generally to serve only for light detection. Most insects have two or three ocelli, and spiders, which do not have compound eyes, may have as many as eight ocelli, depending on species.

Touch Receptors

The body surfaces of terrestrial arthropods are often covered with sensory-receptor units known as sensilla (singular, sensillum), or "little sense organs." Most of the sensilla take the form of fine spines, or setae, composed of hollow shafts of chitin. At the bases of these shafts are sensory cells.

In their simplest form, the sensilla are touch receptors. In these, when the hair is touched or bent, the sensory cell responds and initiates nerve impulses. Such receptors are found, in particular, on the antennae and the legs. In addition to being stimulated by direct contact, they can also be stimulated by vibrations and air currents.

A spider monitors what is going on in its web by sensing vibrations transmitted through the threads when the web is touched. Soldier termites of certain species strike the ground or the walls of their nest with their heads when threatened or disturbed; the vibrations they produce warn their colony mates.

A fly perceives the air currents from the movement of a hand or fly swatter and so escapes; a fly in a glass jar is much less likely to be disturbed by such movements.

Proprioceptors

Proprioceptors are sensory receptors that provide information about the position of various parts of the body and the stresses and strains on them. A type common in the arthropods is the campaniform sensillum. Campaniform sensilla are located in thin, stretchable areas of the cuticle. When the cells are twisted or stretched, a nerve fiber signals the central nervous system.

Touch receptors can also serve as proprioceptors. The praying mantis, for example, is capable of making a lightning-swift strike at a moving object. When it sights a potential victim, the insect moves its entire head to bring it into binocular range, since the eyes themselves do not move.

Movement of the head results in the stimulation of proprioceptive hairs on the head and thorax of the insect. On the basis of the impulses received from these hairs, the position of the prey and the movement of its own legs are automatically coordinated by the mantis. If these hairs are removed, the mantis can strike a moving object only if the object is directly in front of it.

Sound Receptors

Arthropods have a variety of sound receptors. The simplest is a

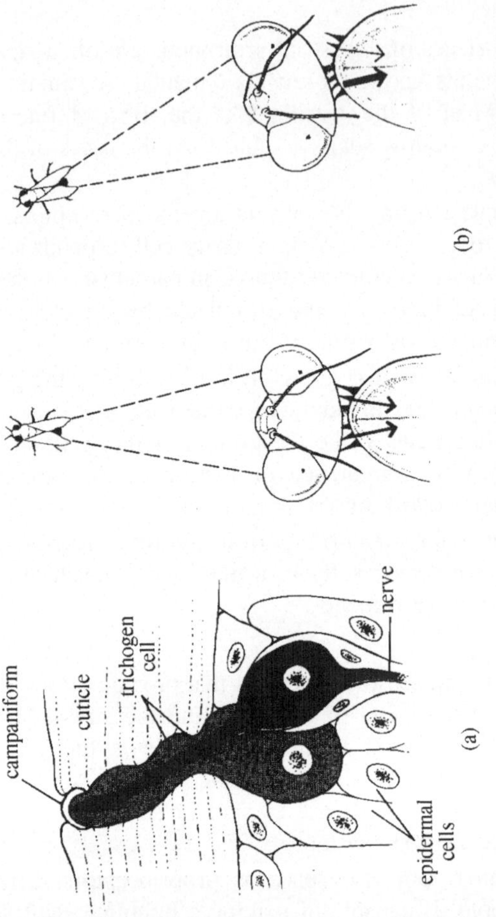

Figure 12.9 : (a) Campaniform sensillum, a type of proprioceptor common in arthropods. (b) Since its eyes do not move, the praying mantis must move its entire head to bring its victim into binocular range.

sensillum with a tactile hair that vibrates as a result of being "touched" by sound waves. The antennae of the male mosquito contain thousands of such hairs, which are responsive to the vibrations made by the wings of the female mosquito in flight and so serve to bring the sexes together.

When the male mosquito first emerges from its pupal shell, it is sexually immature and also deaf, with its antennal hairs lying flat along the shafts. When the male matures sexually, some 24 hours later, the hairs almost simultaneously become erect and are now free to vibrate when a female approaches.

Other insects have developed special groups of cells for hearing; these are known as tympanic organs. In these organs, a fine membrane, the tympanum (or eardrum) is stretched across an air-filled cavity. The tympanic membrane vibrates in response to sounds of certain frequencies, and this vibration is transmitted to underlying receptor cells.

Communication

Communication by Sound

Arthropods, particularly insects, have developed complex forms of sensory communication. A number of species, such as the locusts, grasshoppers, and crickets, call to one another by sounds made by rubbing their legs or wings together or against their bodies. Five distinct types of calls are known:

(1) calling by males and
(2) calling by females, both of which are long-range sounds;
(3) courtship sounds by males and
(4) aggressive sounds by males, both of which are short-range; and
(5) alarm sounds, which may be given either by males or by females.

Recognition of and response to the sound seem to be based on pattern and on rhythm because insects apparently are not able to distinguish frequencies, or the differences between high and low notes, and so are essentially "tone deaf."

The effectiveness of calling songs is often increased by group singing, such as the famous chorus of male seventeen-year cicadas, which can attract females from distances far greater than an individual "voice" would reach. Insects produce songs and respond to appropriate songs without ever having heard a song before.

Communication by Pheromones

The use of chemicals for communication is common among animals, and the substances employed range from the sex attractants of the little algal cell Chlamydomonas to Chanel No. 5. Many insects communicate by chemicals; such chemicals are known as pheromones. Pheromones are chemical messengers.

They are usually produced in special glands and are discharged into the environment, where they act on other members of the same species. Among the best studied of the pheromones are the mating substances of moths.

One female gypsy moth, by the emission of minute amounts of a

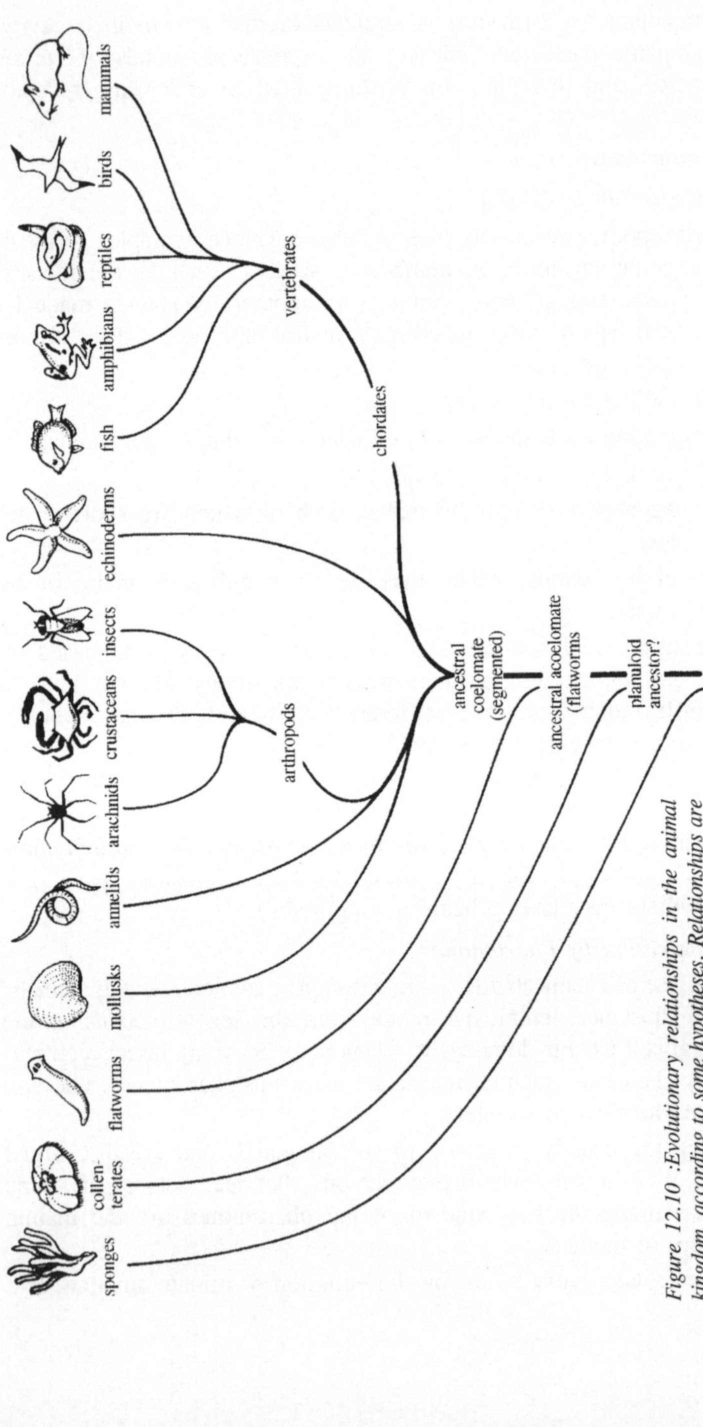

Figure 12.10 :Evolutionary relationships in the animal kingdom, according to some hypotheses. Relationships are based on structural similarities, such as the segmentation in annelids and arthropods, and also on resemblances among larval forms and in developmental patterns.

pheromone commonly known as gyplure, can attract male moths that are several kilometers downwind.

In fact, a single female contains enough gyplure, somewhere around a millionth of a gram, to attract more than a billion males, supposing that it were distributed with maximum efficiency. Since the male can detect as little as a few hundred molecules per cubic centimeter of the attractant, gyplure is still potent even when it has become widely diffused.

The male moth characteristically flies upwind, and the pheromone, of course, disperses downwind. Therefore, when a male moth detects the odour of a female of the species, he will fly toward the source. If he loses the scent, he flies about at random until he either picks it up again or abandons the search.

It is not until he is quite close to the female that he can fly "up the gradient" and use the intensity of the odour as a locating device. Figure elsewhere in this chapter shows the lavishly plumed antennae of a male Cecropia moth by which he detects the pheromone emitted by the female.

Insect Behaviour

Complex patterns of unlearned, genetically transmitted behaviour-such as webbuilding among spiders-are another arthropod characteristic. This rigid programming of behaviour may be a necessary correlate to the shortness of the life span of the smaller arthropods.

It provides an interesting contrast to the more flexible behaviour patterns of the higher mammals, with their comparatively long life spans, long periods of learning, and much larger brains.

PHYLUM CHORDATA

The phylum Chordata comprises three subphyla: the Cephalochordata, or lancelets, which includes *Branchiostoma* (formerly called *Amphioxus);* the Tunicata, or tunicates, of which the most familiar are the sea squirts; and the Vertebrata, or vertebrates.

Branchiostoma is a small, blade-shaped, semitransparent animal found in shallow marine waters all over the warmer parts of the world. Although it can swim very efficiently, it spends most of its time buried in the sandy bottom, with only its mouth protruding above the surface.

This animal exemplifies all four of the salient features of the chordates. The first is the *notochord,* a rod that extends the length of the body and serves as a firm but flexible axis. The notochord is a structural support. Because of it, *Branchiostoma* can swim with strong undulatory motions that move it through the water with a speed unattainable by the flatworms or aquatic annelids.

The second chordate characteristic is the dorsal, hollow nerve cord, a tube that runs beneath the dorsal surface of the animal above the notochord. (The principal nerve cords in other phyla, as you will recall, are ventral.)

The third characteristic is a pharynx with gill slits. The pharyngeal gill slits become highly developed in fishes, in which they serve a respiratory function, and traces of them remain even in the human embryo. In *Branchiostoma,* they serve primarily for collecting food.

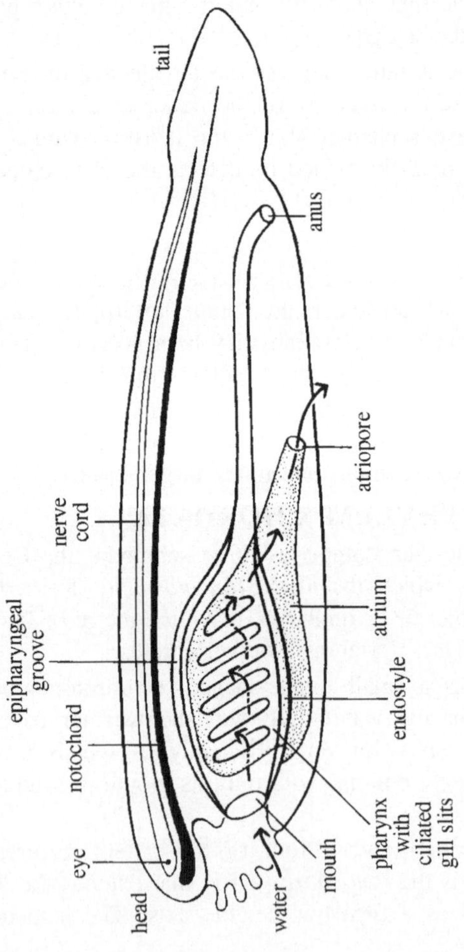

Figure 12.11 : Branchiostoma, a lancelet, exemplifies four distinctive chordate characteristics: (1) a notochord, the dorsal rod that extends the length of the body; (2) a dorsal, tubular nerve cord; (3) pharyngeal gill slits; and (4) a tail.

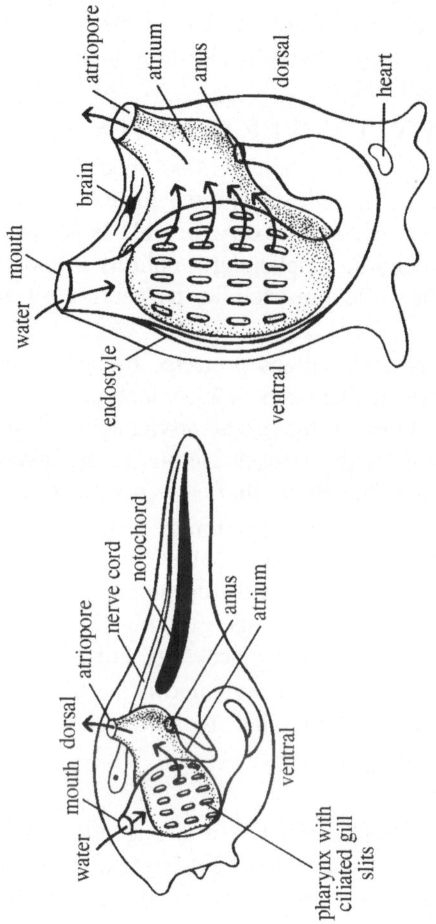

Figure 12.12 : Two stages in the life of a tunicate. At the left is the larva; the adult form is shown on the right. After a brief free-swimming existence, the larva settles to the bottom and attaches at the anterior end.

The cilia around the mouth and at the opening of the pharynx pull in a steady current of water, which passes through the pharyngeal slits into a chamber known as the atrium and then exits through the atrial pore. Food particles are collected in the sievelike pharynx, mixed with mucus, and channeled along ciliated grooves to the intestine.

The fourth characteristic is a tail, posterior to the anus, consisting of blocks of muscle around an axial skeleton. Most of the body tissue of *Branchiostoma* is made up of blocks of muscles, the myotomes.

Although *Branchiostoma* usefully exemplifies the chordates, many biologists believe it is more likely to be a degenerate form of primitive fish rather than a truly primitive member of the phylum. A more probable candidate for the ancestral form is the tunicate. Although the adult form does not have all of the typical chordate features, the larva, which resembles *Branchiostoma, is* clearly a chordate possessing the four chordate characteristics.

SUBPHYLUM VERTEBRATA

The vertebrates are a large (about 43,000 species) and familiar subphylum of the chordates. All vertebrates have a backbone, or vertebral column, as their structural axis-a flexible bony support that develops around the notochord, supplanting it entirely in most species. Dorsal projections of the vertebrae encircle the nerve cord along the length of the spine.

The brain is similarly enclosed and protected by bony skull plates. Between the vertebrae are cartilaginous disks, which give the vertebral column its flexibility. One of the great advantages of this bony endoskeleton, as compared with the exoskeletons of the invertebrates, is that it is composed of living tissue that can grow with the animal.

In the developing embryo, the skeleton is largely cartilaginous, with bone gradually replacing cartilage in the course of maturation. Figure elsewhere in this chapter shows the developing bone tissue of a vertebrate embryo. In the vertebrates, the growing parts of the bones remain cartilaginous until the animal reaches its full adulthood.

There are seven living classes of vertebrates: the fish (comprising three classes), the amphibians, the reptiles, the birds, and the mammals.

Classes Agnatha, Chondrichthyes, and Osteichthyes: Fish

The first fish were jawless and had a strong notochord running the length of their bodies. Today these jawless fish (class Agnatha), once a large and diverse group, are represented only by the hagfish and the lampreys.

They have a notochord throughout their lives, like *Branchiostoma.* Although their ancestors had bony skeletons, modern agnaths have a cartilaginous skeleton. Lacking true bones, they are very flexible; a hagfish can actually tie itself in a knot.

Many cyclostomes ("round mouths"), as they are called, are highly predatory, attaching to other fish by their suckerlike mouths and rasping through the skin into the viscera of their hosts. The juvenile lamprey, which resembles *Branchiostoma,* however, feeds by sucking up mud containing microorganisms and organic debris—as, most probably, did the primitive Agnatha.

The sharks (including the dogfish) and skates, the Chondrichthyes, the second major class of fish, also have a completely cartilaginous skeleton. Like agnaths, their ancestors were also bony animals. Their skin is covered with small, pointed teeth (denticles), which resemble vertebrate teeth structurally and give the skin the texture and abrasive quality of coarse sandpaper.

The third major class of fish includes those with bony skeletons, the Osteichthyes. This group includes the trout, bass, salmon, perch, and many othersmost of the familiar freshwater and saltwater fish.

According to present evidence, fish evolved in fresh water. The chondrichthyans returned to the sea early in their evolution, while the bony fish went through most of their evolution in fresh water and spread to the seas at a much later period.

Some still recapitulate in each lifetime this difficult physiological transition. Salmon, for example, return to fresh water to spawn, while eels leave the fresh waters of Europe and North America to return to the Sargasso Sea at breeding time, from which distant point the young begin the long, difficult journey, often lasting many years, back to the rivers and lakes.

The Transition to Land

Another characteristic of the bony fishes is that the early forms seem to have had lungs or lunglike structures, as well as gills. These lungs, however, were not efficient enough to serve as more than accessory structures to the gills.

They were a special adaptation to fresh water, which, unlike ocean water, may become stagnant (depleted of oxygen) because of decay of organic matter or of algal bloom. Lunged fish were the most common fish in the later Devonian seas, apparently evolving independently several times.

In most of them, the lung evolved into an air bladder, or swim bladder; many modern osteichthyans have gas-filled swim bladders that serve as flotation chambers or organs of sound production. A fish raises or lowers itself in the water by adding gases to or removing them from the air bladder via the bloodstream. Still other primitive fish evolved into the modern lungfish.

These fish can live in water that does not have sufficient oxygen to support other fish life. Lungfish surface and gulp air into their lungs in much the same way that certain aquatic but air-breathing snails bob to the surface to fill their mantle cavities.

In yet others, skeletal supports evolved that served to prop up the thorax of the fish. These fish could gulp air even when their bodies were not supported by water. These osteichthyans could waddle, dragging their bellies on the ground, along the muddy bottom of a drying stream bed to seek deeper water or perhaps even make their way from one water source to another one nearby. Thus the transition to land began as an attempt to remain in the water.

Class Amphibia

Amphibians descended from air-breathing lunged fish. Modern amphibians include frogs and toads (which are tailless as adults) and salamanders (which have tails throughout their lives).

They can readily be distinguished from the reptiles by their thin, usually scaleless skins, which serve as breathing organs. (Frogs have lungs as adults. Some salamanders have lungs, but others breathe entirely through their skins and the mucous membranes of their throats.)

Because water evaporates rapidly through their skins, some amphibians can readily die of desiccation in a dry environment. Those found in deserts spend the drier times of the day far below the surface of the sand.

Most frogs in cold climates have two life stages (hence their name, from *am phi* and *bias,* meaning "two lives"). The eggs are laid in water and are fertilised externally. They hatch into gilled larvae (tadpoles). The tadpoles later develop into adults that lose their gills and develop lungs.

The adults may live out of the water, at least in the summer. However, there are many variations on this theme. Some of the American salamanders fertilise their eggs on land; the males deposit sperm packets that are picked up by the females. Many amphibians are now known to skip the free-living larval stage.

The eggs, which may be laid on land, in a hollow log or cupped leaf, or even carried by the parent, hatch into miniature versions of the adult. Some salamanders, such as the mud puppy and the axolotl, never complete their metamorphosis, remaining essentially aquatic larval forms.

In some species, these larvalike forms can be induced to metamorphose into adult forms by administration of hormones, indicating that the genetic capacity for this later developmental stage has not been lost.

Class Reptilia

As you will recall, the vascular plants freed themselves from the water by the development of the seed. Analogously, the vertebrates became truly terrestrial with the evolution in the reptiles of the amniote egg, an egg that retains its own water supply and so can survive on land.

The reptilian egg, which is much like the familiar hens egg in basic design, contains a large yolk, the food supply for the developing embryo; abundant albumen; and a water supply. A membrane, the amnion, surrounds the developing embryo with a liquid-filled space that substitutes for the ancestral pond.

The gilled stage is passed in a shelled egg or in the maternal oviduct or uterus. In mammals also, although their eggs typically develop internally, the embryos are enclosed in water within an enveloping membrane, the amnion, and pass through a gilled stage (although the gills are never functional) before birth.

Reptiles are characteristically four-legged, although the legs are absent in most snakes and some lizards. In keeping with their terrestrial existence, reptiles have a dry skin, usually covered with protective scales. Modern reptiles, of which there are 5,400 species, include lizards, snakes, turtles, and crocodiles.

Evolution of the Reptiles

By late in the Carboniferous period, the first reptiles had begun to evolve from closely similar amphibian ancestors. During the succeeding Permian period, there was an explosive increase in the number of reptilian species. (During this same period, conifers began to replace the ferns and other "amphibious" plants, suggesting that a drier climate may have been a primary selective force in both of these events.)

During the Permian and much of Triassic time, the dominant land vertebrates were mammal-like reptiles, an abundant and diverse group, members of which were later to give rise to the mammals. Around the beginning of the Triassic period, several of the more specialised reptile groups arose, which include, among the surviving forms, turtles and lizards, and also, the thecodonts, ancestors of the Archosauria, or ruling reptiles, perhaps the most spectacular of all the land's inhabitants so far.

The origin and rise of the Archosauria was associated with improvements in reptilian locomotion. Vertebrates first came to the land with all four limbs sprawled far out to the side; turtles have retained this sprawling gait. Among the early Archosauria, there was a progressive tendency toward bipedalism, with a great increase in the strength and running capabilities of the hind legs, with the concomitant freeing of the front legs for other purposes—for example, flight. There were three major groups of archosaurs: the pterosaurs, or flying reptiles; the crocodilians, which reverting to four-legged posture, became our modern crocodiles and alligators; and the dinosaurs, a varied and splendid group of reptiles.

The largest of the dinosaurs, *Brachiosaurus,* was *25* meters in length and weighed, it is estimated, *50* tons, far larger than any land animal that has succeeded it. Throughout the long Mesozoic era, the dinosaurs dominated the life of the land, rulers of the earth for *150* million years.

Then, they vanished; the reasons for their extinction are not known, but it did occur during a period of climatic change and may have been related to problems of temperature regulation or changes in the vegetation or the disappearance of swampy habitats. They left only a single line of descendants, the birds.

Class Aves: Birds

Birds are essentially reptiles specialised for flight. Their bodies are lightened by air sacs and also by having hollow bones. The frigate bird, a large seagoing bird with a wingspread of more than 2 meters, has a skeleton that weighs only 110 grams (about 4 ounces).

The most massive bone in the bird skeleton is the keel, or breastbone, to which are attached the huge muscles that operate the wings. Flying birds have jettisoned all extra weight; the female's reproductive system has been trimmed down to a single ovary, and even this becomes large enough to be functional only in the mating season.

Birds have feathers, which is their outstanding, unique physical characteristic, and they maintain a high and constant body temperature, which distinguishes them from most of the modern reptiles (although a few, such as leatherback turtles, show some degree of endothermy).

In modern birds, feathers serve both to aid in flight and as insulation. (Only animals that are endothermic require insulation; animals that warm their bodies by exposure to the environment would find insulation a disadvantage.) Birds also have scales, a reminder of their reptilian ancestry. Many birds that are born at an immature stage require a long period of parental care.

Evolution of Flight

How did flight evolve? Biologists agree that evolution occurs by a series of small changes, each of which, to be conserved by natural selection, must be of survival value. Being able to fly not very well is a dubious advantage. Until recently, the most popular theory for the origin of flight has been that the ancestors of the birds were tree-dwelling reptiles and that flight evolved as a way to extend or brake jumps from branch to branch.

However, John Ostrom of Yale, having studied the anatomy of the five known specimens of *Archaeopteryx* and many related forms as well, has come to support a second theory: that the protobirds were ground-dwelling reptiles. *Archaeopteryx,* according to the fossil evidence, is a close relative of small, bipedal, carnivorous dinosaurs known as theropods.

The only major distinctions are that *Archaeopteryx* has feathers and fused collar bones ("wish bone"), like modern birds. But why should feathers evolve in a ground-dwelling organism? According to Ostrom, feathers were originally an adaptation not for flight but for insulation. This raises an interesting question, because "cold-blooded" animals, such as reptiles, warm themselves from outside, and so, to these organisms, insulation is a disadvantage.

Only the "warm-blooded" organisms, such as birds and mammals, require insulation as a help in conserving heat produced by a high metabolic rate. In other words, the theropods, according to this hypothesis, were warm-blooded.

Evidence that the original function of feathers was not flight is provided by anatomical studies showing that the wing feathers apparently were not attached to the bones of the "hand" in *Archaeopteryx,* as they are in modern birds, but were merely embedded in the skin. Also the breastbone and its keel are lacking, indicating that wing muscles were not well developed.

Archaeopteryx was clearly not a good flyer, if indeed it could fly at all. As Ostrom reconstructs it, the early stages in flight began with a feathered, warm-blooded, carnivorous dinosaur running after its prey, flapping its long feathered arms, and leaping. (The fact that the feathered forelimbs of *Archaeopteryx* end in claws, as did the elongated arms of the theropods, lends support to this image.)

The long "wing" feathers may have originated to serve as cagelike trapsnatural nets-for capturing prey; some modern predatory birds use their wings in this way. Thus flight is seen as the culmination of a long, successful predatory leap.

Class Mammalia

Mammals also descended from the reptiles. Characteristics

distinguishing mammals from other vertebrates are that mammals (1) have hair, (2) provide milk for their young from specialised glands (mammae), and (3) like birds, but unlike other vertebrates, maintain a high body temperature by generating metabolic heat.

In nearly all mammalian species, the young are born alive, as they are in some fish and reptiles, which retain the eggs in their bodies until they hatch. Some very primitive mammals, however, the *monotremes,* such as the duckbilled platypus, lay eggs with shells but nurse their young after hatching.

The *marsupials,* which include the opossum and the kangaroo, also bear their young alive, but they differ from the major group of mammals in that the infants are born at a tiny and immature stage and, in some species, are kept in a special protective pouch in which they suckle and continue their development.

Most of the familiar mammals are *placentals, so* called because they have a more efficient nutritive connection, the placenta, between the uterus and the embryo. As a result, the young develop to a much more advanced stage before birth. Thus the young are afforded protection during their most vulnerable period.

The earliest placentals were small, shy, and probably nocturnal, thus avoiding the carnivorous dinosaurs. They undoubtedly lived mostly on insects, grubs, worms, and eggs. Shrews, which are believed to closely resemble these primitive mammals, have retained their elusive habits.

Mammals have fewer, but larger, skull bones than the fish and reptiles, an example of the fact that "simpler" and "more primitive" may have quite opposite meanings. In the mammals, a bony platform or partition has developed that separates nasal and food passages far back in the throat, making it possible for the animal to breathe while eating.

The lower mammalian jaw consists of a single bone. Mammals, unlike snakes or lizards, cannot move the upper jaw in relation to the brain case. They have lost the capacity of many reptiles to unhinge their jaws-an ability that makes it possible for a large anaconda, for example, to swallow a pig whole.

The primates, the order to which we belong, are placental mammals characterised by three kinds of teeth (canines, incisors, and molars), opposable first digits (thumbs and usually toes), two pectoral mammae, expanded cerebral cortex, and a tendency toward single births. We are distinguished from the other primates by our upright posture, long legs and short arms, high forehead and small jaw, and lack of general body hair.

Among all the mammals, we are one of the least specialised. Humans are omnivores. Unlike the Carnivora, which are meat eaters, and the several orders of herbivores, we eat a wide variety of fruits, vegetables, and other animals.

Our hands closely resemble those of a primitive reptile, in contrast to the highly specialised forelimbs developed by, for example, whales, bats, and horses. We cannot see as well as an eagle. Our sense of smell is much less keen than a dog's, and our sense of taste far less sensitive than a housefly's.

Many animals can run faster, swim more powerfully, and climb trees with more agility (though few can do all three). Humans have, however, one area of extreme specialisation: the brain. Because of our brain, we are unique among all the other animals in our capacity to reason, to speak, to plan, to learn, and so, to some extent, to control our own future and those of the other organisms with which we share this planet.

13

AUTOTROPHIC ORGANISMS

For most of earth's history, the land was bare. A billion years ago, seaweeds clung to the shores at low tide and perhaps some gray-green lichens patched a few inland rocks, but had anyone been there to observe it, the earth's surface would generally have appeared as barren and forbidding as the surface of Mars does today.

According to the fossil record, plants first began to invade the land a mere half billion years ago. Not until then did the earth's surface truly come to life. As a film of green spread from the edges of the waters, other forms of life, the heterotrophs, were able to follow.

The shapes of these new forms and the ways in which they lived were determined by the plant life that preceded them. Plants supplied not only their food-their chemical energy-but also their nesting, hiding, stalking, and breeding places.

And so it is today. In all terrestrial communities except those of human creation, the character of the plants still determines the character of the animals and other forms of life that inhabit a particular area. Even we members of the human species, who have seemingly freed ourselves from the life of the land and even, on occasion, from the surface of the earth, are still dependent on the photosynthetic events that take place in the green leaves of plants.

Plants, as defined in this text, are multicellular photosynthetic organisms adapted for life on land. In this section, we shall focus on the class of plants that evolved the most recently, the angiosperms. This class is characterised by specialised structures-flowers-in which sexual reproduction takes place, in which the seed is formed, and from which the fruit develops.

The angiosperms are by far the most abundant class of plants, with about 235,000 species. The group is divided into two large subclasses, the dicots (170,000 species) and the monocots (65,000 species). The differences between the two groups are summarised in Figure elsewhere in this chapter on the next page.

THE PLANT BODY AND EVOLUTION

As we noted in other chapter of this book, the ancestor of the plants was probably a single-celled alga that floated on or just below the water's surface. Like modern plants, its photosynthetic pigments were chlorophylls a and b and carotenoids, especially beta-carotene, all of which were contained in chloroplasts.

It had a membranebound nucleus and mitochondria and other cellular organelles, as well as an external cell wall of cellulose. Its energy source was sunlight, and it obtained oxygen, carbon dioxide, and the minerals it required from the waters in which it lived.

Plants have the same few and relatively simple requirements: light, water, oxygen, carbon dioxide, and certain minerals. From these simple materials they, like their ancestors, make the sugars, amino acids, and all other organic substances on which all plant and animal life depends. But there is an important difference.

In the simplest photosynthesizing organism-the single green cell or filament of cellseach of the needed materials is immediately available to every cell. In a plant, however, the individual cells can no longer function autonomously but can survive only through cooperation and division of labor among the many cells and tissues forming the plant body.

The reasons for this division of labor are easy to understand. The water and minerals needed by plants are found mostly below the surface of the earth; the development of a complex and extensive root system can be seen as a response to this selection pressure. Sunlight cannot reach these belowground structures, however, and photosynthesis is relegated to another part of the plant body.

As the plants began to crowd each other and compete for light, selection pressures favoured those with more extensive and efficient light-collecting surfaces-leaves.

The stem raises these photosynthesizing surfaces into the sunlight. Through the specialised vascular tissues of the stem, water and minerals from the ground travel to the leaves, and the products of photosynthesis formed in the leaves are transported to flowers, roots, and other nonphotosynthetic parts of the plant.

LEAVES

Leaf Structure

A leaf is a compromise between two conflicting evolutionary pressures. The first is to expose a maximum photosynthetic surface to sunlight; the second is to conserve water while, at the same time, providing for the exchange of gases necessary for photosynthesis.

The photosynthetic cells of leaves are of a general type known as *parenchyma.* They are many-sided cells with thin, flexible cell walls. In many leaves, there are two types of parenchyma cells: *palisade parenchyma,* consisting of long columnar cells in which most of the photosynthesis takes place, and *spongy parenchyma,* which consists of more rounded cells with larger air spaces surrounding them.

These spaces are filled with gases, including water vapor. Palisade and spongy parenchyma make up the *mesophyll,* or "middle leaf." The mesophyll is completely enclosed in an almost airtight wrapping made up of epidermal cells. These cells secrete a fatty substance called *cutin,* which forms a coating, the cuticle, over the outer surface of the epidermis.

The epidermal cells and the cuticle are transparent, permitting light to penetrate to the photosynthetic cells of the mesophyll. Materials move into and out of the leaf by two quite different routes: veins and stomata. Veins supply water and minerals to the leaf cells.

The veins pass through the petioles (leaf stalks) and are continuous with the rest of the vascular system of the plant. (Note that they are called veins only when they are in the leaf; in the stem and root these same structures are called vascular bundles.

It is correct to refer to veins as vascular bundles but not vice versa.) The tissue in vascular bundles that is concerned primarily with water transport is known as the *xylem.* Other groups of cells, the *phloem* (pronounced "flow-em"), transport sugars and other products from the photosynthetic (autotrophic) cells to the other (heterotrophic) cells of the plant.

Veins form distinctive patterns in leaf blades. There is a conspicuous difference between the veins of monocots and dicots: In monocots, the major veins are usually parallel; in dicots, the venation (vein pattern)

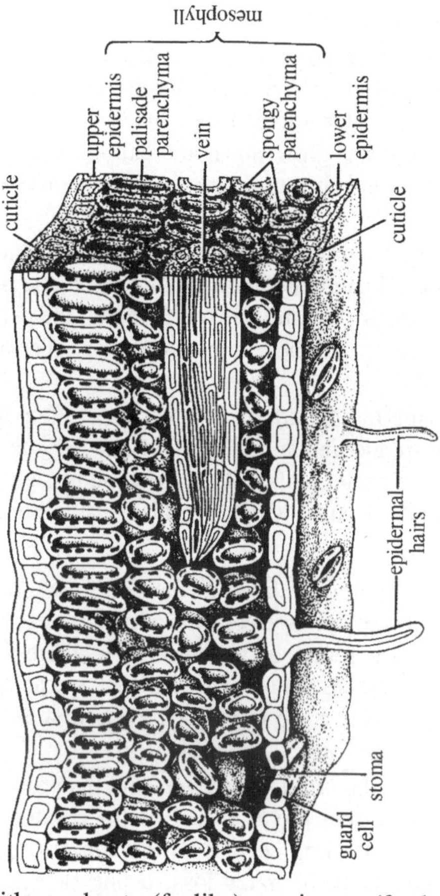

Figure 13.1 : Diagram of the interior of a leaf. Chloroplasts, indicated in green, occur in the guard cells as well as in the cells of the mesophyll.

is netted, either palmate (fanlike) or pinnate (featherlike), as shown in Figure elsewhere in this chapter.

Gases-oxygen and carbon dioxide-move into and out of the leaf by means of *stomata*. (A stoma, as we define it, includes both the opening, or pore, and the guard cells surrounding it.) This exchange of gases is, as we saw in other chapter of this book, necessary for photosynthesis.

However, as gases are exchanged, water escapes from the leaf; 90 percent of the water that leaves the plant body is lost through the stomata. The stomata open and close in response to a variety of stimuli, both internal and external.

Stomata may be very numerous; for example, in tobacco leaves, there are 12,000 stomata per square centimeter of leaf surface. They are usually most abundant on the undersurface.

Leaf Shapes and Adaptations

Leaves come in all shapes and sizes, ranging from broad fronds to tiny scales. Some of these differences can be correlated with the environments in which the plants live. Large leaves with broad surfaces are often found in plants that grow under the canopy in a tropical rain forest, where water is plentiful but where there is intense competition for light.

Leaves of such plants sometimes have "drip tips," which facilitate the runoff of rainwater. Leaves with small photosynthetic surfaces are associated with dry climates. In conifers, for example, the photosynthetic surfaces are greatly reduced and there is an extra-thick layer of epidermis and cuticle.

Similarly, angiosperms found in dry habitats often have small, leathery leaves. This reduction in leaf surface reaches its extreme in desert cacti, which have no leaves at all. In these plants, photosynthesis takes place in the fleshy stems, which are also water-storage organs.

Leaf Abscission

Another type of adaptation related to the conservation of water is found in the leaves of deciduous trees. Deciduous trees, which drop their leaves annually, are found in regions where there is a marked seasonal variation in available water. The fall of the leaf comes about when special enzymes dissolve the middle lamellae in a layer of weak, thin-walled cells in the petiole.

These cells compose the *abscission layer,* and the process is known as *abscission*. Deciduous trees are able, unlike the conifers, to present a broad, efficient light-collecting surface to the sun during favourable periods, while minimising their water loss during dry periods. Thus deciduous trees are far better energy collectors. On the other hand, they must pay the relatively high price, energetically speaking, of replacing all their leaves annually.

Some Leaf Modifications

In some plants, leaves are modified as spines, which are hard, dry, and nonphotosynthetic. (The terms "spine" and "thorn" are often used interchangeably; however, thorns are technically modified branches.) In other plants, such as the garden pea, leaves are modified as tendrils. In many plants, leaves are succulent; that is, they are adapted for water storage.

Other leaves are specialised for food storage. A bulb, such as the onion, is a large bud consisting of a short stem with many leaves modified for food storage. (In the onion, food is stored as sugar rather than as starch.) The "head" of a cabbage also consists of a compressed stem bearing numerous thick, overlapping leaves. In some plants, the petioles become thick and fleshy: Celery and rhubarb are two familiar examples.

In the flower-pot plant, which is an epiphyte (a plant that grows on other plants but is not parasitic on them), some of the leaves form tubes. Rainwater and debris collect in these tubes. Roots of the plant grow into the leaf tubes and collect water and minerals from them.

In addition, ants colonise the tubes, adding to the nitrogen supply with their excreta and dead bodies. Among the most spectacular modified leaves are those of the carnivorous plants, such as the pitcher plant, Venus flytrap, and sundew. These plants capture insects by various means and then digest them with enzymes secreted by the leaf cells. The insects are an additional source of nitrogen for the plant.

THE STEM

The Structure of the Stem

The stem holds the leaves up to the light and provides for the transportation of substances to and from the leaves. The outer surface of a young green stem, like that of the leaf and the root, is made of epidermal cells. Like the leaf, the green stem is covered with a fatty cuticle, contains stomata, and is photosynthetic.

Ground Tissue

The bulk of the tissue of a young stem is known as the *ground tissue*. Like the mesophyll of the leaf, ground tissue is composed mostly of parenchyma cells. The turgor of these cells provides the chief support for young green stems.

Stems also may contain specialised supporting tissues formed from *collenchyma* or *sclerenchyma* cells. Collenchyma cells differ from the thin-walled parenchyma cells of the stem in having primary cellulose walls that are thickened at the corners or in some other uneven fashion. Their name derives from the Greek word *colla,* meaning "glue," which refers to their characteristic thick, glistening walls.

Collenchyma cells are often located just inside the epidermis, forming either a continuous cylinder or distinct vertical strips of supporting tissue.

Sclerenchyma cells are of two types: fibers and sclereids. The name is derived from the Greek *skleros,* meaning "hard." Fibers, which are elongated, somewhat elastic cells, typically occur in strands or bundles arranged in patterns characteristic of the plant. These supporting cells are often associated with the vascular tissues.

Plant fibers such as flax, hemp, jute, sisal, and raffia have long been used in human artifacts, including baskets, rope, and cloth. Sclereids, or stone cells, which are variable in form, are less common in stems than are fibers. Layers of sclereids are found more frequently in seeds, nuts, and fruit stones, where they form the hard outer coverings.

Sderenchyma cells differ from collenchyma in three respects: (1) They have secondary walls; (2) the walls often contain lignin, a complex macromolecule that impregnates the cellulose and toughens and hardens it; and (3) the cells are sometimes dead at maturity, with only their cell walls remaining.

Conducting Tissues

Phloem, as we noted previously, conducts the products of photosynthesis, chiefly in the form of sucrose, from the leaves to the nonphotosynthetic cells of the plant. In angiosperms, the conducting cells of the phloem are called *sieve-tube elements*.

A *sieve tube* is a vertical column of sieve-tube elements joined by their end walls. These end walls, called *sieve plates,* have openings leading from one sieve-tube element to the next.

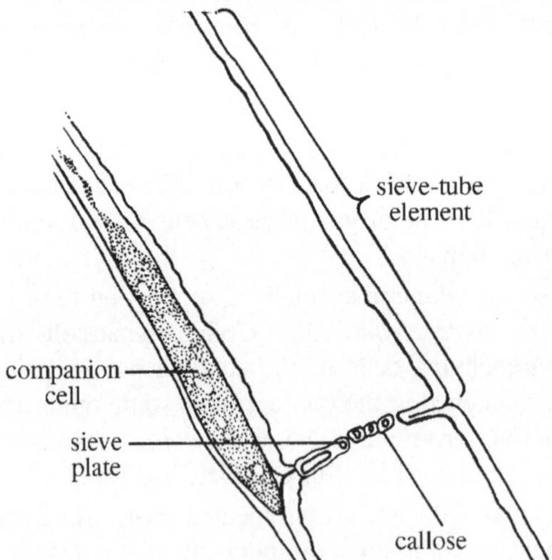

Figure 13.2 : In angiosperms, the conducting elements of the phloem are sieve tubes, made up of individual cells, the sieve-tube elements. These cells, which lack nuclei at maturity, are usually found in close association with companion cells, which do have nuclei. Sieve-tube elements are joined by a sieve plate.

The sieve-tube elements, which are alive at maturity, are filled largely with a watery cytoplasm. They are characterised by the presence of a protein-containing substance called P-protein (or sometimes, slime). In mature sieve-tube elements,

P-protein lies along the inner surfaces of the cell. It is continuous from one cell to the next through the sieve plates. The nucleus of a sieve-tube element disintegrates as the cell matures, as do many of the organelles.

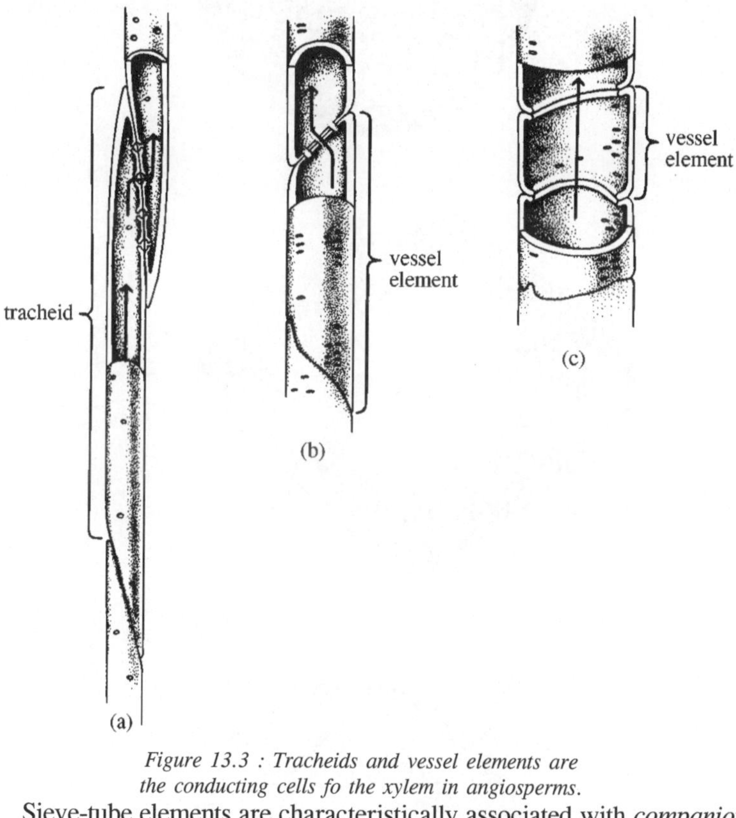

Figure 13.3 : Tracheids and vessel elements are the conducting cells fo the xylem in angiosperms.

Sieve-tube elements are characteristically associated with *companion cells*, which are thought to provide nuclear control and energy for the sieve tubes. A sieve-tube element can function only if its cell membrane is intact, and it is likely that the companion cell helps to maintain the membrane.

Xylem conducts water and minerals from the roots to other parts of the plant body. It is customary to think of xylem as transporting

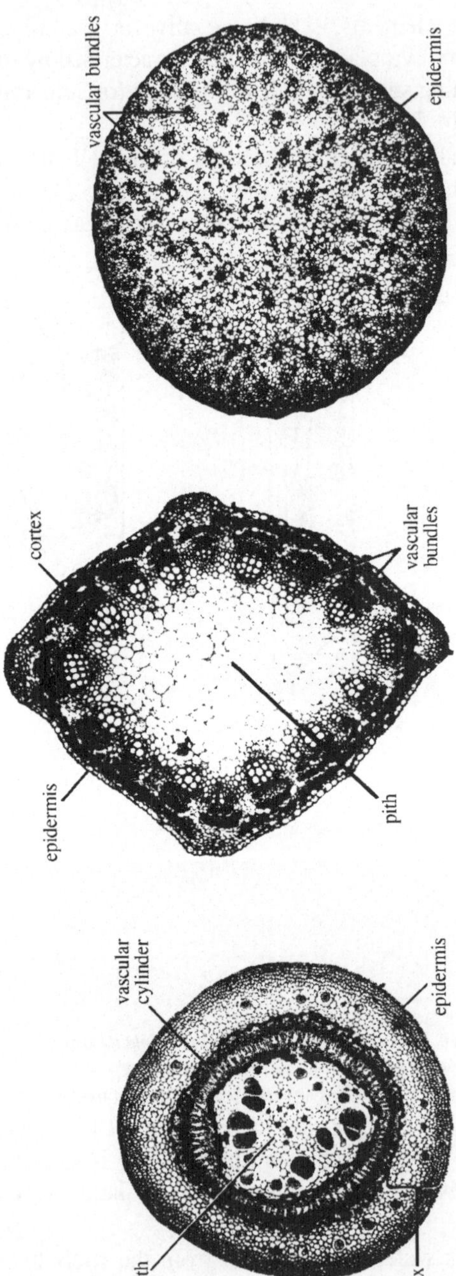

Figure 13.4 : Cross sections of two dicot stems and one monocot stem.

water up and phloem as transporting sugars down, but if you think of the various shapes of plants you can see that water must also often be transported laterally, as along a tendril, or even down, as to the branches of a weeping willow. Conversely, sugars must often go upward, as into a flower or fruit.

In angiosperms, the conducting cells of the xylem are *tracheids* and *vessel elements*. Both of these cell types have thick secondary walls impregnated with lignin, and both are dead at maturity. Tracheids are long, thin cells that overlap one another on their tapered ends.

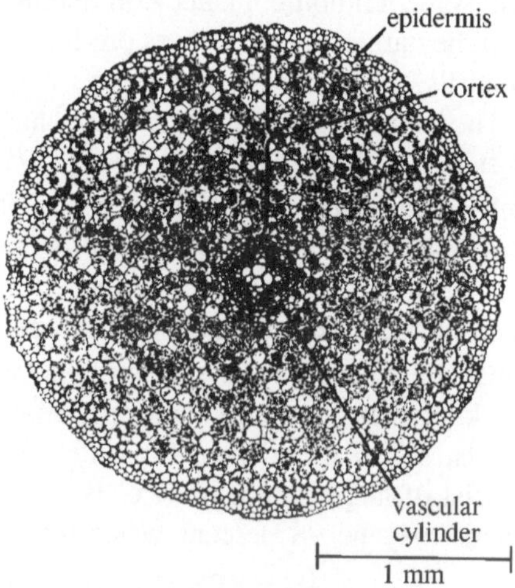

Figure 13.5 : Root of a buttercup in cross section.

These overlapping surfaces contain thin areas, pits, where no secondary wall has been deposited. Water passes from one tracheid to the next through the pits. Vessels, which are much larger, also differ from tracheids in that their end walls contain one or more perforations or are broken down entirely.

Thus, the vessel elements form a continuous *vessel*, which is a more effective conduit than a series of tracheids. Lower vascular plants and most gymnosperms have only tracheids. Most angiosperms have both tracheids and vessels.

Both phloem and xylem tissue contain parenchyma cells, which store food and water, and supporting fibers.

Stem Patterns

In green stems, the xylem and the phloem are usually arranged in longitudinal parallel strands, the vascular bundles, which are embedded in the ground tissue. In young dicot stems, the vascular bundles form a ring, the vascular cylinder, around a central area of ground tissue called the *pith*.

The cylinder of ground tissue outside the vascular bundles is called the *cortex*. Within each bundle, the xylem is characteristically on the inside, adjacent to the pith, and the phloem is on the outside, adjacent to the cortex. In monocots the vascular bundles are scattered throughout the ground tissue.

Special Adaptations of the Stem

The stems of some climbing plants coil themselves around the structures on which they are growing. Others produce modified branches in the form of tendrils. (As we saw previously, tendrils may also be modified leaves.) The tendrils of English ivy, grape, and Virginia creeper are all modified stems.

Runners, such as those found in most varieties of strawberry, are long, slender stems that grow along the surface of the soil. Rhizomes are underground stems that often, as in the grasses, form buds and from these buds produce upright stems bearing leaves and flowers.

Stems also may be adapted for food storage. White potatoes are enlarged rhizomes known as tubers. In some species of plants that grow in arid environments, stems are adapted for water storage. The water-storing tissues consist of large parenchyma cells that lack chloroplasts; the stem of a cactus may be 98 percent water by weight.

ROOTS

Roots anchor the plant and, as we noted at the beginning of the chapter, are specialised for taking up water and essential minerals. In an older plant, the root system may make up more than half of the plant body. The lateral spread of tree roots is usually greater than the spread of the crown of the tree.

In a study made on a four-month-old rye plant, the total surface area of the root system, including root hairs, was calculated by extrapolation to be 639 square meters, 130 times the surface area of the leaves and stem. Root growth is affected by soil conditions and availability of water. The deepest known root was that of a pine growing on sandy, porous soil. It had penetrated to a depth of about 6.5 meters.

The Structure of the Root

The internal structure of the root is comparatively simple. There are three concentric layers: the *epidermis,* the *cortex,* and the *vascular cylinder*.

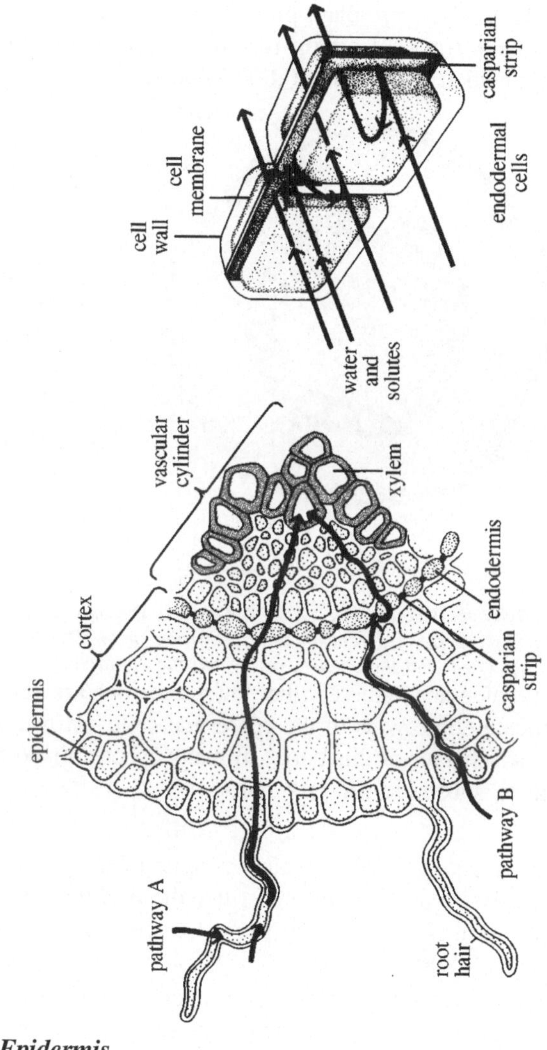

Figure 13.6 : Cross section of the root of a corn plant, showing the vascular cylinder enclosing the pith. Part of a branch root can be seen at the lower right.

The Epidermis

The epidermal cells of the root, which enclose the entire surface of the root, absorb water and minerals from the soil. As you would expect, they lack the cuticle found on the surface of the epidermal cells of the leaf.

They are also characterised by fine, threadlike outgrowths, known as root hairs. Root hairs are slender extensions of the epidermal cells themselves; the nucleus of the epidermal cell is often found within the root hair. In the study of the rye plant previously mentioned, the roots were estimated to have some 14 billion root hairs; placed end to end, they would have extended more than 10,000 kilometers.

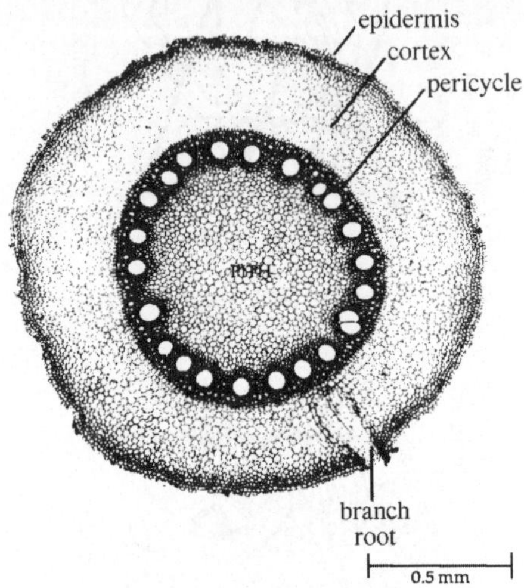

Figure 13.7 : The endodermis is considered part of the cortex. The outermost layer of the vascular cylinder is the pericycle, from which branch roots arise. The conducting tissues, the xylem and the phloem, are within the pericycle.

Much of the water and minerals that enter the root are taken up through these delicate outgrowths of the epidermal cells. (However, as we shall see in other chapter of this book, in many species mycorrhizal associations seem to substitute for root hairs.

The Cortex

The cortex occupies by far the greatest volume of the young root. The cells of the cortex are parenchyma cells, like those of the mesophyll of the leaf and the ground tissue of the stem; however, as you would expect, they lack chloroplasts.

They store starch and other organic substances. The tissue of the cortex contains many air spaces. Oxygen-containing air enters these spaces through the epidermal cells and is used by the cortical cells in respiration.

Unlike the rest of the cortex, the cells of the innermost layer, the *endodermis*, are compact and have no spaces between them. Each endodermal cell is encircled by a *Casparian strip*, a fatty band within the cell wall.

The strip is continuous and is not permeable to water. Therefore, water and dissolved substances, which pass freely around the other

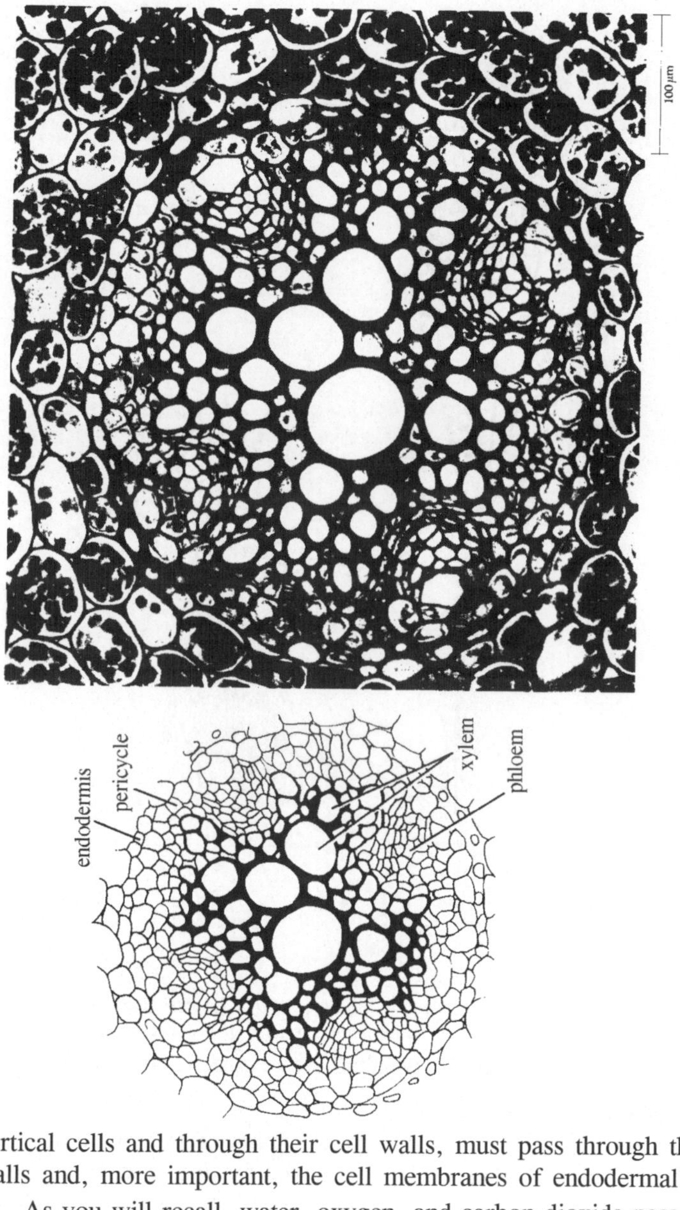

Figure 13.8 : The endodermis is considered part of the cortex. The outermost layer of the vascular cylinder is the pericycle, from which branch root arise.

cortical cells and through their cell walls, must pass through the cell walls and, more important, the cell membranes of endodermal cells.

As you will recall, water, oxygen, and carbon dioxide pass freely through cell membranes, but many ions and other substances do not. Therefore, the membranes of the endodermal cells regulate the passage of such substances into the vascular tissues of the root and so determine

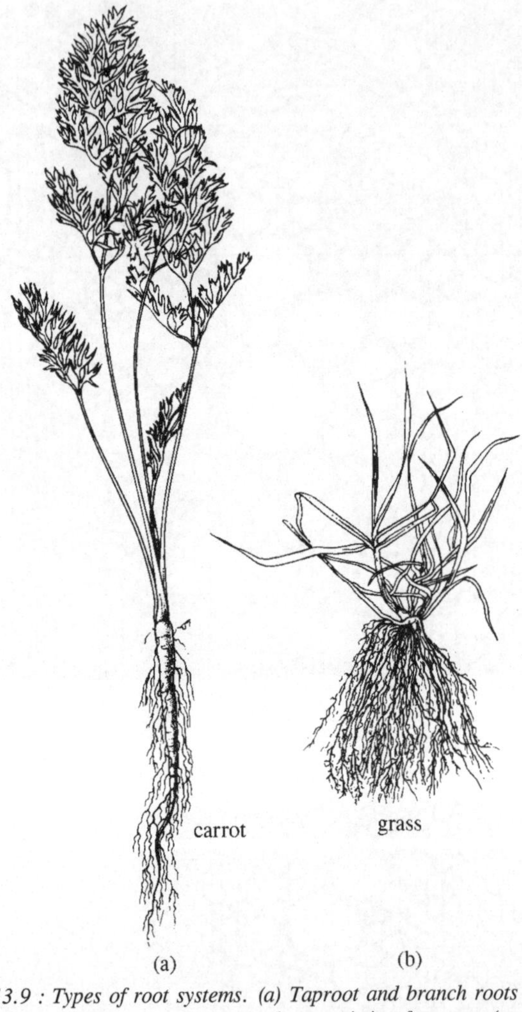

Figure 13.9 : Types of root systems. (a) Taproot and branch roots of a carrot (a dicot). (b) Fibrous root system characteristic of grasses (monocots).

what enters the plant body, as we shall see in other chapter of this book.

The Vascular Cylinder

The vascular cylinder of the root consists of the vascular tissues (xylem and phloem) completely surrounded by one or more layers of cells, the *pericycle*. Branch roots arise from the pericycle. In most species, the vascular tissues are grouped in a solid cylinder, as shown in figure elsewhere in this chapter.

In some, however, they form a hollow cylinder around a pith, a central core of ground tissue. Figure elsewhere in this chapter shows the details of the vascular cylinder of a buttercup.

Patterns of Root Growth

The first root of a plant, which originates in the embryo, is called the radicle. In many dicots, this root develops into a *taproot* that, in turn, gives rise to lateral or branch roots. In monocots, the primary root is usually short-lived and the final root system develops from the base of the stem; such roots are called adventitious roots. (Adventitious describes any structure growing from an unusual place.) The adventitious roots and their branches develop into a fibrous root system.

Special Adaptations of Roots

Aerial roots are adventitious roots produced from aboveground structures. Some aerial roots, such as those of English ivy, cling to vertical surfaces and thus provide support for the climbing stem. In some plants, such as corn, aerial roots serve as prop roots.

Trees that grow in swamps, such as the red mangrove and the bald cypress, often have prop roots. In swampy areas the soil is low in oxygen, and, in some species, the prop roots are believed not only to anchor the plant but also to supply the root cells with the oxygen needed for respiration.

Black mangroves have roots whose tips grow upward out of the mud and serve this aerating function. Many special root adaptations are found among epiphytes, such as the flowerpot plant. In some species of orchids, for instance, the root is the only photosynthetic organ.

Most roots are storage organs, and in some species the roots are highly specialised for this function, with an abundance of storage parenchyma. Beets, carrots, and sweet potatoes are examples of such roots.

14

Embryology of Plants

Unlike the higher animals, whose reproduction is almost exclusively sexual, many plants reproduce both sexually and asexually. (Asexual reproduction is often referred to as vegetative reproduction.) Organisms produced by asexual reproduction are genetically identical to their single parent, whereas organisms produced by sexual reproduction, which involves meiosis and fertilization, are different from both parents.

ASEXUAL REPRODUCTION

There are many forms of asexual reproduction among plants. One of the most familiar occurs by means of runners or rhizomes. Strawberries are a common example of plants that propagate by runners, as are spider plants, commonly grown as hanging plants.

Plants that reproduce by rhizomes include potatoes, many flowering garden perennials, such as lilies-of-the-valley, irises, and dahlias, and the sod-forming grasses of lawns and pastures. Both runners and rhizomes develop adventitious roots.

Many members of the lily family, which includes onions and tulips as well as lilies, reproduce asexually by bulbs. Some species of plants with arching stems, such as raspberries, develop new roots from stem tips that touch the soil.

New plants may form if the stem is subsequently broken, separating it from the parent plant. The leaves of some plants, such as African violets, develop adventitious roots when they are detached from the parent plant and may give rise to new individuals in that way. Some

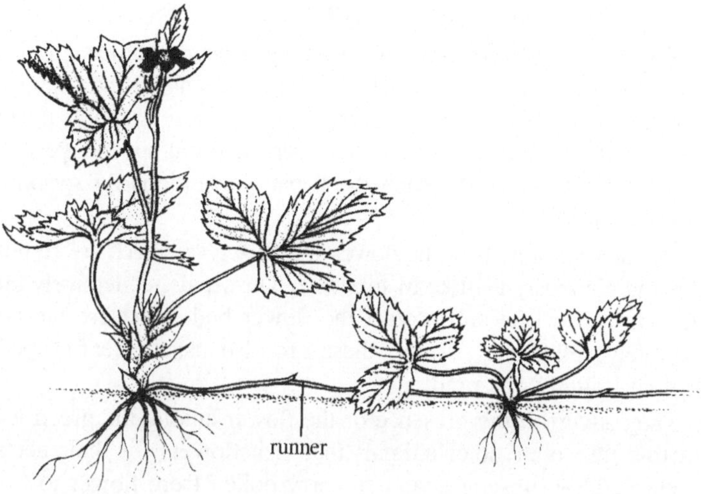

Figure 14.1 : Wild strawberry plants reproduce asexually by means of aboveground stems, or runners. Roots and leaves develop at every second node along the modified stems. These plants also form flowers and reproduce sexually.

species of *Kalanchoe* produce plantlets in the margins of leaves, which later drop to the ground and develop into separate plants. If the taproot of a dandelion is injured or broken near the soil line, a callus (a mass of undifferentiated cells) forms, plugging the wound.

Eventually several new plants grow from this callus tissue. Thus both lawn mowers and grazing animals have highly beneficial effects on the dandelion population.

The capacity of many species of plants to reproduce asexually has been exploited in the development of cultivated varieties of plants for food or ornamental use. Such plants are, of course, genetically identical to the parent stock, and so vegetative reproduction is a way of preserving uniformity.

Many plants are reproduced by stem cuttings, which simply involves sticking young stems in the ground and protecting them from drying out until adventitious roots appear. Rooting can often be facilitated by hormone treatment.

Another artificial form of plant propagation is grafting, in which a stem cutting is attached to the main stem of a rooted woody plant. Most fruit trees and roses are propagated in this way. Many economically important plants are sterile and can only be propagated vegetatively; these include pineapples, bananas, seedless grapes, navel oranges, and numerous ornamental plants.

SEXUAL REPRODUCTION

The flower is the structure of sexual reproduction of the angiosperms. Unlike the gonads of animals, which are permanent organs that develop in the embryo, flowers are transitory, developing seasonally. A perfect flower, as it is called, consists of four sets of floral appendages, which grow in spirals or whorls; each floral part, evolutionarily speaking, is a modified leaf.

The outermost parts of the flower are the *sepals,* which are commonly green and obviously leaflike in structure. The sepals, collectively known as the *calyx,* enclose and protect the flower bud. Next are the *petals,* collectively called the *corolla;* these are also usually leaf-shaped but are often brightly coloured.

They advertise the presence of the flower among the green leaves, attracting insects or other animals that visit flowers for their nectar or for other edible substances and so carry pollen from flower to flower. Calyx and corolla together are known as the *perianth.*

Within the corolla are the *stamens.* Each stamen consists of a single elongated stalk, the *filament,* and at the end of the filament, the *anther.* The pollen grains, when they are ripe, are released-often in large numbers-from the anther, usually through narrow slits or pores. The pollen grains are immature male gametophytes.

The centermost appendages of the flower are the *carpels,* which contain the female gametophytes. Typically a single carpel consists of a *stigma,* which is a sticky surface specialised to receive the pollen; a slender stalk, the *style,* down which the pollen tube grows; and a base, the *ovary.*

Within the ovary are the *ovules,* each of which encloses a female gametophyte with a single egg cell. When the egg cell is fertilised, the ovule develops into a seed. A single flower may have one carpel or several carpels. The carpels may be separate or fused together.

In some species, flowers are either male (staminate) or female (carpellate). Male and female flowers may be present on the same plant, as in corn, squash, oaks, and birches, or on different plants, such as the tree of heaven *(Ailanthus),* the date palm, and the American mistletoe.

Species in which both male and female flowers are borne on the same plant are known as monoecious ("in one house"); species in which the male and female flowers are on separate plants are known as dioecious ("in two houses").

POLLINATION OF THE FLOWER

For flowering plants, a new cycle of life begins when a grain of pollen-often brushed from the body of a foraging insect-comes into contact with the stigma of a flower of the same species. By the time this pollen grain is released from its parent flower, it usually consists of three haploid cells (two sperm cells and a "vegetative," or tube, cell), enclosed by the thickened outer wall of the pollen grain.

Pollen is commonly produced in great quantities; the probability of any particular pollen grain reaching the stigma of an appropriate flower is very small. The pollen grain contains its own nutrients and has so tough an outer coating that intact grains thousands of years old have been found in peat bogs.

In lower plants, you will recall, there is a distinct cycle of alternation of generations in which the sporophyte produces spores that produce gametophytes that produce gametes, with gametophyte and sporophyte having separate existences.

In the course of plant evolution, the gametophyte stage has been steadily reduced and, in the angiosperms, all that remains of the male gametophyte is the tough, tiny pollen grain and the pollen tube. The sperm cells are the gametes.

Once on the stigma, the pollen grain germinates, and, under the influence of the tube nucleus, a pollen tube grows down through the style into an ovule. The ovule contains the female gametophyte, which has also become reduced in size in the course of evolution.

In many species it consists of seven cells, with a total of eight haploid nuclei. One of the seven cells is the egg, containing a single haploid nucleus.

On either side of the egg are two small cells known as synergids. At the opposite end of the gametophyte are three small cells, the antipodal cells, whose function, if any, is unknown.

The large central cell contains two haploid nuclei, called the polar nuclei because they move to the center from each end, or pole, of the gametophyte.

FERTILIZATION

One of the sperm cells carried by the pollen tube unites with the egg. This fertilised cell, the zygote, develops into the young sporophyte, or embryo. The nucleus of the second sperm cell unites with the two nuclei of the central cell. From the resultant *3n* cell, a specialised

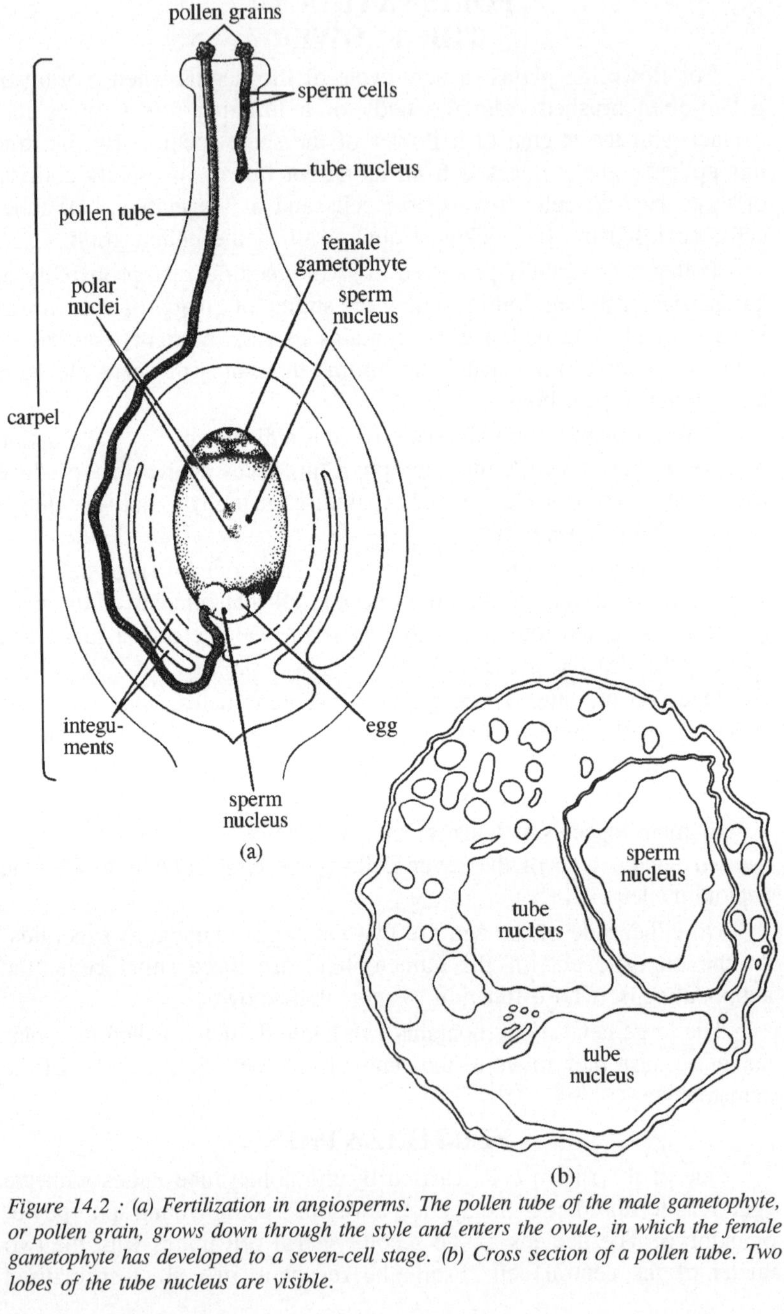

Figure 14.2 : (a) Fertilization in angiosperms. The pollen tube of the male gametophyte, or pollen grain, grows down through the style and enters the ovule, in which the female gametophyte has developed to a seven-cell stage. (b) Cross section of a pollen tube. Two lobes of the tube nucleus are visible.

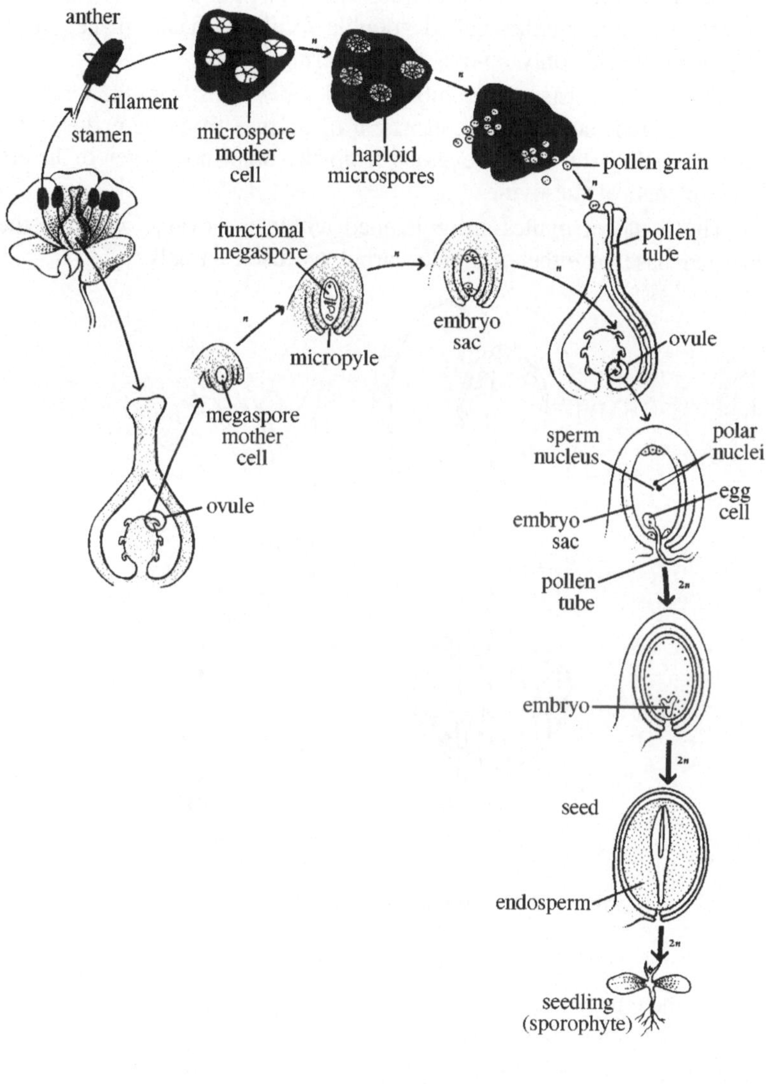

Figure 14.3 : Life history of an angiosperm.

tissue called the *endosperm* develops. It completely surrounds and nourishes the embryo. These extraordinary phenomena of fertilization and triple fusion-together called "double fertilization take place, in all the natural world, only among the flowering plants.

The seed consists of the embryo, which develops from the fertilised egg; the stored food, which consists of or derives from the endosperm; and the seed coat, which develops from the outermost layer or layers (integuments) of the ovule.

The ovule or ovules are contained within the ovary, which is the enlarged base of either a single carpel or fused carpels.

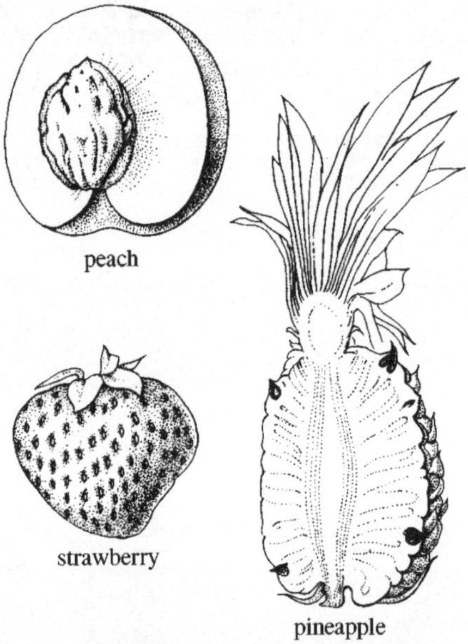

Figure 14.4 : A simple fruit, an aggregate fruit, and, on the right, a multiple fruit.

THE FRUIT

As the embryo develops, the ovary wall (pericarp) develops into the fruit. As you know from your own observations, fruits have many forms. They are generally classified as simple, aggregate, or multiple, depending on the arrangement of the carpels from which they develop.

Simple fruits develop from one carpel or the united carpels of a single flower. Aggregate fruits, such as magnolia, raspberry, and strawberry, are formed from a number of separate carpels of one flower. Multiple fruits consist of the carpels of more than one flower.

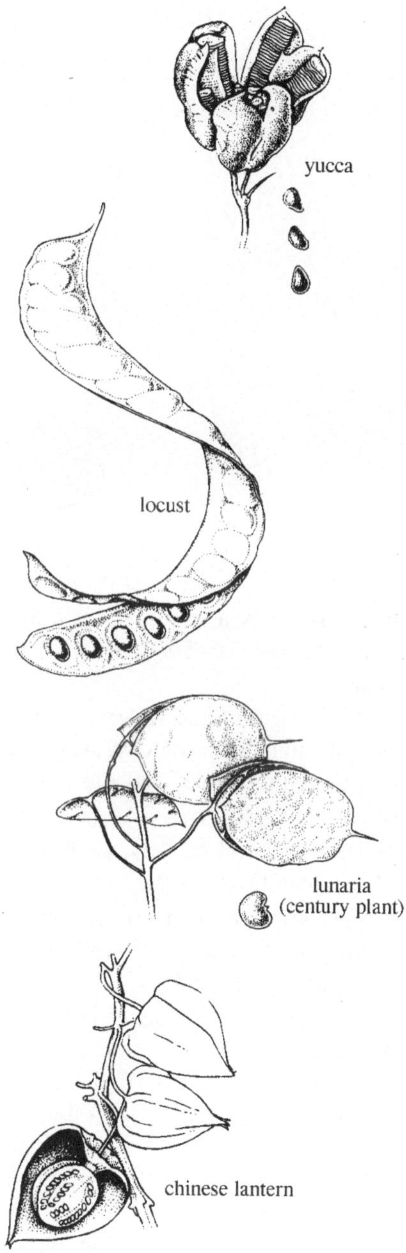

(a) *(Fig. Contd.)*

Figure 14.5 : Examples of (a) dehiscent and (b) indehiscent fruits.

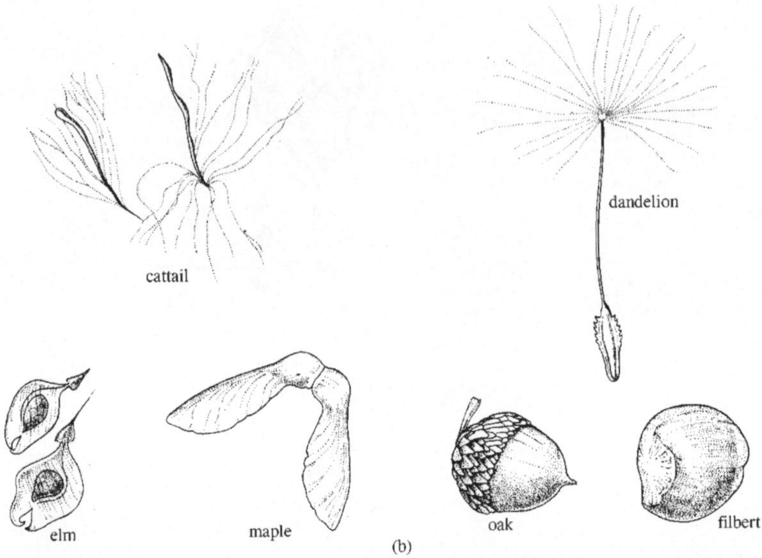

Figure 14.5 : Examples of (a) dehiscent and (b) indehiscent fruits. (Contd.)

A pineapple, for example, is a multiple fruit formed from a flower cluster of many separate flowers. The ovaries of these flowers become fused as they mature.

Simple fruits are by far the most diverse of the three groups. When ripe, they may be soft and fleshy or dry. There are three main types of fleshy fruit-the berry, the drupe, and the pome.

In the berry type, examples of which are tomatoes, dates, and grapes, there are one to several carpels, each of which may have one or many seeds. The inner layer of the pericarp is usually fleshy.

In the drupe, there are also one to several carpels, but each usually contains only a single seed. The inner wall of the fruit is stony and usually tightly adherent to the seed.

Some familiar drupes are the peach, cherry, olive, and plum. The peach is a typical drupe; the skin, the succulent, edible portion of the fruit, and the stone are three layers of the mature ovary wall. The almond-shaped structure within the stone is the seed. The coconut is a drupe whose outer covering is fibrous rather than fleshy.

A highly specialised sort of fleshy fruit is the pome, which is characteristic of the subfamily of roses that produces rose hips. The pome is derived from an inferior ovary in which the fleshy portion comes largely from the perianth. Apples and pears are pomes.

Dry fruits are classified into two groups, dehiscent and indehiscent. In dehiscent fruits, the tissues of the mature ovary wall break open, releasing the seeds. In indehiscent fruits, the seeds remain in the fruit after the fruit is shed from the parent plant.

There are several sorts of dehiscent fruits. A fruit derived from a single carpel in which the ovary wall splits down one side is known as a follicle; the fruits of columbines and milkweeds are examples. In the pea family (legumes), the ovary splits down two sides; the pod is the mature pericarp and the peas are the seeds. Other examples of dehiscent fruit are shown in figure elsewhere in this chapter.

Indehiscent fruits are characteristic of a great variety of plant families. The most common is the achene, a small, single-seeded fruit. Winged achenes, such as those found in the elm and the ash, are called samaras. The most familiar kind of indehiscent fruit is the nut, which resembles the achene but has a stony coat and is derived from a compound ovary (an ovary formed from fused carpels).

Examples of nuts are acorns and hazelnuts. Note that the word nut is used very indiscriminately in common speech: Peanuts are legumes; pine nuts are seeds; almonds and coconuts are drupes.

SEED DORMANCY

The seeds of most wild plants require a period of dormancy before they will germinate. This genetic requirement ensures that the seed will "wait" at least until the next favourable growth period. Seeds can remain dormant and yet viableùwith the embryo in a state of suspended animation-for hundreds of years.

The record for dormancy, as far as is known, has been set by some seeds of Arctic tundra lupine found in a lemming burrow in the Yukon. Deeply buried in the permanently frozen silt, they are estimated to be at least 10,000 years old. But when a sample was planted, the seeds germinated within 48 hours.

The seed coat apparently plays a major role in maintaining dormancy. In some species, the seed coat seems to act primarily as a mechanical barrier, preventing the entry of water and gases, without which growth is not possible.

In these cases, growth is initiated by the seed coat's being worn away in various ways—such as being washed by rainfall, abraded by sand or soil, burned away by a forest fire, decomposed by microbial action, or partially digested as it passes through the digestive tract of a bird or other animal. In other species, dormancy seems to be maintained chiefly by chemical inhibitors in the seed coat. These inhibitors undergo chemical changes in response to various environmental factors, such as light or prolonged cold or a sudden rise in temperature, which neutralise their effects, or they may be washed or eroded away. Eventually, the embryo resumes growth.

The dormancy requirement in seeds apparently evolved only recently, geologically speaking, among groups of plants subjected to the environmental stress of increasing winter cold characteristic of the most recent Ice Age.

By this time-only 1 to 2 million years ago-the angiosperms were already a highly diversified group, and different populations responded to these pressures in different ways. This explains why even closely related plants have different mechanisms for maintaining and breaking dormancy.

GROWTH OF THE PLANT

As we saw earlier, the "double fertilization" of angiosperms produces a 3n cell and the zygote (the fertilised egg cell). The 3n cell divides mitotically to produce endosperm, the tissue that nourishes the developing embryo and, in many cases, the young seedling. The fertilised egg cell also divides mitotically, and as the embryo grows, its cells begin to *differentiate*—become different from one another-and the embryo begins to take on a characteristic form, a process known as *morphogenesis*.

In its earliest stages, the embryo proper consists of a globular mass of cells. Suspensor cells, also formed from divisions of the fertilised egg cell, are believed to push the developing embryo into the endosperm and to be actively involved in the absorption of nutrients from the endosperm.

As development of the embryo proceeds, changes in its internal structure result in the beginnings of the tissue systems of the plant. At the same time, or slightly later, emergence of the one cotyledon in monocots, or the two in dicots, occurs. The stages in the development of a dicot embryo are shown in figure elsewhere in this chapter.

In the earliest stages of embryonic growth, cell division takes place throughout the body of the young plant. As the embryo grows older, however, the addition of new cells becomes gradually restricted to certain parts of the plant body: the *apical meristems* of the root and the shoot.

During the rest of the life of the plant, all the primary growth-which chiefly involves the elongation of the plant body-originates in these meristems.

The existence of such meristematic areas, which add to the plant body throughout the life of the plant, is one of the principal differences between plants and animals. Higher animals stop growing when they reach maturity, although the cells of certain "turnover" tissues, such as nails, hair, skin, or the lining of the intestine, continue to divide.

Plants, however, continue to grow during their entire life span. Growth in plants is the counterpart, to some extent, of mobility in animals. Plants "move" by extending their roots and shoots, both of which involve changes in size and form.

By growth, a plant modifies its relationship with the environment, turning toward the light and extending its roots. The sequence of growth stages in plants thus corresponds to a whole series of motor acts in animals, especially those concerned with the search for food and water. In fact, growth in plants serves many of the functions that we group under the term "behaviour" in animals.

PRIMARY GROWTH

A seed characteristically contains very little moisture (only about 5 to 10 percent of its total weight). Germination begins with a massive entry of water into the seed.

The seed coat ruptures and the young sporophyte emerges.

Primary growth, which begins immediately, involves the elongation of stems and roots, the formation of branches, and the differentiation of the conducting tissues and other specialised tissues of the young shoot and root. All primary growth originates in the apical meristems of the shoot and root.

Primary Growth of the Root

The first part of the embryo to break through the seed coat, in nearly all seed plants, is the embryonic root, the radicle. Figure elsewhere in this chapter diagrams the growing zone of the young root of a dicot. At the very tip is the root cap, which protects the apical meristem as the root is pushed through the soil.

The cells of the root cap wear away and are constantly replaced by new cells from the meristem. The cells in the meristem designated as *apical initials* are those that produce new cells. All the other cells in the root are the progeny of these relatively few meristematic cells. The apical initials are always capable of dividing.

Some of the daughter cells remain in the tip of the meristem to maintain the apical initial population. Others differentiate as they divide, some becoming cells of the root cap and others forming the complex

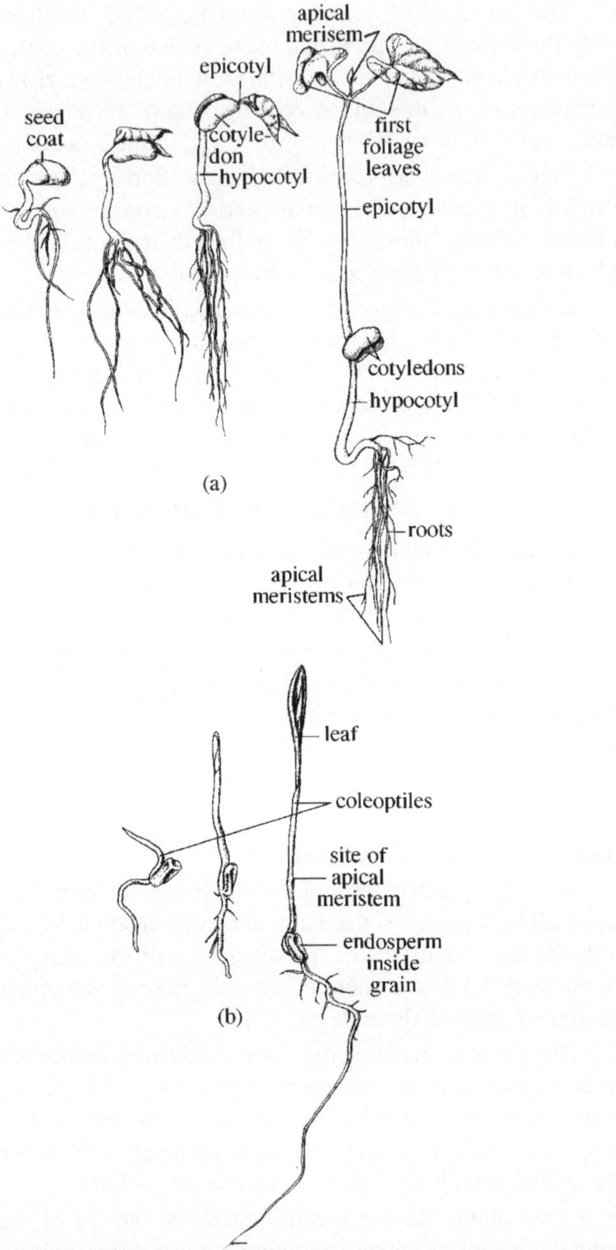

Figure 14.6 :(a) Development of a bean seedling. Prior to germination, the seed imbibes water and swells, bursting the seed coat.(b) Development of a corn seedling.

tissues of the root. The maximum rate of cell division occurs at a point well above the tip of the meristem. Then, just above the point where cell division ceases, the cells gradually elongate, growing to 10 or more times their previous length, often within the span of a few hours.

This process of elongation without cell division is the principal cause of root growth, although, of course, growth is ultimately dependent on the production of the new cells that become part of the zone of elongation.

As the cells stop dividing, some begin to differentiate, forming first the sievetube elements, the conducting cells of the phloem, and then vessel elements, the conducting cells of xylem. At the level of xylem differentiation, the endodermis takes shape, and to the inside of the endodermis, the pericycle forms.

This tissue gives rise to branch roots. At about this same stage, the epidermal cells differentiate and begin to extend root hairs into the crevices between the soil grains.

This same basic pattern of growth is seen in the first root of a seedling and is repeated over and over again in the growing root tips of a tree 50 meters tall.

Primary Growth of the Shoot

The organisation of the developing shoot tip is somewhat similar to that seen in the root: first, a zone in which most of the cell division takes place; next, a zone of cell elongation; and finally, a zone of differentiation.

These zones are not as distinct in the shoot as they are in the root, however, because of the regular occurrence of nodes and their appendages. Also, no covering analogous to the root cap is produced over the shoot tip.

As in the root, the outermost layer of cells develops into the epidermis. In the shoot, these cells have an outer covering, the cuticle. Other cells differentiate to form ground tissue, which in dicots includes the cortex and the pith, and the primary vascular tissues-the primary xylem and the primary phloem.

The pattern of development is more complicated, however, than in the root tip since the apical meristem of the shoot is the source of tissues that give rise to new leaves, branches, and flowers. (At the time of flowering the apical meristem forms the floral parts and ceases to exist.)

Figure elsewhere in this chapter shows the shoot tip of a lilac.

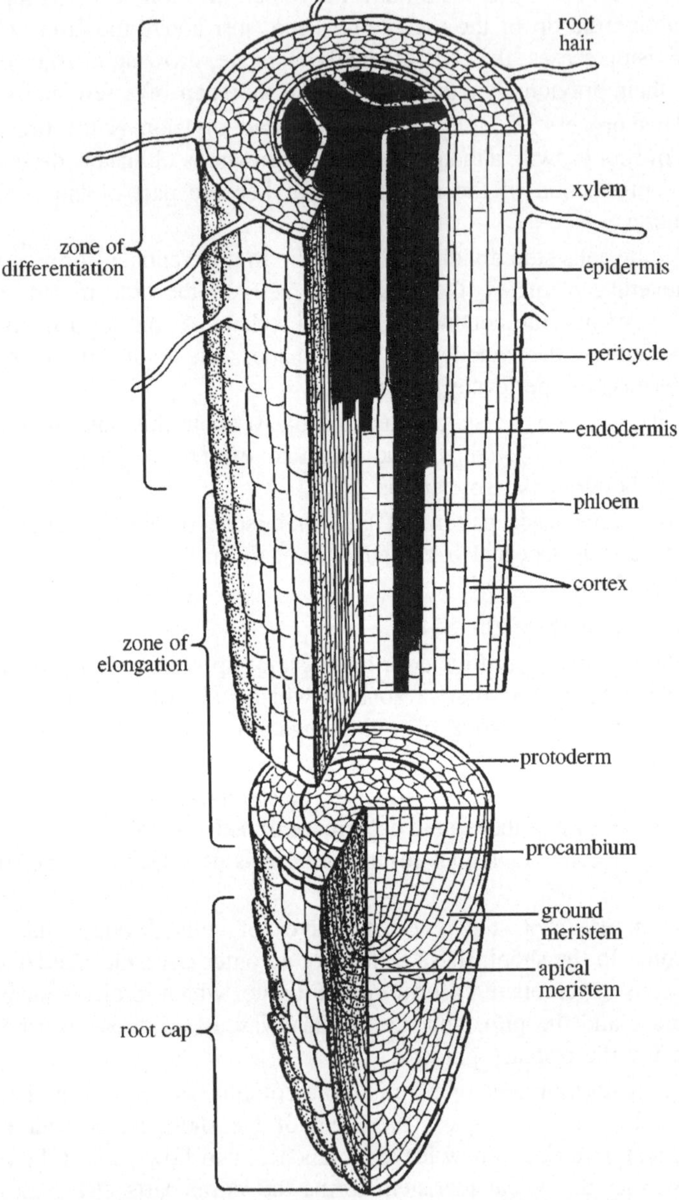

Figure 14.7 : The growth regions of a dicot root. New cells are produced by the division of cells within the apical meristem.

Here you can see the apical meristem, which is very small, and the beginnings-primordia-of leaves. As you can see, leaves are formed in an orderly sequence at the shoot tip. The leaf originates by the division of cells in a localised area along the side of the shoot apex.

The vascular tissue differentiates upward, becoming part of the general vascular system that connects the plant from root to leaf tip. In some species, leaves arise simultaneously in pairs opposite one another, as in our figure. In other species, the leaves occur spirally or in circles (whorls) at the nodes.

As the internodes elongate, the young leaves become separated so that the leaves clustered so tightly together around the apex in Figure elsewhere in this chapter will eventually be spaced out along the stem of the plant.

Buds, Flowers, and Branches

As the growing tip of the shoot elongates, small masses of meristematic tissue are left just above the point at which the leaf joins the stem (the leaf axil). These new meristematic regions, the buds, remain dormant until after the growth of the adjacent leaf and internode is complete.

In many species, the buds do not develop at all unless the apical meristem of the shoot is damaged or removed. (This phenomenon, known as apical dominance, will be discussed further in other chapter.)

In some species, some buds are destined to become lateral branches, or a specialised shoot, such as a rhizome or a tuber or a flower. In other species, whether or not a particular bud will become a flower or a branch is determined by environmental conditions, particularly day length.

SECONDARY GROWTH

Secondary growth is the process by which woody plants increase the thickness of trunks, stems, branches, and roots after primary growth has ceased. The so-called "secondary tissues" are not derived from the apical meristems; they are the result of the production of new cells by the vascular cambium and cork cambium. The cambiums are called *lateral meristems*.

The *vascular cambium* is a thin, cylindrical sheath of tissue in between the xylem and the phloem. In plants with secondary growth, the cambium cells divide continually during the growing season, adding new xylem cells-that is, secondary xylem—on the outside of the primary xylem, and secondary phloem on the inside of the primary phloem.

Some daughter cells remain as a cylinder of undifferentiated cambium. As the tree grows older, the living parenchyma cells of the xylem in the center of the trunk die, and those vessels cease to function. This nonfunctional wood is called heartwood, as distinct from sapwood, which consists of living parenchyma cells and functional vessels.

As the girth of stems and roots increases by secondary growth, the epidermis becomes stretched and torn. In response to this tearing process, a new type of cambium, the *cork cambium*, forms from the cortex.

Cork (phellem), which is a dead tissue at maturity, is produced from the cork cambium. The cork cambium forms anew each year, moving further inward until, finally, there is no cortex left. The tissues outside the vascular cambium, including the phloem, constitute the bark.

Figure elsewhere in this chapter shows the cross section of the stem of a young dicot, in which some secondary growth has taken place. In the center of the stem is the pith, composed of loosely packed parenchyma cells.

The first cylinders of tissues around the pith are layers of xylem, composed of vessels and other cell types. Around the outermost layer of xylem is a layer of meristematic tissue, the vascular cambium. Each year, during the growing season, the cambium undergoes a number of mitotic divisions, forming new xylem (secondary xylem) on its inner surface and new phloem (secondary phloem) on its outer surface. By this continuous formation of layers of xylem and (to a small extent) phloem, tree trunks increase their diameter as primary growth increases their height.

Season after season the new xylem forms visible growth layers, or rings. Each growing season leaves its trace, so that the age of a tree can be estimated by counting the number of growth rings in a section near its base. Since the rate of growth of a tree depends on climatic conditions, it is possible to determine from the width of the annual growth layers of ancient trees fluctuations in temperature and rainfall that occurred hundreds of years ago.

ADAPTATIONS TO CLIMATE CHANGE

As we noted in other chapter of this book, the angiosperms evolved during a relatively mild period in the earth's history. As the climate became colder, water became locked in snow and ice for part of the year. As a consequence, the angiosperms, which already possessed some adaptations to drought (perhaps because of highland origins), were placed under new environmental stress. Some did not survive, and some were pushed toward the Equator.

Those that did survive in colder, drier areas did so because of selection for existing characteristics that offered advantages in these relatively unfavourable environments. Chief among such characteristics is the capacity to remain dormant during periods when water is in short supply and when climatic conditions are unfavourable for delicate growing buds, shoots, new leaves, and root tips.

Depending on their characteristic patterns of active growth, dormancy, and death, modern plants are classified as annuals, biennials, and perennials.

Annuals, Biennials, and Perennials

Among annual plants, the entire cycle from seed to vegetative plant to flower toseed again takes place within a single growing season. Annuals include many of our weeds, wild flowers, garden flowers, vegetables, and grasses and most other monocots.

Such plants usually show little or no secondary growth. All vegetative organs (roots, stems, and leaves) die, and only the dormant seed bridges the gap between one generation and the next. Plants with nonwoody stems, such as most annuals, are known as herbs.

In biennial plants, the period from seed germination to seed formation spans two growing seasons. The first season of growth often results in a rosette of leaves near the soil surface, a short stem, and a root, sometimes a storage root, such as a carrot.

In the second growing season, extensive stem elongation, flowering, fruiting, and seed formation occur. This completes the life cycle and the vegetative organs die. Biennials may be herbaceous or woody.

Perennials are characteristically woody plants that live for many seasons and whose vegetative structures persist from year to year. In a woody plant, the stem increases in diameter and becomes firm due to the xylem inside. On the outside, a protective layer of dead tissue, the cork, accumulates.

The ancestral angiosperm is believed to have been a woody plant. Modern plants in favourable climates, such as a tropical rain forest, may live year after year with little change during the annual cycle, just as did the ancestral plants.

Perennials that live in areas where part of the year is unfavourable to growth show a variety of adaptations. Some, such as cacti and most conifers, undergo little apparent change, although their rates of metabolism, and therefore of growth, change with the seasons.

Most dicots living in the temperate zones undergo both structural and functional changes that allow them to take maximum advantage of the growing season and still survive the rest of the year. In some, all of the aboveground structures die, and the plants overwinter as underground roots, stems (rhizomes or tubers), or buds (bulbs). Others, including many of the common vines, shrubs, and trees, are deciduous.

15

VASCULAR SYSTEMS IN PLANTS

After William Harvey discovered the circulation of the blood, botanists began an eager search for the analogous pathways and pumping mechanisms of plants. It was to no avail. Although plants do have a vascular system, as we noted in other chapter, the ways that fluids move in the plant body are quite different from the circulation of fluids in the bodies of animals.

As long ago as 1727, Stephen Hales, in *Vegetable Staticks,* showed that fluids do not recirculate in plants, as blood does in animals, but that water moves predominantly toward the leaves. However, despite these remarkable early studies, it is only comparatively recently that plant physiologists have begun to understand the principles of the transport of water, sugar, and minerals in plants. Some aspects of the problem are, as you will see, still controversial.

One striking point of difference between plants and animals is that animals have a single major transport system, the blood vessels, and plants have two, the xylem and the phloem. In this chapter, we shall discuss first the movement of water in the xylem; second, the transport of sugars and other nutrients in the phloem; and, at the end of the chapter, a related subject, the uptake by the plant of nutrients from the soil.

THE MOVEMENT OF WATER: TRANSPIRATION

In order to carry out photosynthesis, plants must exchange gases

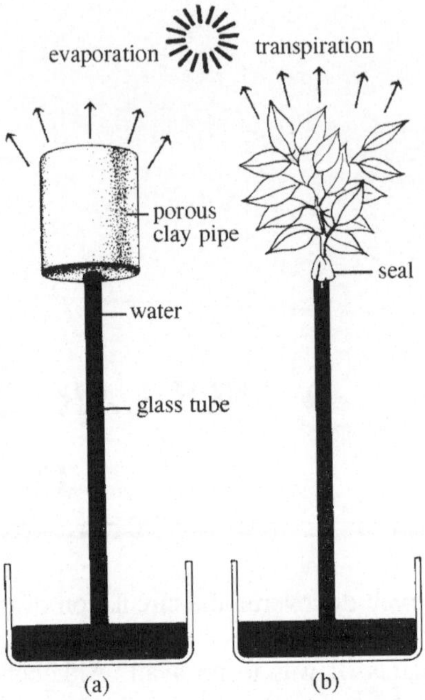

Figure 15.1 : (a) A simple model that illustrates the cohesion-tension theory. A piece of porous clay pipe, closed at both ends, is filled with water and attached to the end of a long, narrow glass tube also filled with water. (b) Transpiration from plant leaves results in sufficient water loss to create a similar negative pressure.

with the surrounding air. In the course of this exchange, as we noted in previous chapter, they lose water, which diffuses as vapor into the surrounding air.

The quantity of water passing through a plant is enormous-far greater than that used by an animal of comparable weight. An animal requires less water because, as we noted, most of its water remains in its body and recirculates again.

By contrast, in plants, more than 90 percent of the water that enters the roots is given off into the air as water vapor. A single corn plant needs 160 to 200 liters of water from seed to harvest, and a hectare of corn requires almost 5 million liters of water a season. The loss of water vapor from the plant body is known as *transpiration.*

Water enters the body of most plants almost entirely through the roots. During periods of rapid transpiration, water may be removed from around the roots so quickly that the soil in the vicinity of the roots becomes depleted; water will then move slowly by diffusion and capillary action through the soil toward the depleted region near the roots.

Root cells, like other living parts of the plant, contain a higher concentration of solutes (both organic and inorganic) than does soil water, and so water from the soil enters the roots by osmosis. Osmosis is sufficient to move water a short distance up the stem, a phenomenon known as root pressure.

Guttation is a visible consequence of root pressure. But how can water reach 20 meters high to the top of an oak tree, travel three stories up the stem of a vine, or move 125 meters up in a tall redwood?

One important clue is the observation that during times when the most rapid transpiration is taking place-which is, of course, when the flow of water up the stem must be the greatest-xylem pressures are characteristically negative (less than atmospheric pressure).

The existence of negative pressure can be demonstrated readily. If you peel a piece of bark from a transpiring tree and make a cut in the xylem, no sap runs out. In fact, if you place a drop of water on the cut, the drop will be drawn in.

What is the pulling force? It is not simple suction, as the negative pressure might indicate. Suction simply removes air from a system so that the water (or other liquid) is pushed up by atmospheric pressure. But atmospheric pressure is only enough to raise water (against no resistance) about 11 meters at sea level, and many trees are much taller than 11 meters.

According to the now generally accepted theory, the explanation is to be found not in the properties of the plant but in the remarkable properties of water, to which the plant has become exquisitely adapted. As we pointed out in other chapter, in every water molecule, the pair of hydrogen atoms is linked to a single oxygen atom.

The hydrogen atoms are also held to the oxygen atoms of the nearest water molecules by hydrogen bonds. This secondary attraction can produce a tensile strength of as much as 140 kilograms per square centimeter (2,000 pounds per square inch) in a thin column of water. In the leaf, water evaporates, molecule by molecule, from the cells into the intercellular spaces within the leaves.

The water potential of the leaf cell falls, and water from the vessels or tracheids moves, molecule by molecule, into the leaf cells. But each molecule in the xylem vessel is linked to other molecules in the vessel, and they, in turn, are linked to others, forming one long, narrow, continuous thread of water reaching right down to a root tip. As the molecule of water moves into the leaf, it tugs the next molecule along behind it.

Because the diameter of the vessels is very small and because the water molecules adhere to the walls, even as they are cohering to one another, gas bubbles, which could rupture the column, do not usually form. The pulling action, molecule by molecule, causes the negative pressure observed in the xylem.

The technical term for a negative pressure is *tension,* and this theory of water movement is known as the *cohesion-tension theory*.

The principle of cohesion-tension is illustrated in figure elsewhere in this chapter. As indicated in the diagram, the power for this process comes not from the plant, which plays only a passive role in transpiration, but directly from the energy of the sun.

FACTORS INFLUENCING TRANSPIRATION

Transpiration, as we noted, is costly, especially when water supply is limited. Various factors affect the rate of water loss. One is temperature; the rate of evaporation doubles for every temperature rise of about 10°C. Humidity is also important.

Water is lost much more slowly into air already laden with water vapor. Air currents also affect transpiration. A breeze cools your skin on a hot day because it blows away the water vapor that has accumulated near the skin surface and so facilitates evaporation.

Similarly, wind blows away the water vapor from leaf surfaces, which makes the concentration gradient steeper and so hastens the diffusion of water molecules.

Leaves of plants that grow in exposed, windy areas are often hairy; these hairs are believed to protect the leaf surface from the wind and so retard transpiration. By far the most important factor affecting transpiration, however, is the regulatory effect exercised by the opening and closing of the stomata.

Mechanism of Stomatal Movements

As shown in figure elsewhere in this chapter, each stoma has two surrounding guard cells. Stomatal movements are caused by changes in the turgor of these cells. When the guard cells are turgid, they bow out, opening the stoma; when they lose water, they collapse, and the stoma closes.

Turgor, as we saw in other chapter of this book, is maintained or lost due to the osmotic movement of water into or out of cells along a gradient of solute concentration. Solute concentration in the guard cells can change as a result of the loss of water, the production of more solutes within the cells, or the transport of solutes into the guard cells.

Factors Influencing Stomatal Movements

A variety of environmental factors influence the opening and closing of the stomata. The principal one is the availability of water: When the plant body begins to lose water, the stomata close. This is not a direct effect; closing of the stomata occurs before the leaf begins to wilt. It is, however, an overriding one.

Stomatal changes also occur quite independently of the loss or gain of water.

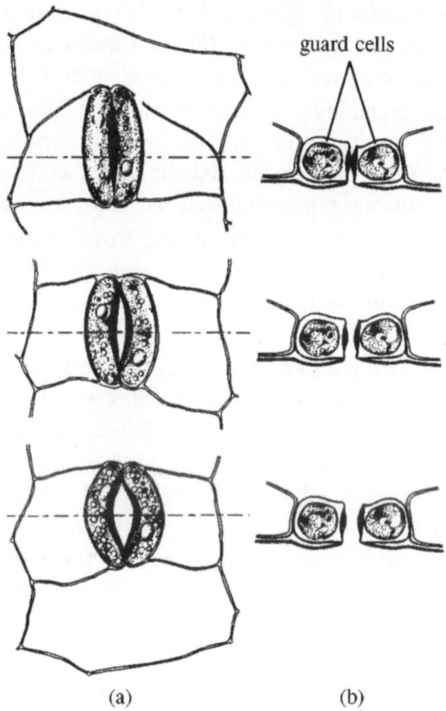

Figure 15.2 : Mechanism of stomatal movement. A surface view is shown in (a) and a cross section in (b). Each stoma has two guard tells that open the stoma when they are turgid and collapse and close it when they lose turgor.

The simplest and most common example is found in the many species in which the stomata close regularly in the evening, when photosynthesis is no longer possible, and open in the morning. These stomatal movements in response to light occur even when there are no changes in the water available to the plant.

An increase in temperature causes stomatal closing in many species. Carbon dioxide concentration also affects the stomata. An increase in carbon dioxide concentration in the intercellular spaces of the leaf causes the stomata to close. Conversely, in some species, exposure of the leaf to CO_2-free air causes the stomata to open. These changes occur even though the water supply and the light remain constant.

As long ago as the 1920s the so-called classic theory of stomatal function was formulated. According to this hypothesis, a decrease in carbon dioxide in the guard cells causes a slight increase in pH as a consequence of the decrease in the carbonic acid (H_2CO_3) concentration.

In response to this increase in pH, the enzyme (amylase) that catalyzes the hydrolysis of starch to sugar becomes more active. As we noted in other chapter, the size of the molecules of a solute has little effect on osmosis; it is the number of molecules that counts.

Therefore the breakdown of large starch molecules into many smaller molecules rapidly changes the osmotic equilibrium, causing water to move rapidly into the guard cells and the guard cells to open. Carbon dioxide decreases during photosynthesis and increases during respiration.

Thus opening in the light and closing in the dark may be a result of the changes in carbon dioxide concentration. Similarly, heat increases the rate of respiration, so the heat effect may also be mediated by the CO_2-H_2CO_3 effect.

More recent data indicate, however, that this pleasing theory does not explain stomatal movements in all species. For example, some plants-onions, for instance-do not form starch, yet their stomata open and close. Also, the action spectrum for photosynthesis does not match that for stomatal opening; the greatest effect for the latter is in the blue region of the spectrum.

As a consequence of such findings, a search has been underway for an alternative explanation. New techniques that permit the measurement of ion concentrations within single guard cells show that potassium (K^+) ions are accumulated in guard cells in the light and lost from these cells in the dark. Apparently, the K^+ ions are brought in by active transport, and the water follows.

The relative roles of these two mechanisms are still under debate. It is possible, of course, that different plants have evolved different mechanisms of stomatal regulation.

CAM Photosynthesis

As we mentioned, the stomata of most plants are open during the day, when photosynthesis takes place, and, closed at night. This is not true of all plants, however. Many succulents-including cacti, pineapples, and members of the stonecrop family-close their stomata during the hot, dry days and open them at night. The carbon dioxide taken in during the night is converted to malic and isocitric acids. During the day, when the stomata are closed, the carbon dioxide is released from these organic acids and used in photosynthesis.

This process is known as Crassulacean acid metabolism (from Crassulaceae, the plant family to which the stonecrops belong), and is generally referred to as CAM photosynthesis. It is analogous to the C_4 pathway in photosynthesis described in other chapter, although it apparently evolved independently. (As you can see, this is another instance of stomatal movement not explained by the CO_2 mechanism.)

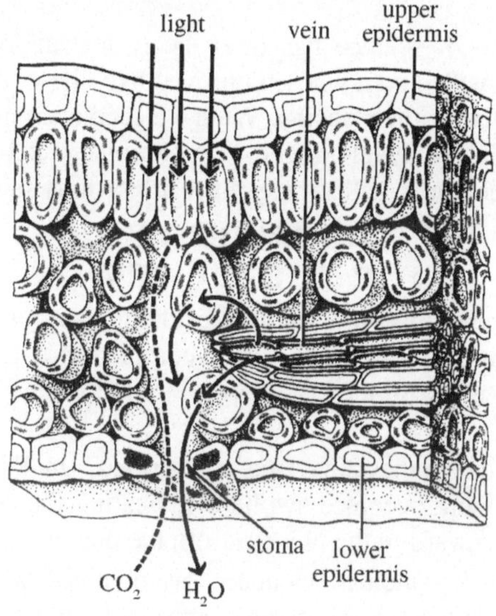

Figure 15.3 : As carbon dioxide, essential for photosynthesis, enters the leaf through the stomata, water vapor is lost.

Photosynthesis and Water Loss

In short, photosynthesis requires carbon dioxide. Uptake of carbon dioxide involves loss of water. Evolution has not yet produced a way that a plant can maintain a free flow of carbon dioxide without water loss. It has, however, produced a number of ingenious ways of reducing water loss, through structural modifications and by regulation of stomatal movements. The way in which various external and internal stimuli act upon the membranes of guard cells to produce closing and opening of the stomata is not known.

THE MOVEMENT OF SUGARS: TRANSLOCATION

The fact that water is transported by vessels in the xylem was recognised by botanists 300 years ago. The role of phloem in the movement of sugar was not generally agreed upon, however, until well into the twentieth century. One reason for this long delay is that the sieve-tube elements are so delicate.

When they are disturbed, callose and P-protein plug the pores in the sieve plates, impeding or preventing the movement of substances through them. Many botanists of the eighteenth and nineteenth centuries believed that sugars, like water, move through the xylem, and they developed elaborate theories involving the properties of water to support this contention.

The direction of science has often been determined by brilliant, articulate, strong-willed men whose unproved hypotheses dominated their fields, even until after their deaths. We have seen examples of this both in genetics and in the development of evolutionary theory. It is likely that this phenomenon is still taking place in various fields of science.

THE EVIDENCE FOR THE PHLOEM

Early evidence supporting the role of the phloem in transport came from observations of trees that had had a complete ring of bark removed from them. As we saw in the last chapter, bark contains the phloem but not the xylem.

When a photosynthesizing tree is "girdled" in this manner, the tissue above the ring becomes swollen, indicating the accumulation of fluid moving downward in the phloem from the photosynthesizing leaves.

Much more convincing evidence was obtained when radioactive tracers became available. If plants carry out photosynthesis in air containing carbon dioxide made with carbon 14 ($^{14}CO_2$), the sugars produced will include the radioactive ^{14}C label.

If a tissue sample is taken from a plant containing ^{14}C-labeled sugars and placed on a photographic emulsion, emissions from the radioactive isotope will make tracks on the emulsion. These tracks reveal the concentration of radioactive material in the plant . Such studies have shown conclusively that sugars are transported in the sieve tubes of plants.

ASSISTANCE BY APHIDS

Cutting into a sieve tube with even the most delicate dissecting blade results,surging of sap from the severed sieve tubes and the plugging up of the sieve-I pores with slime and callose. This technical problem has been clever.. circumvented with the help of aphids, which are very small sap-sucking insects. The aphid drives its sharp mouthparts, or stylets, through the epidermis of a plant, traversing cortical cells, and then taps the contents of a single sieve-tube element. If the aphid is anesthetized, it is possible to sever the stylets, leaving them in place in the cell.

The solution will continue to exude through the stylets from the sieve tube for several days, and pure samples of phloem fluid can be collected for analysis. Many of the findings reported here were made possible 'by this simple and ingenious technique.

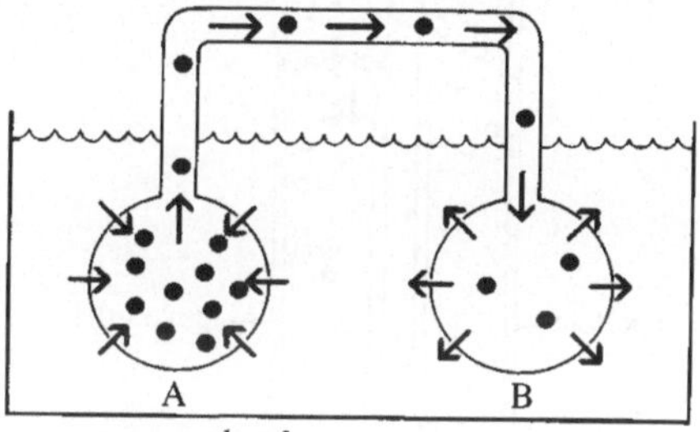

● sugar molecule
→ movment of water
→ movement of sugar solution

Figure 15.4 : Model of pressure flow hypothesis.

Data gathered by this technique and from radioactive tracers indicate that sieve-tube sap contains (by weight) 10 to 25 percent solutes, 90 percent or more of which are sugars, mostly sucrose. Low concentrations of amino acids and other nitrogen-containing substances are also present.

The rate of movement of these substances along the sieve tube is remarkably fast: In one set of experiments, for example, it was estimated that the sap was moving at a rate of about 100 centimeters an hour, far faster than could be accounted for by diffusion.

Pressure-Flow Hypothesis

The most popular current explanation for translocation is the *pressure-flow hypothesis,* which proposes that solutes move in solutions that, in turn, move because of differences in water potential.

The principle underlying this theory can be illustrated by a simple physical model consisting of bulbs permeable only to water and connected by glass tubes. The first bulb contains a solution in which there is a dissolved material, such as sucrose, and the second, to make the example as simple as possible, contains only water.

When these interconnected bulbs are placed in distilled water, water will enter the first by osmosis. The entry of water will increase

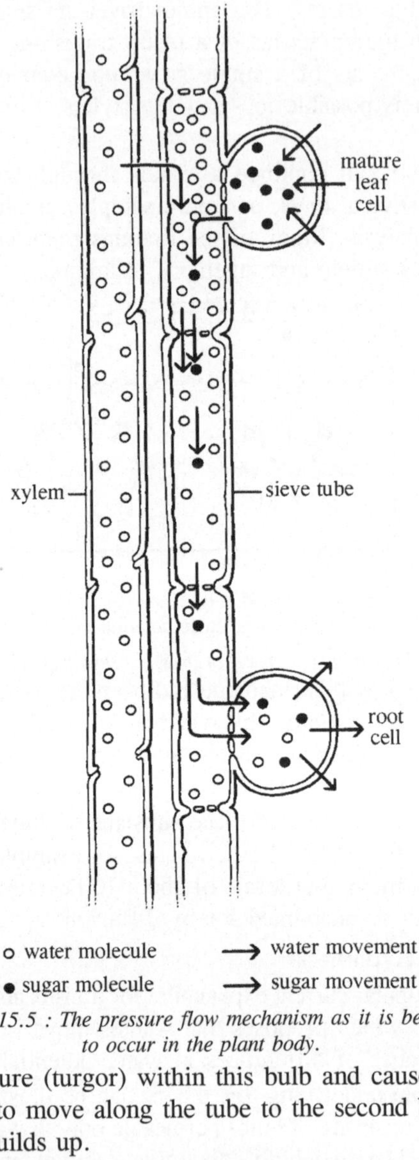

Figure 15.5 : The pressure flow mechanism as it is believed to occur in the plant body.

hydrostatic pressure (turgor) within this bulb and cause the water and the solutes in it to move along the tube to the second bulb, where the pressure again builds up.

If the second bulb is connected with a third one containing water or a sucrose concentration lower than that now in the second one, the solution will flow from the second to the third by the same process, and so on indefinitely down the sucrose gradient.

This hypothesis is supported by the fact that distinct gradients in the concentrations of sucrose and other sugars have been demonstrated along the phloem tissues during the summer months. Moreover, it can account for the known rates of movement in the phloem.

According to the proponents of the pressure-flow mechanism, the sieve tubes play a passive role in the movement of the sugar solution through them. Active transport is also involved, however; the active transport is not directly involved with long-distance transport through the sieve tube, but with the movement of sugars and other substances into and out of the sieve tubes.

In addition, the energy required for this active transport is expended not by the sieve tubes, but by other phloem cells (parenchyma cells and companion cells) bordering the sieve tubes. The energy requirements of this active transport would account for the comparatively high rate of respiration often found in phloem.

Some alternative hypotheses are under consideration. However, all of them apparently have serious deficiencies, leaving the pressure-flow hypothesis by far the most creditable explanation for the movement of substances through the phloem.

SOILS AND PLANT NUTRITION

Minerals

The earth is composed of about 100 different elements; oxygen and silicon are by far the most abundant of these, followed by aluminum and iron. Elements are found in the earth in the form of *minerals*. A mineral is a naturally occurring inorganic substance, usually solid, with a definite chemical composition.

Some minerals, such as diamond, sulfur, and copper, consist of single elements. Others, such as quartz (SiO_2) and calcite (CaCO), are compounds.

The mineral elements required by plants are usually classified either as macronutrients, which are generally expressed in percentage of dry weight of the plant and which range from about 0.5 to 3 or 4 percent, or as micronutrients, of which as little as a few parts per million may be present.

Determination of many of the elements is generally made by burning the plant completely, which permits the carbon, hydrogen, oxygen, nitrogen, and sulfur to escape as gases; the ash is then analyzed. Proportions of each element vary in different species and in the same species grown under different conditions. Also, the ash will often contain elements, such as silicon, which are present in the soil and are taken up by plants but which are not generally thought to be required for plant growth.

Uptake of Minerals

Minerals are taken up in solution by the roots and travel through plants with the transpiration stream. As you saw in figure elsewhere in this chapter, the cells of the endodermis play a major role in determining which elements enter the xylem.

The mineral composition of plant cells is far different from the mineral composition of the medium in which the plant grows. For example, in one study, cells of pea roots were found to have a concentration of potassium ions 75 times greater than that of the nutrient solution.

Similarly, in another study, the vacuoles of rutabaga cells were shown to contain 10,000 times more potassium than the external solution.

Thus it seems evident that minerals are brought into plant cells by active transport. Support for this hypothesis comes from observations indicating that the uptake of minerals is an energy-requiring process.

For instance, if roots are deprived of oxygen or poisoned so that respiration is curtailed, mineral uptake is drastically decreased. Also, if a plant is deprived of light, it will cease to absorb minerals and eventually will release them back into the soil.

Ion Pumps

One way that roots move ions such as potassium against a concentration gradient is by the action of carrier proteins in the cell membrane. Such a protein combines with the ion and then, utilising the energy of ATP, carries it to the other side of the membrane and releases it.

Because the membrane is partially impermeable to ions such as potassium, the continued action of the "pump proteins" results in differences in the concentration of the transported ions on one side of the membrane as compared to the other.

As a result of these differences in ion concentrations, there is often a difference of electric charge on either side of the membrane. In the nerve cells of animals, as we shall see, stimulation of the cell membrane results in an abrupt change in its permeability to ions.

The rapid movement of ions across the membrane is the basis for transmission of nerve impulses. Similar events apparently involved in certain plant responses will be described in other chapter.

Functions of Minerals in Plants

Plants require mineral elements for many different functions. For example, mineral ions affect osmosis and so regulate water balance. Because in many plants several mineral ions can serve interchangeably in this role, this requirement is described as nonspecific.

On the other hand, a mineral element may be a functional part of an essential biological molecule, and in this case the requirement is highly specific. An example is the magnesium atom in the chlorophyll molecule. Some minerals are required constituents of cell membranes, and some control membrane permeability.

Others are indispensable components of a variety of enzyme systems that catalyze biological reactions in the cell. Still others provide a proper ionic environment in which biological reactions can occur.

Because mineral elements are involved in many fundamental processes, the effects of mineral deficiencies are typically very wide-ranging, affecting a number of structures and functions in the plant body.

The mineral elements required by plants, the form in which they usually are absorbed, and some of the uses plants make of them. You might anticipate that organisms make use of what is most readily available; indeed, they seem to have done this to a considerable extent when life originated from elements in the gases of the primitive atmosphere.

But the table reveals some findings that you might not expect. Sodium, for instance, which is one of the most abundant of the elements, is apparently not required at all by most plants.

The fact that plants evolved with no functions requiring sodium is even more striking when you consider that sodium is vital to animals. (Sodium is the principal osmoregulator in animals and, as we shall see in the next section, is necessary for transmission of the nerve impulse.)

In the seas, where both plant and animal life seem to have originated, sodium is the most abundant mineral element and is far more readily available than potassium, which it closely resembles in its essential properties. Potassium, however, is the principal osmoregulator in plants.

Similarly, although silicon and aluminum are almost always present in large amounts in soils, few plants require silicon and apparently none requires aluminum. On the other hand, most plants need molybdenum, which is relatively rare.

SYMBIOSES AND MINERAL UTILISATION

Mycorrhizae

Two types of symbiotic relationships play important roles in plant nutrition. One of these is *mycorrhizae* ("fungus-roots"), which are associations between plant roots and fungi. The importance of mycorrhizae was first recognised in connection with efforts to grow orchids in greenhouses.

Orchids have microscopic seeds that germinate to form a tiny pad of tissue called a protocorm. Cultivators of orchids found that the plants seldom developed beyond the protocorm stage unless they were infected with a particular kind of fungus.

Subsequently it was found that if seedlings of many forest trees are grown in nutrient solutions and then transplanted to prairie and other grassland soils, they fail to grow. Eventually they die from malnutrition despite the fact that soil analysis shows that there are abundant nutrients in the soil.

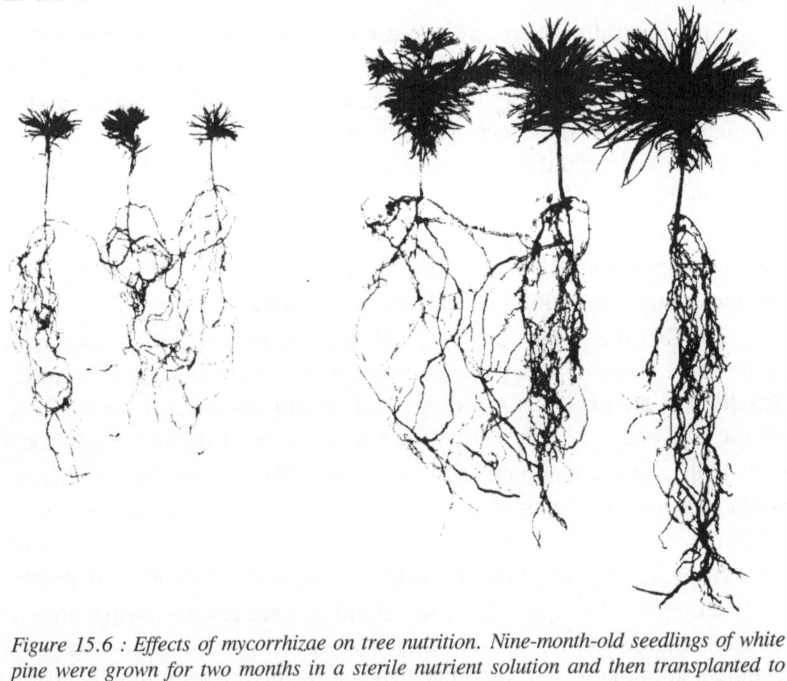

Figure 15.6 : Effects of mycorrhizae on tree nutrition. Nine-month-old seedlings of white pine were grown for two months in a sterile nutrient solution and then transplanted to prairie soil. The seedlings on the left were transplanted directly. The seedlings on the right were placed in forest soil for two weeks before being transplanted to the prairie.

If a small amount (0.1 percent by volume) of forest soil containing fungi is added to the soil around the roots of the seedlings, however, they will grow promptly and normally. Mycorrhizae are now thought to occur in more than 90 percent of all families of plants.

In mycorrhizal associations, the fungus may form a sheath of hyphae, or a fungal mantle, around the root. Only the cortex is actually invaded by the fungus. Roots with mycorrhizae usually lack root hairs, the role of water and mineral uptake from the soil evidently being at least partially assumed by the fungus.

The exact relationship between roots and fungi is not known. Apparently the roots secrete sugars, amino acids, and possibly some other organic substances that are utilised by the fungi. Although the evidence is just now accumulating, it seems that the chief contribution of the fungi is in water uptake and in converting minerals in the soil and in decaying material into an available form.

Rhizobia and Nitrogen Fixation

Molecular nitrogen (N_2), which constitutes about 78 percent of the air, is held together by an exceptionally strong bond. A large quantity of energy is required to break it. The process by which atmospheric nitrogen is incorporated into nitrogen compounds that can be utilised by plants is known as *nitrogen fixation*.

It is carried out to a small extent by abiotic (nonliving) processes, such as the production of nitrogen oxides and ammonia by interactions between nitrogen and other atmospheric gases, with lightning as an energy source.

Nitrogen fixation is carried out commercially by combining 1 mole of nitrogen gas (N) and 3 moles of hydrogen gas (H_2) to produce 2 moles of ammonia (NH_3). The required energy is supplied by fossil fuels.

As the costs of these fuels increase, so do the prices of the nitrogen-containing fertilisers produced. At present, the equivalent of 2 million barrels of oil a day is required for the production of nitrogen-containing fertilisers.

On a worldwide basis, most nitrogen fixation is carried out by a few types of free-living microorganisms, including blue-green algae, some free-living bacteria, and some species of bacteria that live in symbiosis with plants. Of these various classes of nitrogen-fixing organisms, the symbiotic bacteria are by far the most important in terms of total amounts of nitrogen fixed.

The most common of the nitrogen-fixing symbiotic bacteria is

Rhizobium, a type of bacterium that invades the roots of leguminous plants, such as clover, peas, beans, vetches, and alfalfa (Figure 29-13a). Each species of legume is associated with a distinct species of *Rhizobium.*

Rhizobia enter the roots of seedlings by way of the root-hair tips. The cell membrane turns inward, forming an infection thread. The bacteria at this stage are not actually in contact with the protoplasm, but are separated from it by the cell membrane.

Once started, the infection thread branches, becoming populated with the multiplying bacteria. These threads typically pass close to the cell nuclei and seem to cause the nuclei to degenerate. The infection threads pass from one cell to another and finally invade the cortex of the root.

Soon there is a proliferation of the surrounding cortical cells, presumably owing to the effects of hormones released during the growth of the rhizobia. Finally, a vesicle forms in the thread, near a cell nucleus. The vesicle breaks open, and the bacteria enter the cytoplasm of the host cell.

Soon after their release, the bacteria begin to grow, increasing in size some tenfold. Ammonium (NH_4^+) produced by the bacteria is combined with carbon compounds synthesized by the photosynthetic cells of the plant to produce amino acids.

A key molecule in the nitrogen-fixation process is an enzyme called nitrogenase, which is composed of two different polypeptides, one containing iron and the other molybdenum. The enzyme is inhibited by oxygen.

The beneficial effects to the soil of growing leguminous plants are so obvious that they have been recognised for hundreds of years. Where leguminous plants are grown, some of the "extra" nitrogen may be released into the soil; it then becomes available to other plants.

In modern agriculture, it is common practice to rotate a nonleguminous crop, such as corn, with a leguminous one, such as alfalfa. The leguminous plants are then either harvested, leaving behind the nitrogen-rich roots, or, better still, plowed back into the field.

A good crop of alfalfa that is plowed back into the soil may add as much as 450 kilograms of nitrogen to the soil per hectare, frequently enough to grow a crop of a nonleguminous plant.

Genetic mapping of a free-living nitrogen-fixing bacterium has shown that the genes involved in nitrogen fixation are clustered on one portion of the chromosome. In experiments at the University of Sussex, biologists have succeeded in transferring this gene cluster to a plasmid and then introducing the plasmid into *Escherichia coli* cells. The *E. coli* cells then were found to synthesize nitrogenase and to fix nitrogen. These experiments raise the hope, of course, that nitrogen-fixing genes can be transferred to the cells of plants such as corn, which could then, in effect, make their own nitrogen-containing compounds. However, it is generally agreed that the technical problems involved are so formidable that this prospect is remote.

16

Plant Hormones

As we study in the other chapter of this book that as a plant grows it does far more than increase its mass and volume. It differentiates, forming a variety of cells, tissues, and organs, and undergoes morphogenesis, taking on the shape characteristic of the adult sporophyte.

Moreover, many of its activities are finely tuned to its environment and to the changing pattern of the seasons. Many of the details of how these processes are regulated are not known, but it is clear that plant development and growth depend on the interplay of a number of internal and external factors.

Chief among the internal factors are the plant hormones. Hormones, by definition, are substances that are produced in one tissue and transported to another, where they exert highly specific effects. Hormones help the plant integrate the growth, development, and metabolic activities of its various tissues.

Typically they are active in very small quantities. In the shoot of a pineapple plant, for example, only 6 micrograms of auxin, a common growth hormone, are found per kilogram of plant material. One enterprising plant physiologist calculated that the weight of the hormone in relation to 1 kilogram of shoot is comparable to the weight of a needle in a 22-ton haystack.

The term "hormone" comes from the Greek word meaning "to excite." It is now clear, however, that many hormones have inhibitory influences. So, rather than thinking of hormones as stimulators, it is perhaps more useful to consider them as chemical messengers. But this term also needs qualification. As we shall see, the response to the particular "message" depends not only on its content but also upon how it is "read" by its recipient. All known plant hormones have a multiplicity of effects.

HORMONES AND REGULATION OF PLANT GROWTH

The Auxins

The first plant hormones to be isolated were the auxins. The effects of these hormones were observed by Charl es Darwin and his son Francis and first reported in *The Power of Movement in Plants*, published in 1881. The Darwins were studying the bending toward light, or *phototropism*, of grass seedlings.

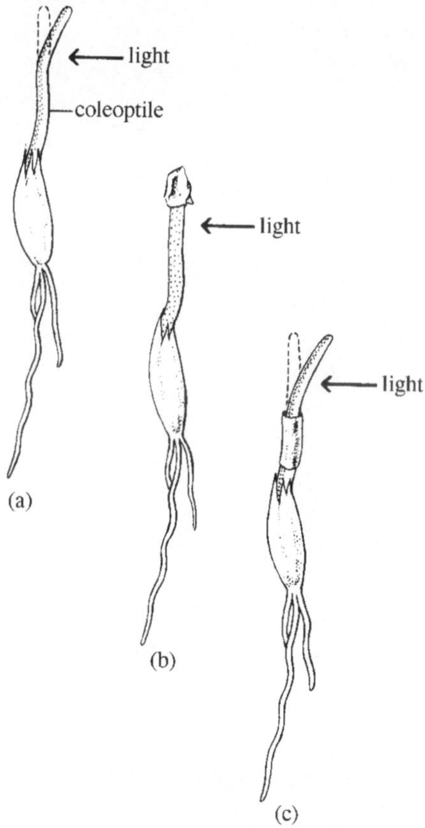

Figure 16.1 : The Darwins' experiment. (a) Light striking a growing coleoptile (such as the tip of this oat seedling) causes it to bend toward the light. (b) Placing an opaque cover over the tip of the seedling inhibits this bending response, but (c) an opaque collar placed below the tip does not.

They noted that the bending takes place below the tip, in the lower part of the coleoptile. Then they showed that if they covered just the terminal portion of the coleoptile with a cylinder of metal foil or a hollow tube of glass blackened with India ink and exposed the plant to a light coming from the side, the characteristic bending of the seedling did not occur.

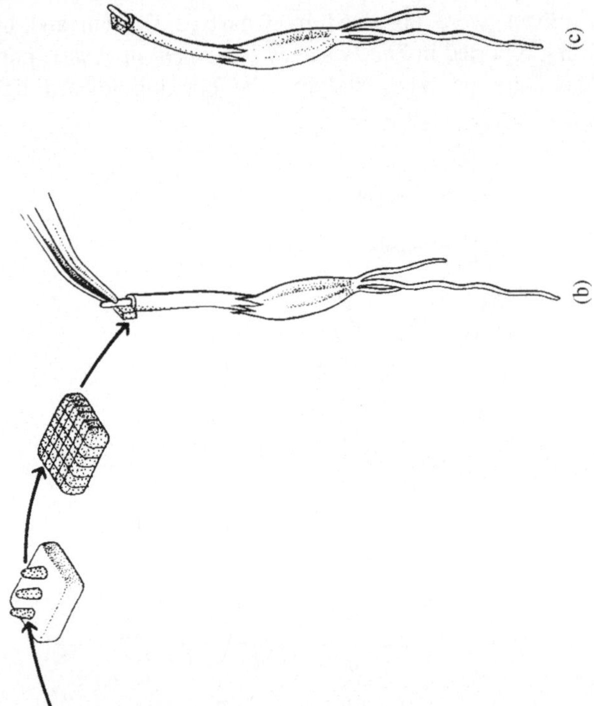

Figure 16.2 : Went's experiment.

If, however, the tip was enclosed in a transparent glass tube, bending occurred normally. Bending also occurred normally when the lightproof cylinder was placed below the tip. "We must therefore conclude," they stated, "that when seedlings are freely exposed to a lateral light some influence is transmitted from the upper to the lower part, causing the material to bend."

In 1926, the Dutch plant physiologist Frits W. Went succeeded in separating this "influence" from the plants that produced it. Went cut off the coleoptile tips from a number of oat seedlings. He placed the tips on a slice of agar (a gelatinlike substance), with their cut surfaces in contact with the agar, and left them there for about an hour.

He then cut the agar into small blocks and placed a block off-center on each stump of the decapitated plants, which were kept in the dark during the entire experiment. Within one hour, he observed a distinct bending *away* from the side on which the agar block was placed.

Agar blocks that had not been exposed to a coleoptile tip produced either no bending or only a slight bending toward the side on which the block had been placed. Agar blocks that had been exposed to a section of coleoptile lower on the shoot produced no physiological effect.

Went interpreted these experiments as showing that the coleoptile tip exerted its effects by means of a chemical stimulus (in short, a hormone) rather than a physical stimulus, such as an electric impulse.

In response to this chemical stimulus, the side of the coleoptile adjacent to the agar block grew more rapidly, causing the coleoptile to bend away from that side. The hormone was named auxin, a term coined by Went from the Greek word *auxein,* "to increase."

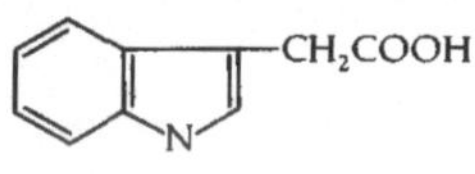

IAA

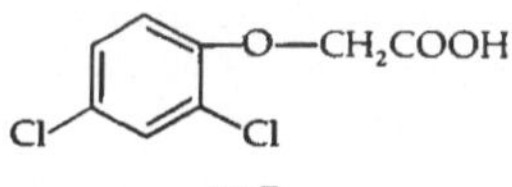

2,4-D

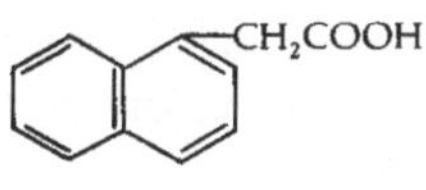

naphthalenacetic acid

Figure 16.3 : Auxins. IAA (indoleacetic acid) is a natural auxin, isolated from plant tissues. 2,4-D is a synthetic auxin used as a weed killer (herbicide). Naphthalenacetic acid, also a synthetic auxin, is commonly used to induce the formation of adventitious roots in cuttings and to reduce fruit drop in orchard crops.

Several different substances with auxin activity have now been isolated from plant tissues, and others have been synthesized in the laboratory; they are all known as auxins. The most common of the natural auxins is indoleacetic acid, abbreviated IAA. One of the synthetic auxins, known as 2,4-D, is commonly used as an herbicide (like many other physiologically active compounds, auxins are toxic in high doses). For reasons not known, 2,4-D and related compounds are effective on broad-leaved plants at concentrations not harmful to grasses and so are commonly used on lawns to control broad-leaved weeds.

Auxins, in massive doses, were among the herbicides used in Southeast Asia during United States' participation in the Vietnam War. The synthetic auxins, unlike IAA, are not readily broken down by natural plant enzymes or by bacteria.

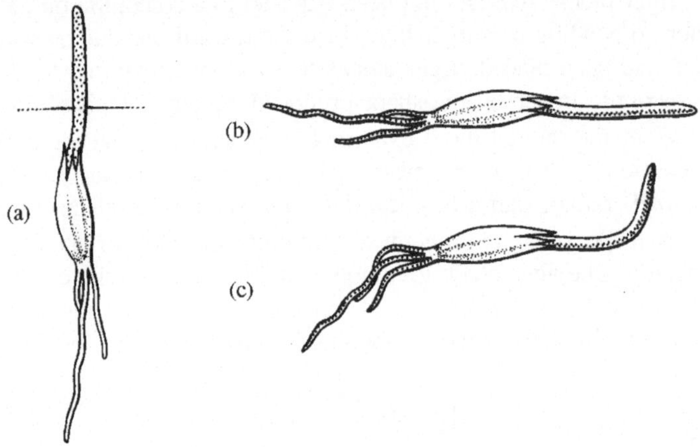

Figure 16.4 : Why shoots grow upward and roots downward. (a) When a seedling is perpendicular, the auxin produced in the tip is distributed evenly and the plant grows erect. (b) However, when a seedling is placed on its side, auxin is transported laterally and accumulates in cells on the lower side of the shoot; (c) these cells then grow more rapidly and so the shoot grows upward.

Their longer effective life makes them better suited for commercial purposes. Their destructive effects on vegetation are long-lasting.

The phototropism observed by the Darwins results from the fact that under the influence of light, auxins migrate from the light side to the dark side of the tip.

The cells on the dark side, having more auxin, elongate more rapidly than those on the light side, causing the plant to bend toward the light. Auxin effects on stems and coleoptiles can be detected within 15 minutes of application of the hormone, suggesting that auxin exerts its effects by producing changes in the permeability of the cell membrane.

The action spectrum for phototropism is not the same as that for photosynthesis; only light in the blue region of the spectrum (less than 500 nanometers in wavelength) produces the phototropic response.

Other Tissue Responses to Auxin

Various plant tissues show other responses to auxin. Shoots elongate in response to auxins produced in the meristem. Apparently, under the influence of auxin, the cell wall becomes more plastic and thus the cell takes up more water and elongates. Because of the construction of the cell walls, expansion of the cell is unidirectional.

When large concentrations of auxins are present, the growth of the main roots is inhibited, and this inhibition is presumed responsible for the capacity of seedlings to orient themselves in the ground. In low concentrations, auxins induce the formation of adventitious roots; rooting preparations used by gardeners contain auxin.

In most dicot species, the growth of lateral buds is inhibited by auxins. If you pinch off the growing tip (meristem) of the stem of the houseplant *Coleus*, for example, the lateral buds begin to grow vigorously, producing a plant with a bushier, more compact body.

If you treat the "eyes" (actually lateral buds) of a potato with auxin, they will be inhibited from sprouting and so the tubers can be stored longer. The formation of the abscission layer has been correlated with diminished production of auxin in the leaf. Auxins are also involved in the growth of fruits.

Mechanism of Action

As we noted earlier, auxin increases the plasticity of the cell wall. This effect is brought about by a complex series of interactions that are not yet fully understood.

During continued growth, auxin stimulates specific RNA and protein biosyntheses, and under the control of this newly forming protein, certain of the old bonds holding the cell wall together are broken as new carbohydrate material is incorporated into the structure.

However, response to auxin by coleoptiles, as we noted, is very rapid, occurring in too short a time for new protein synthesis to be initiated. Current studies indicate that, in these reactions, auxin exerts its effects by binding to the cell membrane and changing its permeability. Auxin responses are associated with a rapid movement of hydrogen ions across the membrane.

THE GIBBERELLINS

The gibberellins were first discovered by a Japanese scientist who was studying a disease of rice plants called "foolish seedling disease." The diseased plants grew rapidly but were spindly and tended to fall over under the weight of the developing seeds. The cause of the symptoms, it was found, was a chemical produced by a fungus, *Gibberella fujikuroi*, which infected the seedlings. The substance, which was named gibberellin, was subsequently isolated not only from the fungus but from many species of plants. These hormones are produced in apical meristems, leaves, and plant embryos.

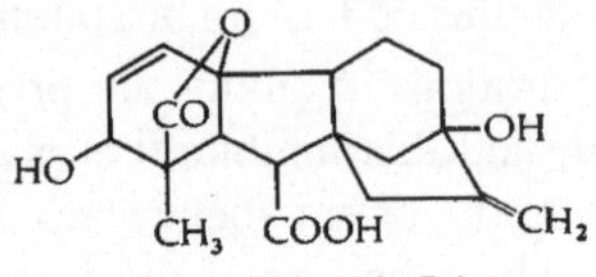

gibberellic acid (GA_3)

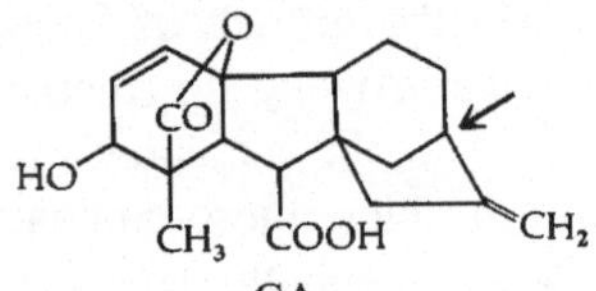

GA_7

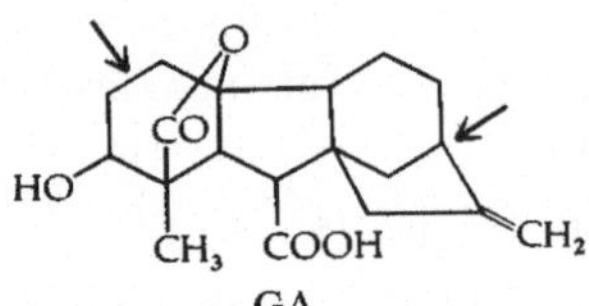

GA_4

Figure 16.5 : Three of the more than 90 gibberellins that have been isolated from natural sources. Gibberellic acid (GA_3) is the most abundant in fungi and the most biologically active in many tests. The minor structural differences that distinguish the other two gibberellins are indicated by arrows.

The most remarkable results are seen when gibberellins are applied to plants that are genetic dwarfs. Under gibberellin treatment, these dwarfs become indistinguishable from normal tall plants.

Some plants-lettuce and cabbage are common examples-first grow as rosettes; the leaves develop but the internodes do not elongate until just before flowering. At that time the stem elongates rapidly, a phenomenon known as bolting.

In the case of cabbage and other biennials, bolting and flowering do not normally occur until after a period of cold; however, bolting and flowering can be induced by the application of gibberellin.

Gibberellins have also been shown to play a role in the growth of plant embryos and seedlings. In grass seeds, there is a specialised layer of cells, the aleurone layer, just inside the seed coat. These cells are rich in protein. During the early stages of germination, the embryo

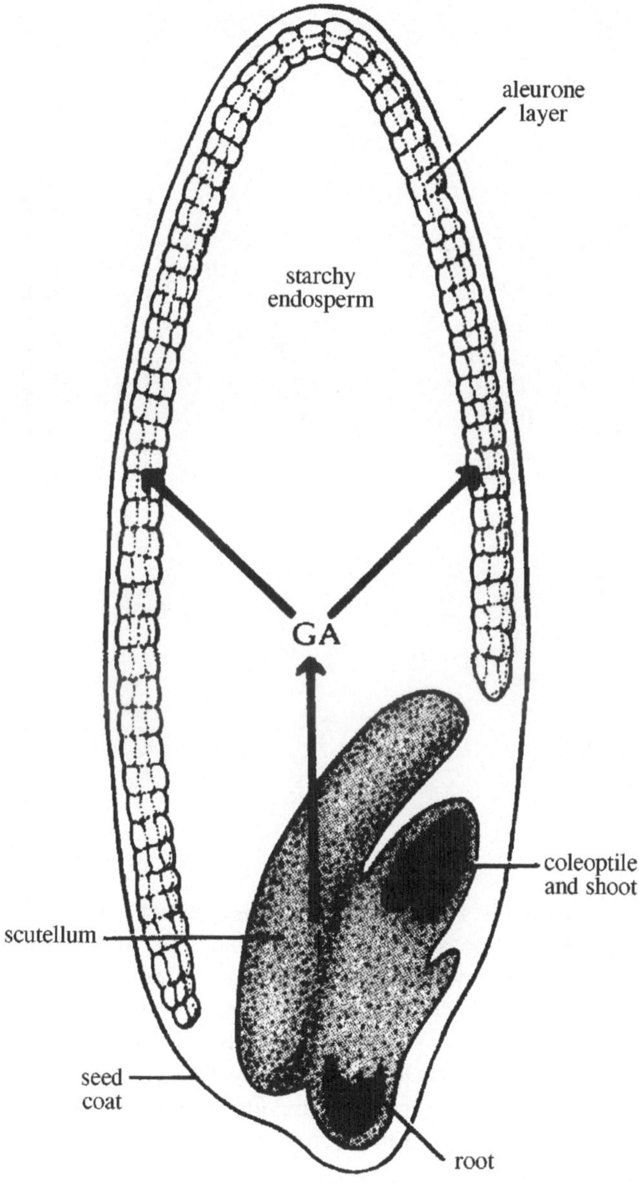

Figure 16.6 : Mechanism of action of gibberellin in a barley seed.

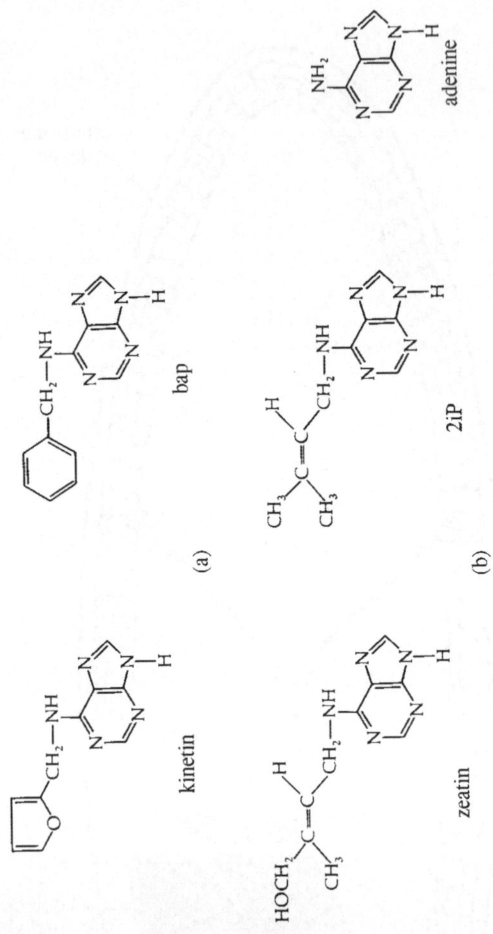

Figure 16.7 : Cytokinins. (a) Kinetin, the first of this group to be discovered, and 6-benzylamino purine (BAP) are commonly used synthetic cytokinins. (b) Zeatin and 2iP have been isolated from plant material.

produces gibberellin, which diffuses to the aleurone layer. In response to the gibberellin, the aleurone cells produce enzymes that hydrolyse the starch, proteins, and other storage products to soluble sugars, amino acids, and other small molecules that the embryo and then the seedling uses for its growth as it pushes up through the soil.

Recent studies by Joseph Varner of Washington University show that, in the germinating barley grain, gibberellin acts directly at the nuclear level, activating formerly repressed genes and so resulting in new messenger RNA formation.

THE CYTOKININS

The cytokinins are a group of hormones originally detected in coconut "milk," which is a liquid endosperm. They were found to promote the division of plant cells isolated in test tubes, and their name is derived from cytokinesis, meaning cell division. They have now been found in numerous plants, largely in actively dividing tissues, including germinating seeds, fruits, and roots.

Responses to Cytokinin and Auxin Combinations

Studies of responses to combinations of auxin and cytokinins are helping physiologists understand how plant hormones work to produce the total growth pattern of the plant.

Apparently, the undifferentiated plant cell-such as the meristematic cell-has two courses open to it: Either it can enlarge, divide, enlarge, and divide again, or it can elongate without cell division. The cell that divides repeatedly remains essentially undifferentiated, or embryonic, whereas the elongating cell tends to differentiate and become specialised.

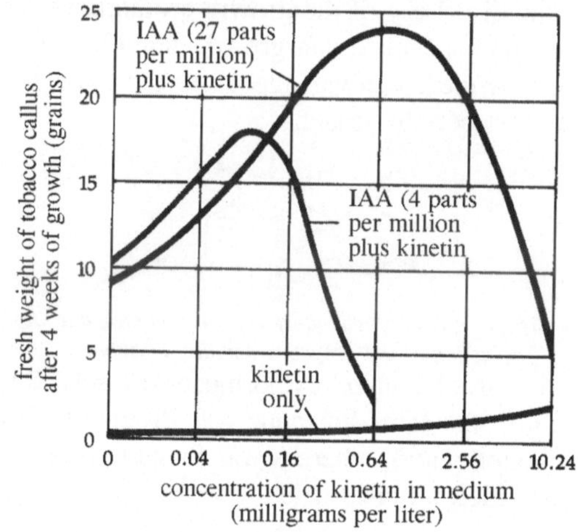

Figure 16.8: The response of tobacco cells in tissue culture to combinations of an auxin and a cytokinin.

In studies of tobacco stem callus, the addition of an auxin to the tissue culture produced rapid cell expansion, so that giant cells were formed. A cytokinin alone had little or no effect. Auxin plus cytokinin resulted in rapid cell division, so that large numbers of relatively small cells were formed.

By slight alterations in the relative concentrations of auxin and cytokinin, investigators have been able to affect the development of undifferentiated cells growing in tissue culture. When a high concentration of auxin is present, undifferentiated tissue gives rise to organised roots.

With higher concentrations of cytokinins, buds appear. However, lest you think this is simple, we shall describe another tissue culture study, in which tuber tissue of the Jerusalem artichoke was used. In this study, it was shown that a third substance, the calcium ion, can modify the action of the auxin-cytokinin combination.

Auxin plus low concentrations of cytokinin was shown to favour cell enlargement, but as calcium ion was added to the culture, there was a steady shift in the growth pattern from cell enlargement to cell division.

High concentrations of calcium ion apparently prevent the cell wall from expanding, and at such concentrations the cell switches course and divides. Thus, not only do hormones modify the effects of hormones, but these combined effects may be, in turn, modified by nonhormonal factors, such as calcium ions and, undoubtedly, many others.

ABSCISIC ACID

Soon after the discovery of the growth-promoting hormones, plant physiologists began to speculate that growth-inhibiting hormones would be found, since it is clearly advantageous to the plant not to grow at certain times and in certain seasons.

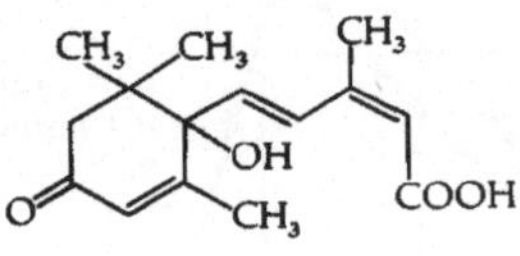

Figure 16.9 : Abscisic acid (dormin), an inhibitor that blocks the action of the growth-promoting hormones.

Not long afterward, an inhibitory hormone was isolated from dormant buds. Subsequently, the same hormone was discovered in cotton bolls (the fruit of the cotton plant), where it was found to promote abscission. The hormone is called abscisic acid.

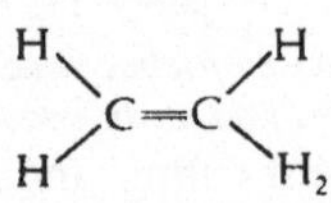

Figure 16.10: Ethylene, a simple hydrocarbon involved in the ripening of fruit. Unlike any other known hormone, it is a gas, raising the question of whether it should properly be considered a hormone at all.

Abscisic acid accelerates the dropping of leaves and of fruit; the presence of auxin inhibits abscission. Application of abscisic acid to vegetative buds changes them to winter buds by converting the outermost leaf primordia to bud scales; these inhibitory effects can be overcome by gibberellin. The appearance of hydrolyzing enzymes induced by gibberellin in barley seeds is inhibited by abscisic acid. Abscisic acid, though it has little effect on dwarf plants, reduces the growth of normal plants; this inhibition can be counteracted by gibberellin. Kinetin inhibits yellowing in excised leaves; abscisic acid causes green leaves to yellow.

In short, abscisic acid, in many of its effects, serves as an inhibitor of the growth-promoting effects of other hormones, emphasizing the concept that growth is the result of a balance of different factors.

Finally, as if the subject of stomatal movements was not already sufficiently complex, abscisic acid has been shown to be a potent effector of stomatal closure.

When leaves lose moisture, abscisic acid synthesis increases and the stomata close. A variety of tomato is known, called a "wilty mutant," that cannot make abscisic acid and cannot close its stomata.

Ethylene

Ethylene is an unusual growth regulator in that it is a gas, a simple hydrocarbon, $H_2C{=}CH_2$. Its effects have been known for a long time. In the early 1900s, many fruit growers made a practice of improving the colour and flavor of citrus fruits by "curing" them in a room with a kerosene stove. (Long before this, the Chinese used to ripen fruits in rooms where incense was being burned.)

It was long believed that it was the heat that ripened the fruits. Ambitious fruit growers, who went to the expense of installing more modern heating equipment, found to their sorrow that this was not the case.

As experiments showed, it was actually the incomplete combustion products of kerosene that were responsible for ripening the fruits. The most active gas was identified as ethylene. As little as 1 part per million of ethylene in the air will speed the ripening process.

Subsequently, it was found that ethylene is produced by plants, as well as by kerosene stoves, that it appears just before and also during fruit ripening, and that it is responsible for a number of changes in colour, texture, and chemical composition that take place as fruits mature.

Auxin at certain concentrations causes a burst of ethylene production in some plants. It is now believed that some of the effects on fruits and flowers generally attributed to auxin are related to the release of ethylene.

Similarly, it is now believed that abscisic acid is not the direct cause of abscission in most cases; rather, it is hypothesized, abscisic acid induces ethylene formation, which accelerates senescence, .which stimulates abscission.

HORMONAL CONTROL OF FLOWERING

Flowering also appears to be under the control of a hormone or hormones, although to date no specific one has been isolated and identified. Some of the earliest experiments on this hypothetical flowering hormone were carried out by a Russian scientist, M. H. Chailakhyan, in the 1930s.

Working with a species of chrysanthemum, Chailakhyan found that if the upper portion of the stem was stripped of its leaves and the leaves on the lower stem were exposed to an appropriate light cycle, the plant would flower, a phenomenon known as *photoinduction.* (We shall have more to say about light cycles and flowering later in this chapter.)

If, however, only the upper, leafless stem and its buds were exposed, no flowering occurred. He interpreted these results as indicating that the leaves form a hormone that moves to the apical meristem of the plant and initiates flowering. He named this hypothetical hormone florigen, the "flower maker."

Subsequent experiments showed that the flowering response does not take place if the leaf is removed immediately after photoinduction. But if the leaf is left on the plant for a few hours after the induction cycle is complete, it can then be removed without stopping flowering.

The flowering hormone can pass through a graft from a photoinduced plant to a noninduced plant. If a branch is girdled, florigen movement ceases. This led to the conclusion that florigen moves by way of the phloem system, the means by which most organic substances are transported.

However, despite this strong evidence for the existence of florigen, the hormone has never been isolated and, also, more recent evidence indicates that other, inhibitory factors are also involved in flowering.

PLANTS AND PHOTOPERIODISM

In many regions of the biosphere, the most important environmental changes affecting plants (and indeed, land organisms, in general) are those that result from the changing seasons.

Plants are able to accommodate themselves to these changes because of their capacity to sense and, more important, to anticipate the yearly calendar of events-the first frost, the spring rains, long dry periods, long growing spells, and even the time that nearby plants of the same species will be in flower.

For many plants, all of these determinations are made in the same way: by measuring the relative periods of light and darkness. This phenomenon is known as *photoperiodism.*

PHOTOPERIODISM AND FLOWERING

The effects of photoperiodism on flowering are particularly striking (Figure 30-18). Plants are of three general types: day-neutral, short-day, and long-day. Day-neutral plants flower without regard to day length. Short-day plants flower in early spring or fall; they must have a light period shorter than a critical length-for instance, the cocklebur flowers when exposed to 15½ hours or less of light.

Other short-day plants are poinsettias, strawberries, primroses, ragweed, and some chrysanthemums. Long-day plants, which flower chiefly in the summer, will flower only if the light periods are *longer* than a critical length. Spinach, potatoes, clover, henbane, and lettuce are examples of long-day plants.

The discovery of photoperiodism explained some puzzling data about the distribution of common plants. Why, for example, is there no ragweed in northern Maine? The answer, investigators found, is that ragweed starts producing flowers when the day is less than 14½ hours long.

The long summer days do not shorten to 14½ hours in northern Maine until August, and then there is not enough time for ragweed seed to mature before the frost. For similar reasons, spinach cannot produce seeds in the tropics. Spinach needs 14 hours of light a day for a period of at least two weeks in order to flower, and days are not this long in the tropics.

Note that the cocklebur and spinach will both bloom if exposed to 14 hours of daylight, yet one is designated as short-day and one as long-day. The important factor is not the absolute length of the photoperiod but rather whether it is longer or shorter than a particular critical interval for that variety.

And in some varieties, 5 or 10 minutes' difference in exposure can determine whether or not a plant will flower.

These early field studies on photoperiodism in plants were carried out by W. W. Garner, H. A. Allard, and co-workers at the U.S. Department of Agriculture, known as the Beltsville group, for the small town in Maryland where they carried out their studies.

Photoperiodism has now been demonstrated in many species of insects, fish, birds, and mammals. It influences such diverse phenomena as the metamorphosis from caterpillar to butterfly, sexual behaviour, migration, molting, and seasonal changes in coat or plumage.

Measuring the Dark

Following the early studies by the Beltsville group, other investigators, Karl C. Hamner and James Bonner, began a laboratory study of photoperiodism. They also used the cocklebur as the experimental organism. As we mentioned previously, the cocklebur is a short-day plant, requiring 15½ hours or less of light per 24-hour cycle to flower.

It is particularly useful for experimental purposes because a single exposure under laboratory conditions to a short-day cycle will induce flowering two weeks later, even if the plant is immediately returned to long-day conditions.

Also, the cocklebur can withstand a good deal of rough treatment. With the cocklebur it was possible to demonstrate that flowering will not occur if the leaves are removed but will occur if even a portion of one leaf remains on the plant. In other words, it is the leaf that "perceives" the light, and this function can, in some cases, be assumed by a fraction of the total leaf surface.

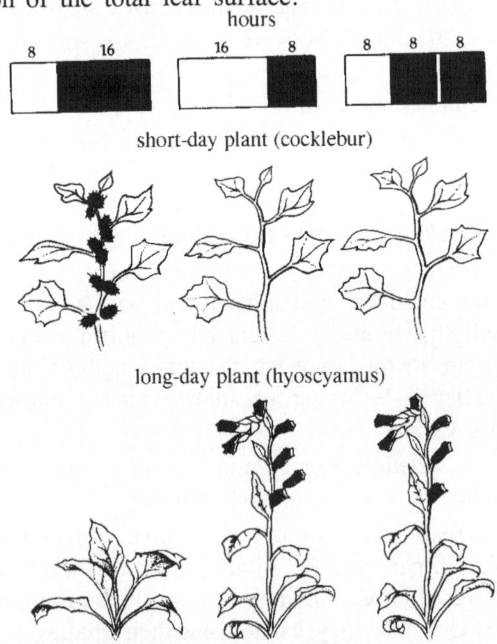

Figure 16.11 : Experiments on photoperiodism showed that plants measure the darkness rather than the light. Short-day plants flower only when the darkness exceeds some critical value.

In the course of these studies, in which they tested a variety of experimental conditions, the investigators made a crucial and totally unexpected discovery.

If the period of darkness is interrupted by as little as a 1-minute exposure to the light of a 25-watt bulb, flowering does not occur. Interruption of the light period by darkness has no effect whatsoever on flowering.

Subsequent experiments with other short-day plants showed that they, too, required periods not of uninterrupted light but of uninterrupted darkness.

What about long-day plants? They also measure darkness. A long-day plant that will flower if it is kept in a laboratory in which there is light for 16 hours and dark for 8 hours will also flower on 8 hours of light and 16 hours of dark if the dark is interrupted by even a brief exposure to light.

A. Lang of Michigan State University has carried out studies involving grafts of day-neutral, long-day, and short-day plants that strongly indicate the presence of a hormone or hormones other than the hypothetical florigen.

For instance, he and his co-workers have shown that if the long-day plant *Hyoscyamus niger* is completely defoliated, flower buds will form irrespective of photoperiod; however, if even one leaf remains, it will flower only on long days.

If a day-neutral plant is grafted to a long-day plant, flowering of the day-neutral plant is accelerated by exposure to long days. Exposure to short days, however, inhibits flowering of a day-neutral plant grafted to a long-day plant. In short, flower-inhibitors as well as flower-promoters are involved.

PHOTOPERIODISM AND PHYTOCHROME

Following up on the clues from the Hamner and Bonner experiments, the Beltsville group was able to detect and eventually to isolate the pigment involved in photoperiodism. This pigment, which they called *phytochrome*, exists in two different forms: One is P_{660} and one is P_{730}.

The numbers refer to the wavelengths of light the two forms absorb; 660 nanometers is red light and 730 nanometers is far-red. P660 absorbs red light and is converted to P_{730}, which is the active form. This conversion takes place in daylight or in incandescent light; in both of these types of light, red wavelengths predominate over far-red. When

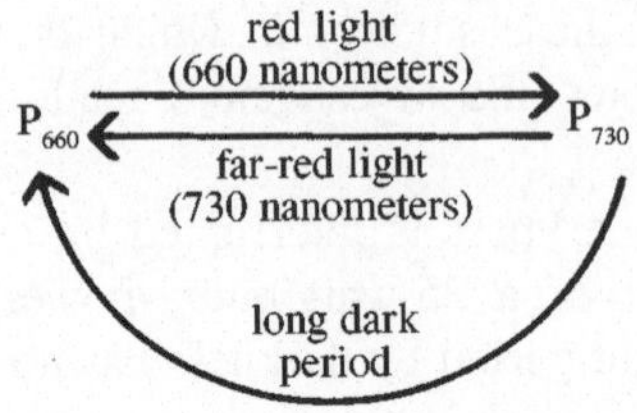

Figure 16.12 : P_{660} changes to P_{730}, the active form, when exposed to red light, which is present in sunlight. P_{730} reverts to P_{660} when exposed to far-red light. In darkness, P_{730} slowly reverts to P_{660}.

P_{730} absorbs far-red light, it is converted back to P_{660}. The P_{730} to P_{660} conversion can also take place in the dark, which is how it usually occurs in nature. P_{730}, the active form of the pigment, promotes flowering in long-day plants and inhibits flowering in short-day plants.

Other Phytochrome Responses

Many types of small seeds, such as lettuce, germinate only when they are in loose soil, near the surface. Otherwise the seedling would have little chance of reaching the light. Red light, a sign that sunlight is present, stimulates seed germination by converting phytochrome to the active form.

Similarly, phytochrome is involved in the early development of seedlings. When a seedling develops in the dark, as it normally does underground, the stem elongates rapidly, pushing the shoot up through the soil layers. Any seedling grown in the dark will be elongated and spindly with small leaves.

It will also be almost colourless, because the chloroplasts do not synthesize chlorophyll until they are exposed to light. Such a seedling is said to be etiolated. When the seedling tip reaches the light, normal growth begins. Phytochrome is involved in the switching of etiolated to normal growth.

If a dark-grown bean seedling is exposed to only one minute of red (660 nanometers) light, it will respond with normal growth. If, however, the exposure to red light is followed by a one-minute exposure to far-red light, etiolated growth continues, thus negating the original exposure. The exposures can be alternated repeatedly and the plant responds only to the last one perceived.

The way in which phytochrome acts is not known. One recent suggestion is that it alters the permeability of the cell membrane, permitting particular substances to enter the cell, or, perhaps, inhibiting their entry, and that these substances, which probably include hormones, regulate the cell's activities.

CIRCADIAN RHYTHMS

Some species of plants have flowers that open in the morning and close at dusk or they spread their leaves in the sunlight and fold them toward the stem at night. As long ago as 1729, the French scientist Jean-Jacques de Mairan noticed that these diurnal (daily) movements continue even when the plants are kept in dim light.

More recent studies have shown that less evident activities, such as photosynthesis, auxin production, and the rate of cell division, also have daily rhythms. The rhythms continue even when all environmental conditions are kept constant. These regular day-night cycles have come to be called *circadian rhythms*, from the Latin words *circa,* meaning "about," and *dies,* "day." Circadian rhythms now have been found throughout the plant and animal kingdoms.

Biological Clocks

Are these rhythms internal-that is, caused by factors within the plant or animal itself-or is the organism keeping itself in tune with some external factor? For a number of years, biologists debated whether it might not be some environmental force, such as cosmic rays, the magnetic field of the earth, or the earth's rotation, that was setting the rhythms.

Attempts to settle this recurrent controversy have led to numerous experiments under an extraordinary variety of conditions. Organisms have been taken down into salt mines, shipped to the South Pole, flown halfway around the world in airplanes, and, most recently, orbited in satellites.

Although there is still a vocal minority that believes that circadian rhythms are under the influence of a subtle geophysical factor, most workers now agree that the rhythms are endogenous-that is, they originate within the organism. Strong evidence in support of this belief is that the rhythms are not exact.

Different species and different individuals of the same species often have slightly different, but consistent, rhythms, often as much as an hour or two longer or shorter than 24 hours. Nothing, however, is known about the physical or chemical nature of this internal timing device, which is often referred to as a *biological clock.*

Another important feature of these rhythms is that they do not speed up as the temperature rises, as you might expect since enzymatic activities must be involved and enzyme reactions take place more rapidly as temperatures increase.

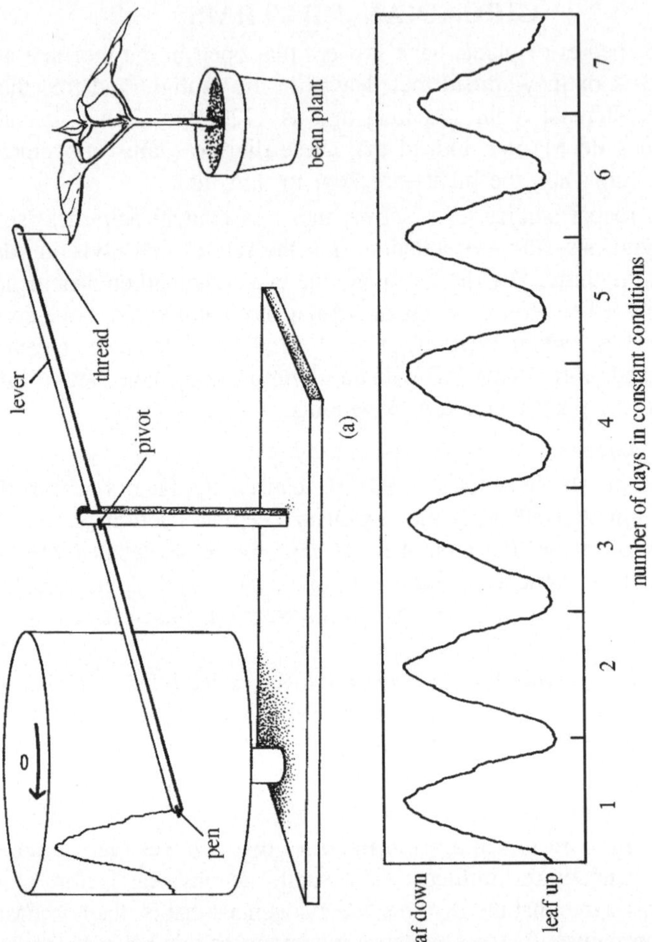

Figure 16.13 : "Sleep movement" rhythms in the bean plant. Many legumes, such as the bean, orient their leaves perpendicular to the rays of the sun during the day and fold them up at night.

Therefore, the clock must contain within its workings some type of compensatory mechanism-a feedback system that adjusts it to temperature changes. This idea is supported by the observation that in some organisms circadian rhythms seem to slow down as the temperature rises, rather than speed up, suggesting that overcompensation may be taking place.

CHANGING THE RHYTHMS

Although circadian rhythms probably originate within the organisms themselves, they can be modified by external conditions-a fact that is, of course, important to the survival of both individuals and species. For instance, a plant whose natural daily rhythm shows a peak every 26 hours when grown under continuous dim light can adjust its rhythm to 14 hours of light and 10 hours of darkness.

It can also adjust to 11 hours of light and 11 of dark (or 22 hours). Such adjustment to an externally imposed rhythm is known as entrainment. If the new rhythm is too far removed from the original one, however, the organism will "escape" the entrained rhythm and revert to its natural one.

A plant that has been kept on an artificial or forced rhythm, even for a long period of time, will revert to its normal internal period when returned to continuous dim light.

CLOCK FUNCTIONS

Biological clocks are believed to play an essential role in many aspects of plant and animal physiology. For instance, insects are more active in the early evening hours. Bats that feed on insects begin to fly each evening just when the insects are most available.

Moreover, caged bats under controlled and constant laboratory conditions continue to show this sort of activity about every 24 hours, indicating that they are following an internal rhythm, not merely responding to environmental cues.

Some plants secrete nectar or perfume at certain specific times of the day. As a result, insects-which have their own biological clocks-become programmed to visit these flowers at these times, thereby ensuring maximum rewards for both the insects and the flowers.

The ability to tell time also appears to be involved in a number of complex and fascinating phenomena such as the extraordinary ability of migrating birds and turtles to navigate.

Biological clocks enable organisms to recognise the changing seasons of the year by "comparing" external rhythms of the environment, such as changes in day length, to their own relatively constant internal rhythms. This capacity is an important factor in regulating the growth cycle of many plants.

Finally, biological clocks are clearly involved in photoperiodism. In order for organisms to detect changes in day length-and remember that in some cases, they are accurate to within 15 minutes-they must have some constant, a clock, with which to compare them. The chemical nature of the biological clock-or indeed if there is just one kind of clock or many-is still not known.

TOUCH RESPONSES IN PLANTS

Many plants respond to touch. One of the most common examples is seen in tendrils or winding stems. They wrap around objects with which they come in contact and so enable the plant to cling and climb. The response can be rapid; a tendril may wrap around a support in less than a minute.

Cells touching the support shrink slightly and those on the other side elongate. There is some evidence that auxin plays a role in this response.

A more spectacular response is seen in the sensitive plant, *Mimosa pudica,* in which the leaflets and sometimes entire leaves droop suddenly when touched. This response is a result of a sudden change in turgor pressure in cells at the base of the leaflets and leaves.

The change in turgor pressure appears to involve the movement of potassium ions, as do the changes in stomata, but again, how the change is triggered is unknown. There is also some controversy about its survival value to the plant.

Mimosa pudica often grows in dry, exposed areas where it may be subjected to drying winds; strong winds may shake the leaves enough to make them fold up, so conserving water. Another suggestion is that the wilting response makes the plant unattractive to grazing animals or startles chewing insects.

The triggering of turgor changes by touch is also involved in the capture of prey by the carnivorous Venus flytrap. The leaves of the Venus flytrap are hinged in the middle, and each leaf half is equipped with three sensitive hairs.

When an insect walks on one of these leaves, attracted by the nectar on the leaf surface, it brushes against the hairs, triggering the traplike closing of the leaf. The toothed edges mesh, the leaf halves gradually squeeze closed, and the insect is pressed against digestive glands on the inner surface of the trap.

The trapping mechanism is so specialised that it can distinguish between living prey and inanimate objects, such as pebbles and small sticks, that fall on its leaves by chance: The leaf will not close unless two of its hairs are touched in succession or one hair is touched twice.

Studies have recently been made by investigators at Washington University in St. Louis on how the sundew traps insects. The club-shaped leaves of the plant are covered with tiny tentacles.

A sticky droplet surrounding the tip of each tentacle attracts insects. When an insect is caught on the tip of a tentacle, the tentacle bends in rapidly, carrying the prey to the center of the leaf, where it is digested by enzymes. N icroelectrodes placed in the tentacles have revealed that the rapid response is accompanied by an electric impulse that moves down the tentacle. This impulse is similar, in principle, to the action potential that forms the basis of the nerve impulse in animals.

The investigators predict that electric signals will be found to coordinate a variety of functions in plants.

INDEX

A

B

C

D

E

F

G

N

O

P

Q

R

S

T

U

V

X

Y